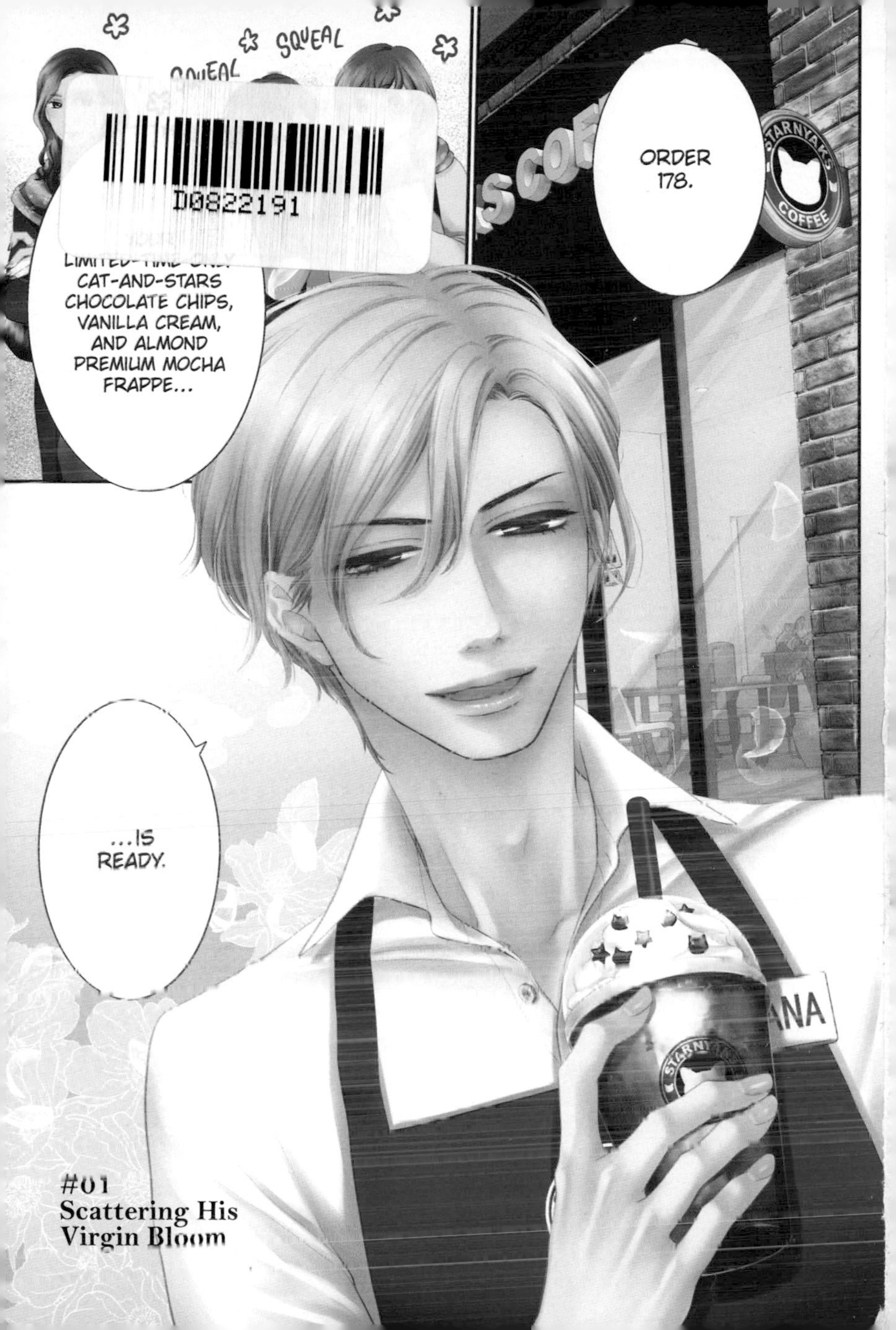
ORDER 178.
STARNYAKS COFFEE
SQUEAL
SQUEAL
LIMITED-TIME ONLY CAT-AND-STARS CHOCOLATE CHIPS, VANILLA CREAM, AND ALMOND PREMIUM MOCHA FRAPPE...
...IS READY.
ANA

#01 Scattering His Virgin Bloom

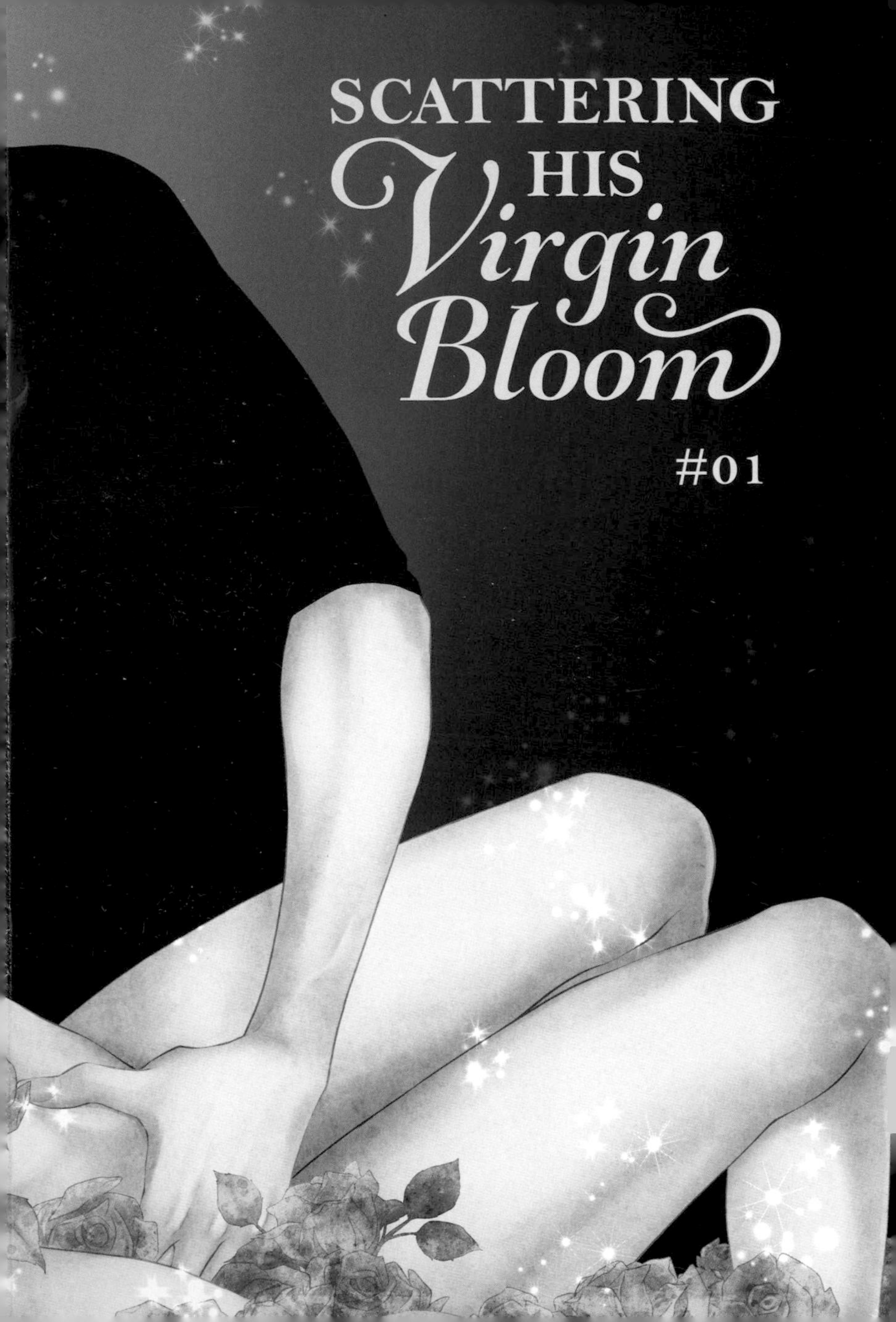
SCATTERING
HIS
Virgin
Bloom
#01

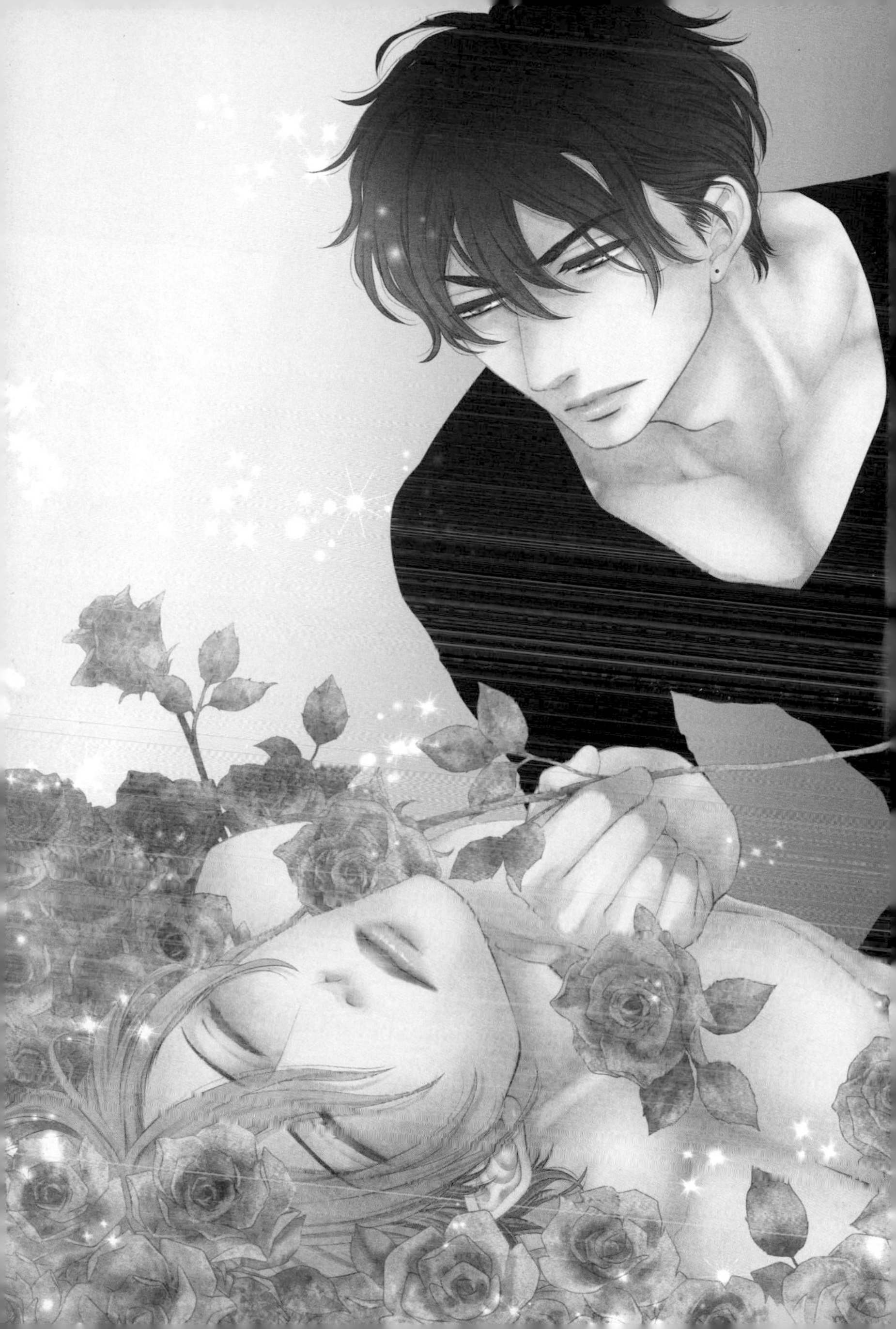

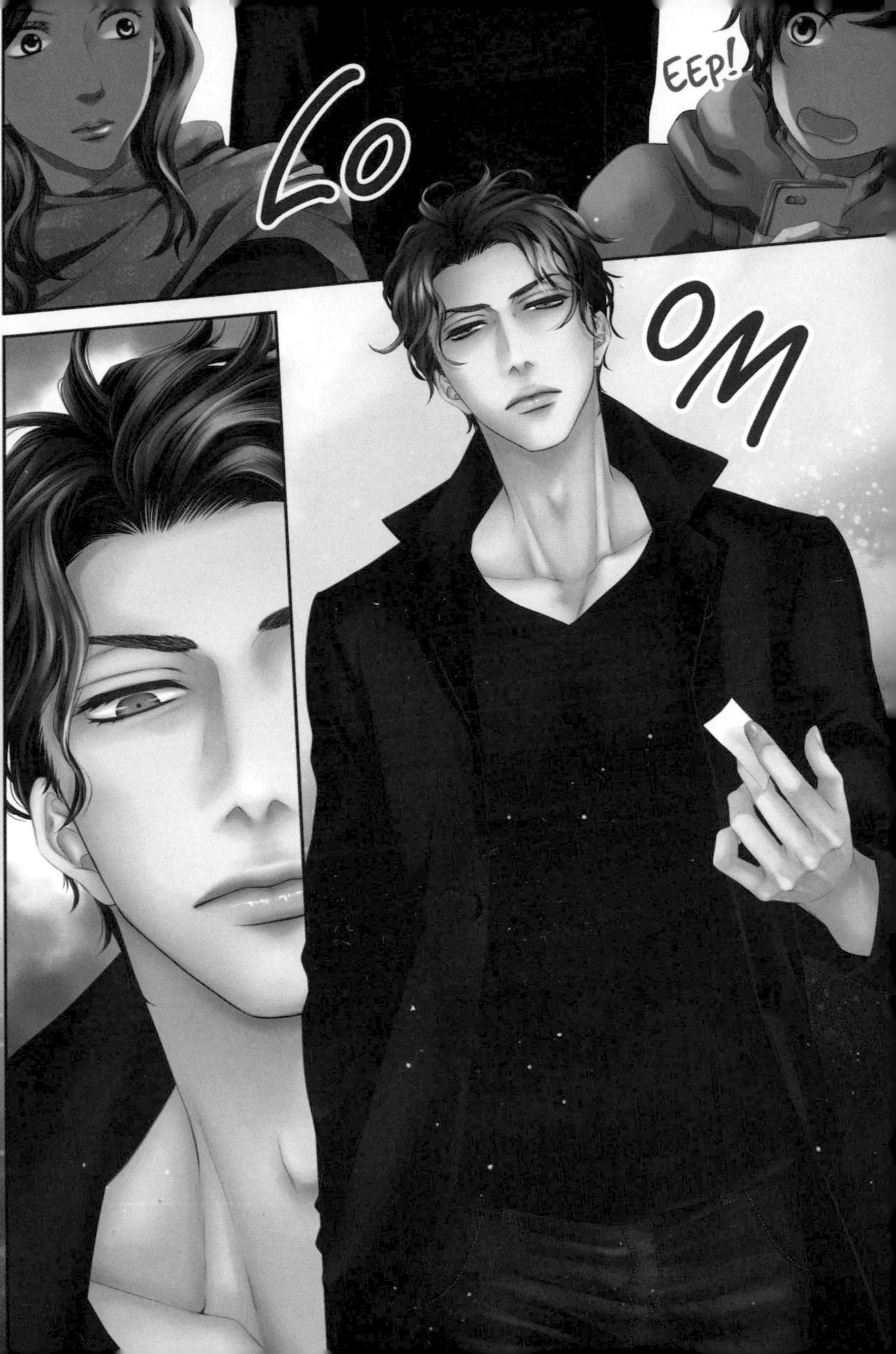
EEP!
LO
OM

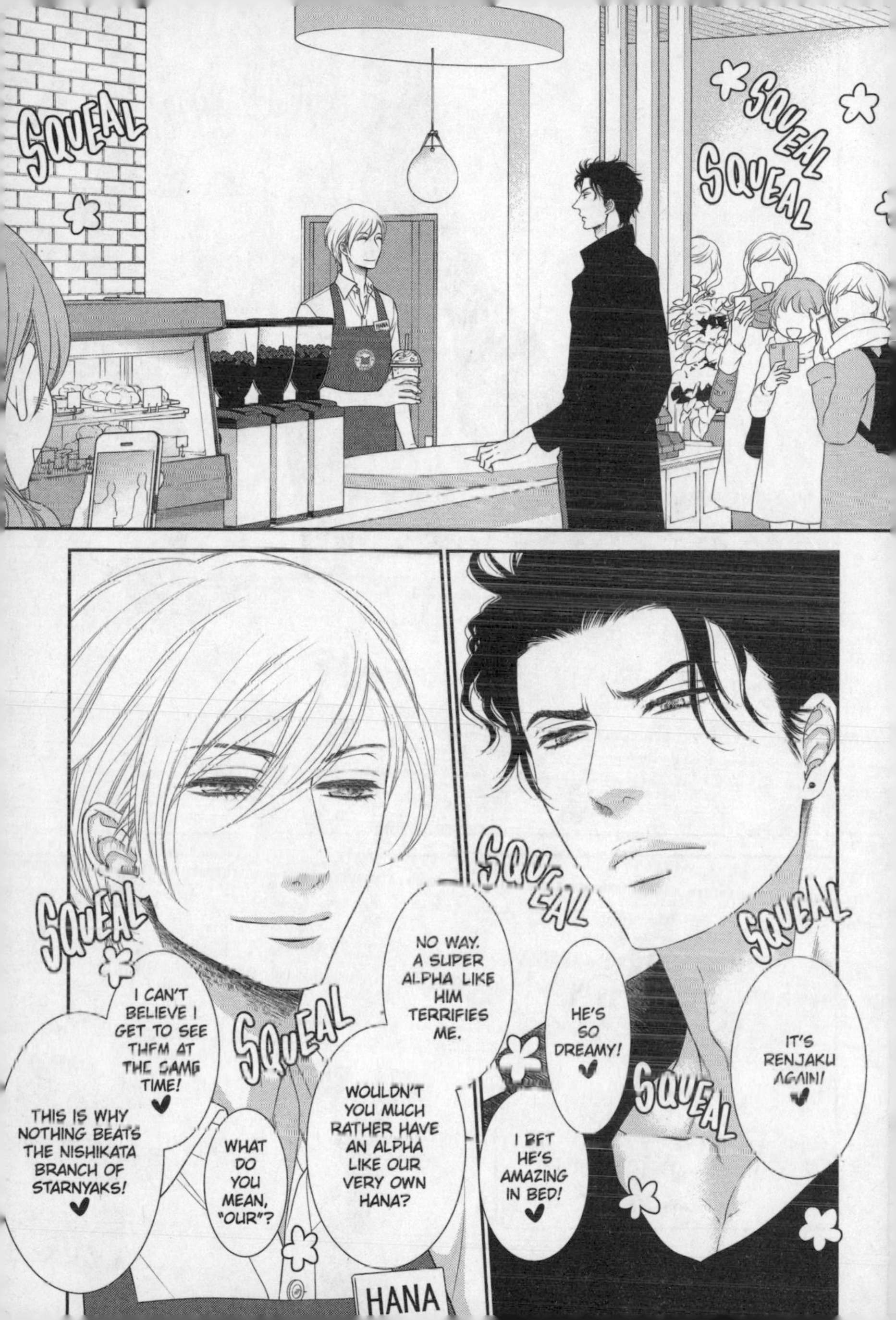
SQUEAL
SQUEAL
SQUEAL
SQUEAL
IT'S RENJAKU AGAIN! ♥
SQUEAL
HE'S SO DREAMY! ♥
SQUEAL
I BET HE'S AMAZING IN BED! ♥
NO WAY. A SUPER ALPHA LIKE HIM TERRIFIES ME.
WOULDN'T YOU MUCH RATHER HAVE AN ALPHA LIKE OUR VERY OWN HANA?
WHAT DO YOU MEAN, "OUR"?
SQUEAL
I CAN'T BELIEVE I GET TO SEE THEM AT THE SAME TIME! ♥
SQUEAL
THIS IS WHY NOTHING BEATS THE NISHIKATA BRANCH OF STARNYAKS! ♥
HANA

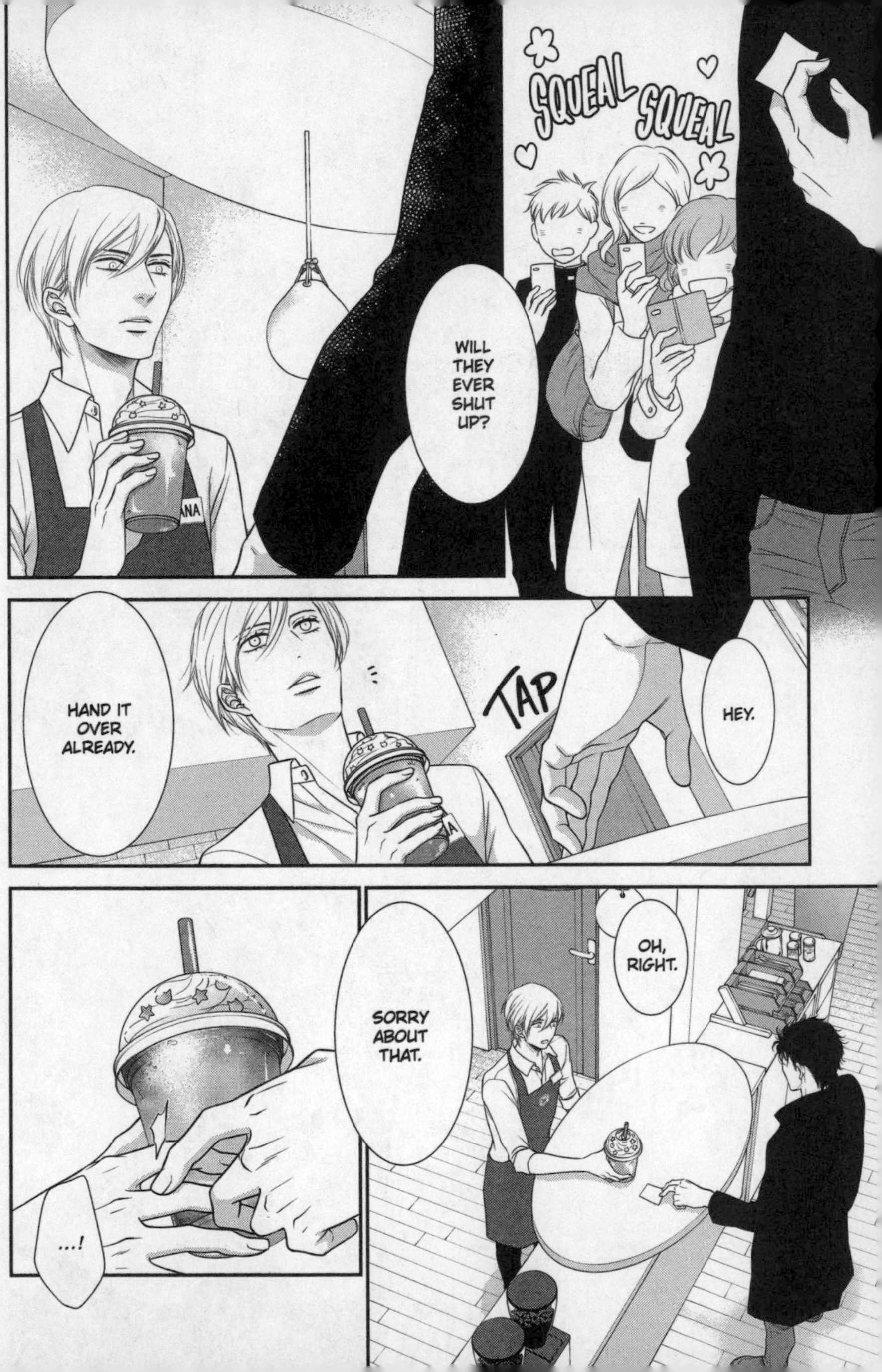
SQUEAL SQUEAL
WILL THEY EVER SHUT UP?
HEY.
TAP
HAND IT OVER ALREADY.
OH, RIGHT.
SORRY ABOUT THAT.
...!

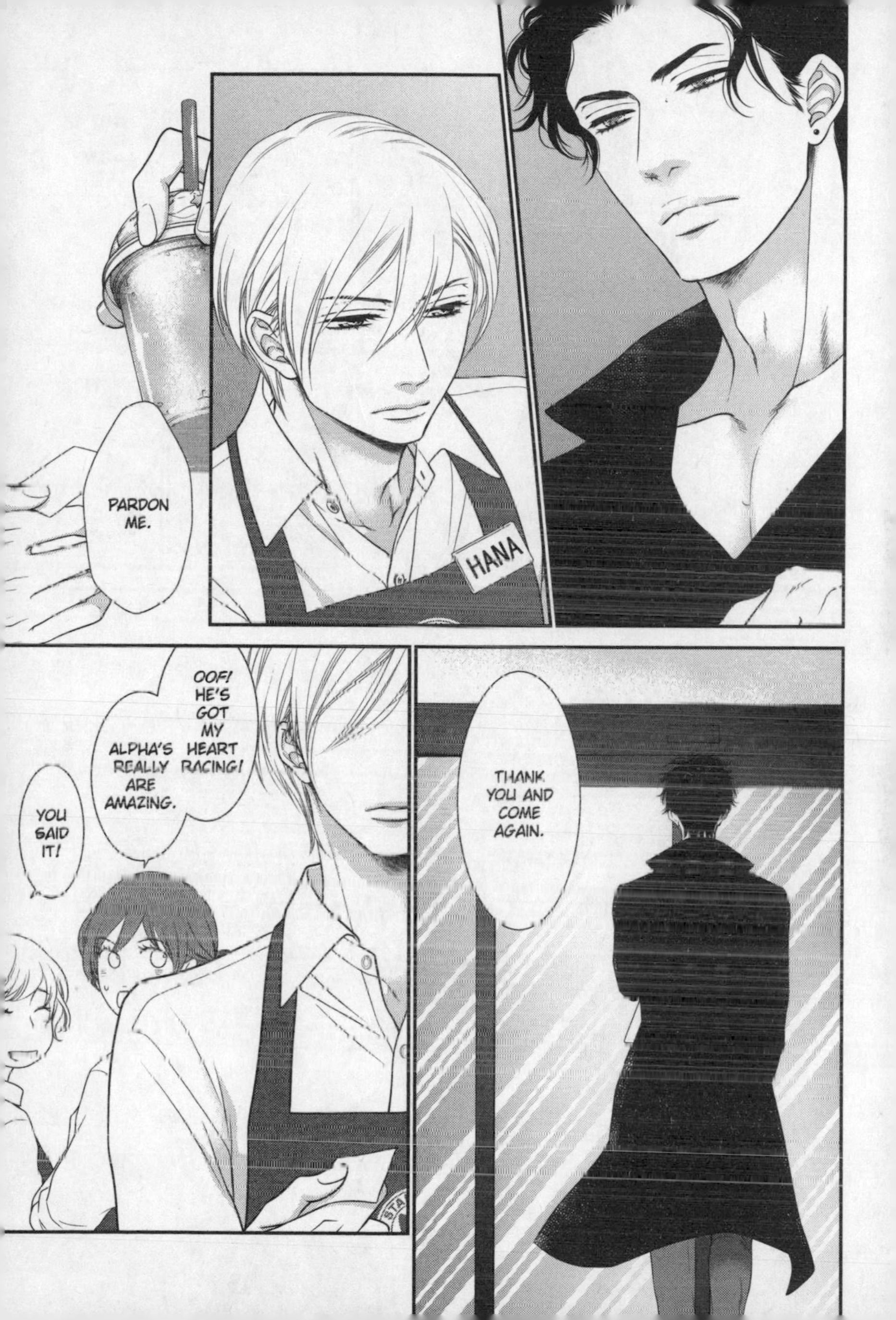
PARDON ME.
HANA
THANK YOU AND COME AGAIN.
OOF! HE'S GOT MY HEART RACING!
ALPHA'S REALLY ARE AMAZING.
YOU SAID IT!

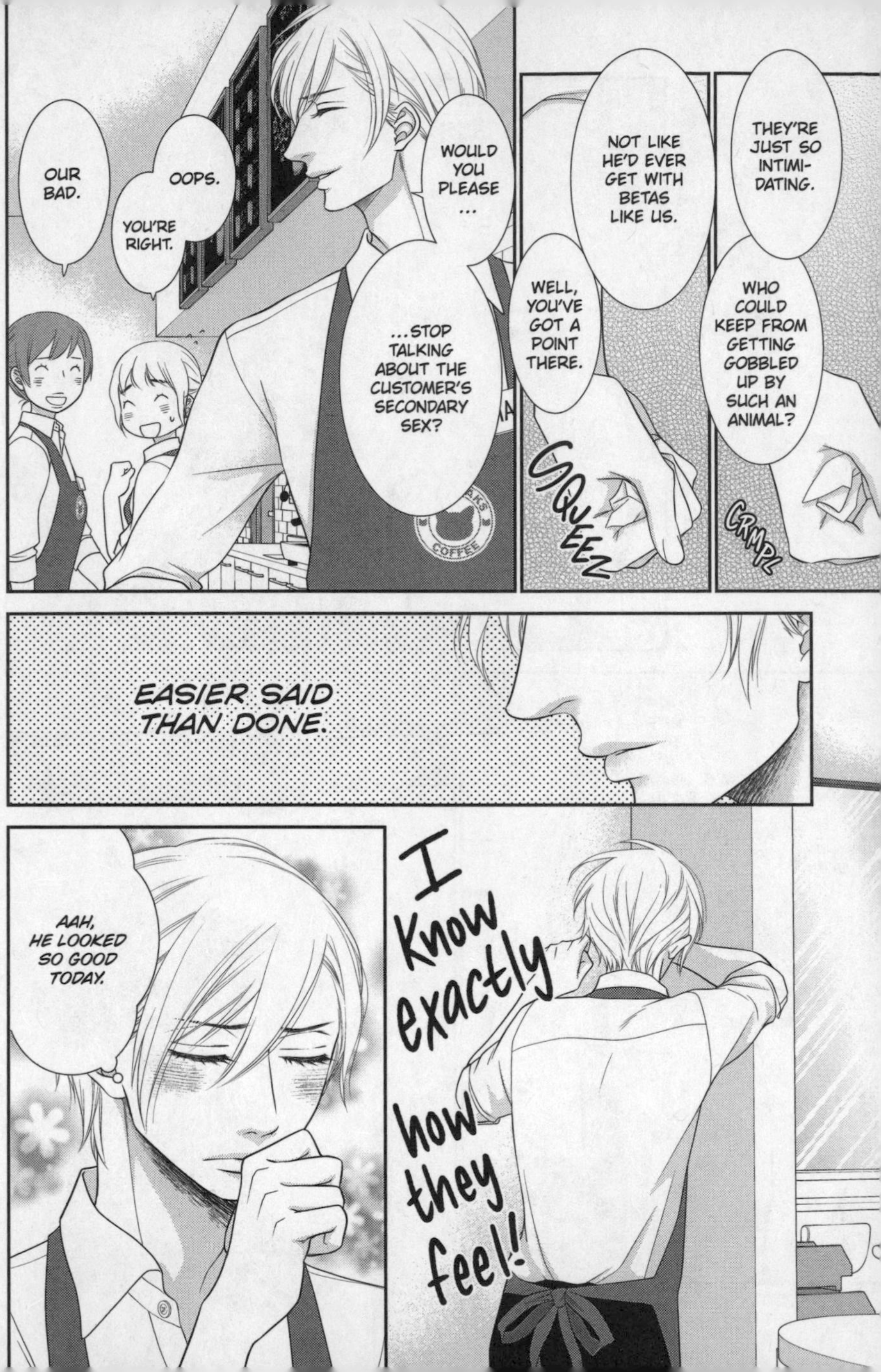
THEY'RE JUST SO INTIMI-DATING.
WHO COULD KEEP FROM GETTING GOBBLED UP BY SUCH AN ANIMAL?
CRMPL
NOT LIKE HE'D EVER GET WITH BETAS LIKE US.
WELL, YOU'VE GOT A POINT THERE.
SQUEEZ
WOULD YOU PLEASE ...
...STOP TALKING ABOUT THE CUSTOMER'S SECONDARY SEX?
OOPS.
YOU'RE RIGHT.
OUR BAD.
EASIER SAID THAN DONE.
I Know exactly how they feel!
AAH, HE LOOKED SO GOOD TODAY.

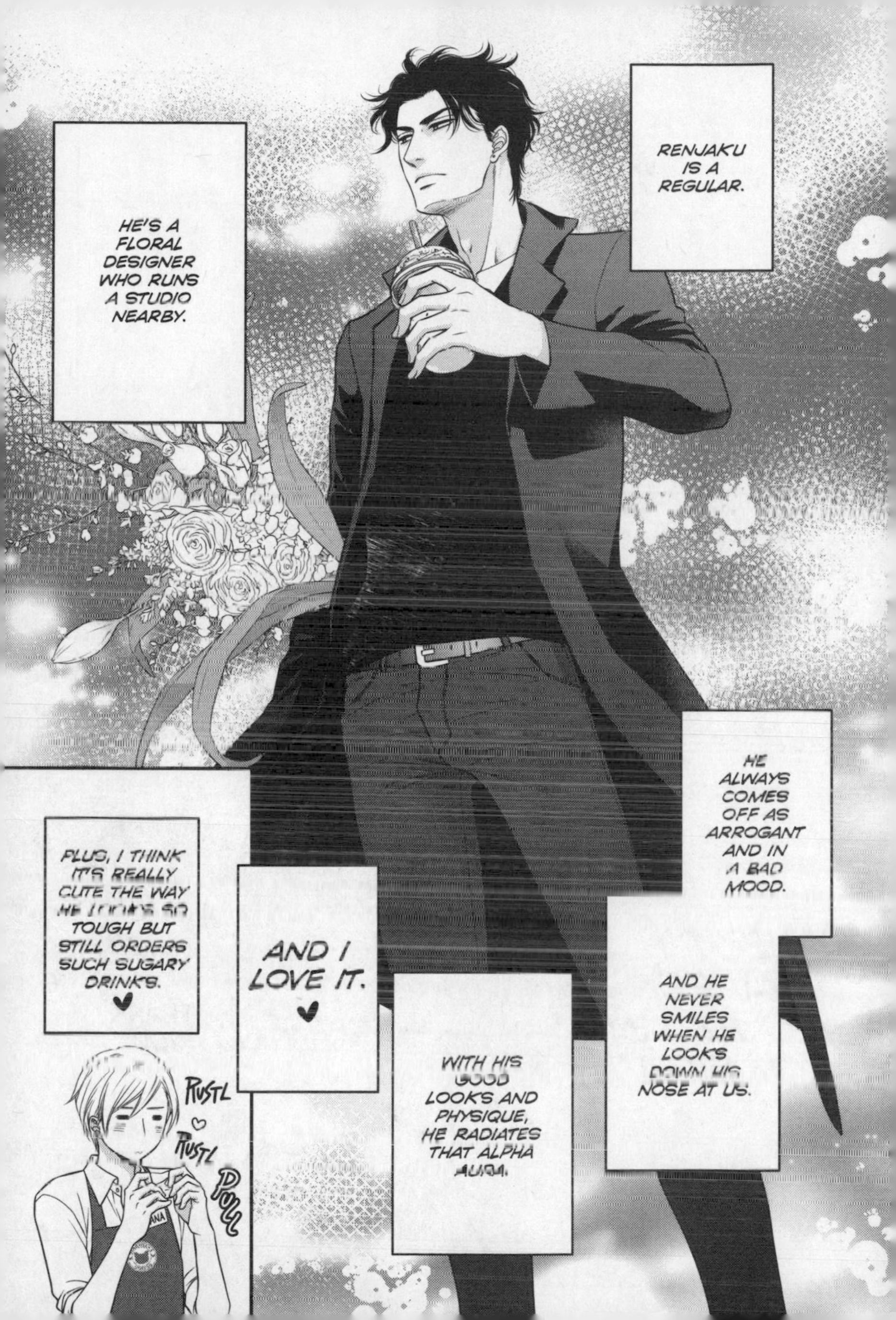
RENJAKU IS A REGULAR.
HE'S A FLORAL DESIGNER WHO RUNS A STUDIO NEARBY.
HE ALWAYS COMES OFF AS ARROGANT AND IN A BAD MOOD.
AND HE NEVER SMILES WHEN HE LOOKS DOWN HIS NOSE AT US.
WITH HIS GOOD LOOKS AND PHYSIQUE, HE RADIATES THAT ALPHA AURA.
AND I LOVE IT. ♥
PLUS, I THINK IT'S REALLY CUTE THE WAY HE LOOKS SO TOUGH BUT STILL ORDERS SUCH SUGARY DRINKS. ♥
RUSTL ♥ RUSTL
PULL

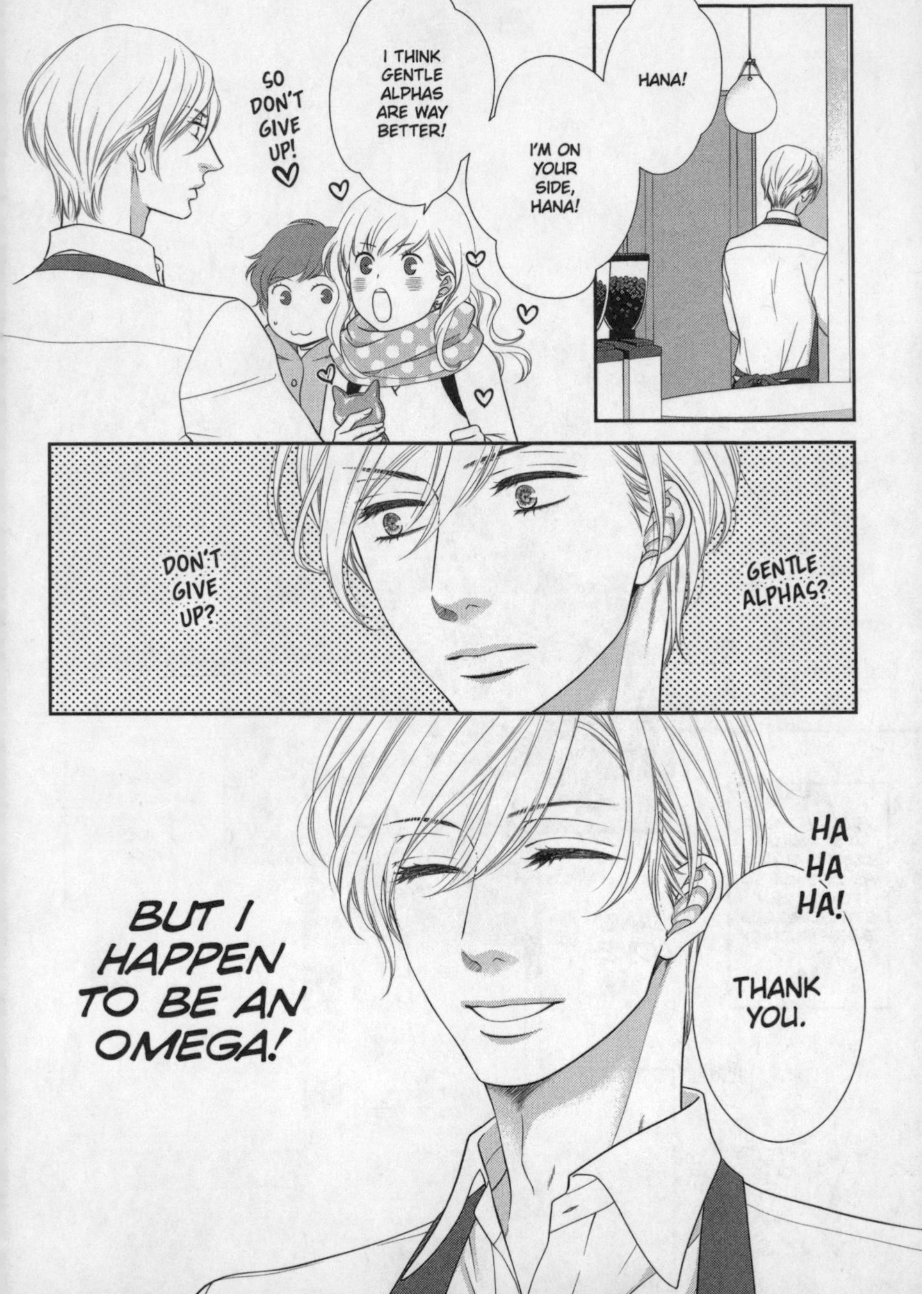
HANA!
I'M ON YOUR SIDE, HANA!
I THINK GENTLE ALPHAS ARE WAY BETTER!
SO DON'T GIVE UP!
GENTLE ALPHAS?
DON'T GIVE UP?
HA HA HA!
THANK YOU.
BUT I HAPPEN TO BE AN OMEGA!

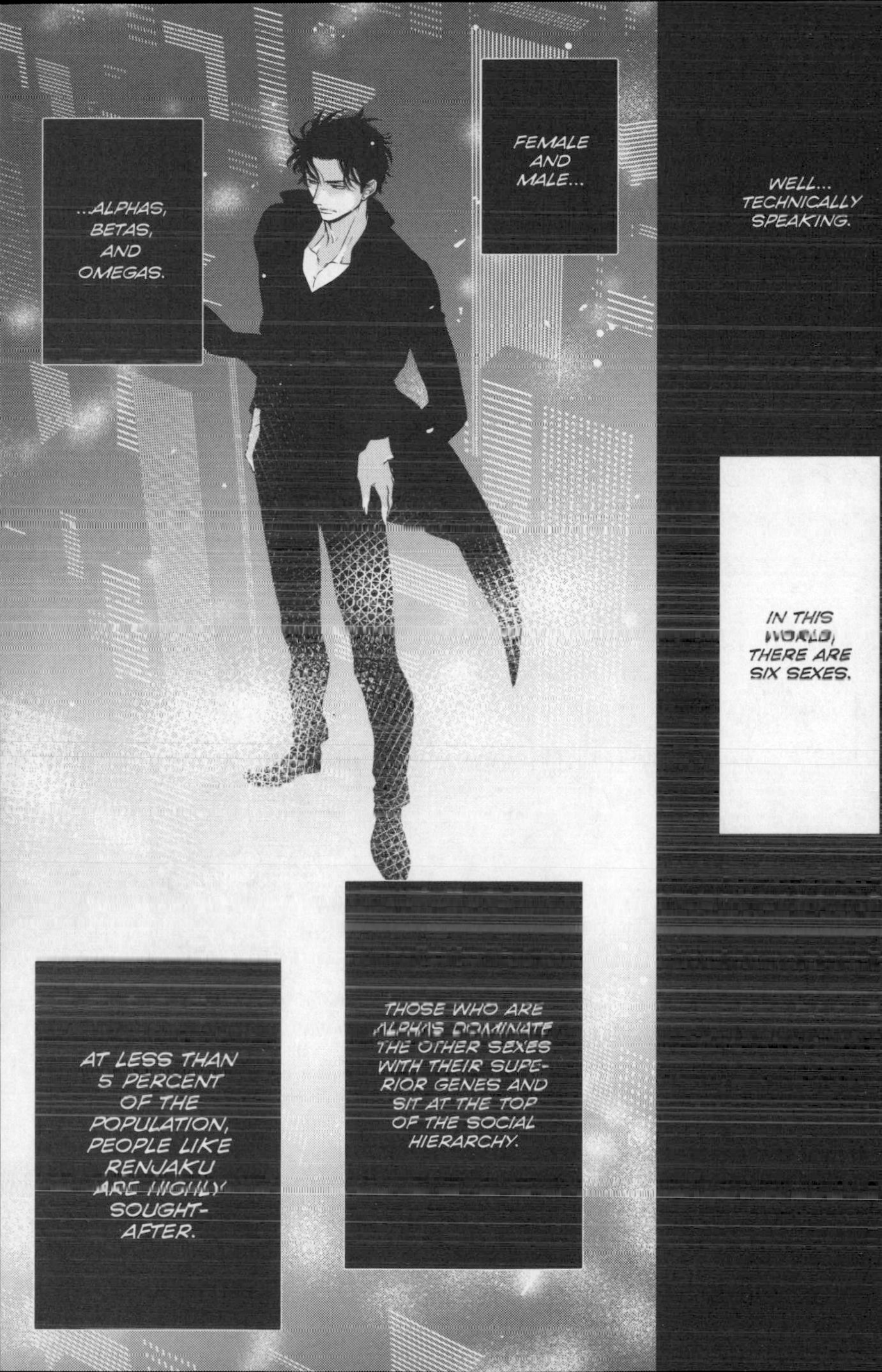
WELL... TECHNICALLY SPEAKING.
IN THIS WORLD, THERE ARE SIX SEXES.
FEMALE AND MALE...
...ALPHAS, BETAS, AND OMEGAS.
THOSE WHO ARE ALPHAS DOMINATE THE OTHER SEXES WITH THEIR SUPE-RIOR GENES AND SIT AT THE TOP OF THE SOCIAL HIERARCHY.
AT LESS THAN 5 PERCENT OF THE POPULATION, PEOPLE LIKE RENJAKU ARE HIGHLY SOUGHT-AFTER.

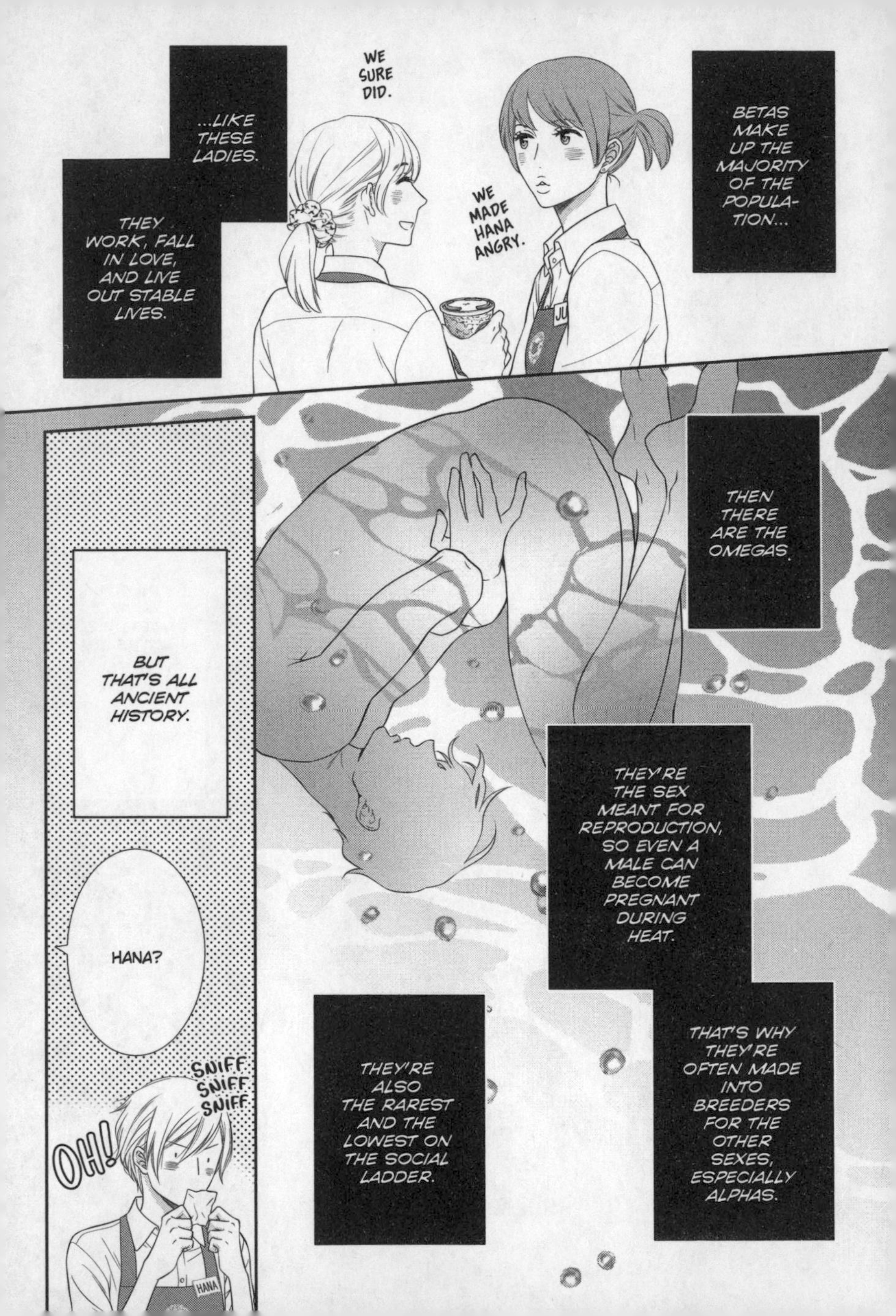
BETAS MAKE UP THE MAJORITY OF THE POPULATION...
WE MADE HANA ANGRY.
WE SURE DID.
...LIKE THESE LADIES.
THEY WORK, FALL IN LOVE, AND LIVE OUT STABLE LIVES.
JU
THEN THERE ARE THE OMEGAS.
THEY'RE THE SEX MEANT FOR REPRODUCTION, SO EVEN A MALE CAN BECOME PREGNANT DURING HEAT.
THAT'S WHY THEY'RE OFTEN MADE INTO BREEDERS FOR THE OTHER SEXES, ESPECIALLY ALPHAS.
THEY'RE ALSO THE RAREST AND THE LOWEST ON THE SOCIAL LADDER.
BUT THAT'S ALL ANCIENT HISTORY.
HANA?
SNIFF SNIFF SNIFF
OH!
HANA

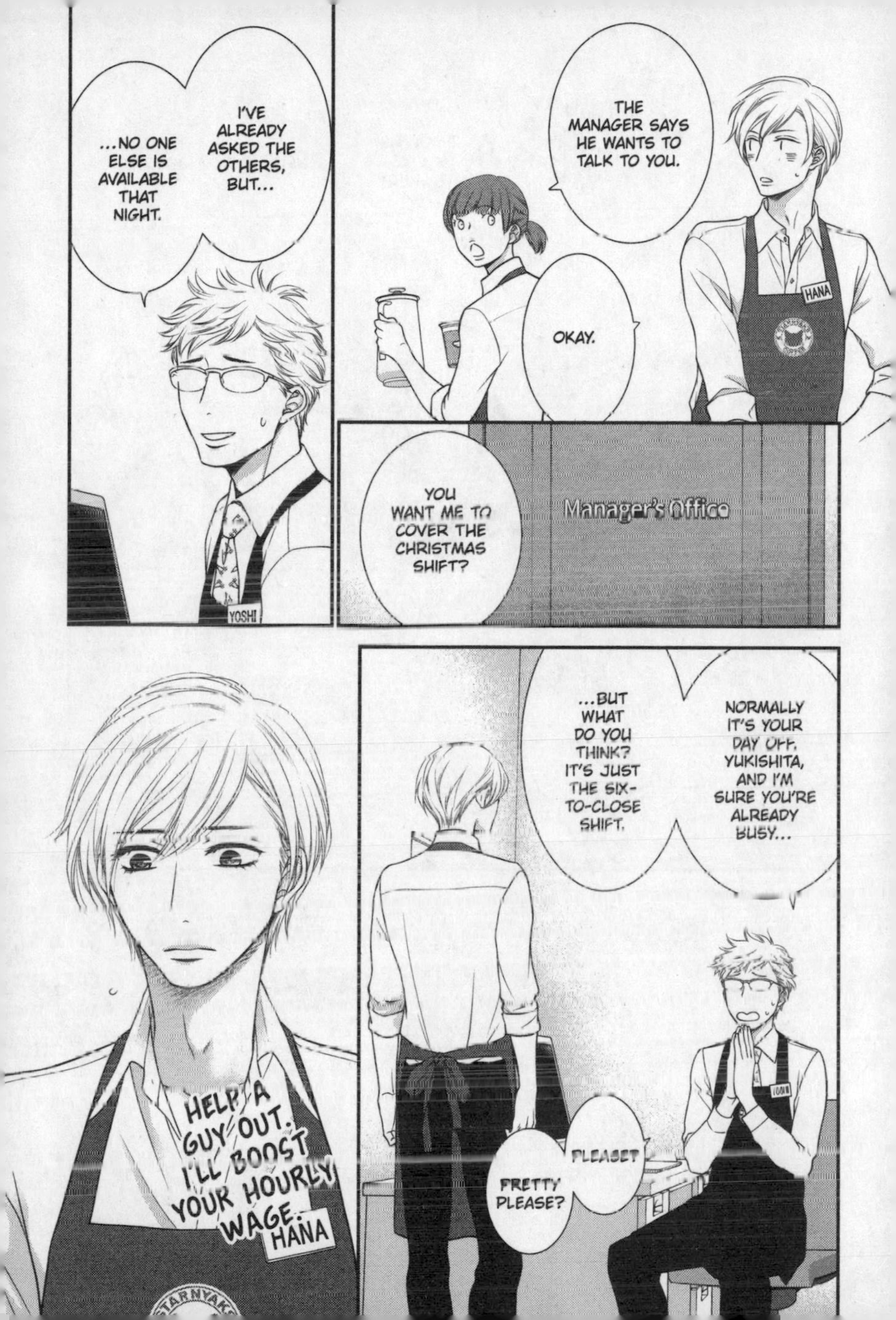
THE MANAGER SAYS HE WANTS TO TALK TO YOU.
HANA
OKAY.
YOU WANT ME TO COVER THE CHRISTMAS SHIFT?
Manager's Office
I'VE ALREADY ASKED THE OTHERS, BUT...
...NO ONE ELSE IS AVAILABLE THAT NIGHT.
YOSHI
NORMALLY IT'S YOUR DAY OFF, YUKISHITA, AND I'M SURE YOU'RE ALREADY BUSY...
...BUT WHAT DO YOU THINK? IT'S JUST THE SIX-TO-CLOSE SHIFT.
PLEASE?
PRETTY PLEASE?
HELP A GUY OUT. I'LL BOOST YOUR HOURLY WAGE.
HANA

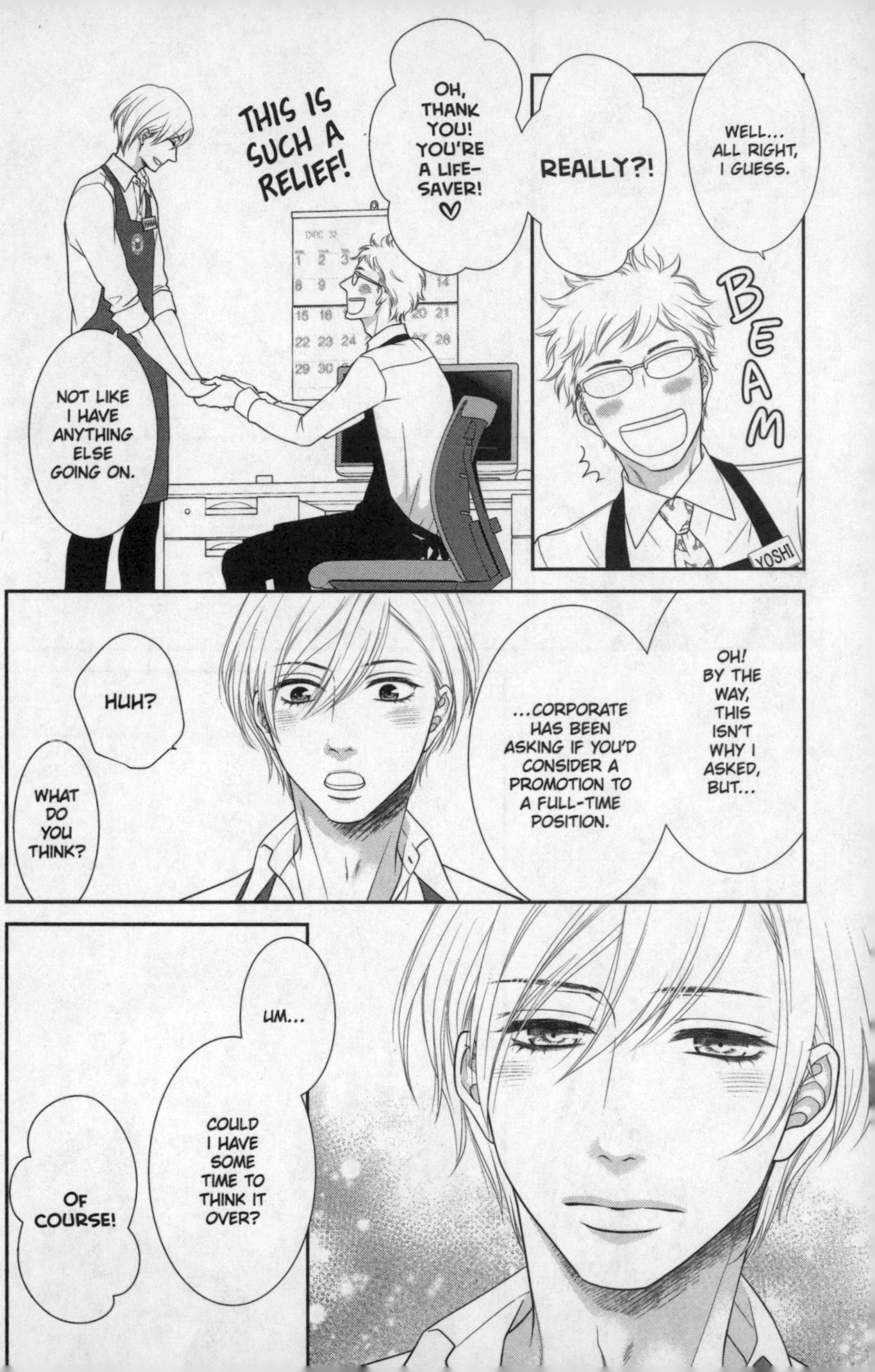
WELL... ALL RIGHT, I GUESS.
REALLY?!
BEAM
YOSHI
OH, THANK YOU! YOU'RE A LIFE-SAVER! ♡
THIS IS SUCH A RELIEF!
NOT LIKE I HAVE ANYTHING ELSE GOING ON.
OH! BY THE WAY, THIS ISN'T WHY I ASKED, BUT...
...CORPORATE HAS BEEN ASKING IF YOU'D CONSIDER A PROMOTION TO A FULL-TIME POSITION.
HUH?
WHAT DO YOU THINK?
UM...
COULD I HAVE SOME TIME TO THINK IT OVER?
OF COURSE!

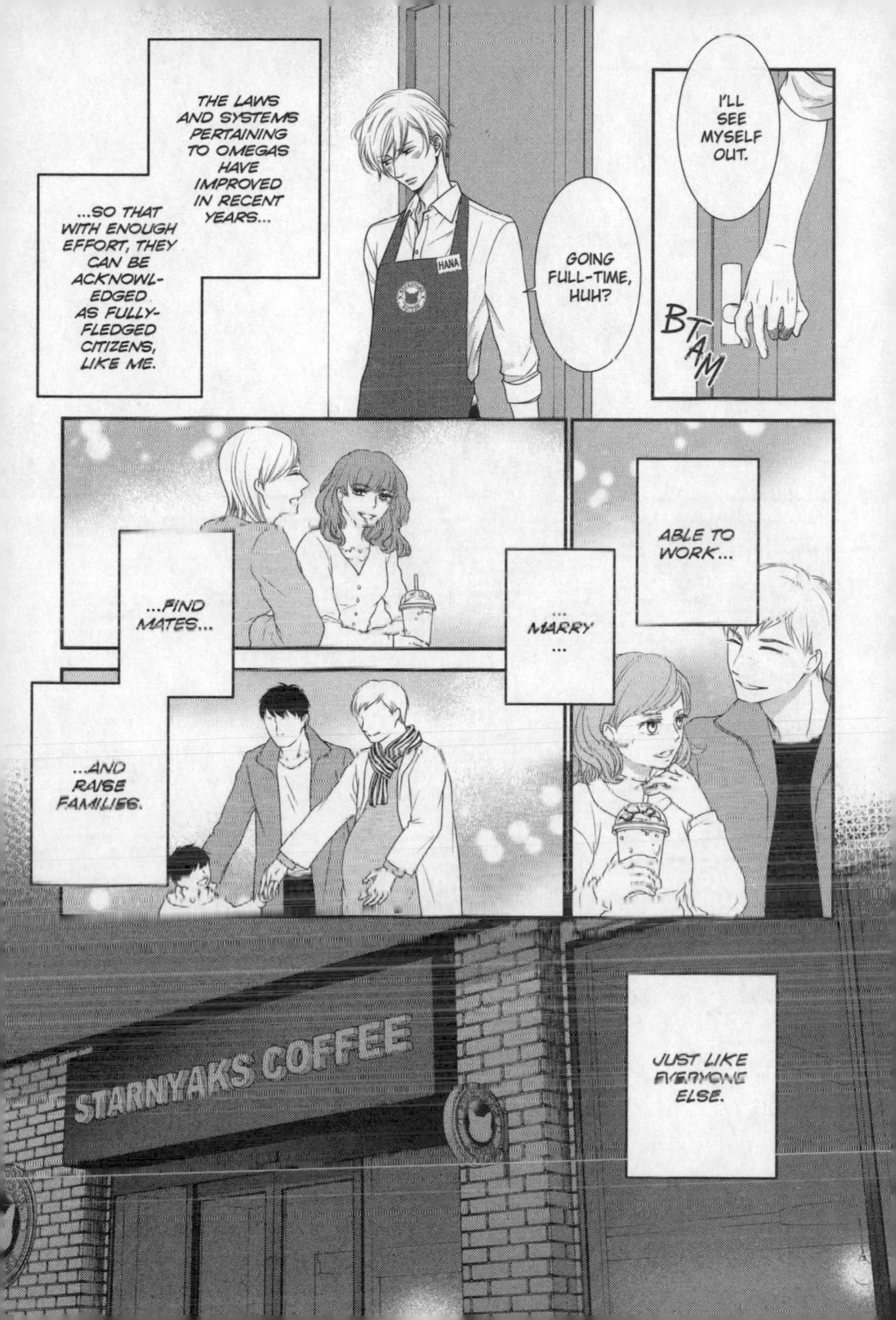
I'LL SEE MYSELF OUT.
BTAM
GOING FULL-TIME, HUH?
HANA
THE LAWS AND SYSTEMS PERTAINING TO OMEGAS HAVE IMPROVED IN RECENT YEARS...
...SO THAT WITH ENOUGH EFFORT, THEY CAN BE ACKNOWL-EDGED AS FULLY-FLEDGED CITIZENS, LIKE ME.
ABLE TO WORK...
...MARRY...
...FIND MATES...
...AND RAISE FAMILIES.
JUST LIKE EVERYONE ELSE.
STARNYAKS COFFEE

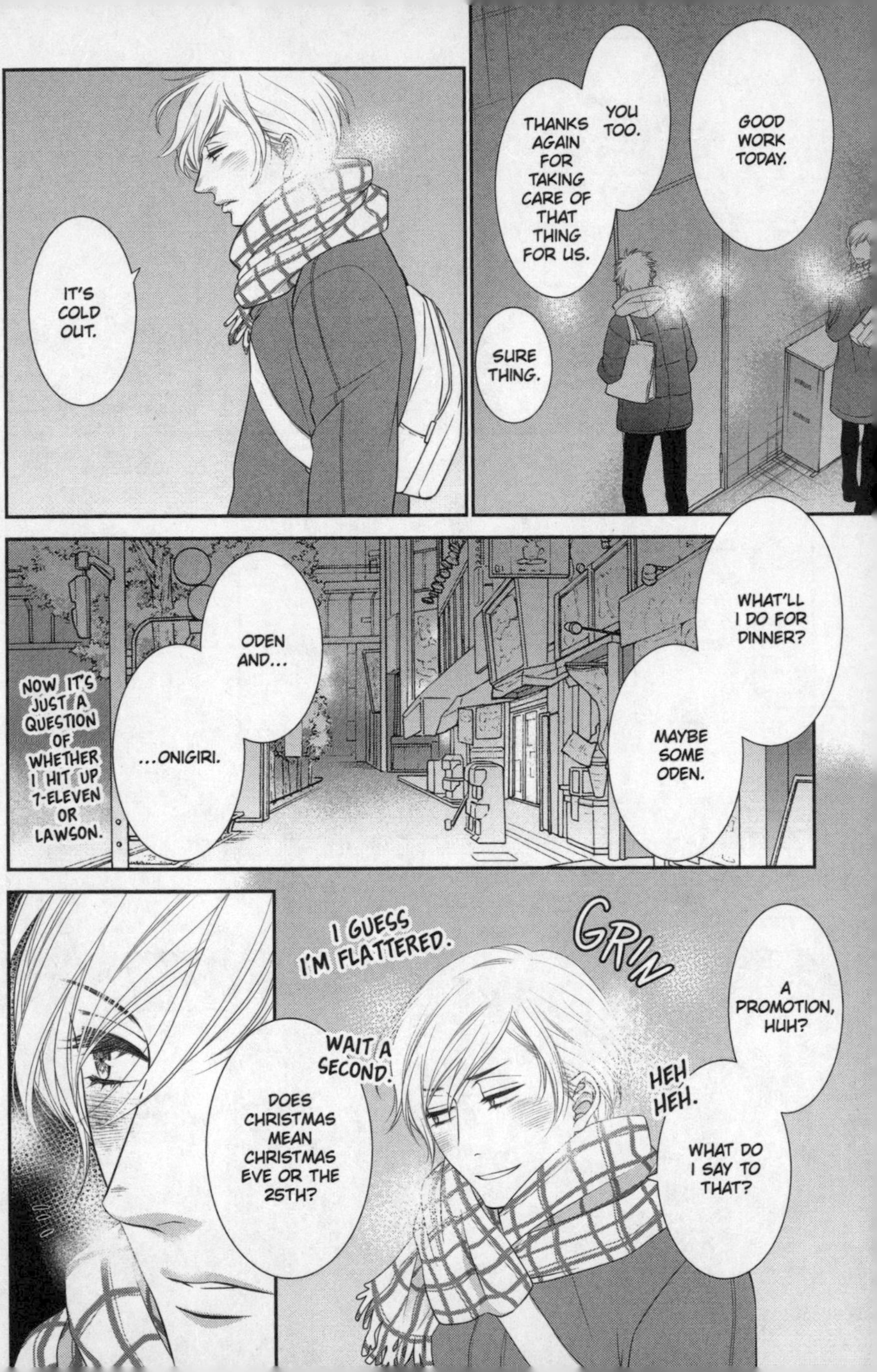
GOOD WORK TODAY.
YOU TOO.
THANKS AGAIN FOR TAKING CARE OF THAT THING FOR US.
SURE THING.
IT'S COLD OUT.
WHAT'LL I DO FOR DINNER?
MAYBE SOME ODEN.
ODEN AND...
...ONIGIRI.
NOW IT'S JUST A QUESTION OF WHETHER I HIT UP 7-ELEVEN OR LAWSON.
A PROMOTION, HUH?
GRIN
HEH HEH.
I GUESS I'M FLATTERED.
WHAT DO I SAY TO THAT?
WAIT A SECOND.
DOES CHRISTMAS MEAN CHRISTMAS EVE OR THE 25TH?

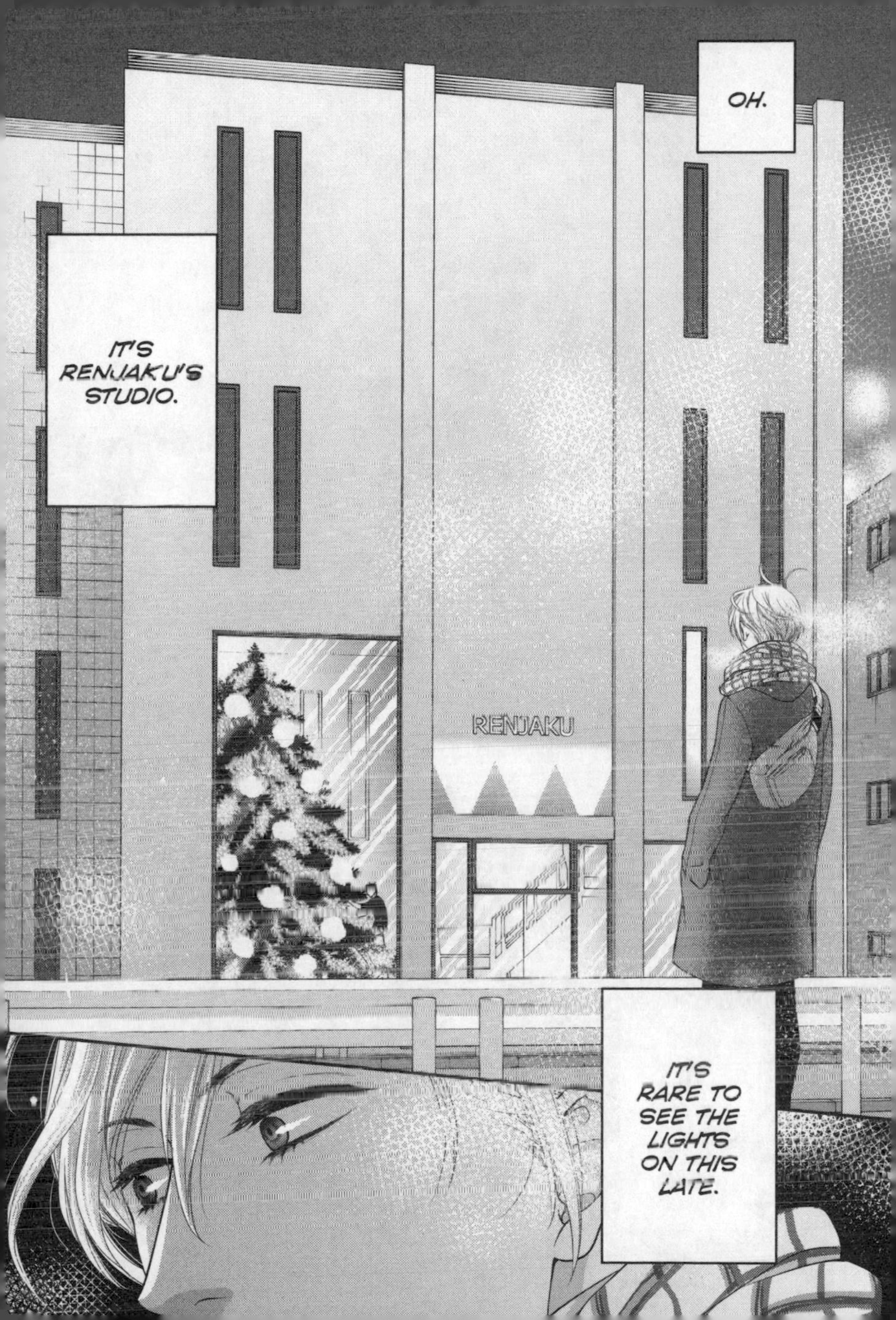
OH.
IT'S RENJAKU'S STUDIO.
RENJAKU
IT'S RARE TO SEE THE LIGHTS ON THIS LATE.

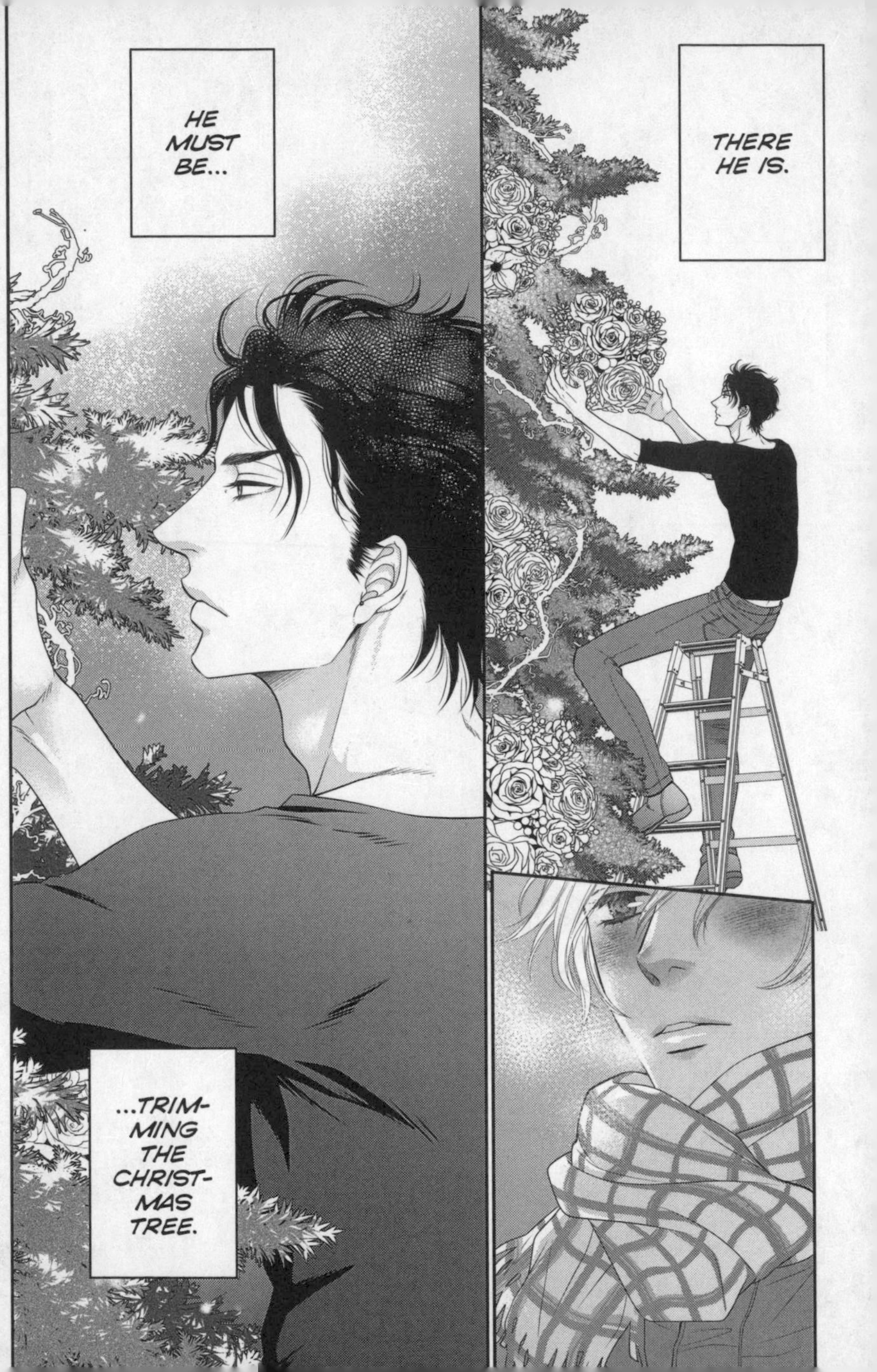
THERE HE IS.
HE MUST BE...
...TRIMMING THE CHRISTMAS TREE.

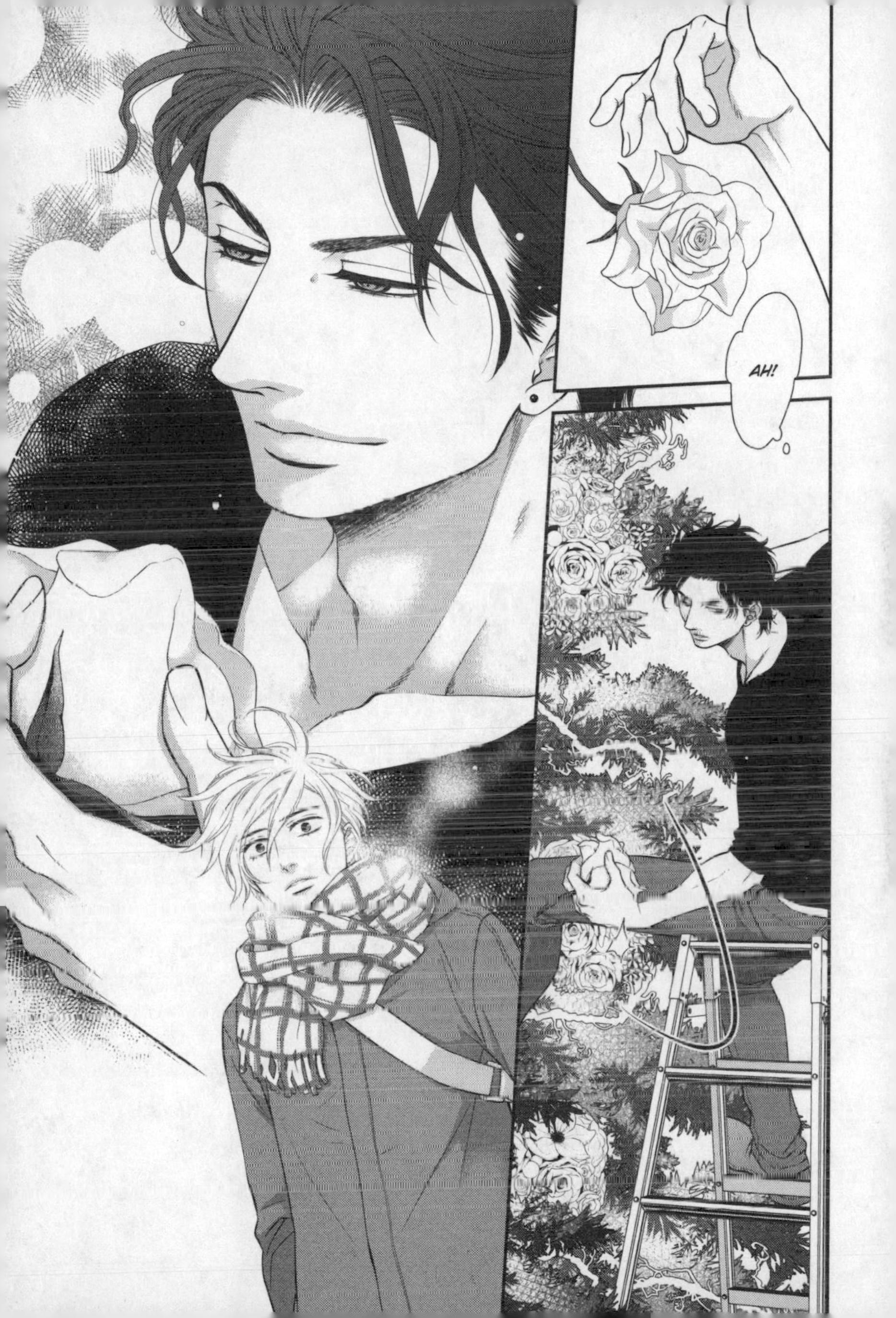
AH!

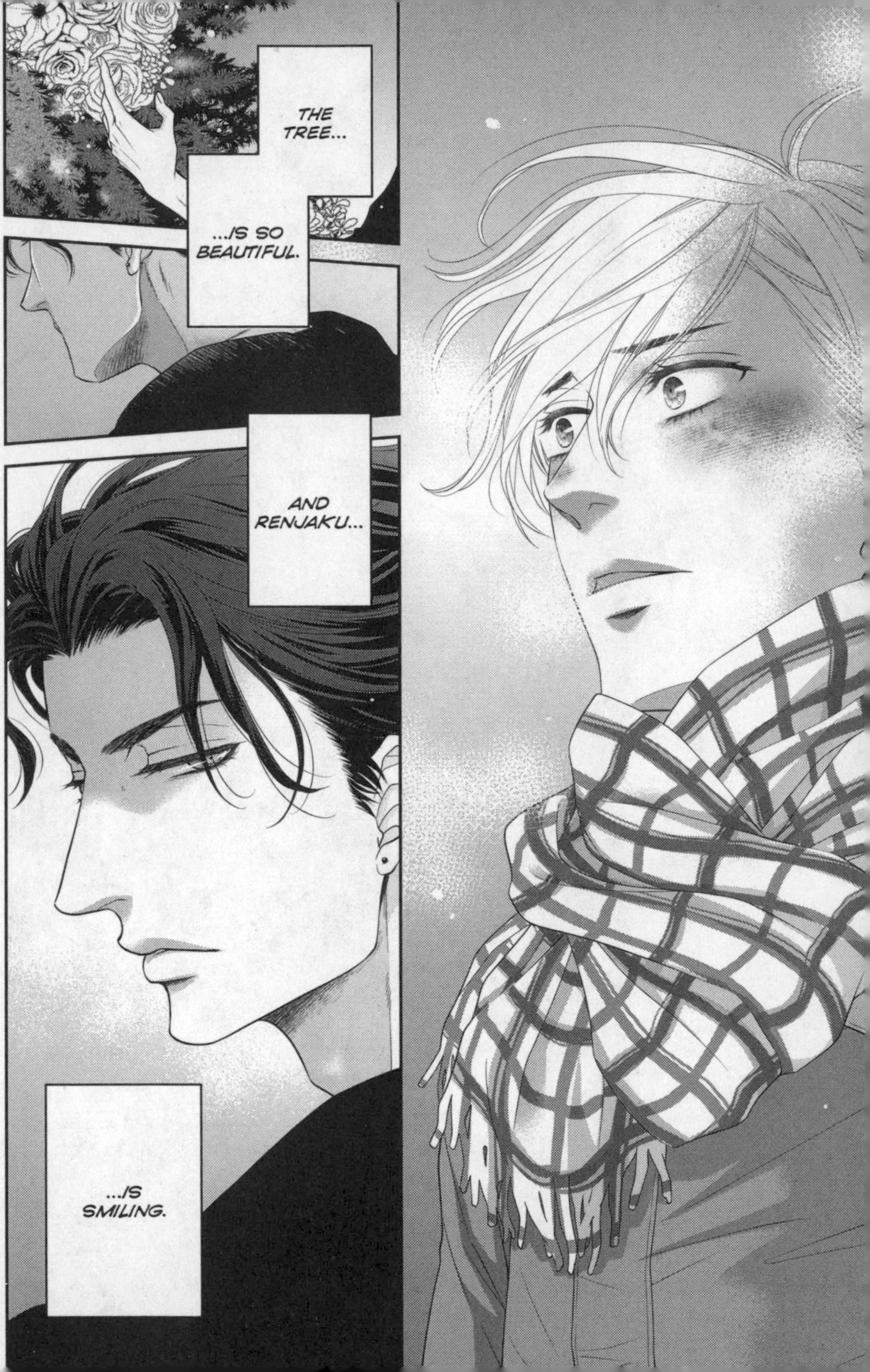
THE TREE...
...IS SO BEAUTIFUL.
AND RENJAKU...
...IS SMILING.

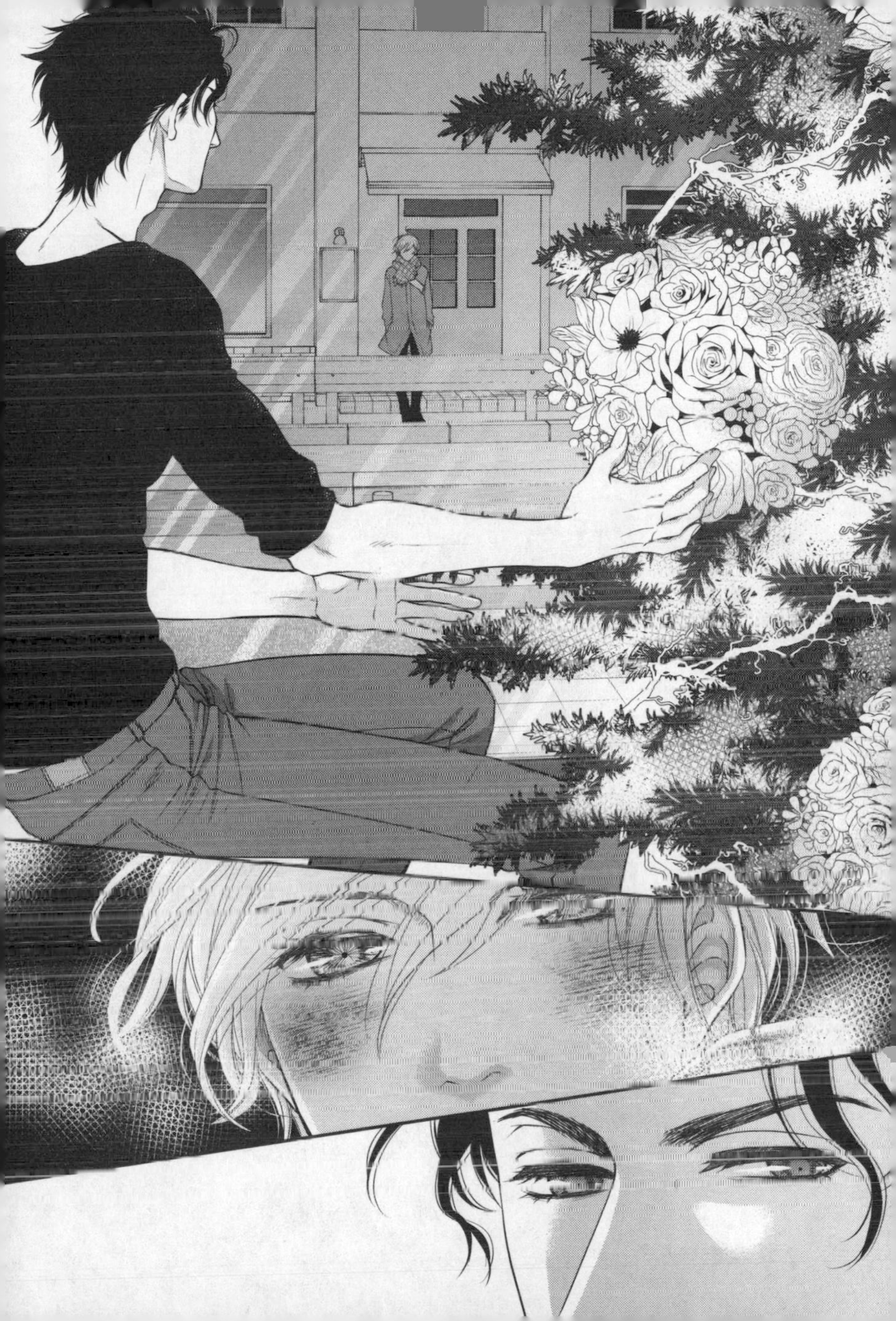

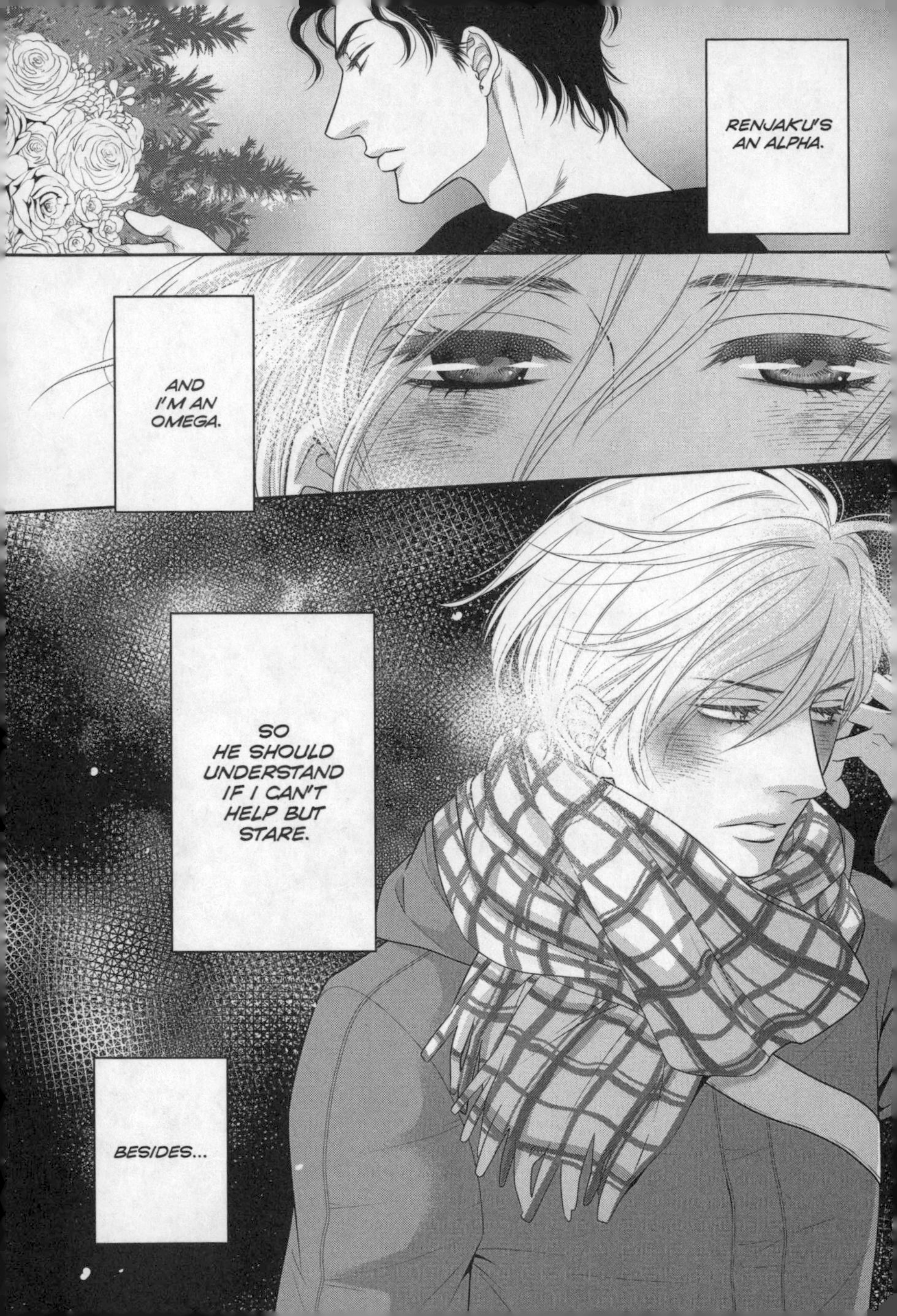
RENJAKU'S AN ALPHA.
AND I'M AN OMEGA.
SO HE SHOULD UNDERSTAND IF I CAN'T HELP BUT STARE.
BESIDES...

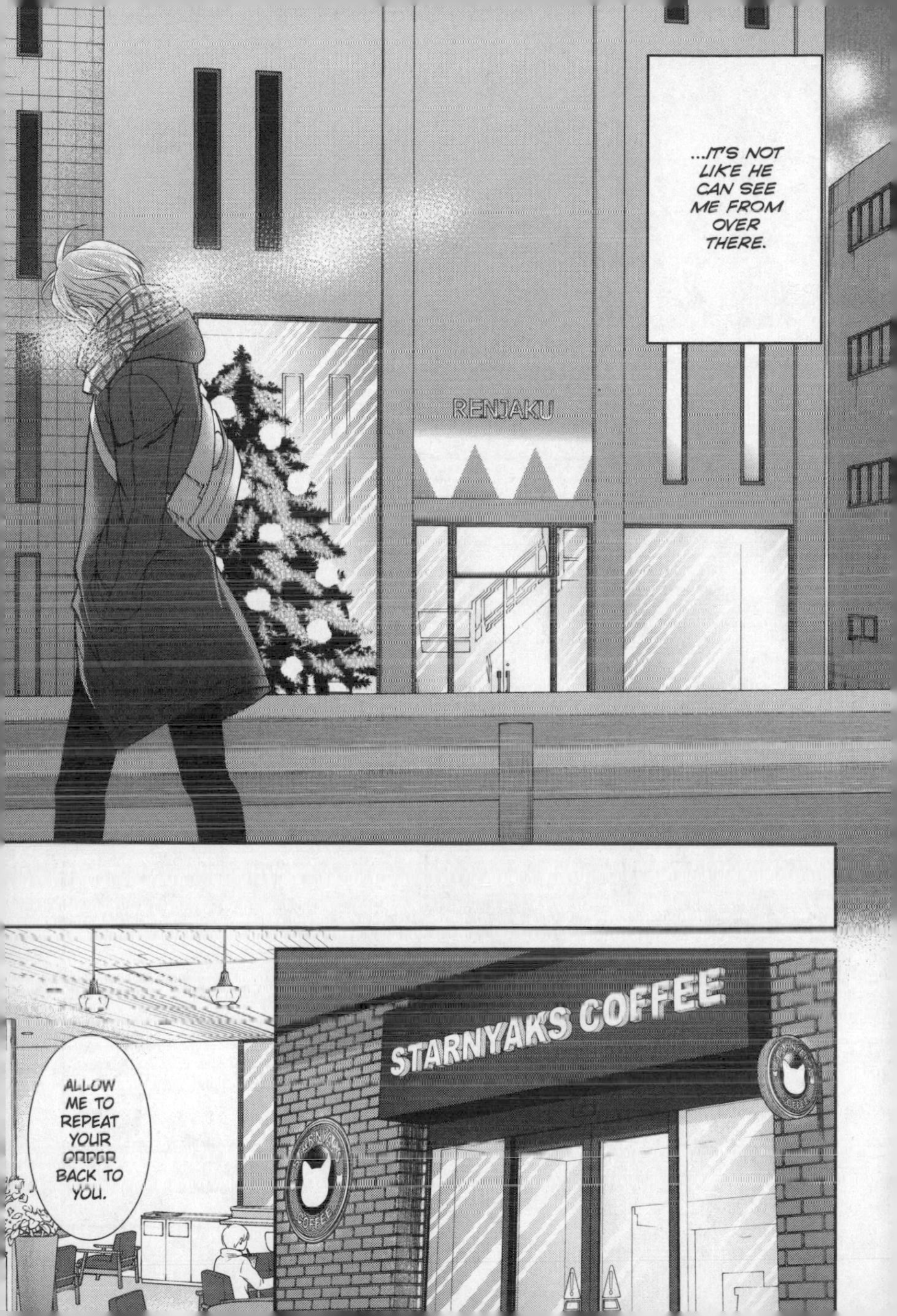
...IT'S NOT LIKE HE CAN SEE ME FROM OVER THERE.
RENJAKU
STARNYAKS COFFEE
ALLOW ME TO REPEAT YOUR ORDER BACK TO YOU.

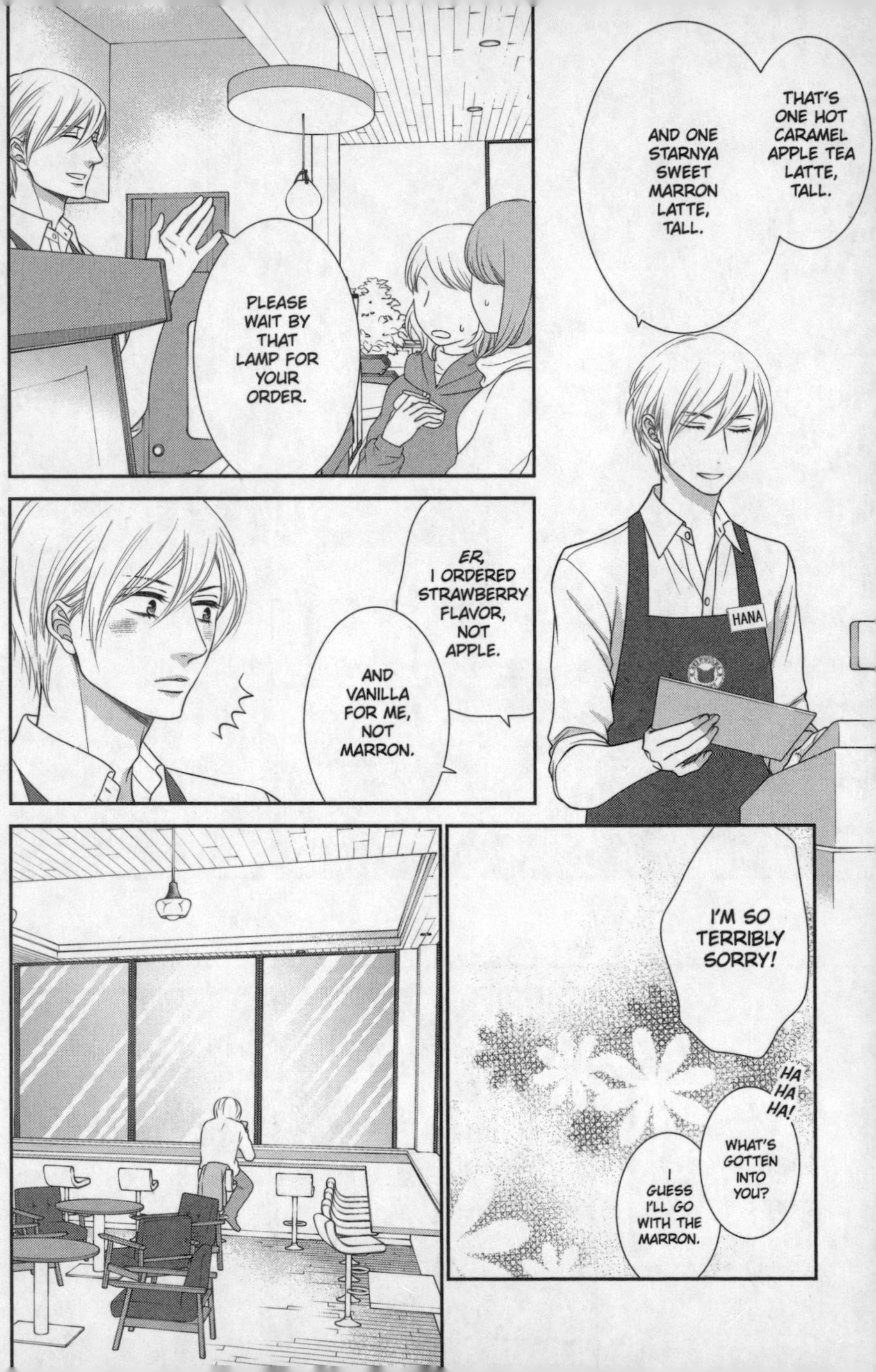
THAT'S ONE HOT CARAMEL APPLE TEA LATTE, TALL.
AND ONE STARNYA SWEET MARRON LATTE, TALL.
HANA
PLEASE WAIT BY THAT LAMP FOR YOUR ORDER.
ER, I ORDERED STRAWBERRY FLAVOR, NOT APPLE.
AND VANILLA FOR ME, NOT MARRON.
I'M SO TERRIBLY SORRY!
HA HA HA!
WHAT'S GOTTEN INTO YOU?
I GUESS I'LL GO WITH THE MARRON.

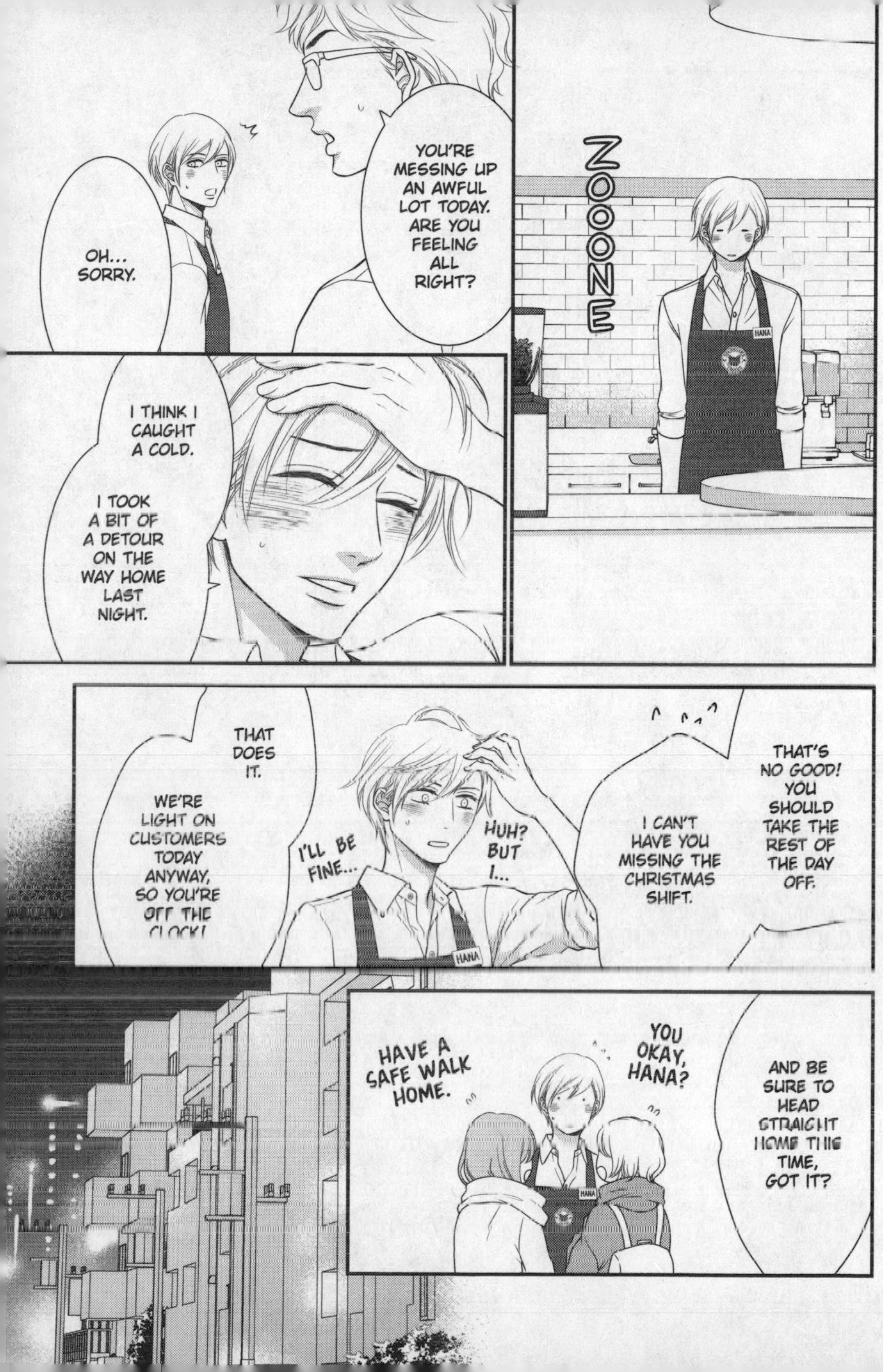
ZOOONE
YOU'RE MESSING UP AN AWFUL LOT TODAY. ARE YOU FEELING ALL RIGHT?
OH... SORRY.
I THINK I CAUGHT A COLD.
I TOOK A BIT OF A DETOUR ON THE WAY HOME LAST NIGHT.
THAT'S NO GOOD! YOU SHOULD TAKE THE REST OF THE DAY OFF.
I CAN'T HAVE YOU MISSING THE CHRISTMAS SHIFT.
HUH? BUT I...
I'LL BE FINE...
THAT DOES IT.
WE'RE LIGHT ON CUSTOMERS TODAY ANYWAY, SO YOU'RE OFF THE CLOCK!
AND BE SURE TO HEAD STRAIGHT HOME THIS TIME, GOT IT?
YOU OKAY, HANA?
HAVE A SAFE WALK HOME.

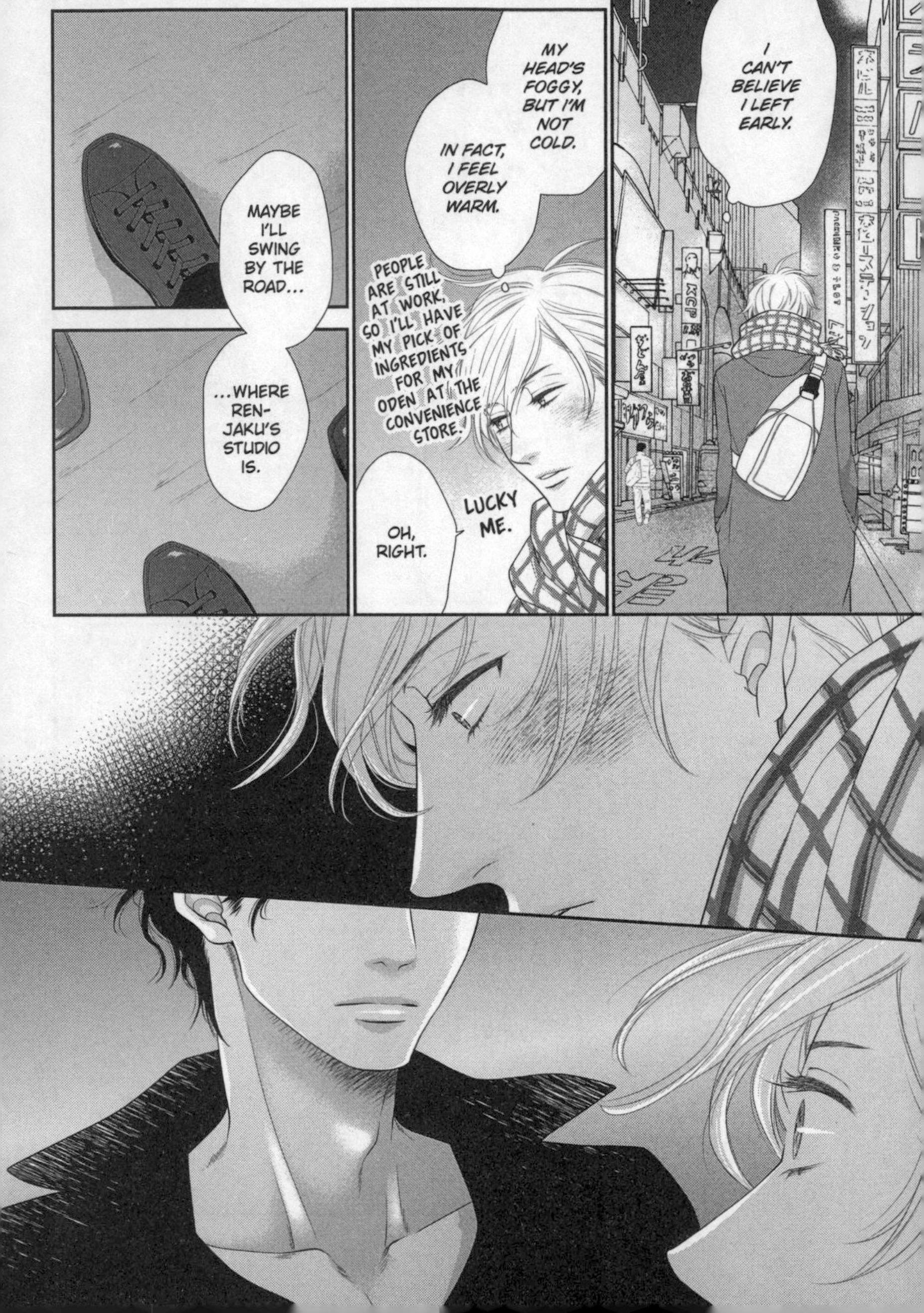
I CAN'T BELIEVE I LEFT EARLY.
MY HEAD'S FOGGY, BUT I'M NOT COLD.
IN FACT, I FEEL OVERLY WARM.
PEOPLE ARE STILL AT WORK, SO I'LL HAVE MY PICK OF INGREDIENTS FOR MY ODEN AT THE CONVENIENCE STORE.
LUCKY ME.
OH, RIGHT.
MAYBE I'LL SWING BY THE ROAD...
...WHERE REN-JAKU'S STUDIO IS.

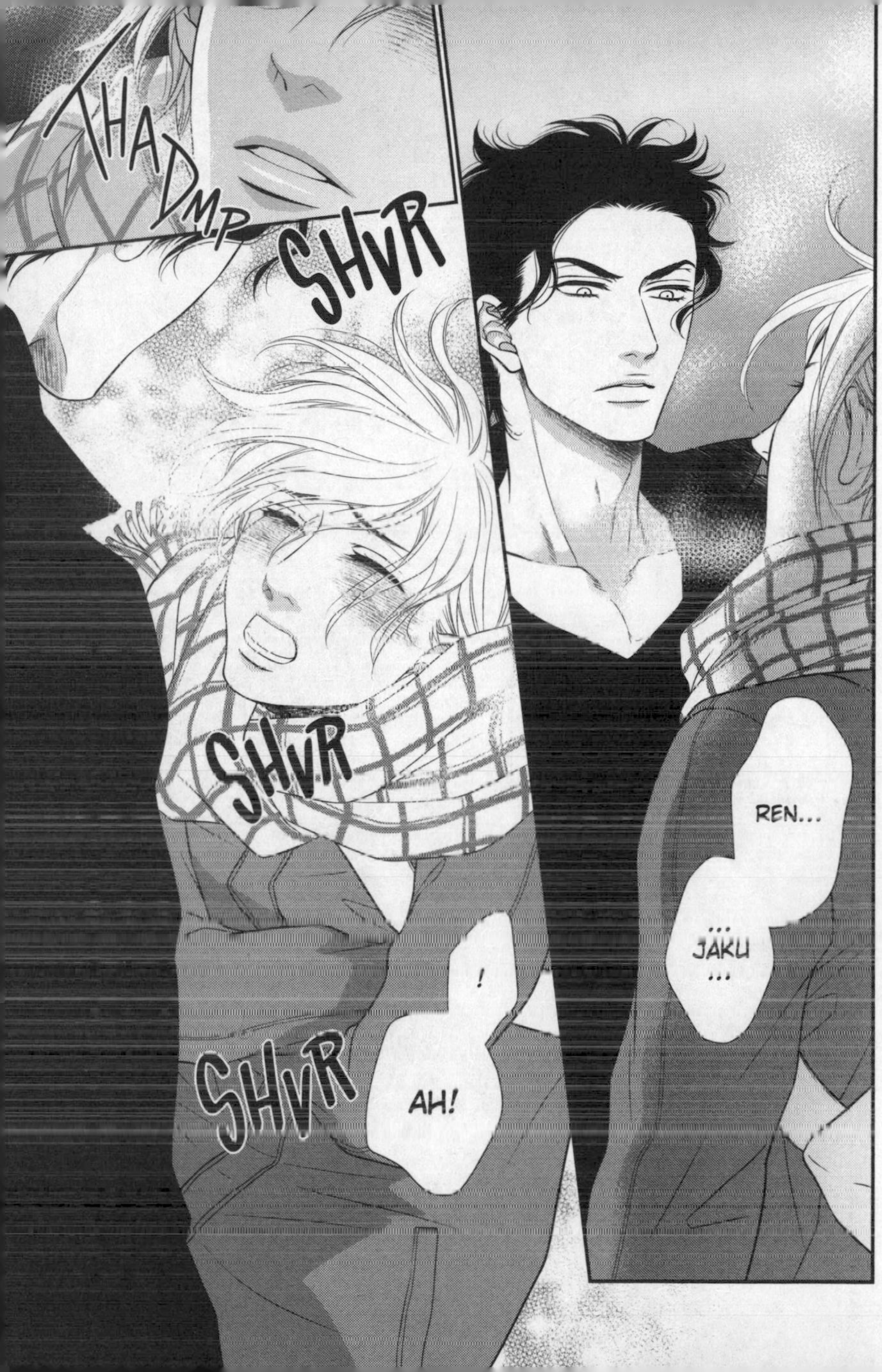
REN...
...JAKU...
THADMP
SHVR
SHVR
!
SHVR
AH!

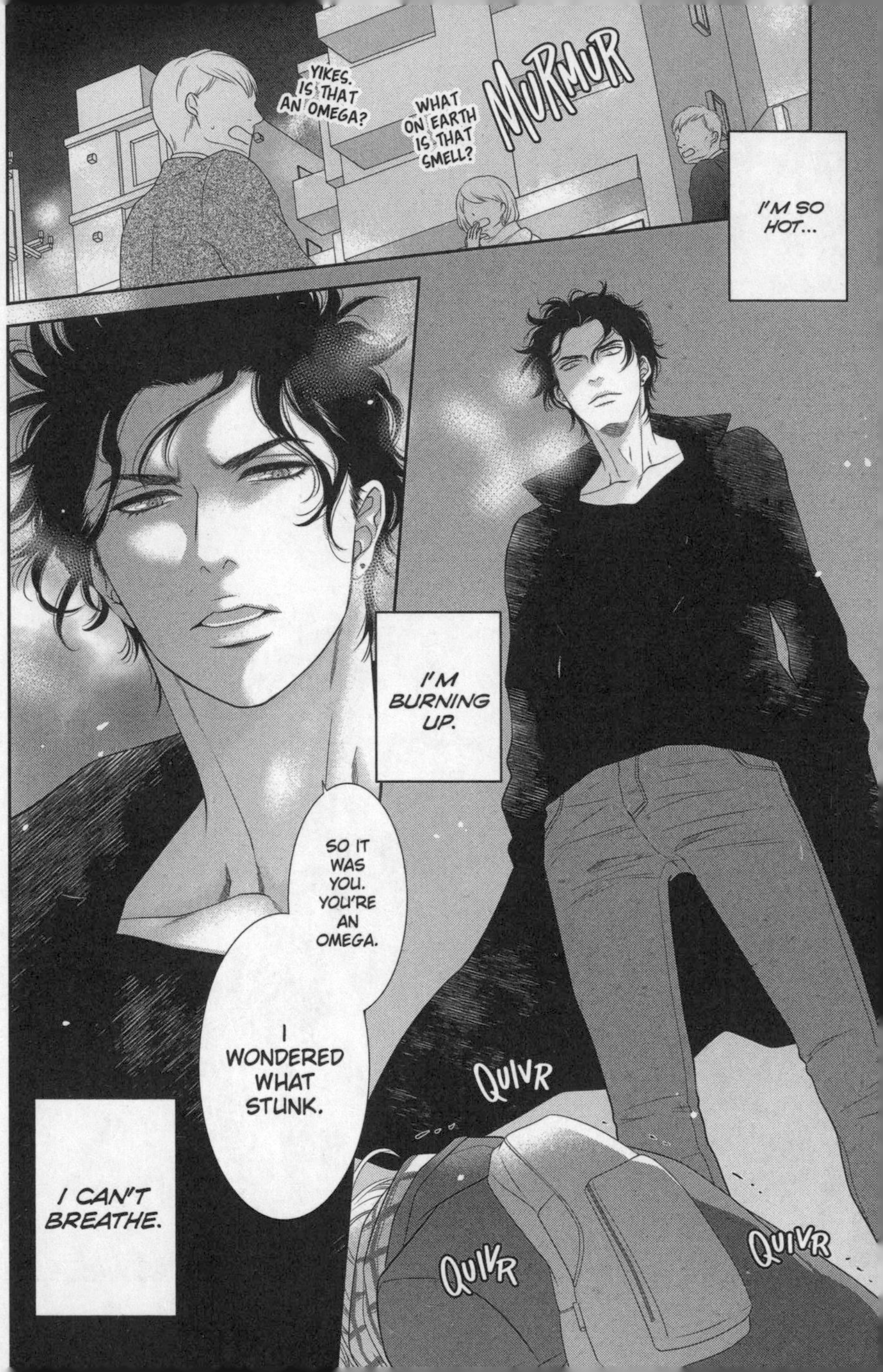
MURMUR
WHAT ON EARTH IS THAT SMELL?
YIKES. IS THAT AN OMEGA?
I'M SO HOT...
I'M BURNING UP.
SO IT WAS YOU. YOU'RE AN OMEGA.
I WONDERED WHAT STUNK.
QUIVR
QUIVR
QUIVR
I CAN'T BREATHE.

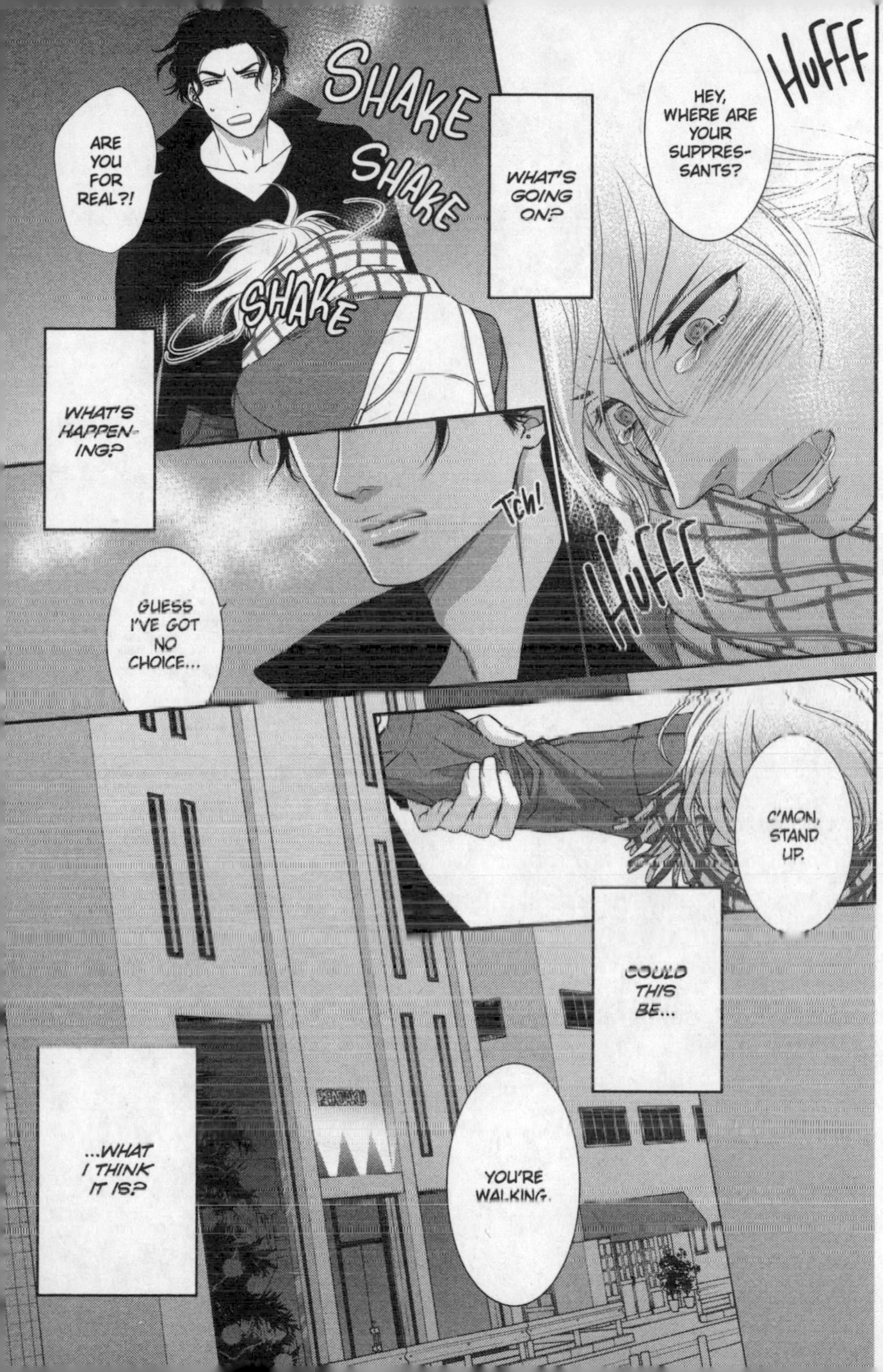
HUFFF
HEY, WHERE ARE YOUR SUPPRES-SANTS?
WHAT'S GOING ON?
HUFFF
ARE YOU FOR REAL?!
SHAKE SHAKE
SHAKE
WHAT'S HAPPEN-ING?
Tch!
GUESS I'VE GOT NO CHOICE...
C'MON, STAND UP.
COULD THIS BE...
YOU'RE WALKING.
...WHAT I THINK IT IS?

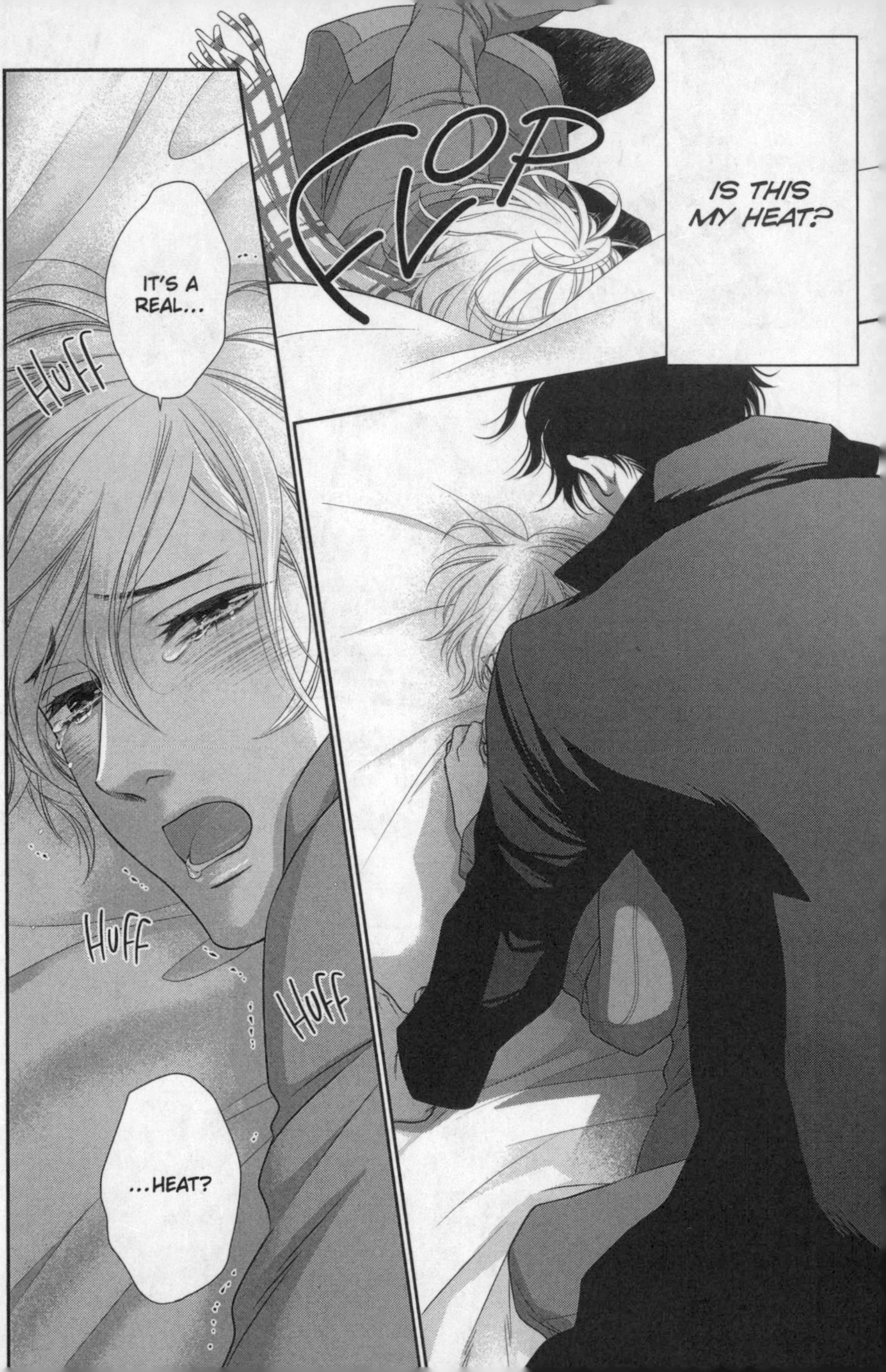
IS THIS MY HEAT?
FLOP
...
IT'S A REAL...
HUFF
HUFF
HUFF
...HEAT?

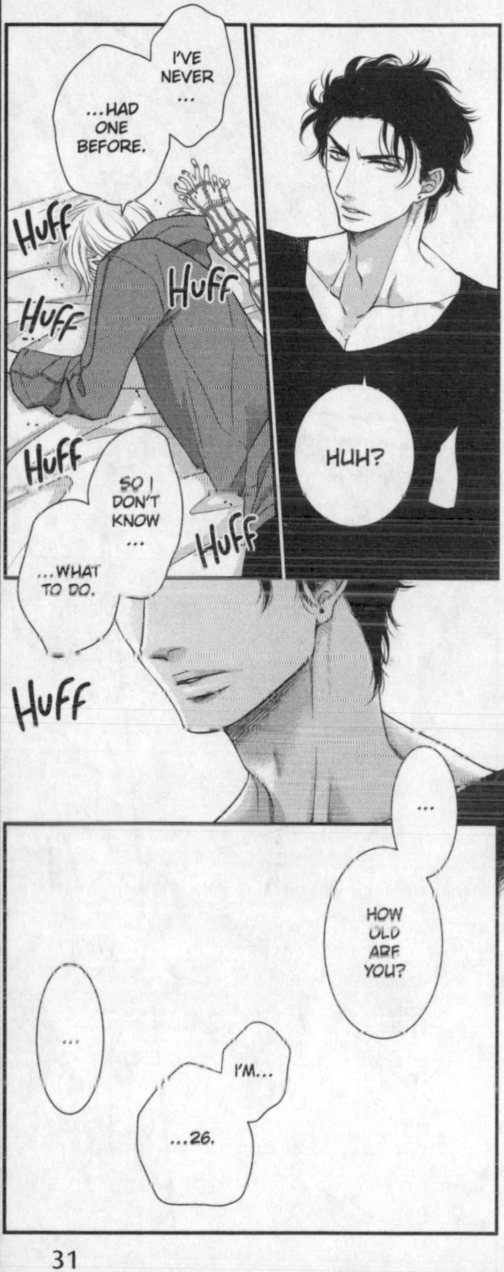
HUH?
I'VE NEVER ...
...HAD ONE BEFORE.
HUFF
HUFF
HUFF
HUFF
HUFF
SO I DON'T KNOW ...
...WHAT TO DO.
HUFF
...
HOW OLD ARE YOU?
...
I'M...
...26.

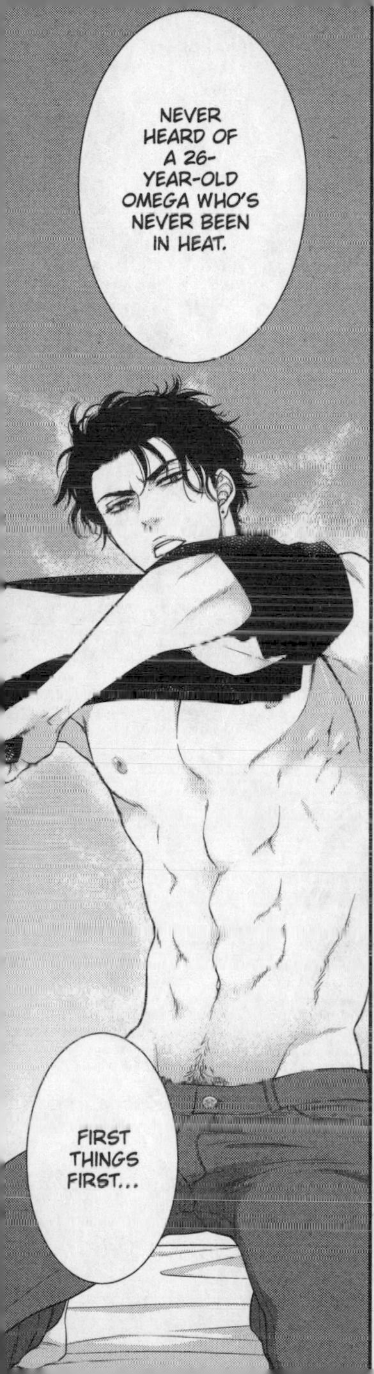
NEVER HEARD OF A 26-YEAR-OLD OMEGA WHO'S NEVER BEEN IN HEAT.
FIRST THINGS FIRST...

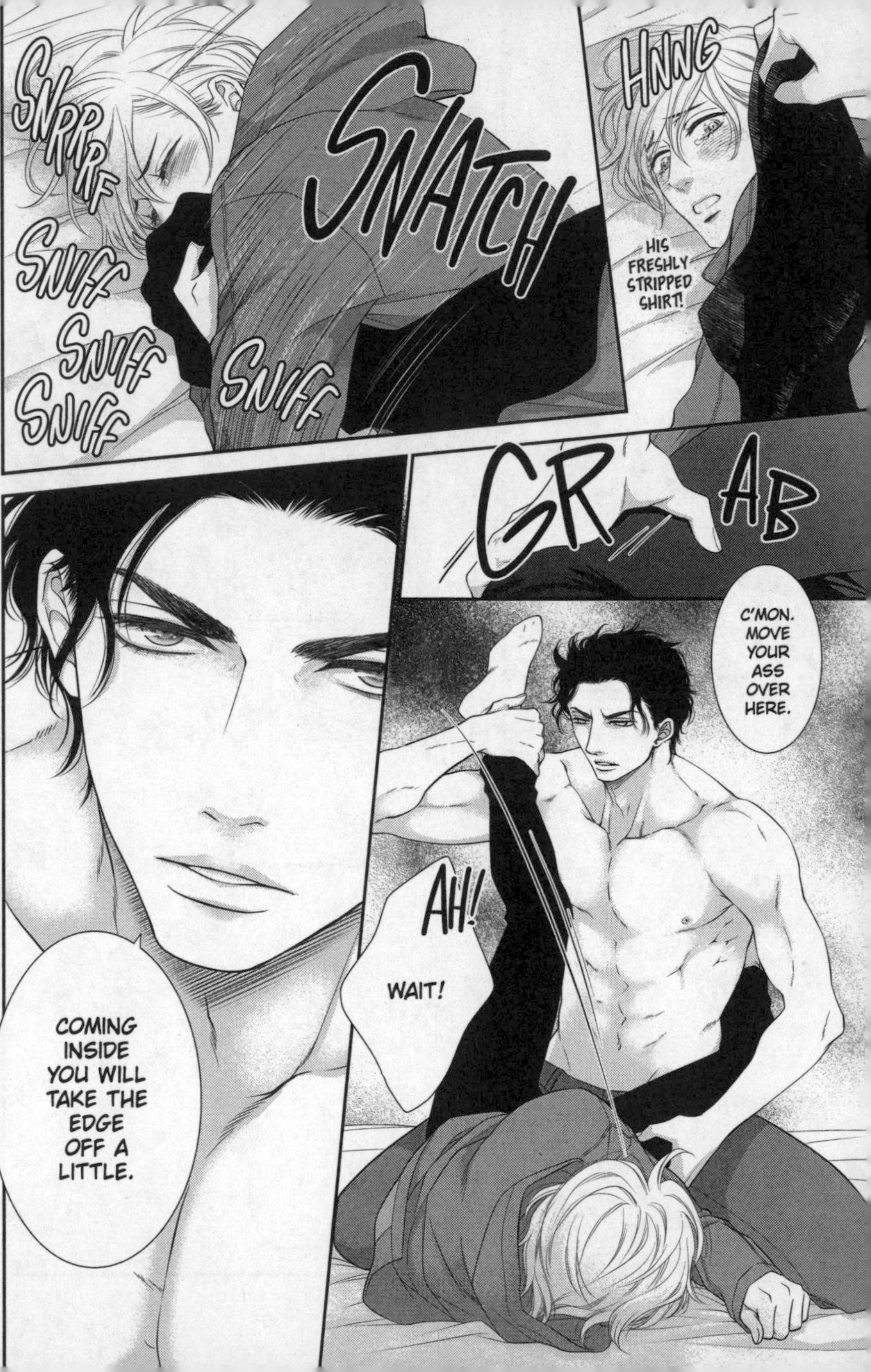
HNNG
HIS FRESHLY STRIPPED SHIRT!
SNATCH
SNIFF
SNRRRF
SNIFF
SNIFF
SNIFF
GR AB
C'MON. MOVE YOUR ASS OVER HERE.
AH!
WAIT!
COMING INSIDE YOU WILL TAKE THE EDGE OFF A LITTLE.

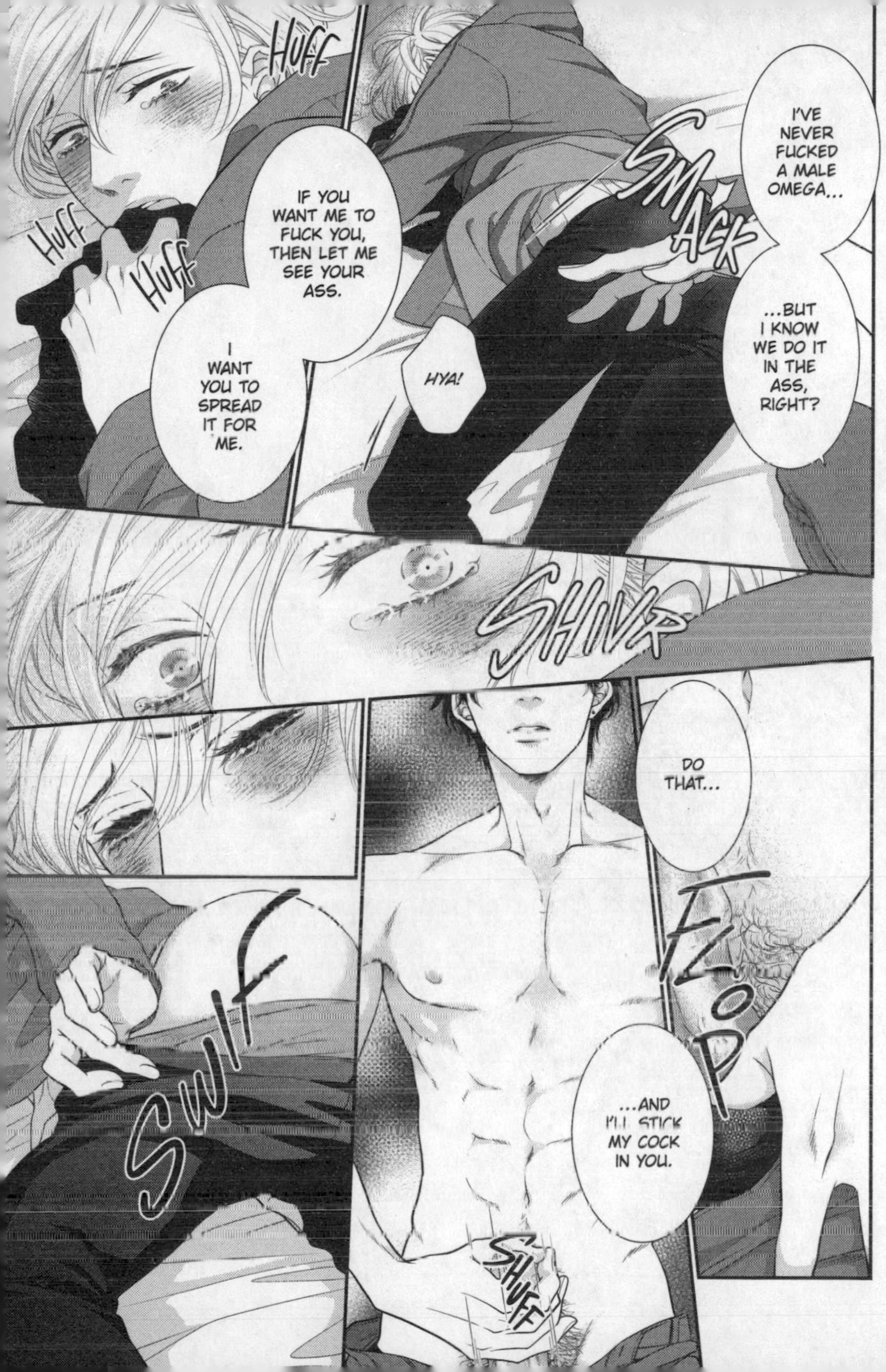
I'VE NEVER FUCKED A MALE OMEGA...
...BUT I KNOW WE DO IT IN THE ASS, RIGHT?
SMACK
HYA!
IF YOU WANT ME TO FUCK YOU, THEN LET ME SEE YOUR ASS.
I WANT YOU TO SPREAD IT FOR ME.
HUFF
HUFF
HUFF
SHIVR
DO THAT...
FLOP
...AND I'LL STICK MY COCK IN YOU.
SHUFF
SWIF

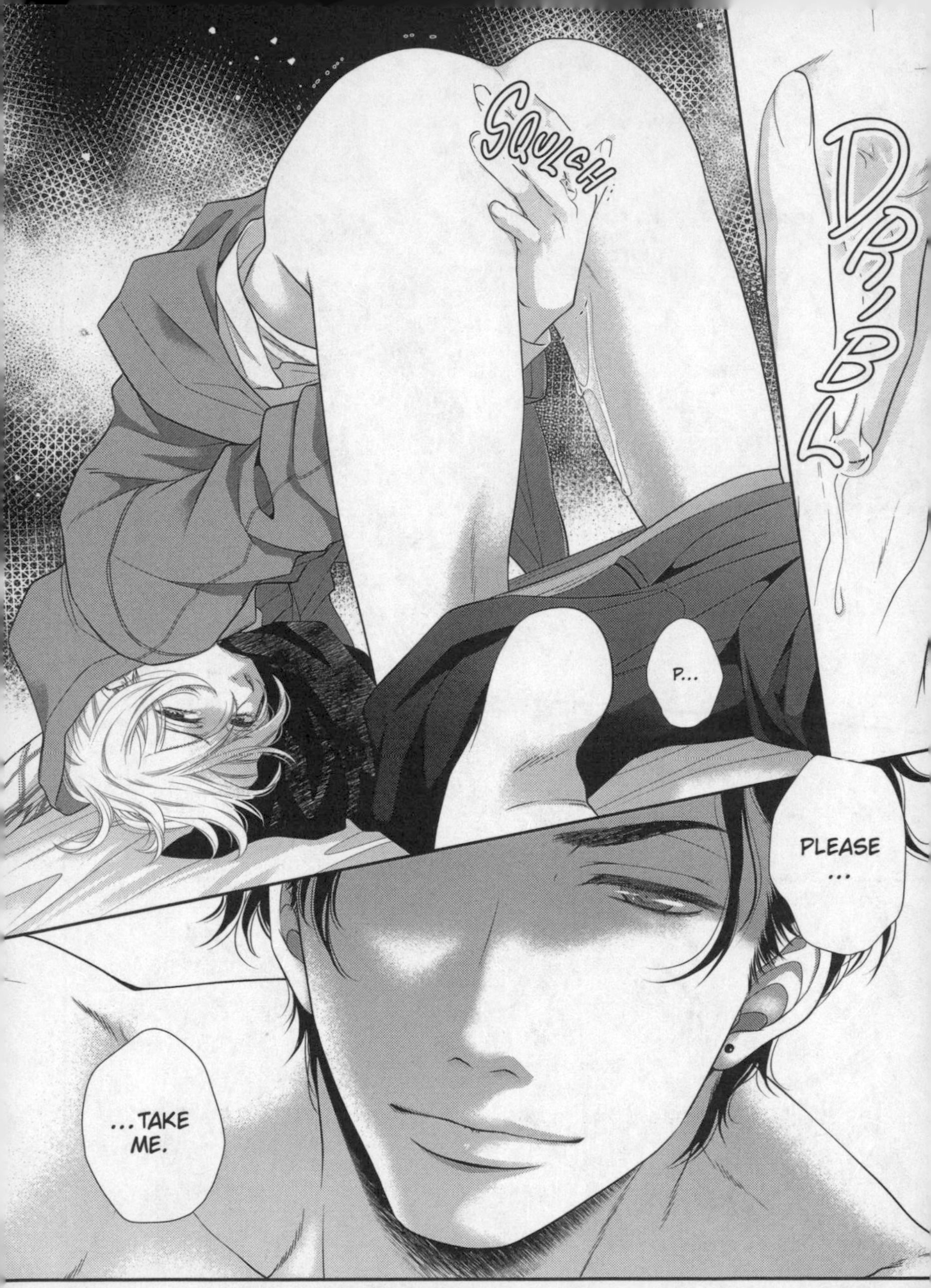
DRIBL
SQULCH
P...
PLEASE ...
...TAKE ME.

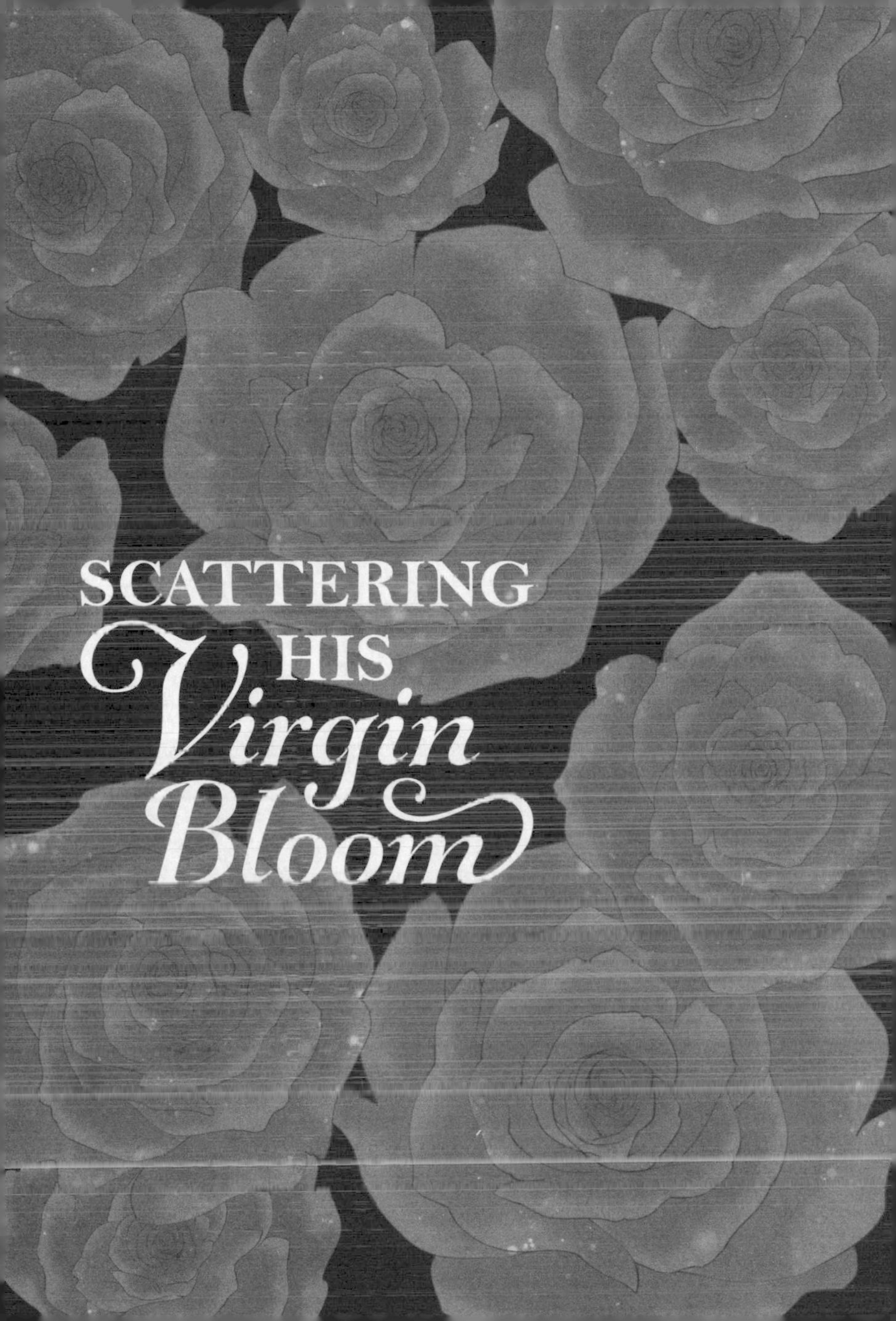
SCATTERING HIS
Virgin
Bloom

#02
Scattering His Virgin Bloom

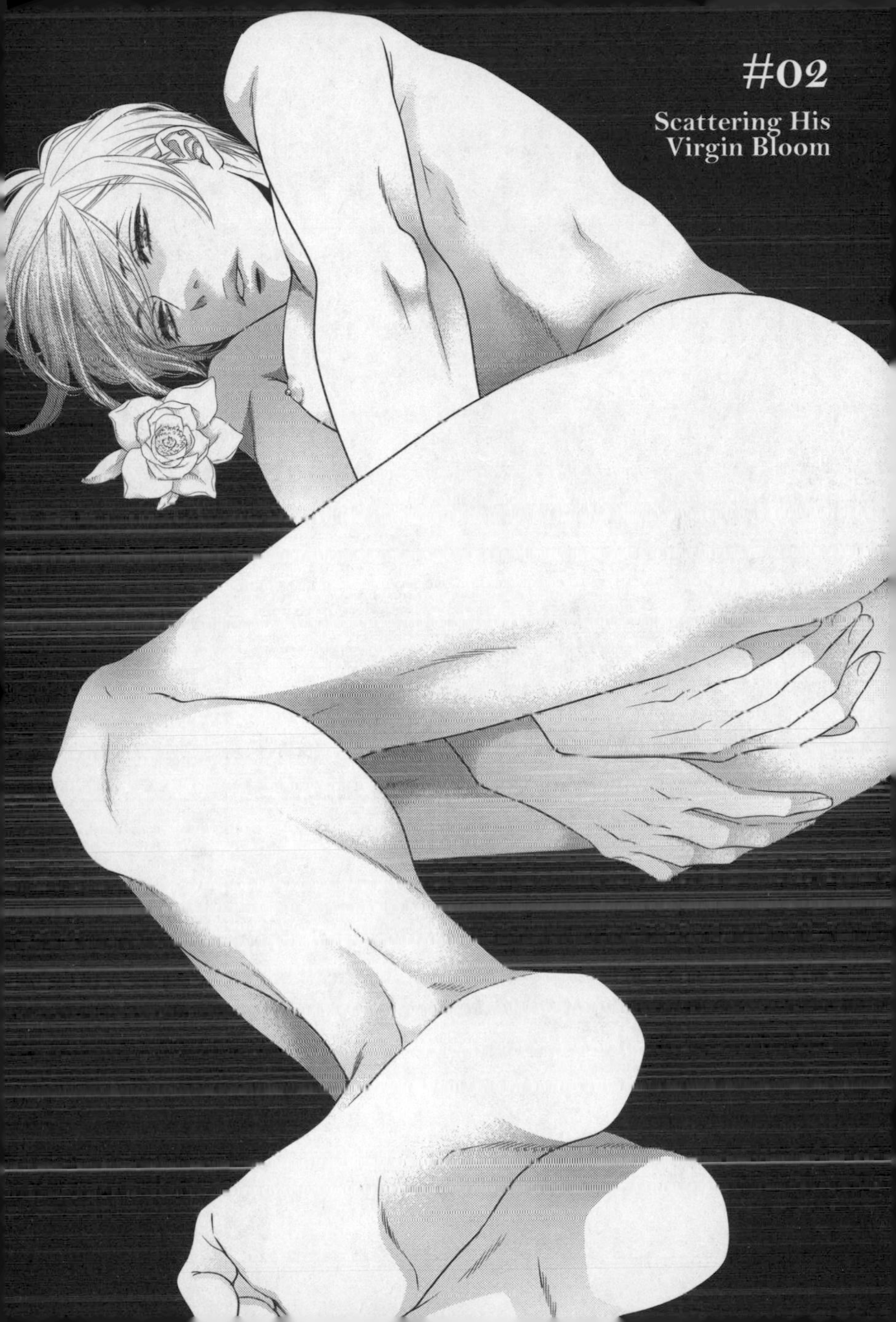

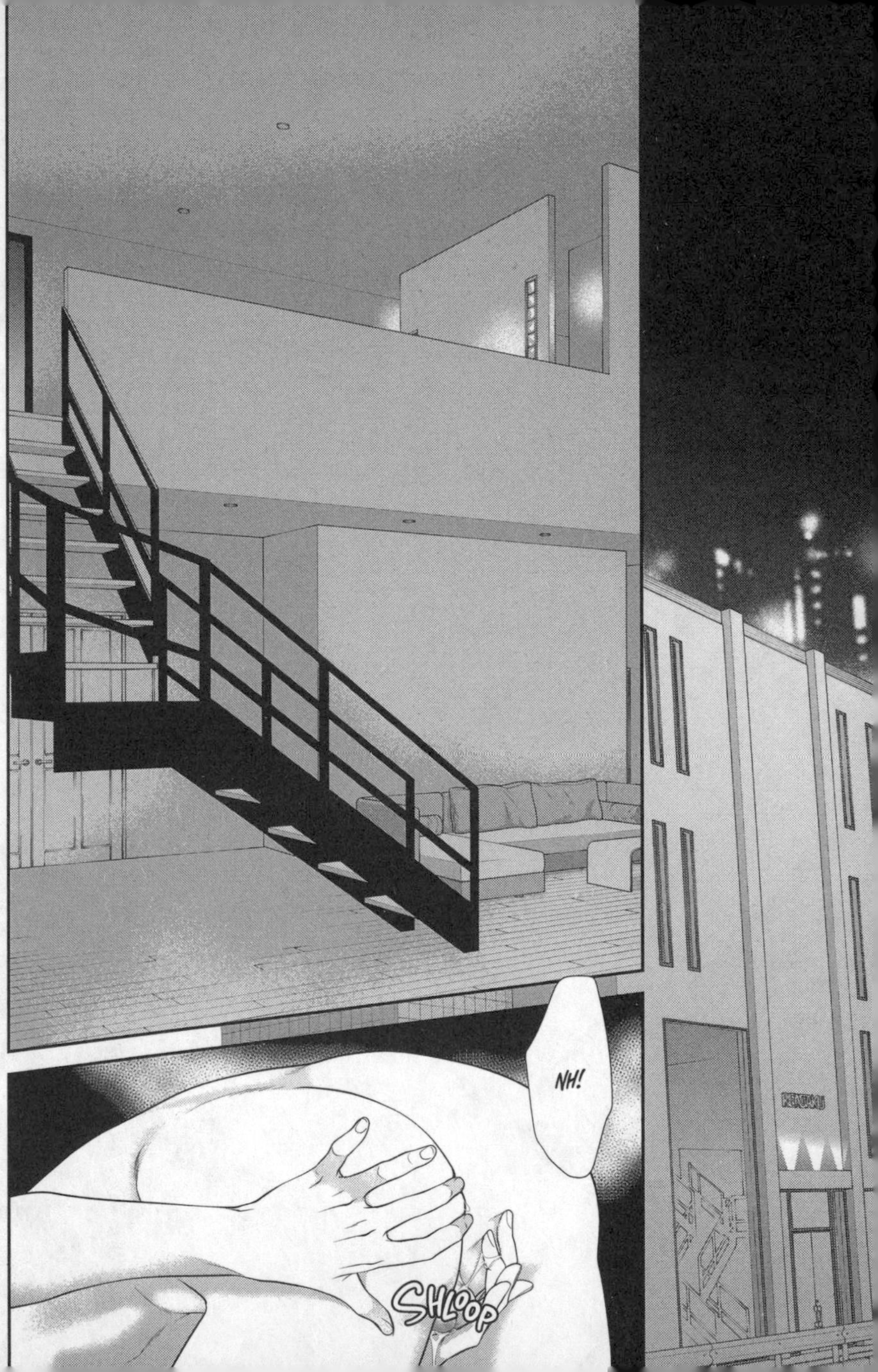
NH!
SHLOOP

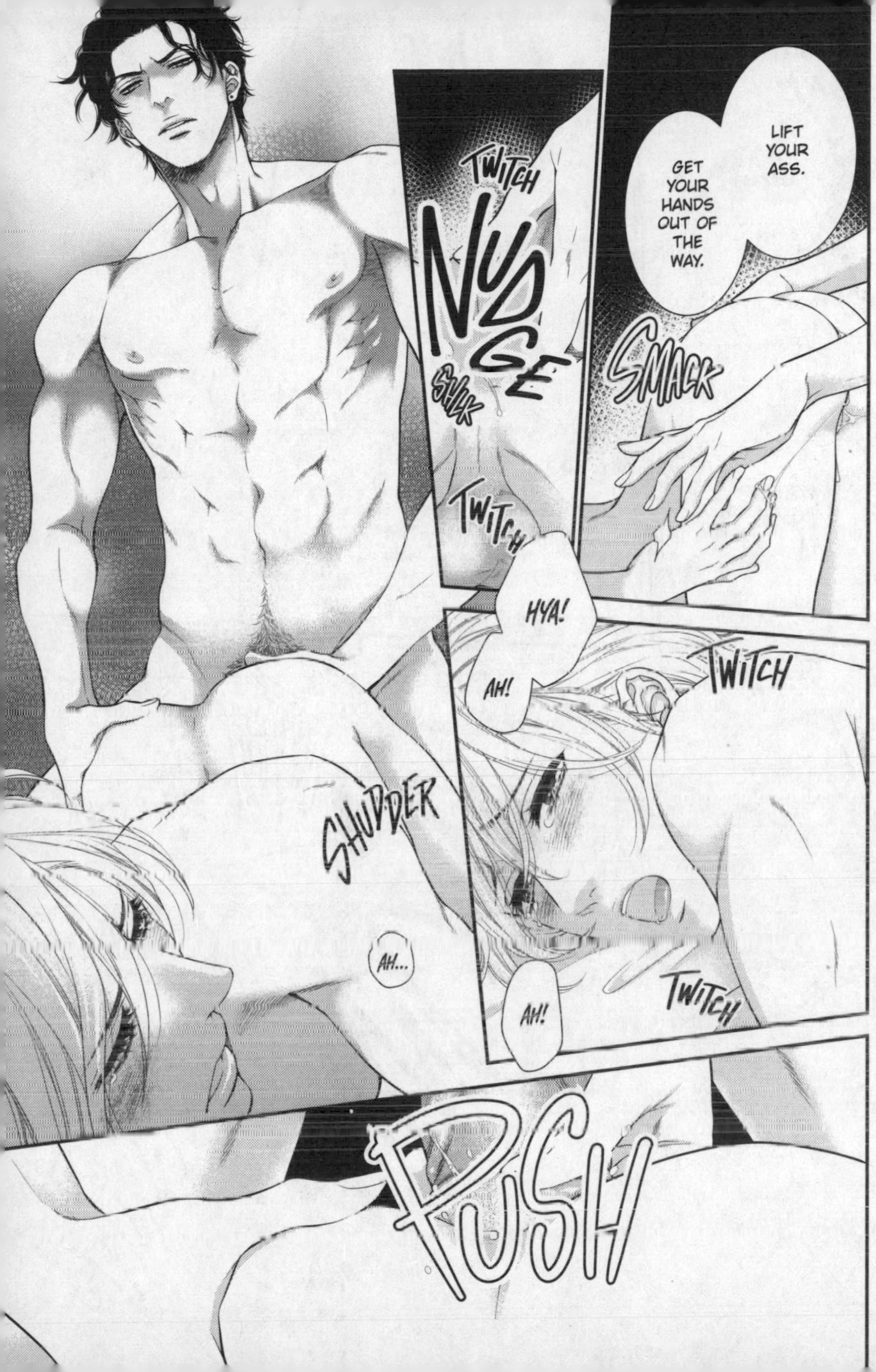
LIFT YOUR ASS.
GET YOUR HANDS OUT OF THE WAY.
SMACK
TWITCH
NUDGE
SHLK
TWITCH
HYA!
AH!
TWITCH
AH!
TWITCH
SHUDDER
AH...
PUSH

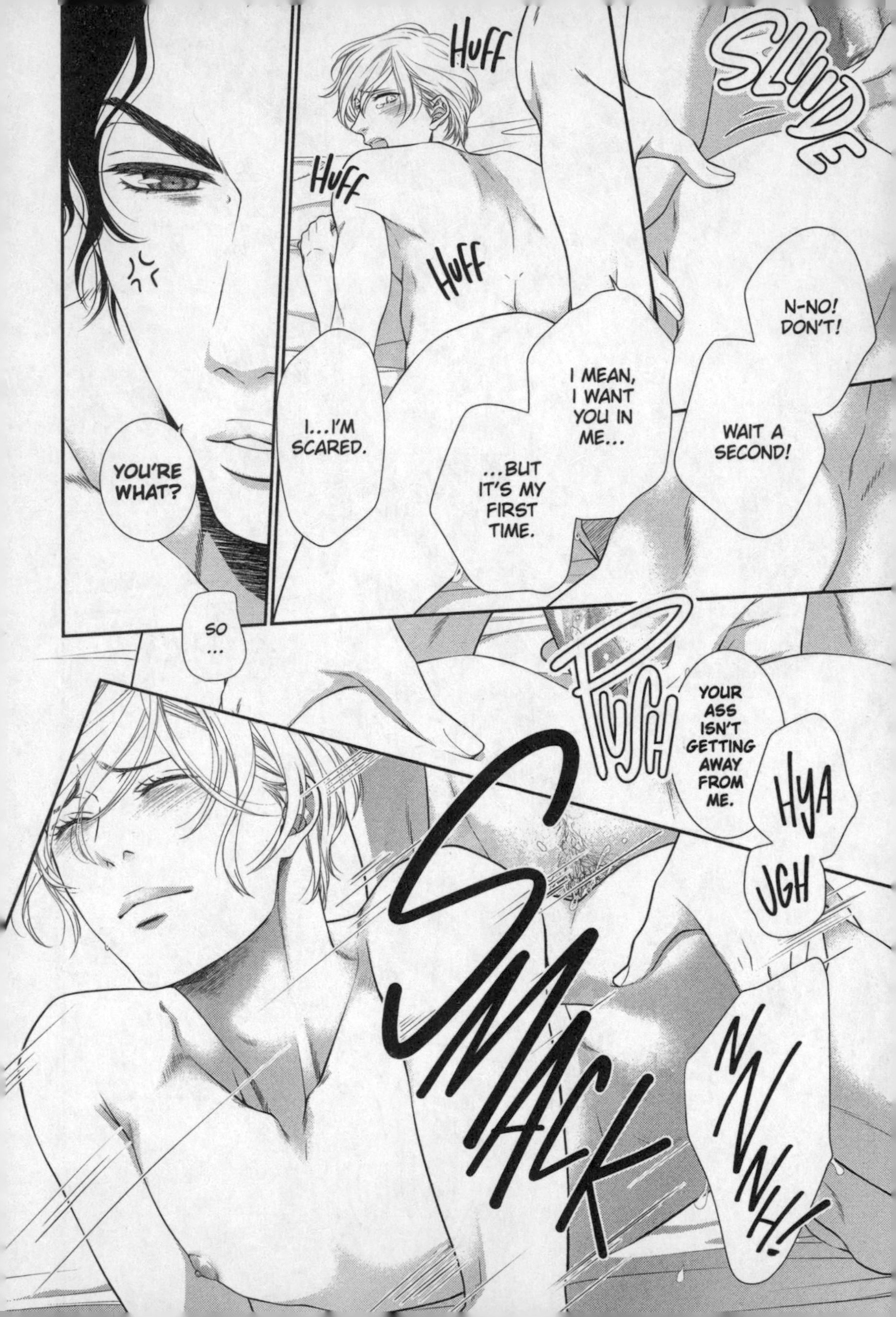
SLIIIDE
N-NO! DON'T!
WAIT A SECOND!
HUFF
HUFF
HUFF
I MEAN, I WANT YOU IN ME...
...BUT IT'S MY FIRST TIME.
I...I'M SCARED.
YOU'RE WHAT?
SO ...
PUSH
YOUR ASS ISN'T GETTING AWAY FROM ME.
HYA
UGH
SMACK
NNNH!

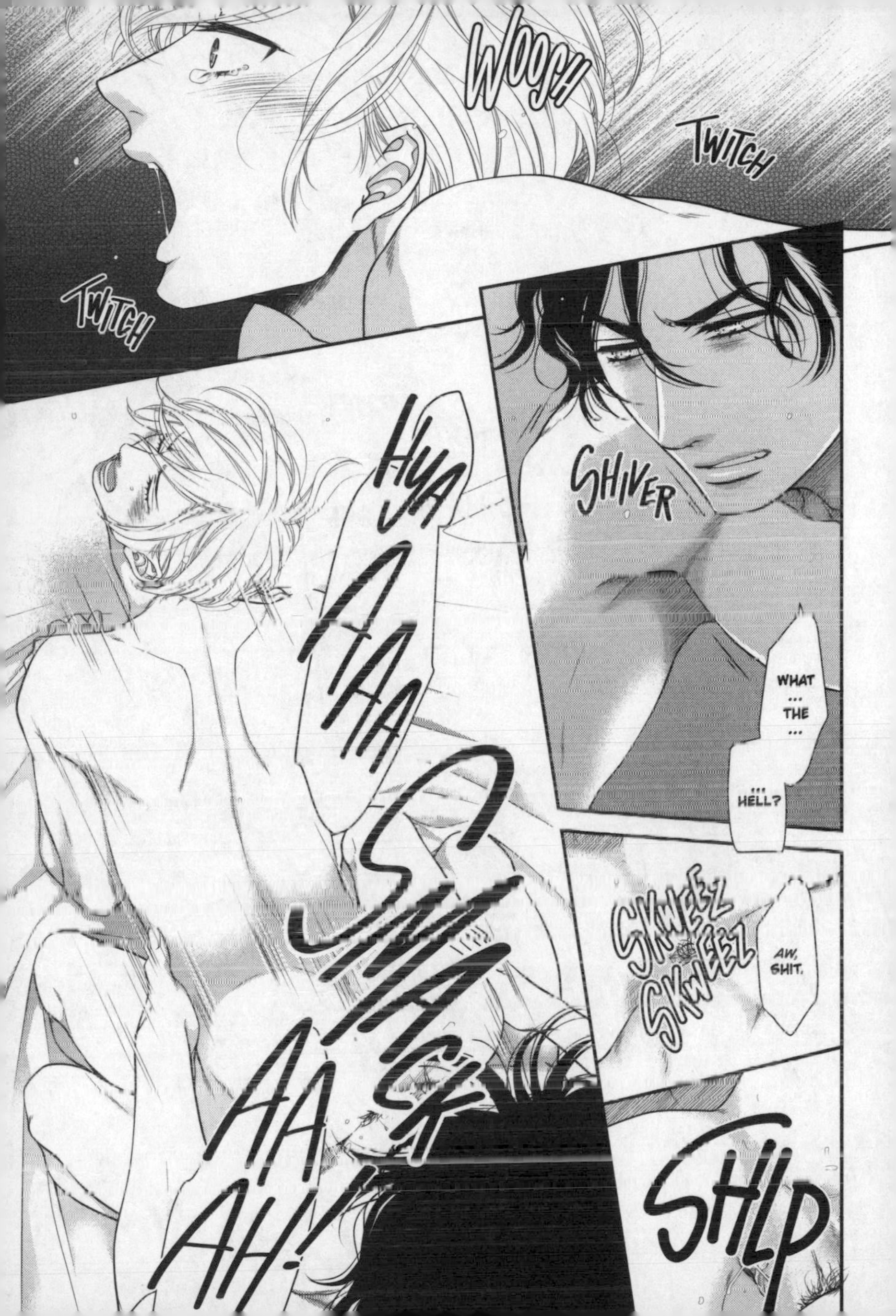
WOOSH
TWITCH
TWITCH
SHIVER
WHAT ... THE ...
... HELL?
SKWEEZ SKWEEZ
AW, SHIT.
SHLP
HYAAAAA
SMACK
AAAAH-!

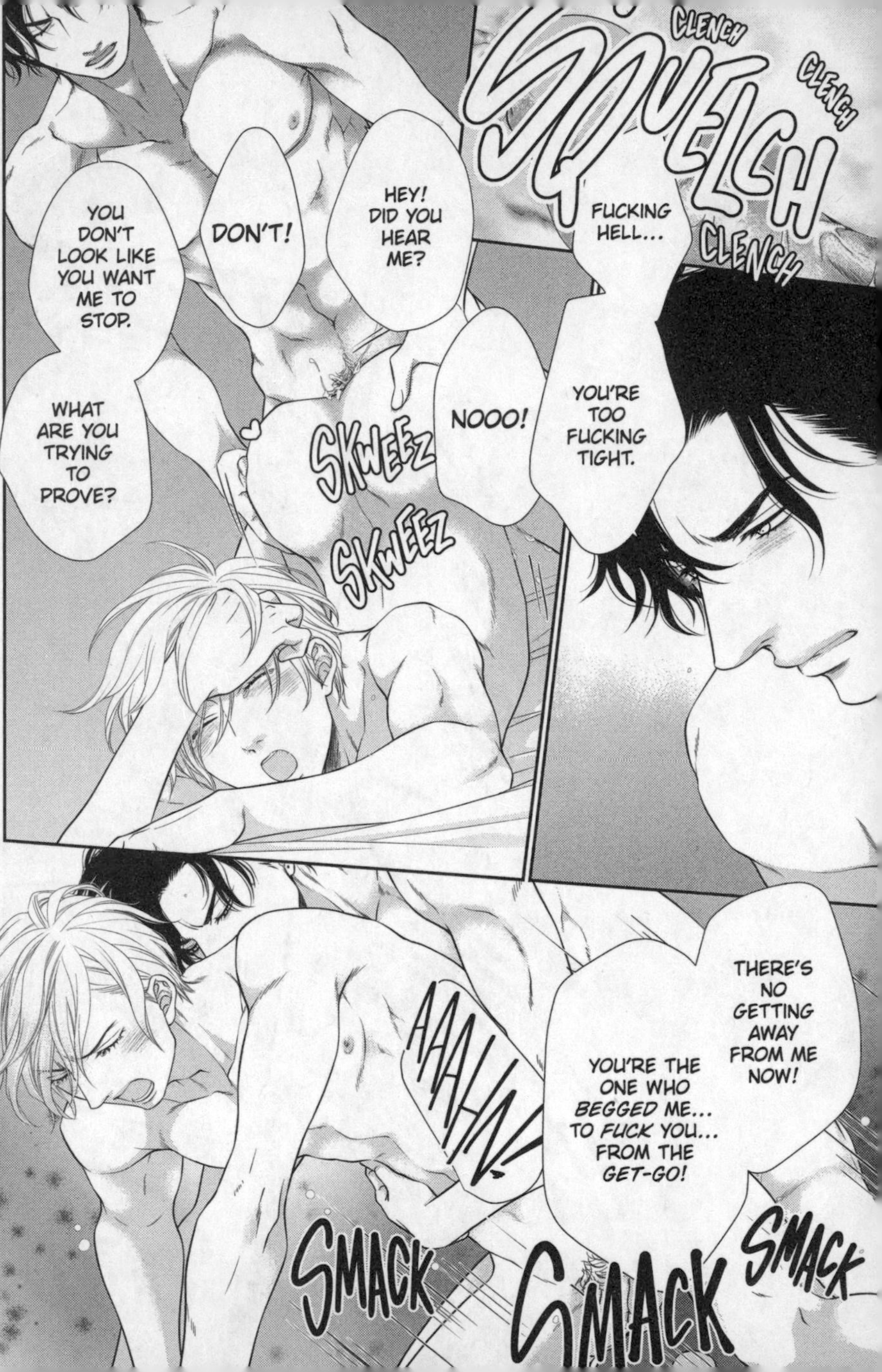
CLENCH
CLENCH
SQUELCH
CLENCH
FUCKING HELL...
YOU'RE TOO FUCKING TIGHT.
HEY! DID YOU HEAR ME?
DON'T!
YOU DON'T LOOK LIKE YOU WANT ME TO STOP.
NOOO!
SKWEEZ
SKWEEZ
WHAT ARE YOU TRYING TO PROVE?
THERE'S NO GETTING AWAY FROM ME NOW!
YOU'RE THE ONE WHO BEGGED ME... TO *FUCK* YOU... FROM THE *GET-GO!*
AAAHN!
SMACK
SMACK
SMACK

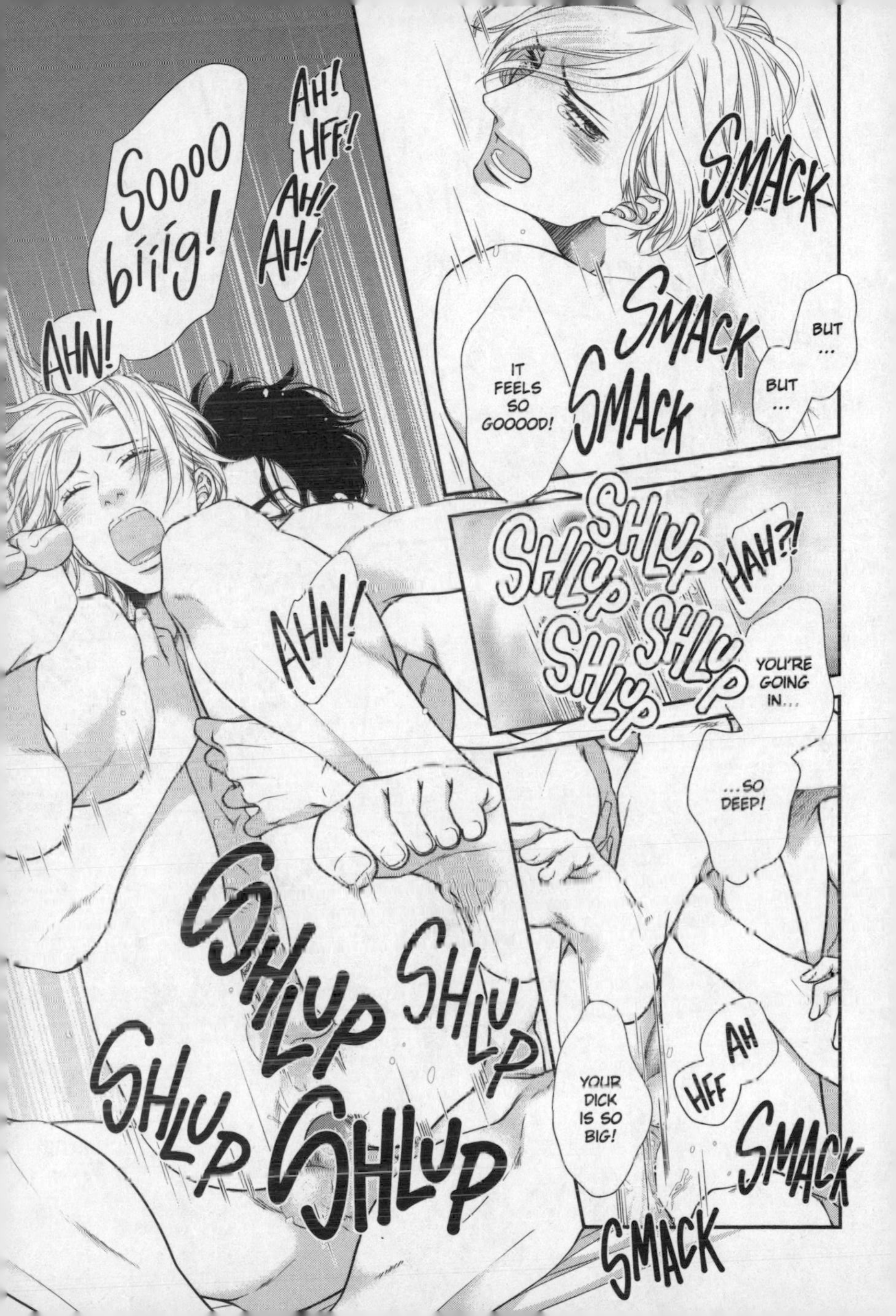
SMACK
BUT... BUT...
SMACK SMACK
IT FEELS SO GOOOOD!
SHLUP SHLUP SHLUP SHLUP SHLUP
HAH?!
YOU'RE GOING IN...
...SO DEEP!
AH HFF
YOUR DICK IS SO BIG!
SMACK SMACK
AH! HFF! AH! AH!
Soooo bíiíg!
AHN!
AHN!
SHLUP SHLUP SHLUP SHLUP

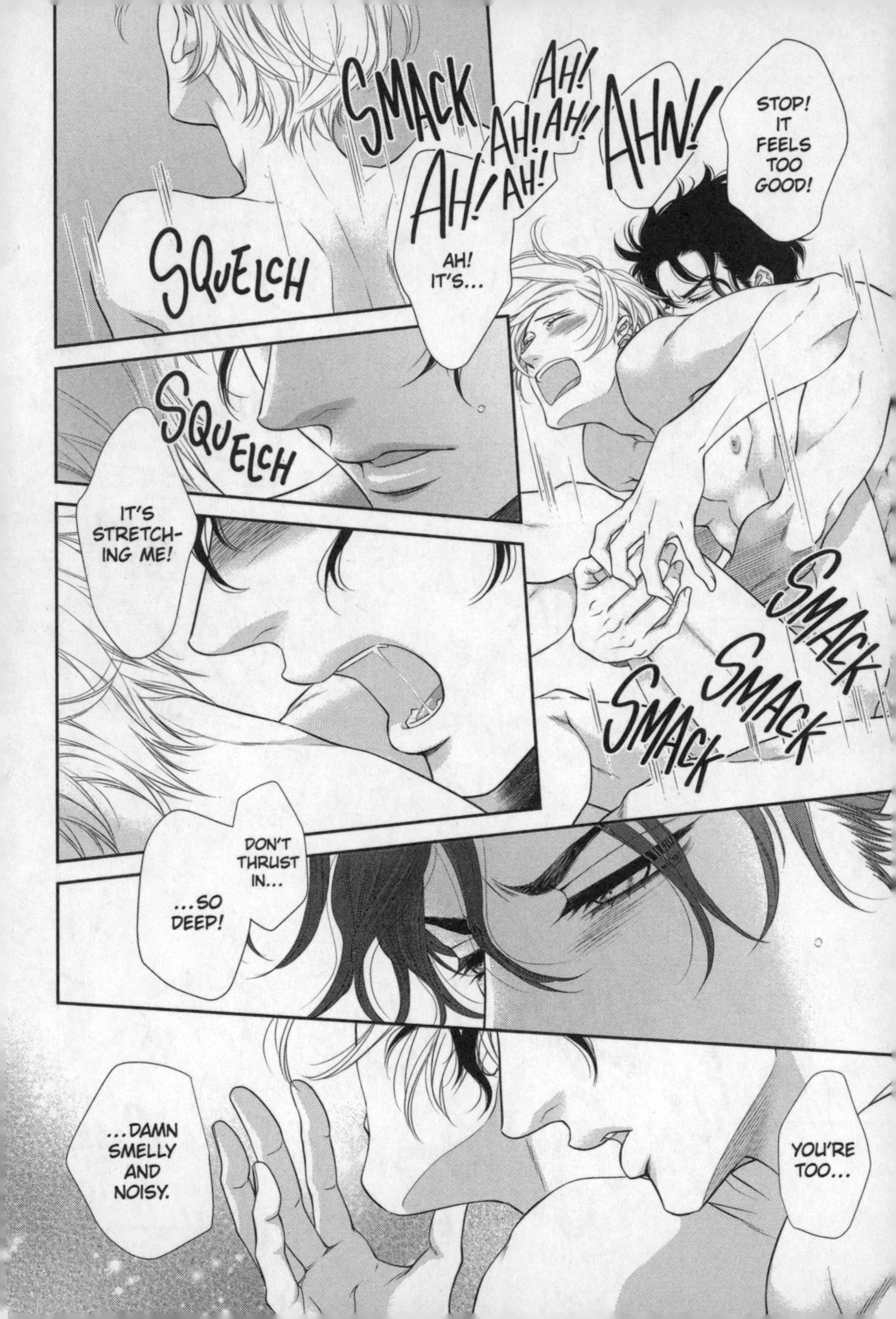
STOP! IT FEELS TOO GOOD!
AHN!
AH! AH! AH! AH! AH!
SMACK
SQUELCH
AH! IT'S...
SMACK SMACK SMACK
SQUELCH
IT'S STRETCHING ME!
DON'T THRUST IN...
...SO DEEP!
YOU'RE TOO...
...DAMN SMELLY AND NOISY.

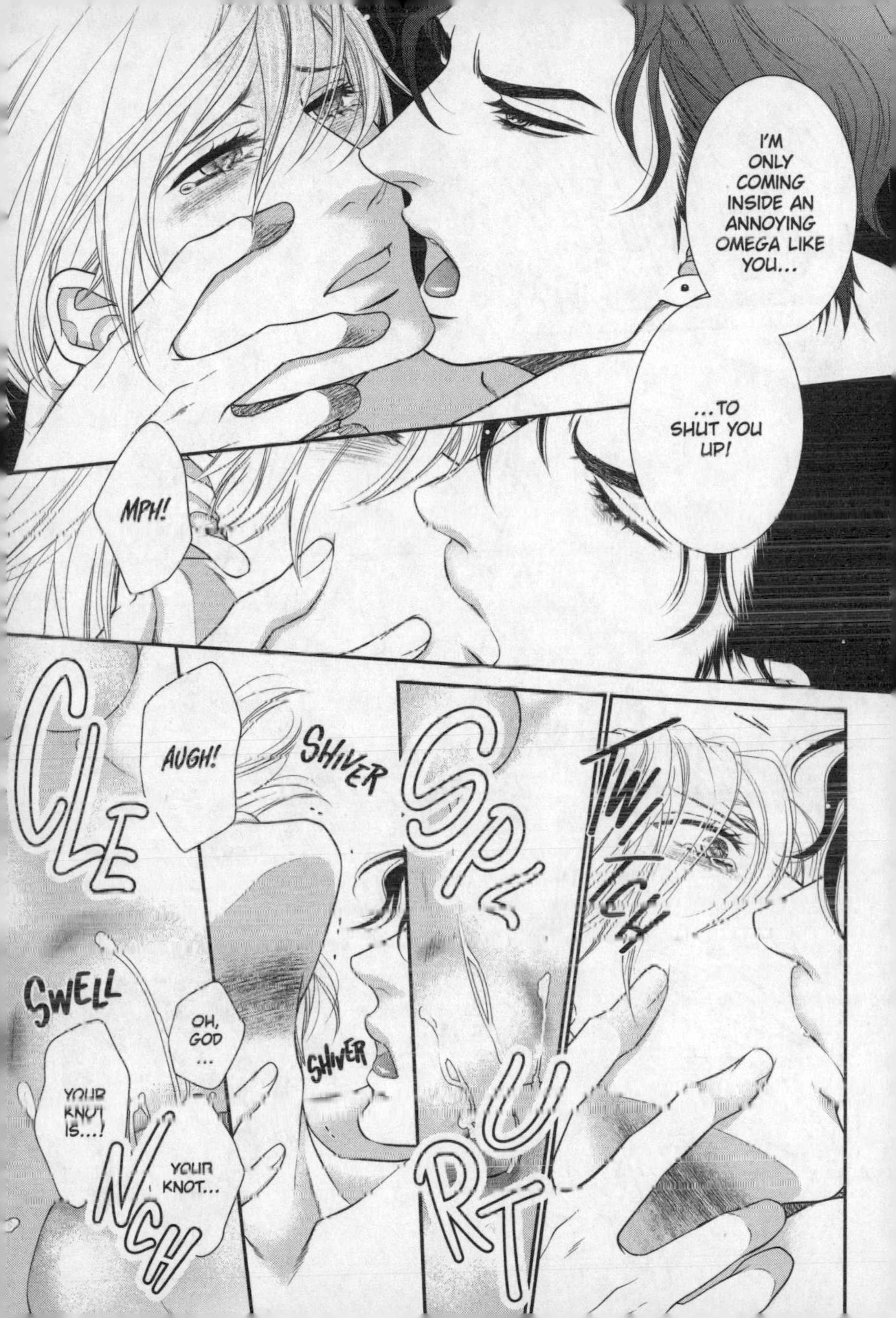
I'M ONLY COMING INSIDE AN ANNOYING OMEGA LIKE YOU...
...TO SHUT YOU UP!
MPH!
TWITCH
SPLURT
CLENCH
AUGH!
SHIVER
OH, GOD ...
SHIVER
SWELL
YOUR KNOT IS...!
YOUR KNOT...

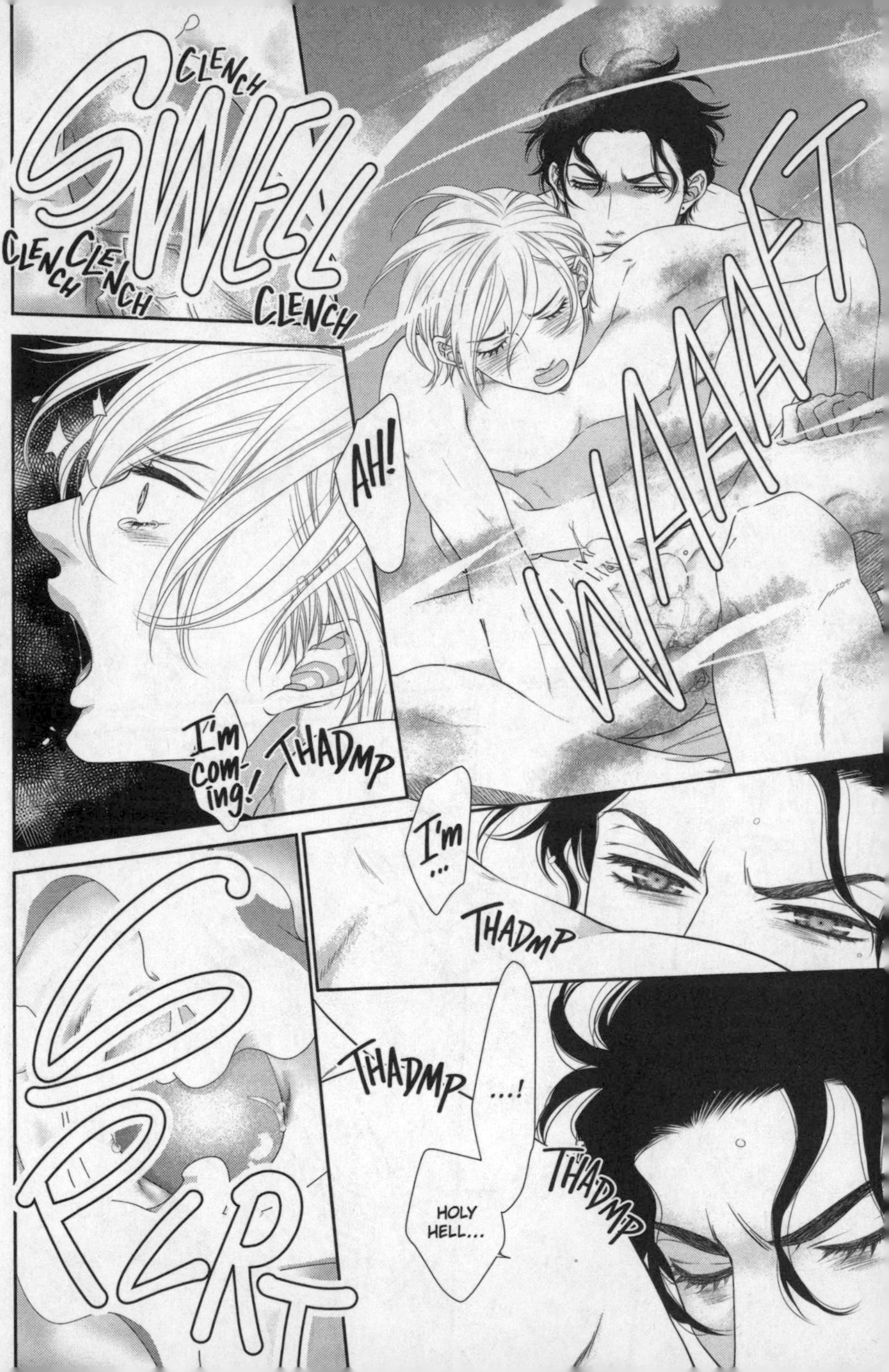
WAAAFT
SWELL
CLENCH
CLENCH CLENCH CLENCH
CLENCH
AH!
I'm com-ing!
THADMP
I'm...
THADMP
...!
THADMP
HOLY HELL...
THADMP
SPLRT

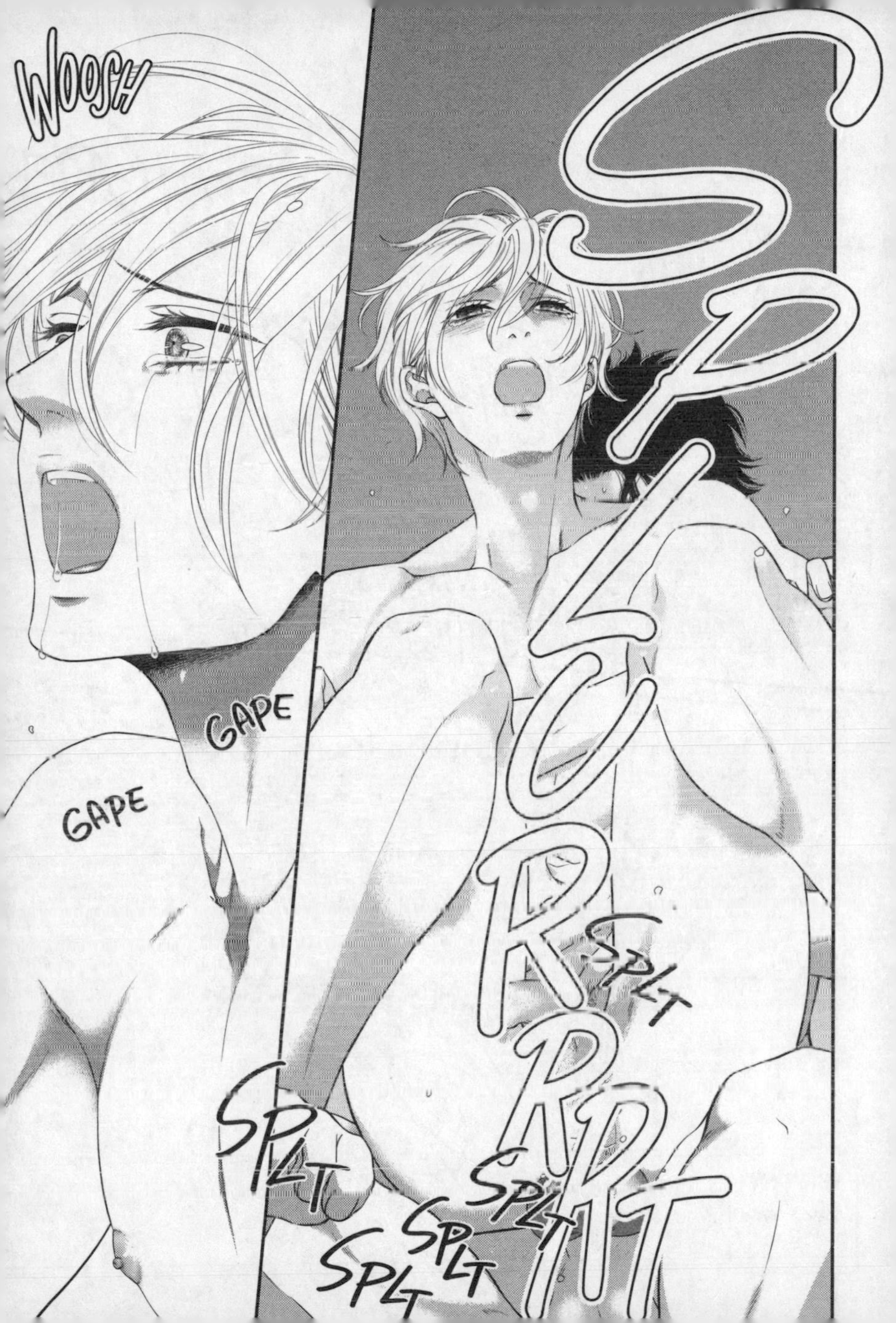
SPLURRT
SPLT
SPLT
SPLT
SPLT
SPLT
WOOSH
GAPE
GAPE

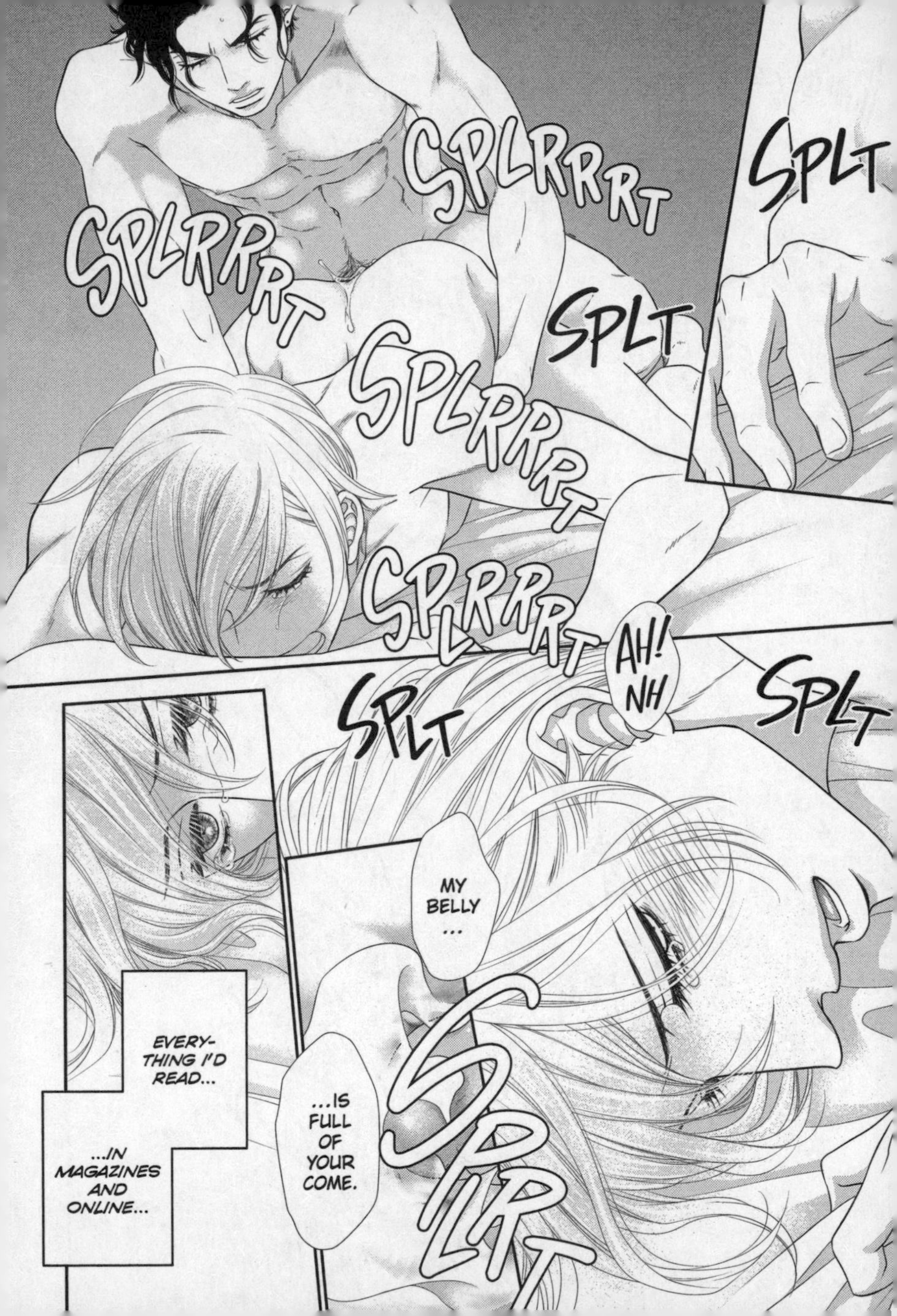
SPLT
SPLRRRRT
SPLRRRRT
SPLT
SPLRRRRRT
SPLRRRRRT
SPLT
AH! NH
SPLT
MY BELLY ...
...IS FULL OF YOUR COME.
SPLRT
EVERY-THING I'D READ...
...IN MAGAZINES AND ONLINE...

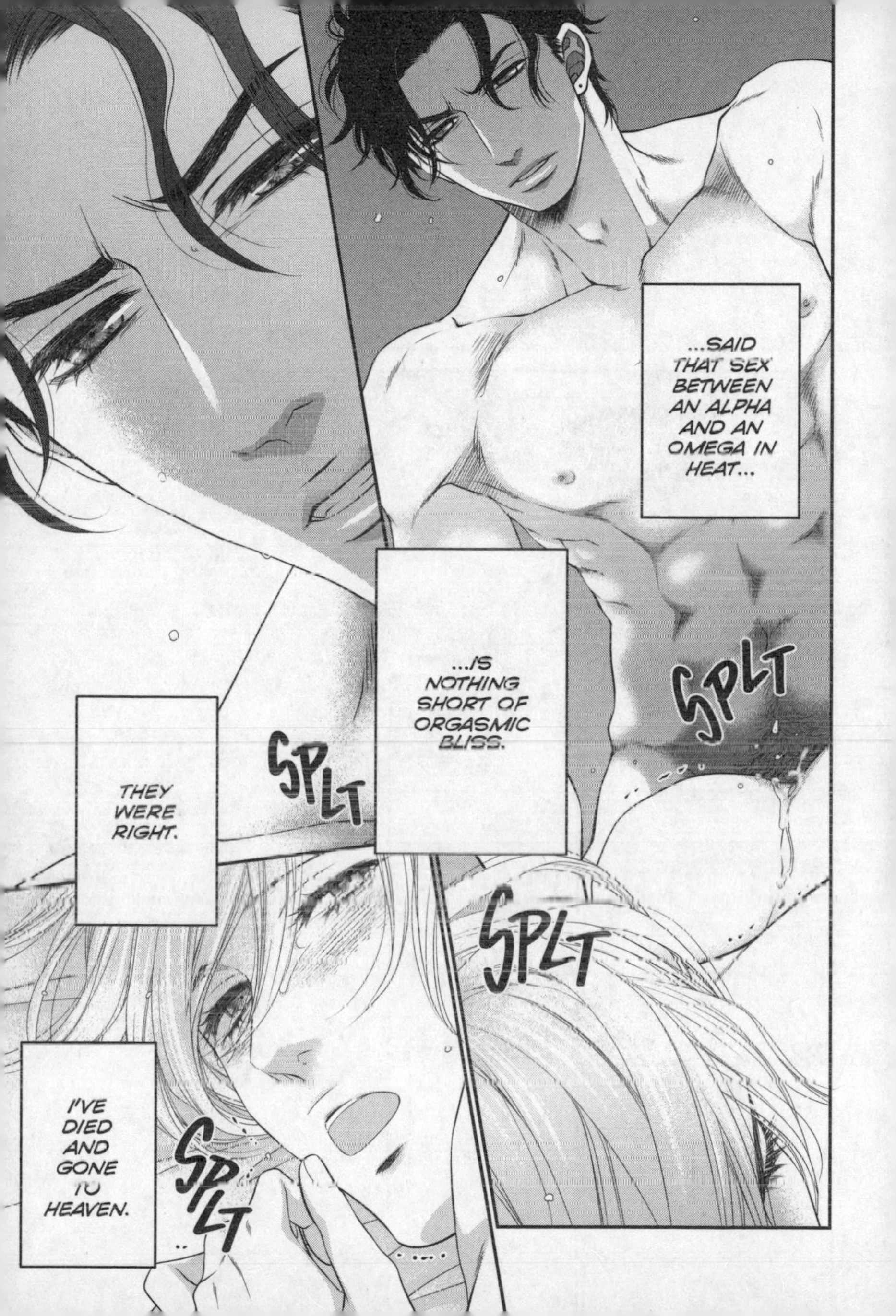
...SAID THAT SEX BETWEEN AN ALPHA AND AN OMEGA IN HEAT...
SPLT
...IS NOTHING SHORT OF ORGASMIC BLISS.
SPLT
THEY WERE RIGHT.
SPLT
I'VE DIED AND GONE TO HEAVEN.
SPLT

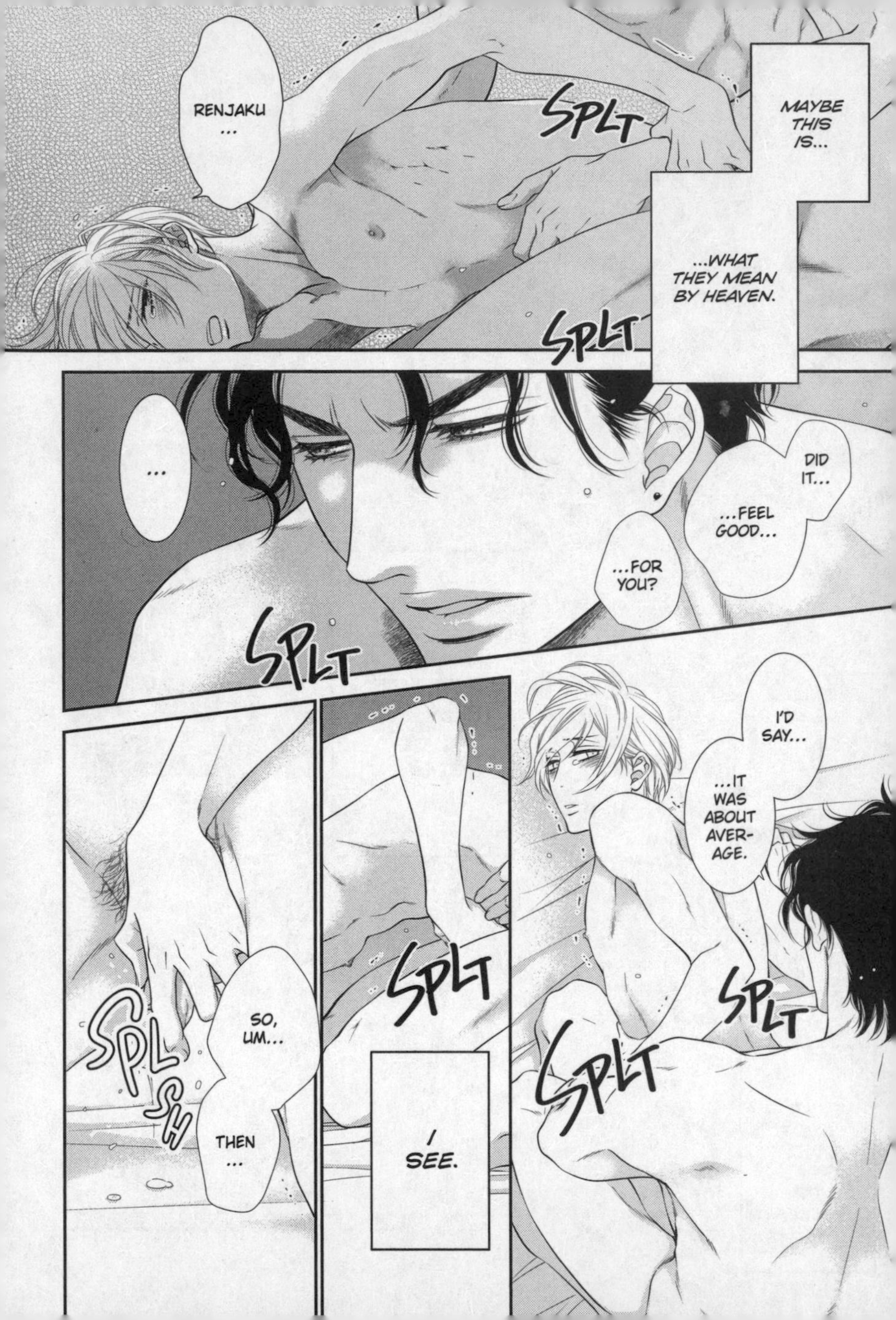
MAYBE THIS IS...
...WHAT THEY MEAN BY HEAVEN.
SPLT
SPLT
RENJAKU ...
DID IT...
...FEEL GOOD...
...FOR YOU?
...
SPLT
I'D SAY...
...IT WAS ABOUT AVER-AGE.
SPLT
SPLT
SPLT
I SEE.
SO, UM...
THEN ...
SPLSH

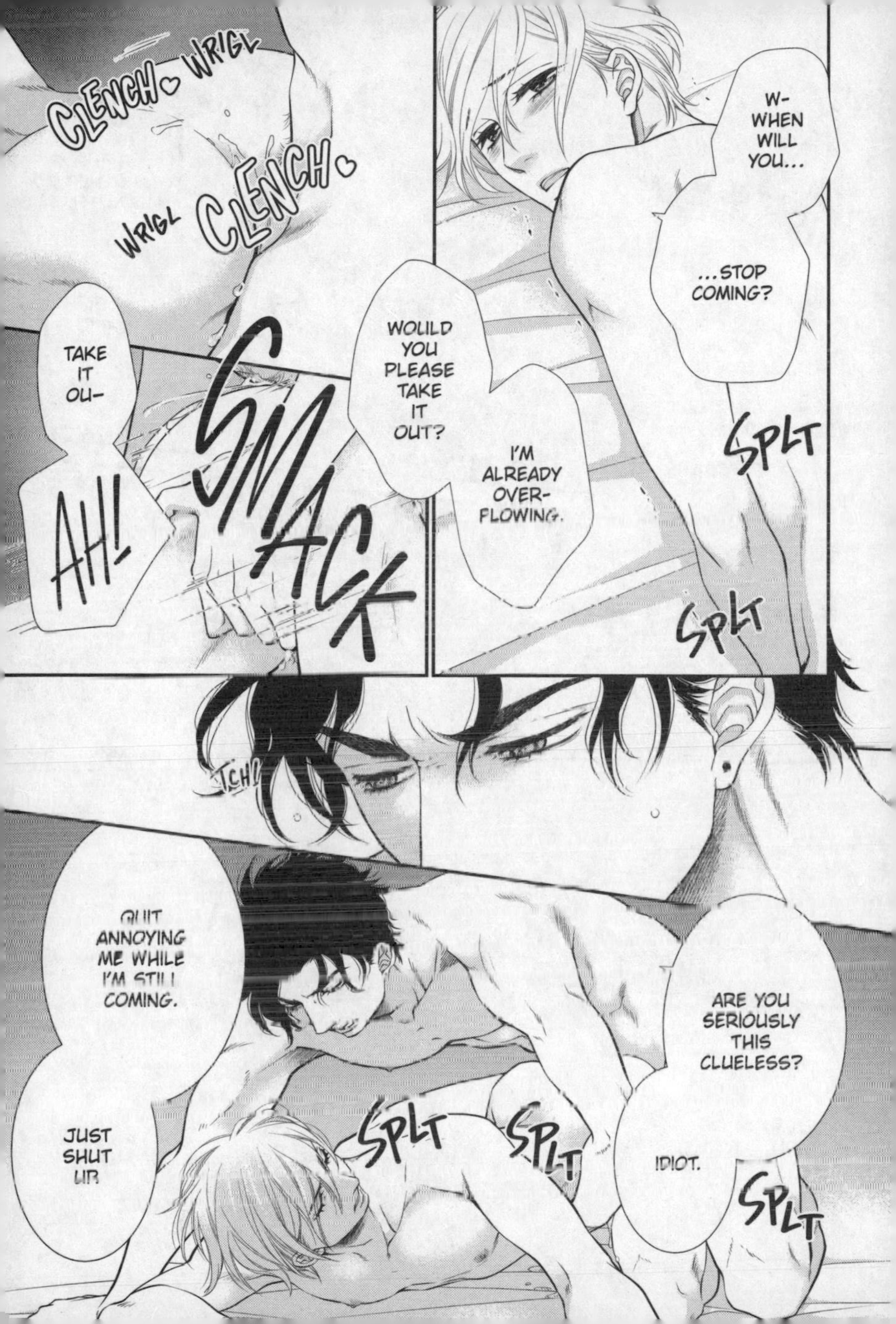
W-WHEN WILL YOU...
...STOP COMING?
WOULD YOU PLEASE TAKE IT OUT?
I'M ALREADY OVERFLOWING.
SPLT
SPLT
CLENCH♥ WRIGL
CLENCH♥
WRIGL
TAKE IT OU-
SMACK
AH!
TCH!
ARE YOU SERIOUSLY THIS CLUELESS?
IDIOT.
SPLT
SPLT
SPLT
QUIT ANNOYING ME WHILE I'M STILL COMING.
JUST SHUT UP.

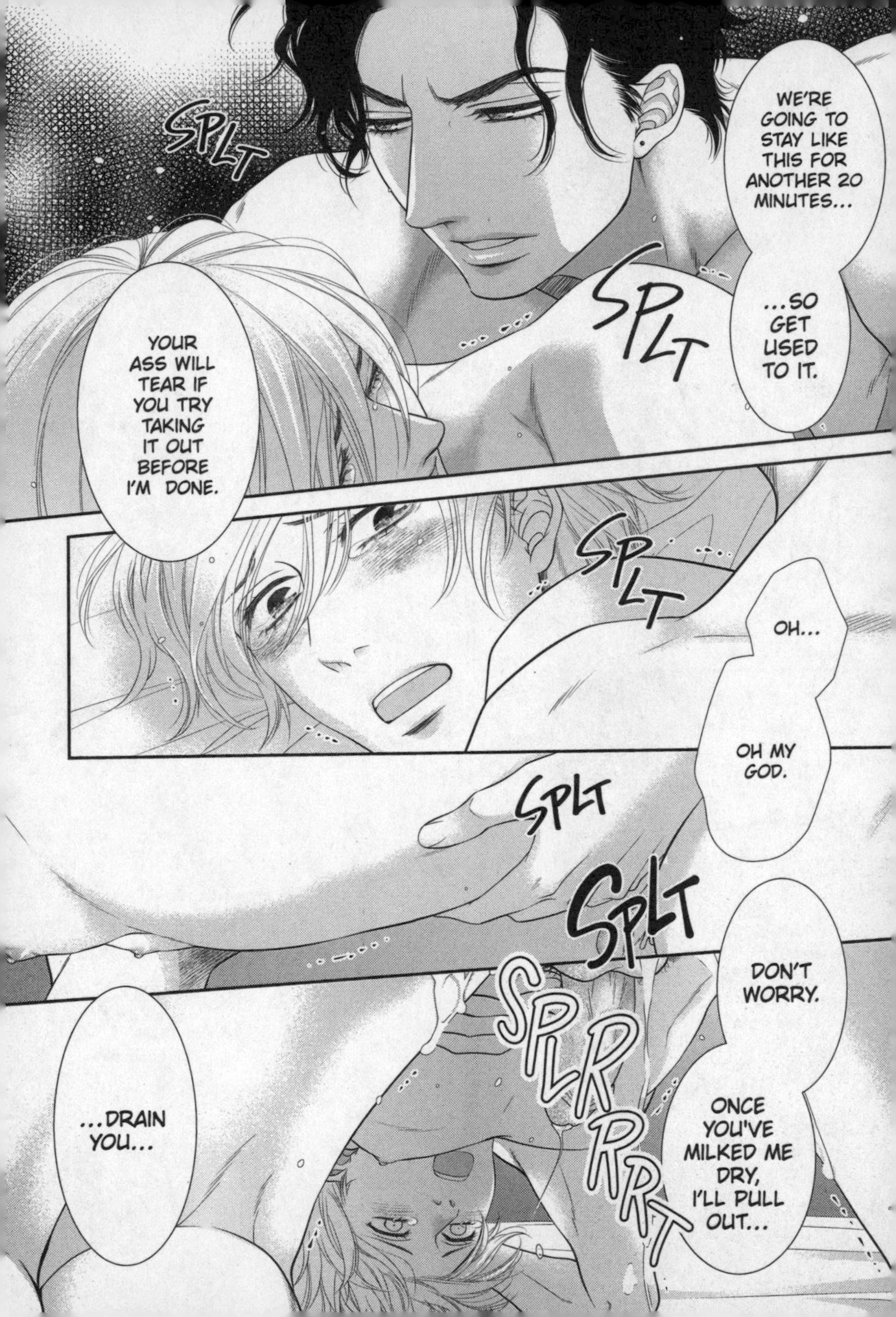
SPLT
WE'RE GOING TO STAY LIKE THIS FOR ANOTHER 20 MINUTES...
SPLT
...SO GET USED TO IT.
YOUR ASS WILL TEAR IF YOU TRY TAKING IT OUT BEFORE I'M DONE.
SPLT
OH...
OH MY GOD.
SPLT
SPLT
DON'T WORRY.
ONCE YOU'VE MILKED ME DRY, I'LL PULL OUT...
SPLRRRT
...DRAIN YOU...

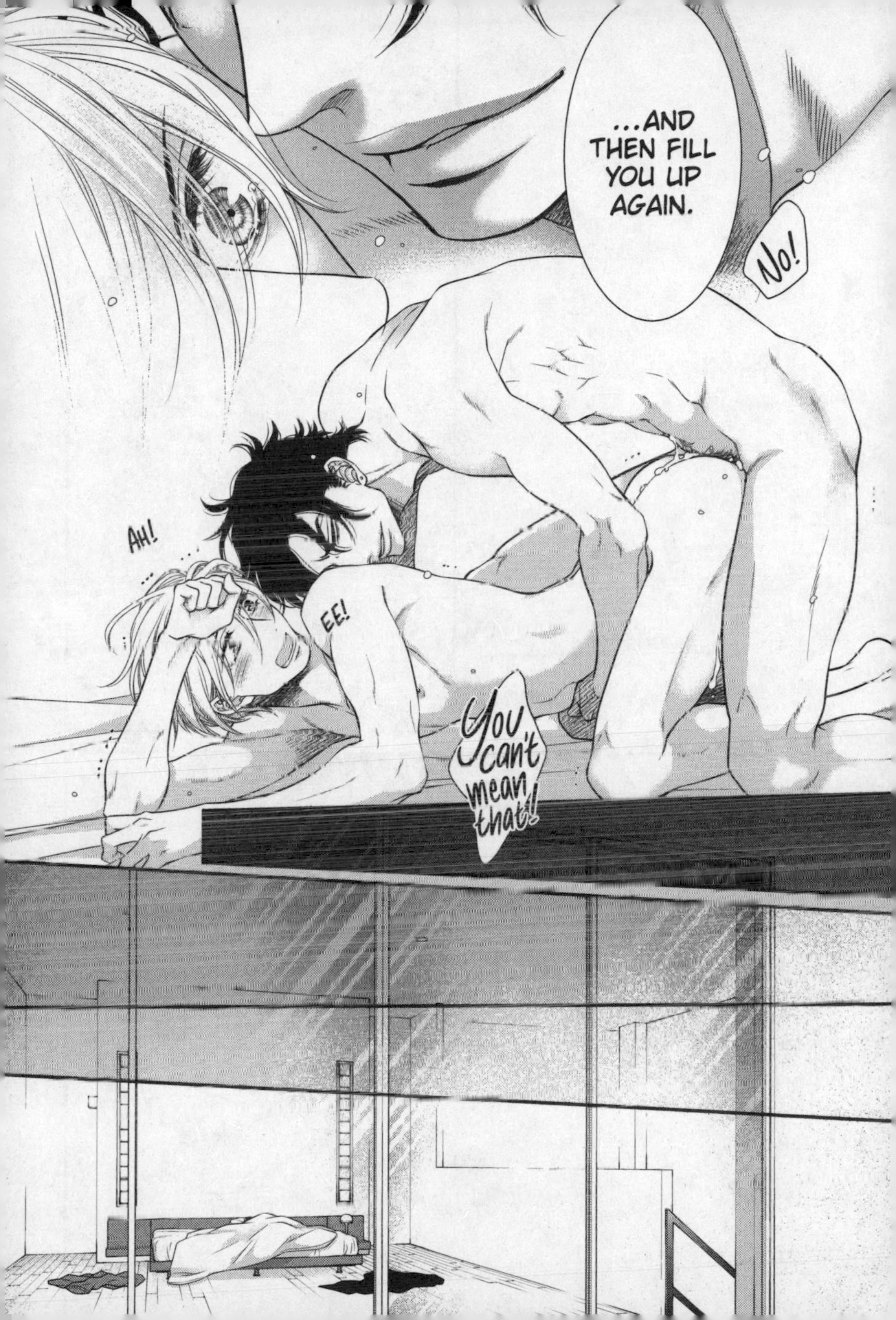
...AND THEN FILL YOU UP AGAIN.
No!
You can't mean that!
EE!
AH!

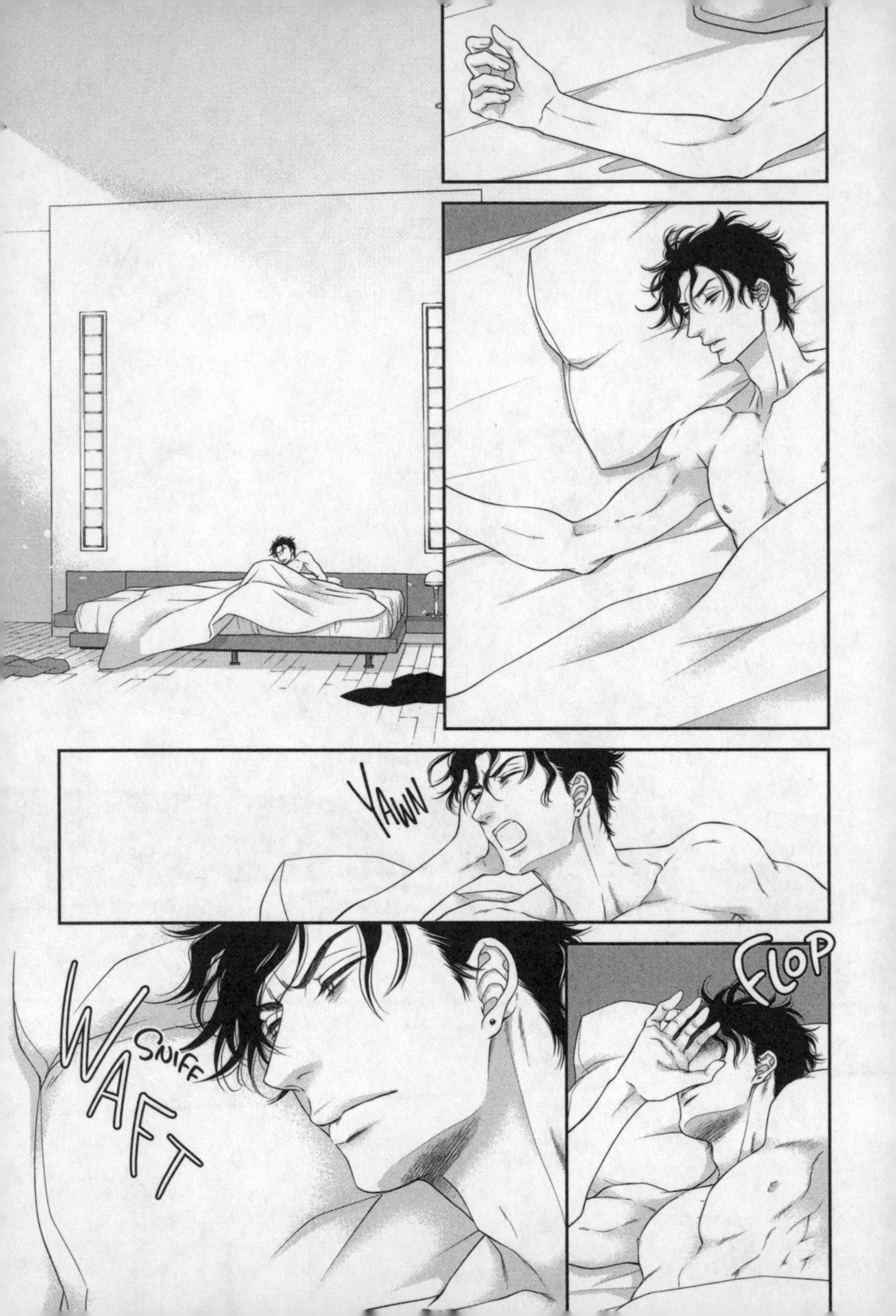
YAWN
FLOP
WAFT
SNIFF

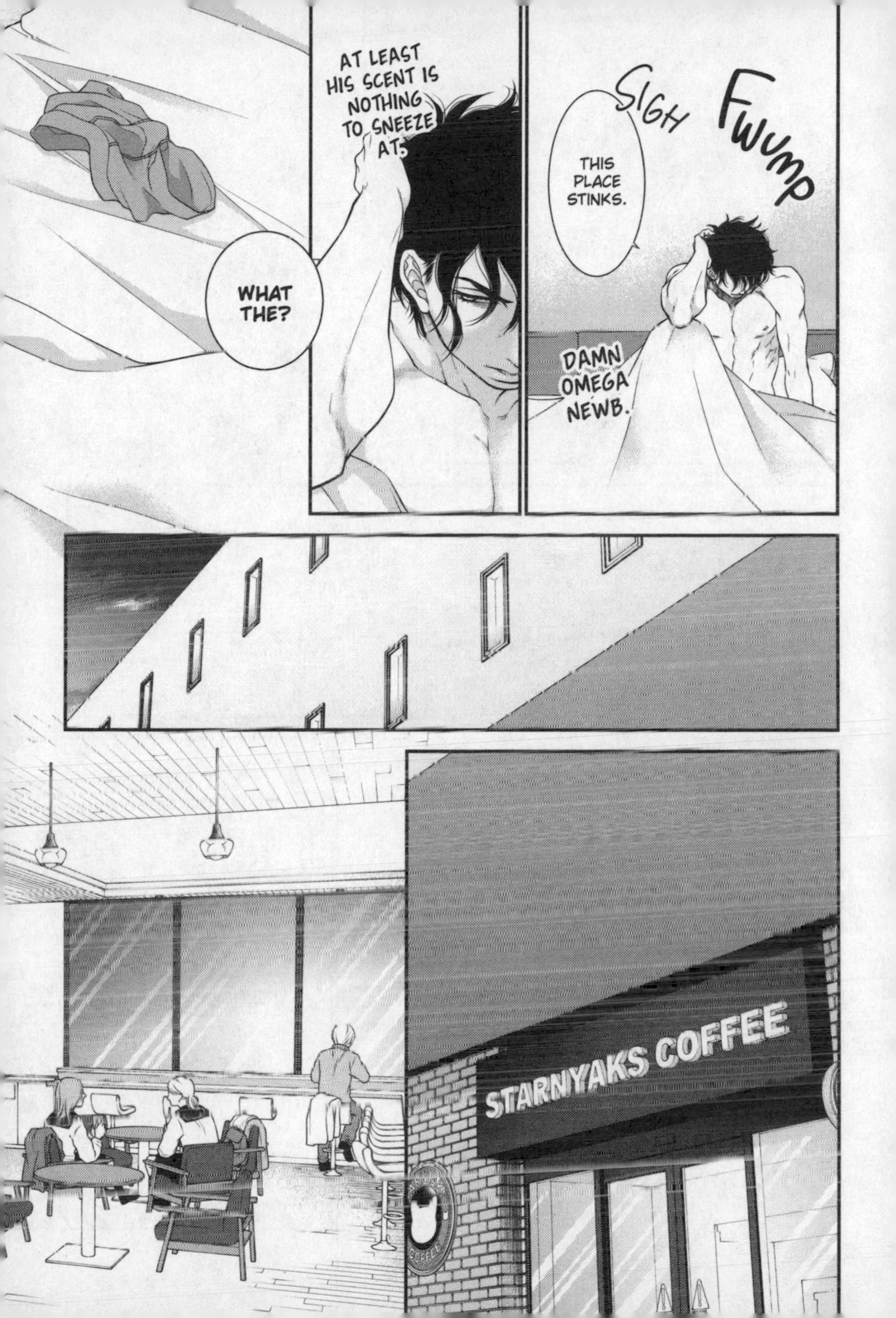
FWUMP
SIGH
THIS PLACE STINKS.
DAMN OMEGA NEWB.
AT LEAST HIS SCENT IS NOTHING TO SNEEZE AT.
WHAT THE?
STARNYAKS COFFEE

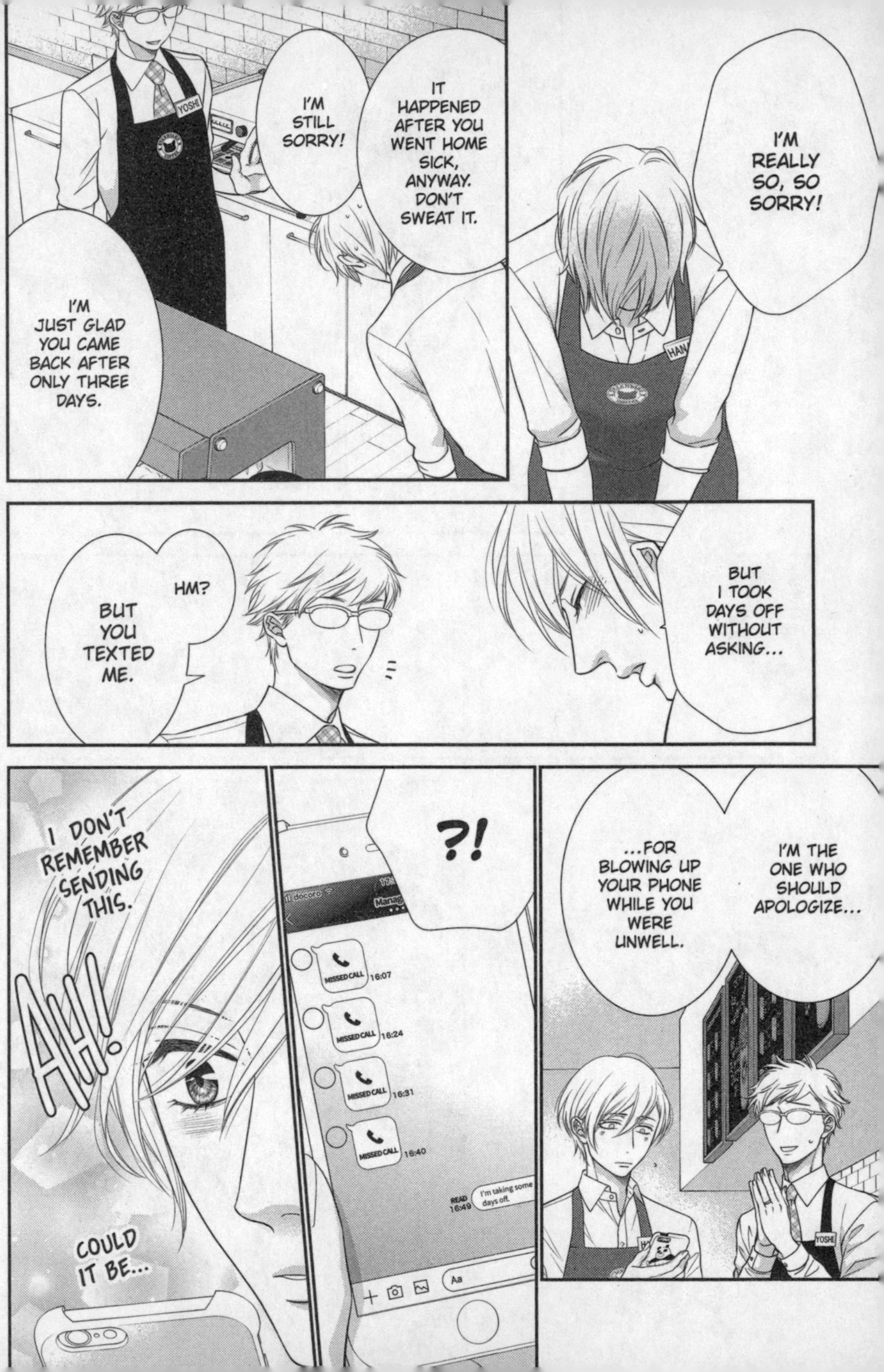
I'M REALLY SO, SO SORRY!
IT HAPPENED AFTER YOU WENT HOME SICK, ANYWAY. DON'T SWEAT IT.
I'M STILL SORRY!
I'M JUST GLAD YOU CAME BACK AFTER ONLY THREE DAYS.
BUT I TOOK DAYS OFF WITHOUT ASKING...
HM?
BUT YOU TEXTED ME.
I'M THE ONE WHO SHOULD APOLOGIZE...
...FOR BLOWING UP YOUR PHONE WHILE YOU WERE UNWELL.
?!
MISSED CALL 16:07
MISSED CALL 16:24
MISSED CALL 16:31
MISSED CALL 16:40
READ 16:49
I'm taking some days off.
Aa
I DON'T REMEMBER SENDING THIS.
AH!
COULD IT BE...

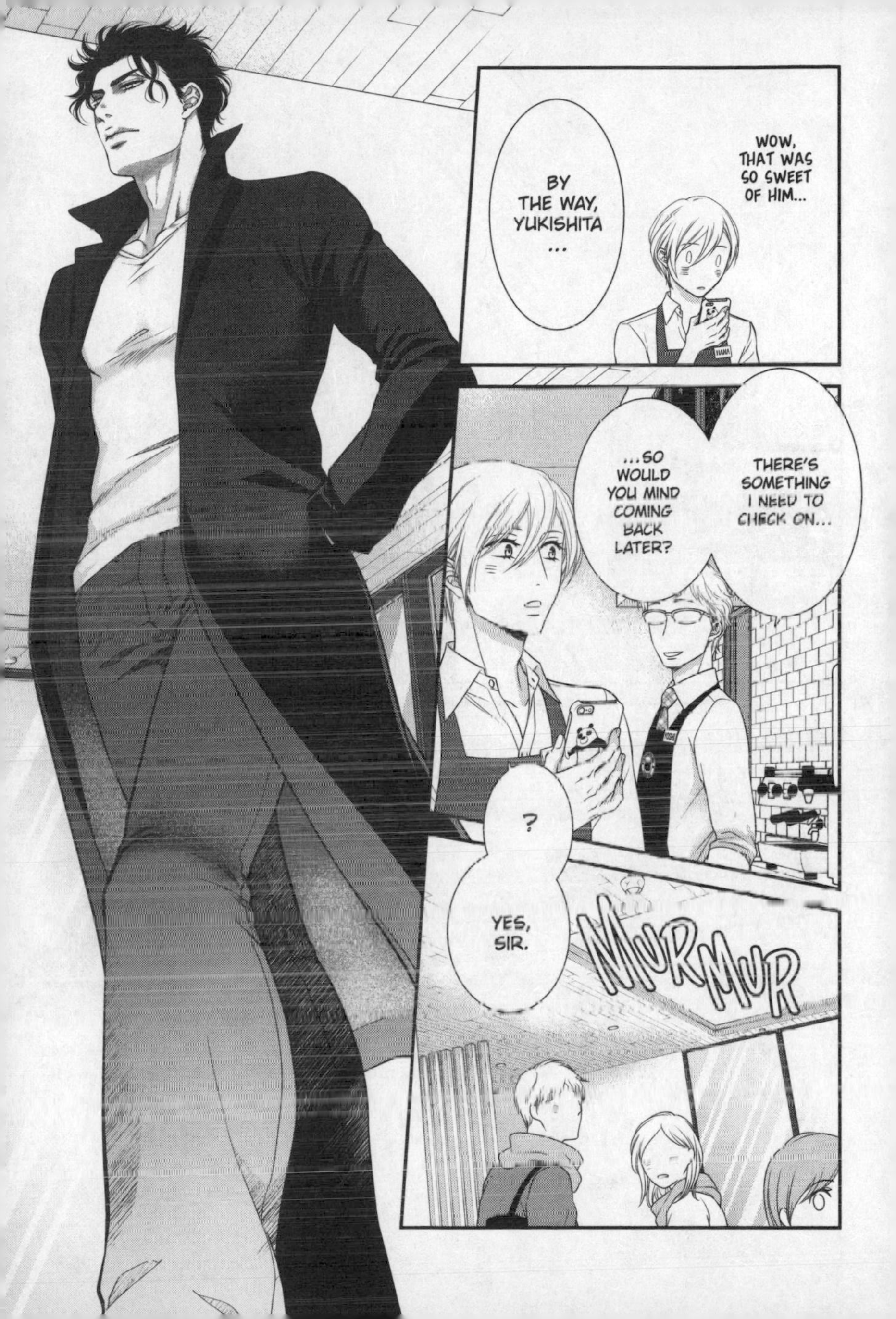
WOW, THAT WAS SO SWEET OF HIM...
BY THE WAY, YUKISHITA...
THERE'S SOMETHING I NEED TO CHECK ON...
...SO WOULD YOU MIND COMING BACK LATER?
?
YES, SIR.
MURMUR

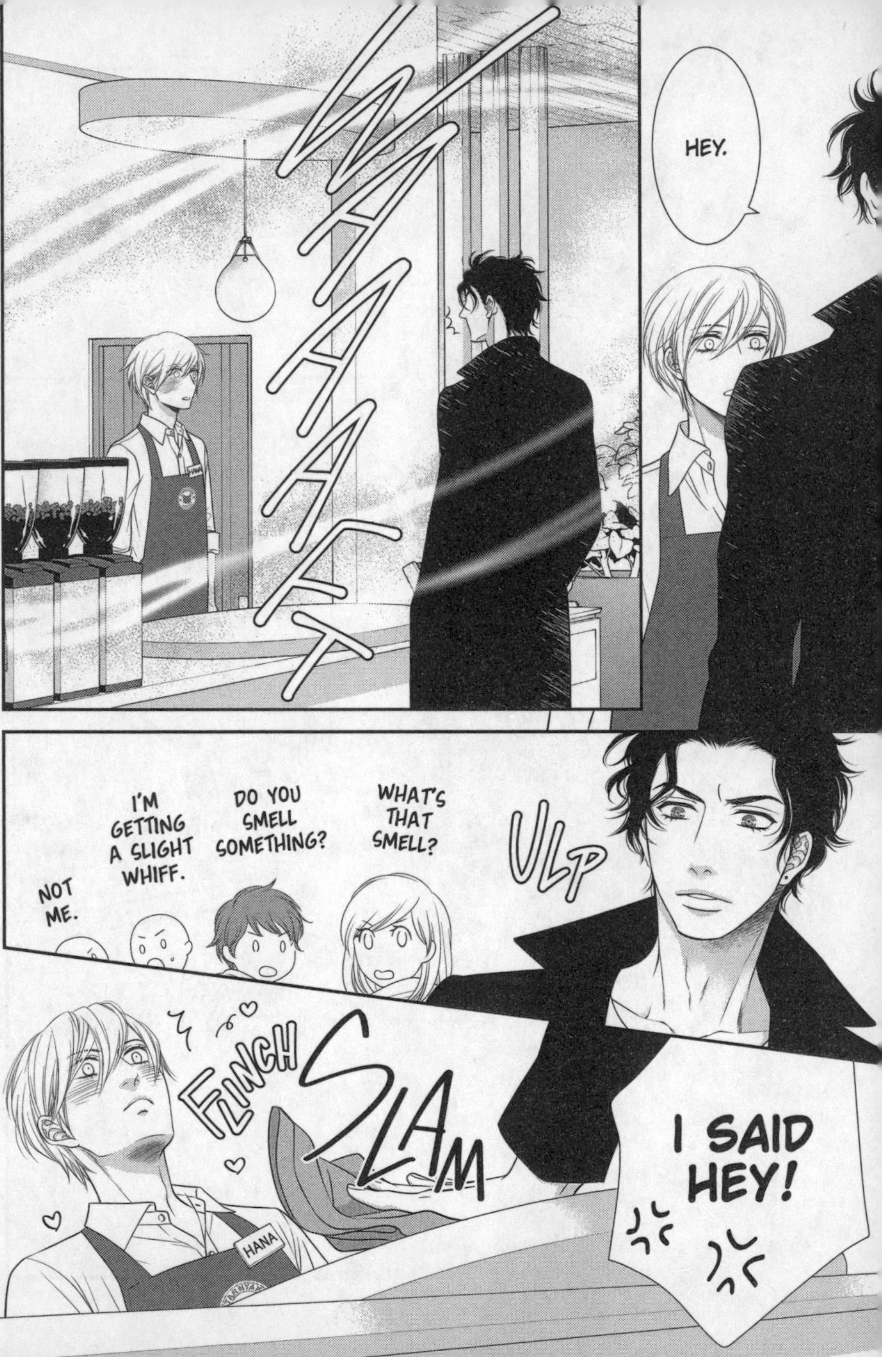
HEY.
WAAAAT
ULP
WHAT'S THAT SMELL?
DO YOU SMELL SOMETHING?
I'M GETTING A SLIGHT WHIFF.
NOT ME.
I SAID HEY!
SLAM
FLINCH
HANA

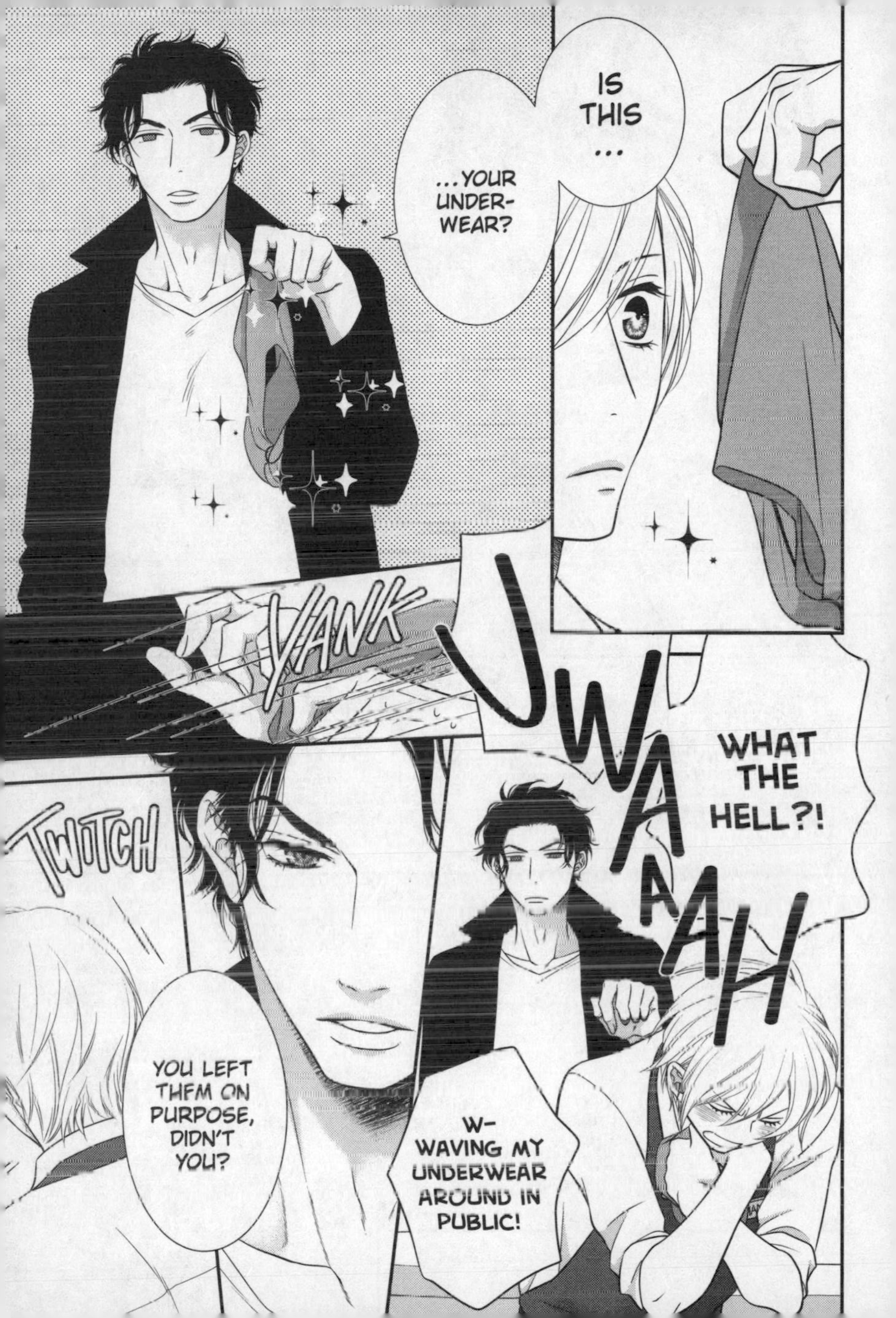
IS THIS ...
...YOUR UNDER-WEAR?
YANK
UWAAAH
WHAT THE HELL?!
W-WAVING MY UNDERWEAR AROUND IN PUBLIC!
TWITCH
YOU LEFT THEM ON PURPOSE, DIDN'T YOU?

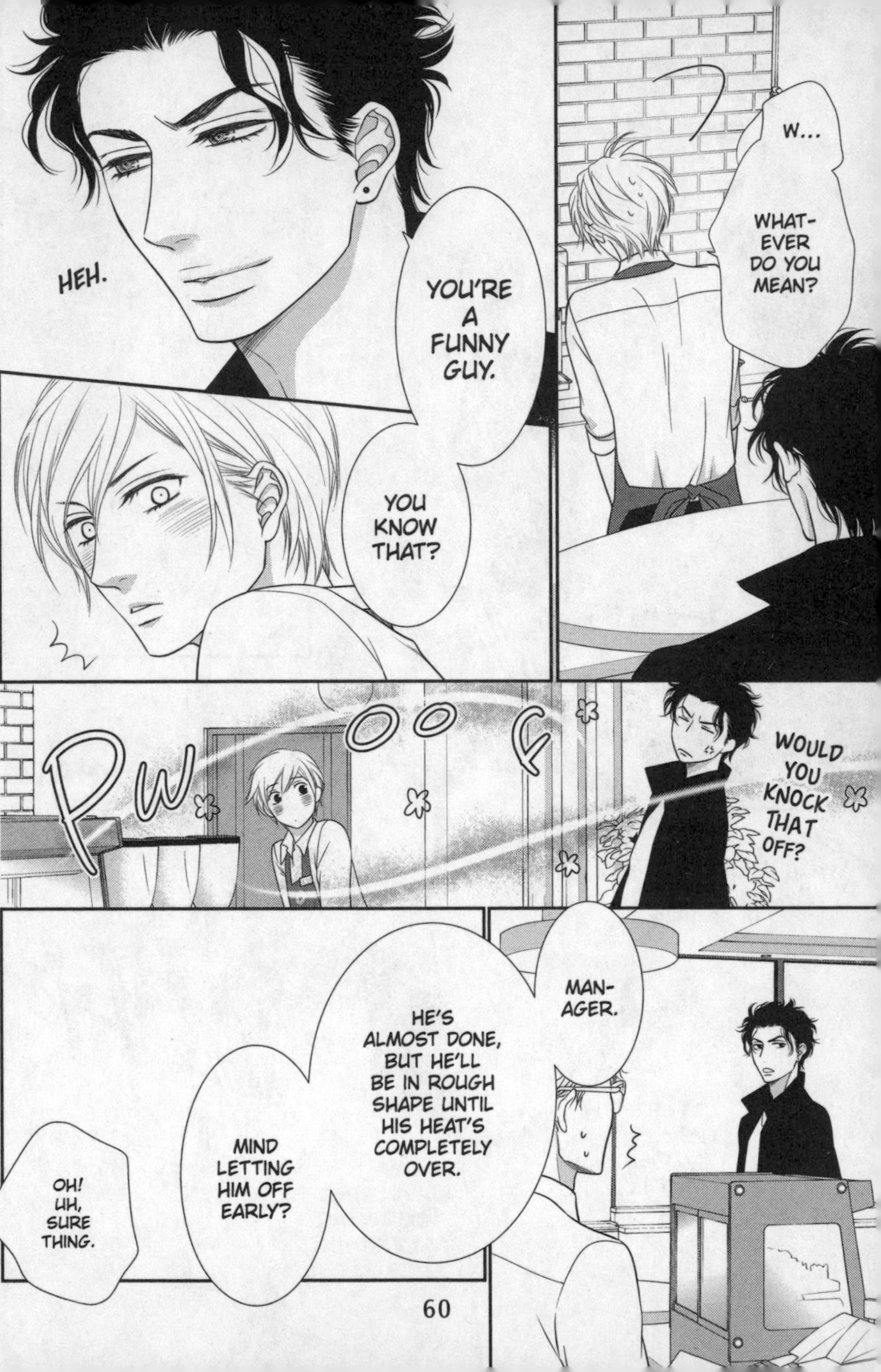
W...
WHATEVER DO YOU MEAN?
HEH.
YOU'RE A FUNNY GUY.
YOU KNOW THAT?
WOULD YOU KNOCK THAT OFF?
PWOOF
MANAGER.
HE'S ALMOST DONE, BUT HE'LL BE IN ROUGH SHAPE UNTIL HIS HEAT'S COMPLETELY OVER.
MIND LETTING HIM OFF EARLY?
OH! UH, SURE THING.

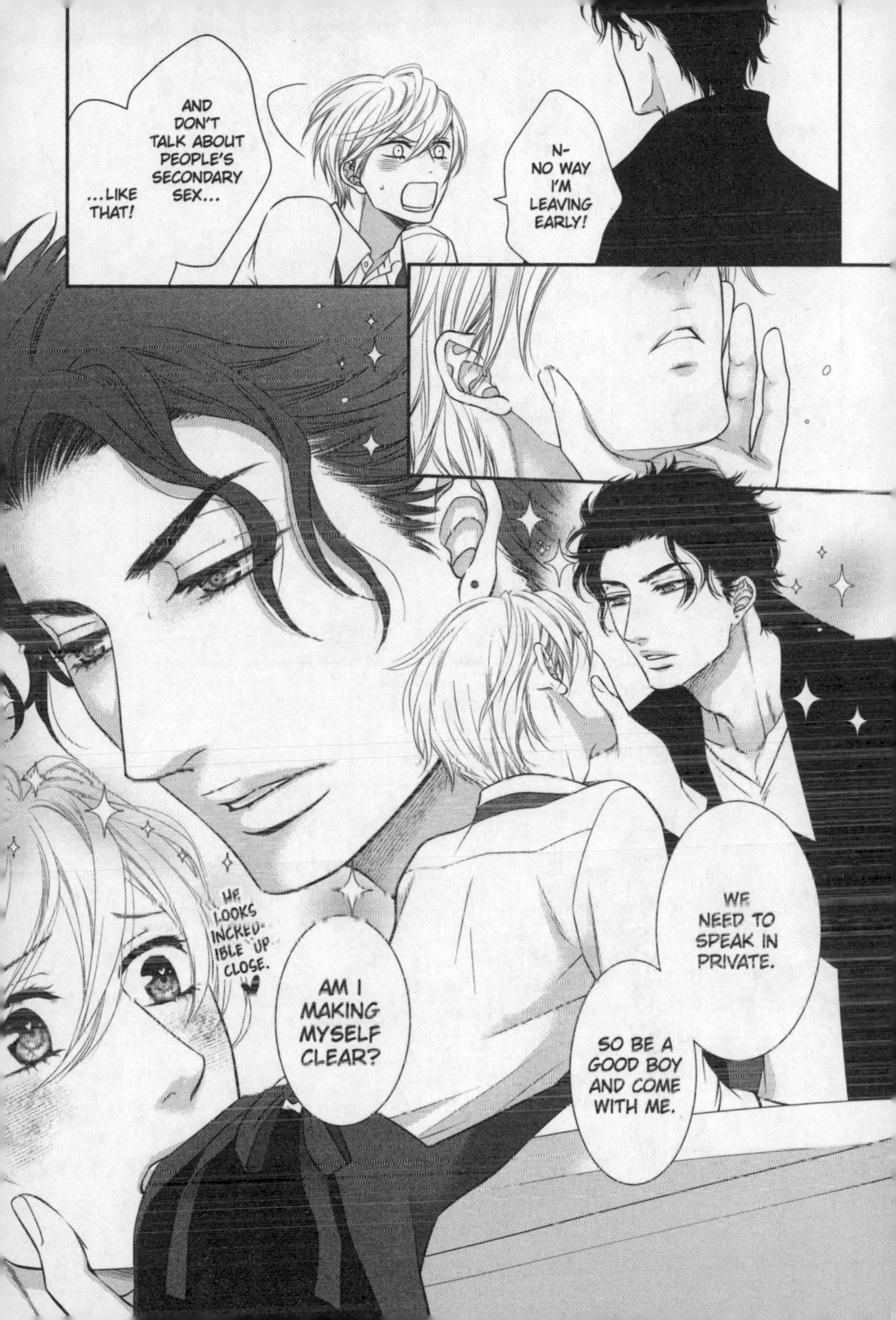
N- NO WAY I'M LEAVING EARLY!
AND DON'T TALK ABOUT PEOPLE'S SECONDARY SEX...
...LIKE THAT!
WE NEED TO SPEAK IN PRIVATE.
SO BE A GOOD BOY AND COME WITH ME.
AM I MAKING MYSELF CLEAR?
HE LOOKS INCRED-IBLE UP CLOSE.

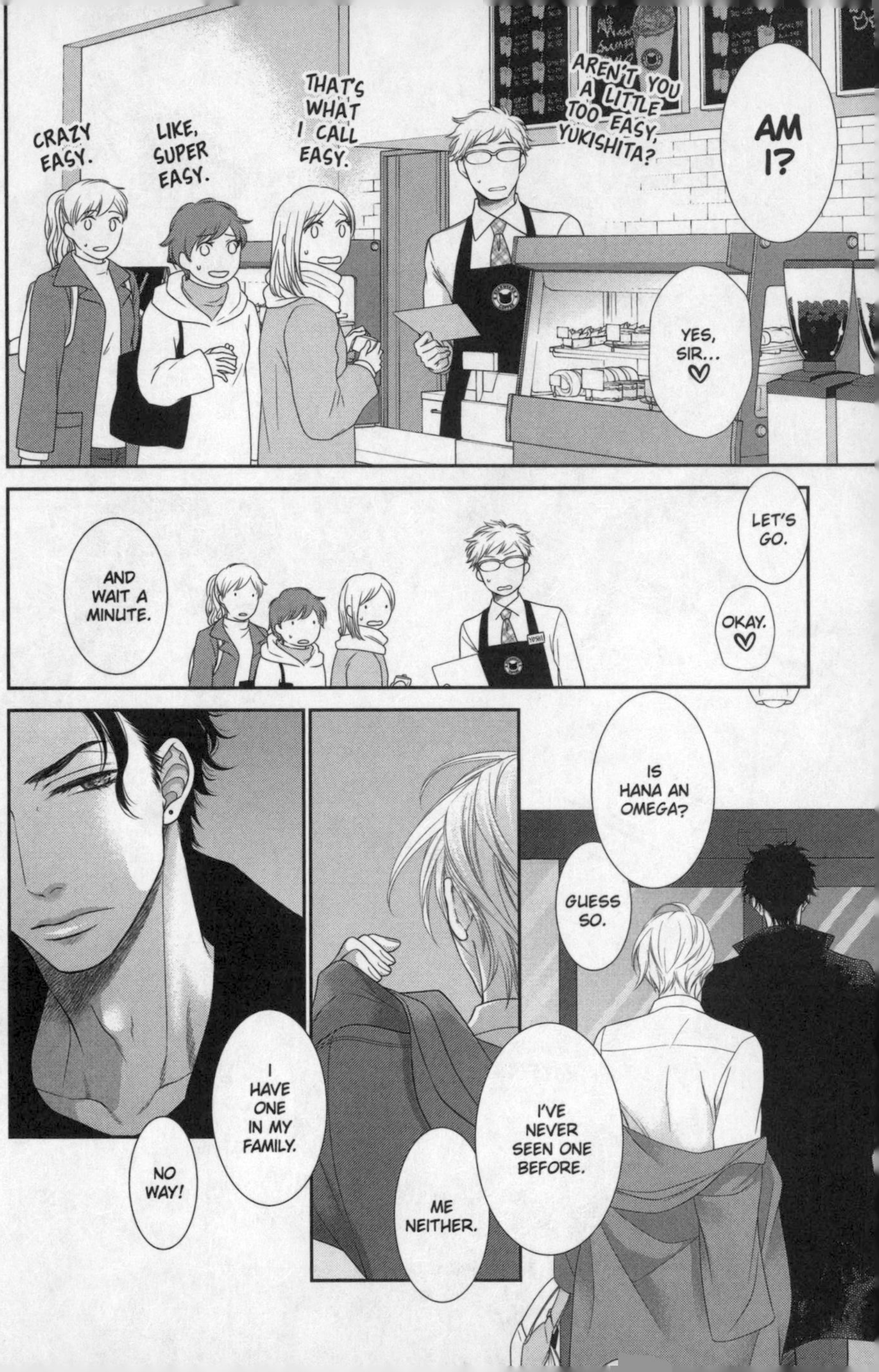
AM I?
AREN'T YOU A LITTLE TOO EASY, YUKISHITA?
YES, SIR... ♥
THAT'S WHAT I CALL EASY.
LIKE, SUPER EASY.
CRAZY EASY.
LET'S GO.
OKAY. ♥
AND WAIT A MINUTE.
IS HANA AN OMEGA?
GUESS SO.
I'VE NEVER SEEN ONE BEFORE.
ME NEITHER.
I HAVE ONE IN MY FAMILY.
NO WAY!

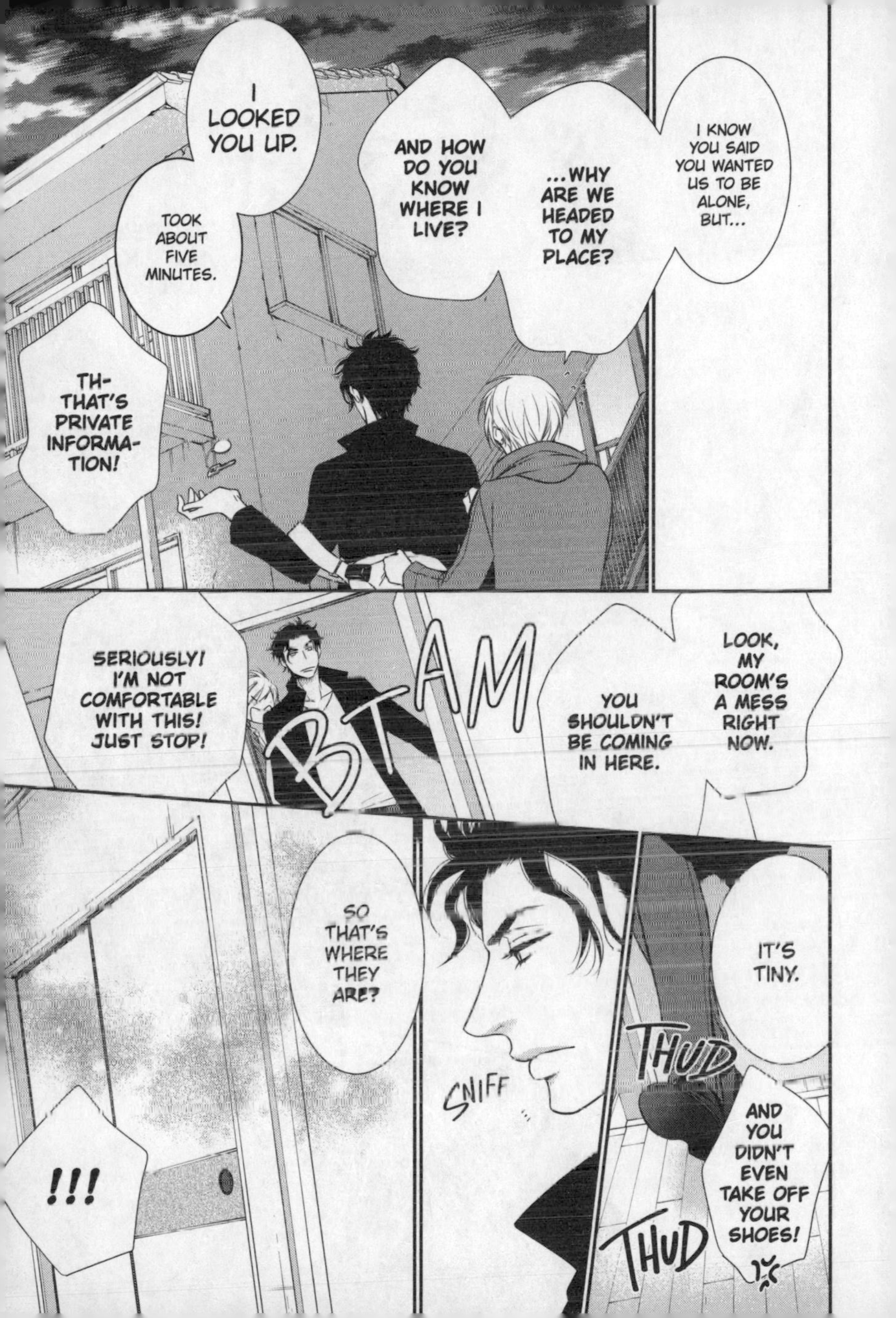
I KNOW YOU SAID YOU WANTED US TO BE ALONE, BUT...
...WHY ARE WE HEADED TO MY PLACE?
AND HOW DO YOU KNOW WHERE I LIVE?
I LOOKED YOU UP.
TOOK ABOUT FIVE MINUTES.
TH-THAT'S PRIVATE INFORMATION!
LOOK, MY ROOM'S A MESS RIGHT NOW.
YOU SHOULDN'T BE COMING IN HERE.
BTAM
SERIOUSLY! I'M NOT COMFORTABLE WITH THIS! JUST STOP!
IT'S TINY.
THUD
AND YOU DIDN'T EVEN TAKE OFF YOUR SHOES!
THUD
SNIFF
SO THAT'S WHERE THEY ARE?
!!!

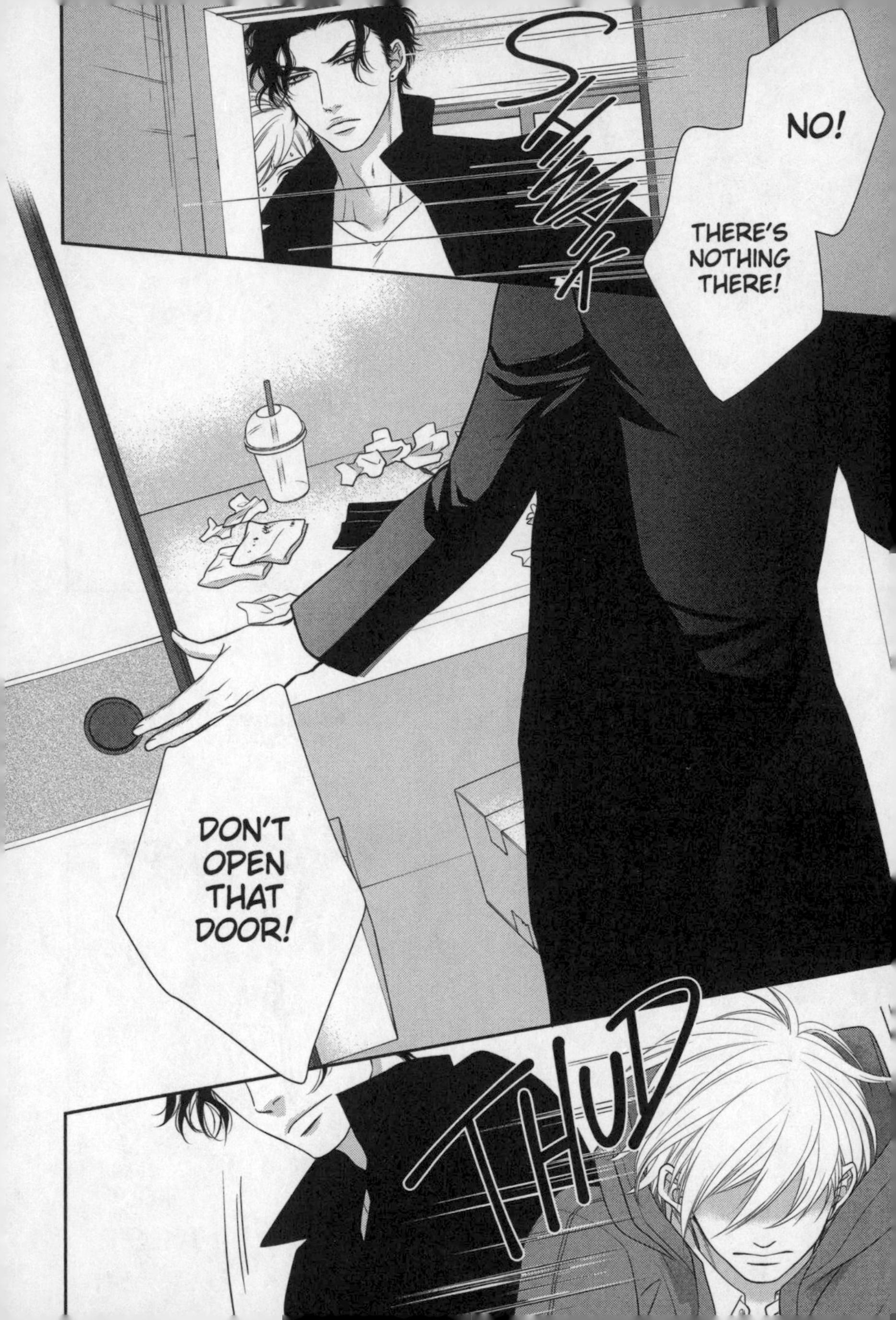
SHWAK
NO!
THERE'S NOTHING THERE!
DON'T OPEN THAT DOOR!
THUD

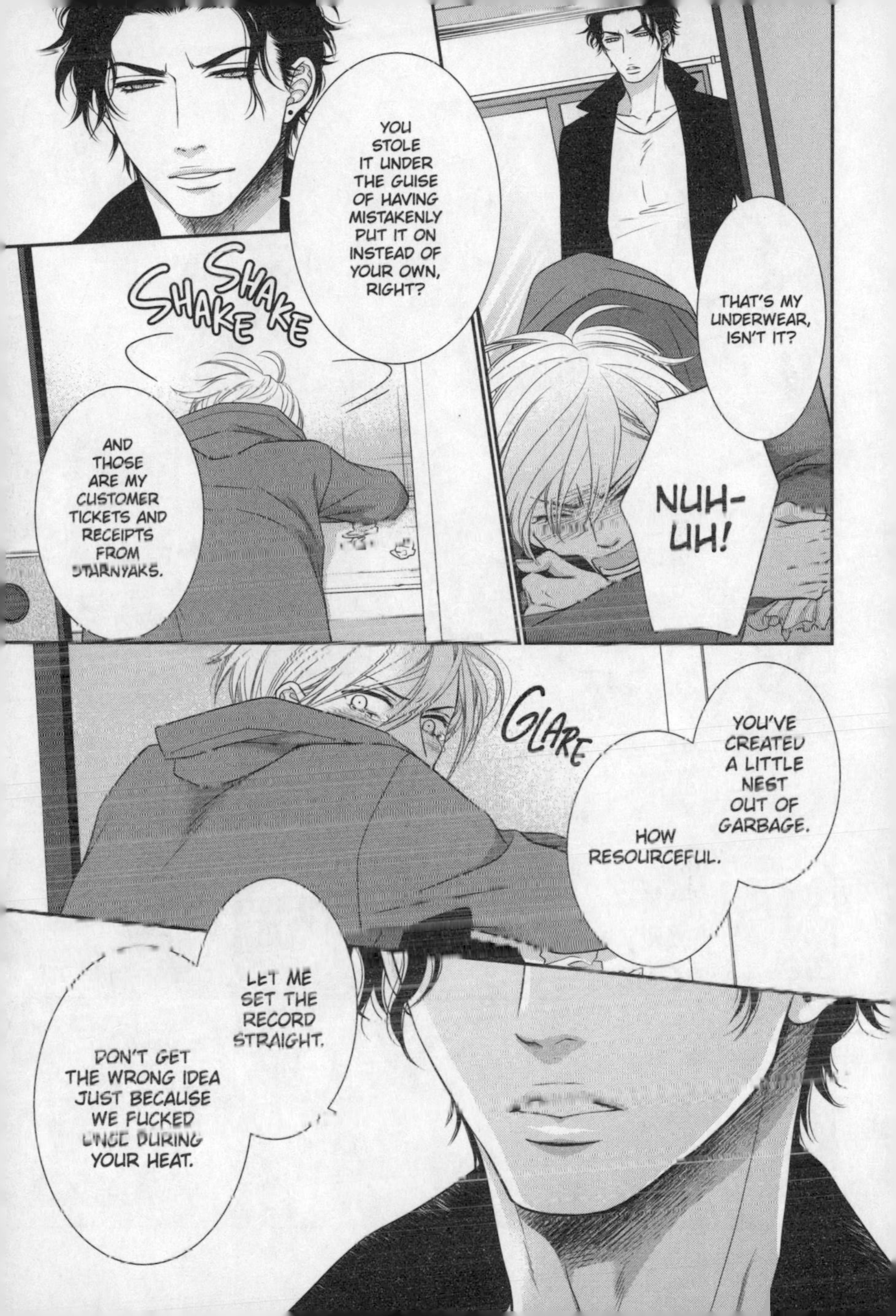
THAT'S MY UNDERWEAR, ISN'T IT?
NUH-UH!
YOU STOLE IT UNDER THE GUISE OF HAVING MISTAKENLY PUT IT ON INSTEAD OF YOUR OWN, RIGHT?
SHAKE SHAKE
AND THOSE ARE MY CUSTOMER TICKETS AND RECEIPTS FROM STARNYAKS.
GLARE
YOU'VE CREATED A LITTLE NEST OUT OF GARBAGE.
HOW RESOURCEFUL.
LET ME SET THE RECORD STRAIGHT.
DON'T GET THE WRONG IDEA JUST BECAUSE WE FUCKED ONCE DURING YOUR HEAT.

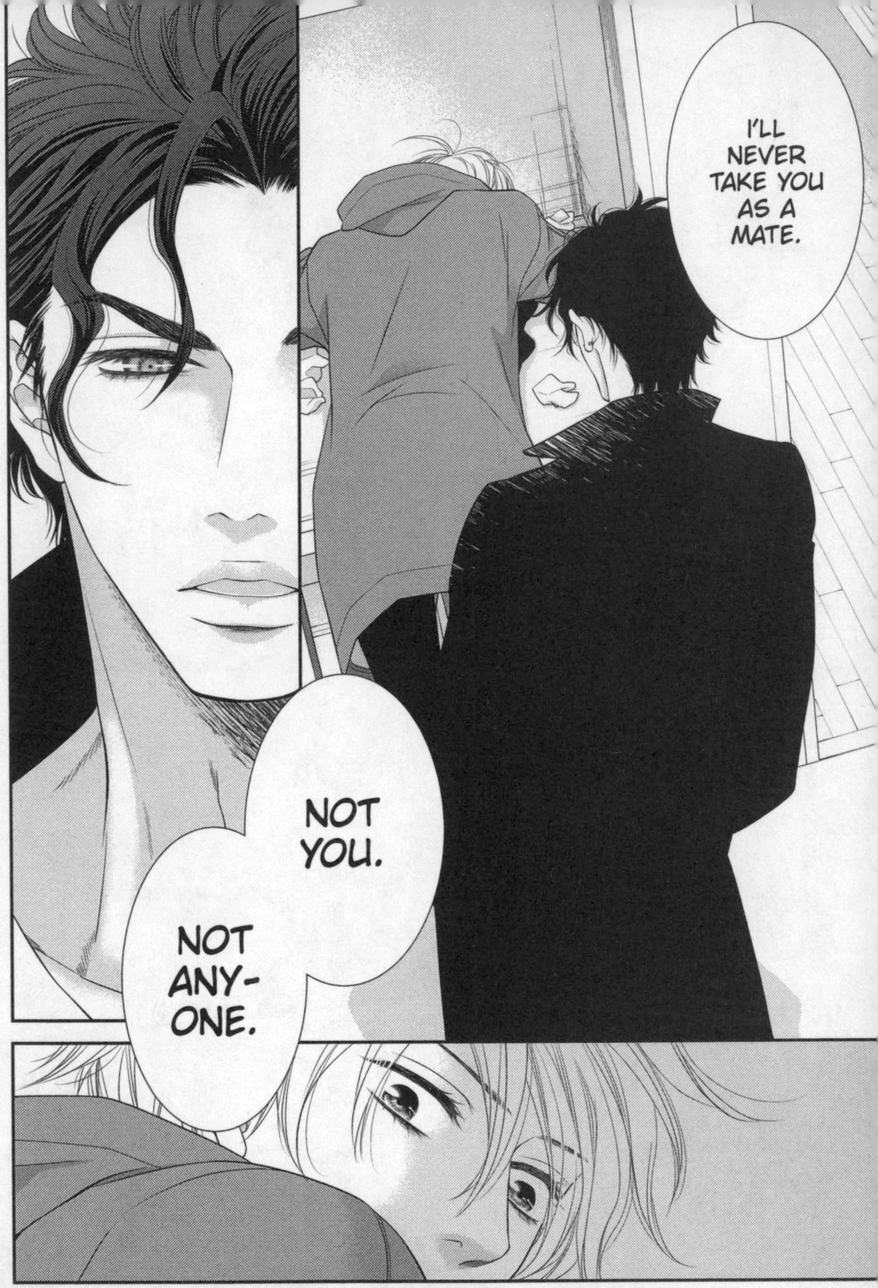
I'LL NEVER TAKE YOU AS A MATE.
NOT YOU.
NOT ANY-ONE.

SCATTERING HIS *Virgin Bloom*

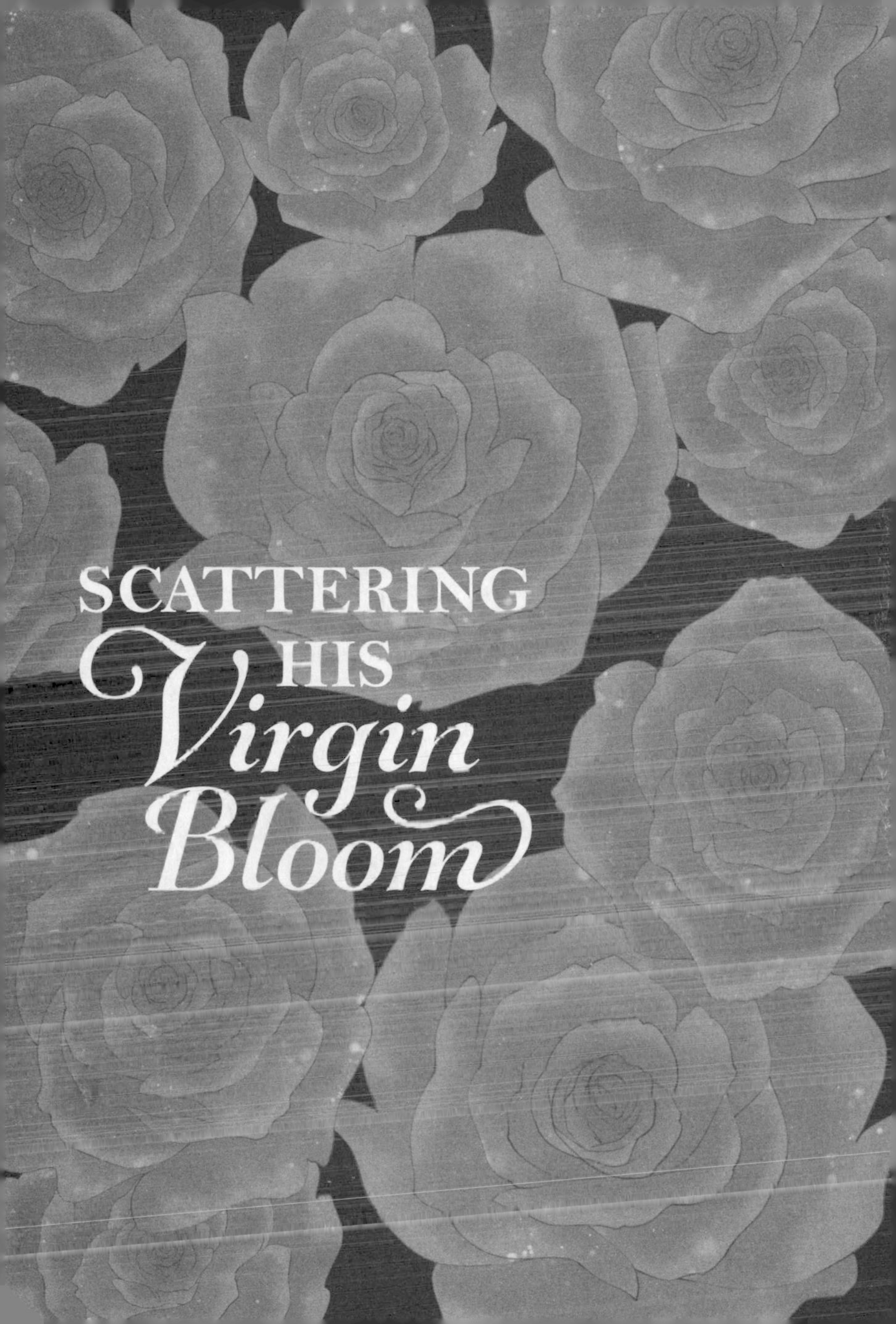

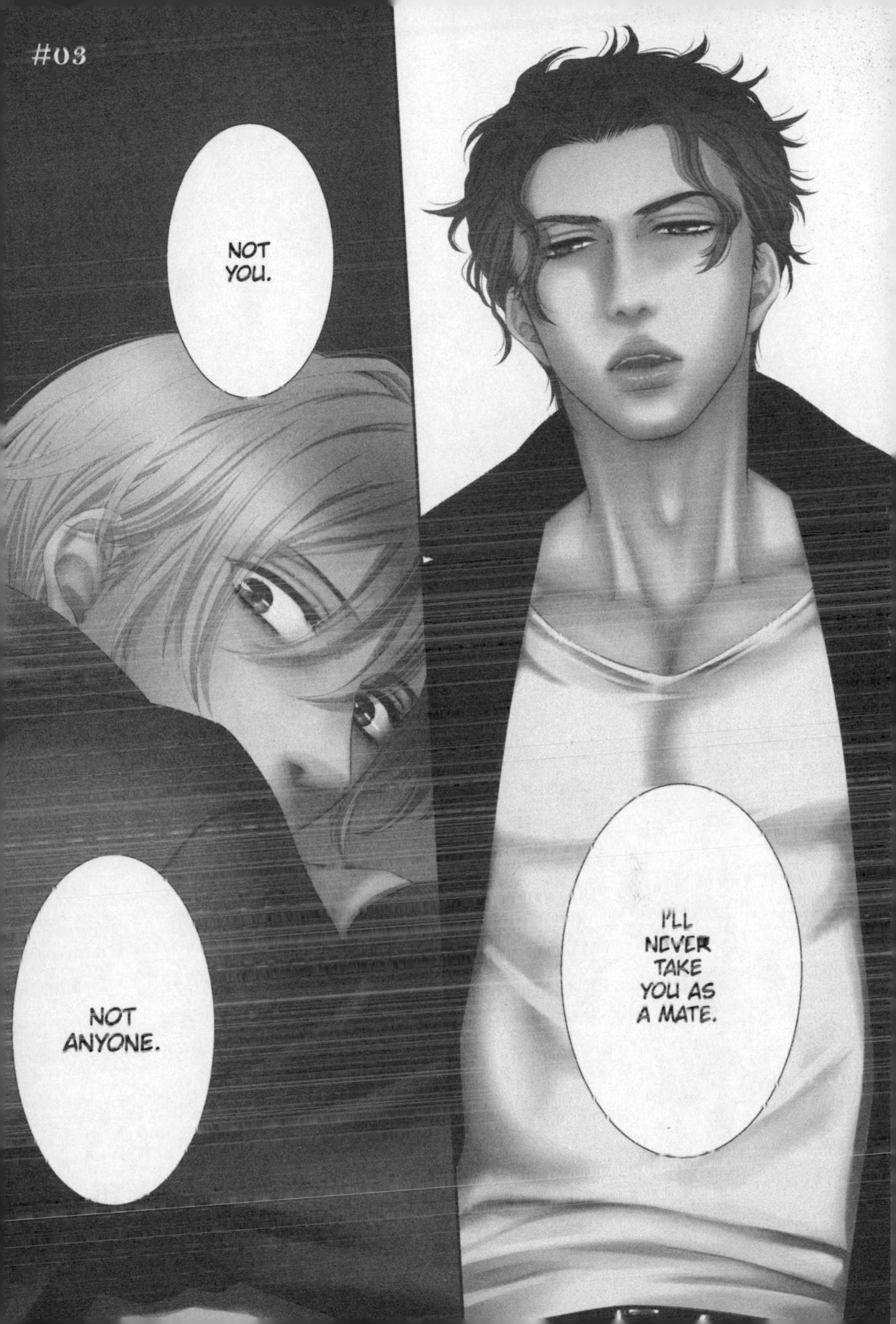
#03
I'LL NEVER TAKE YOU AS A MATE.
NOT YOU.
NOT ANYONE.

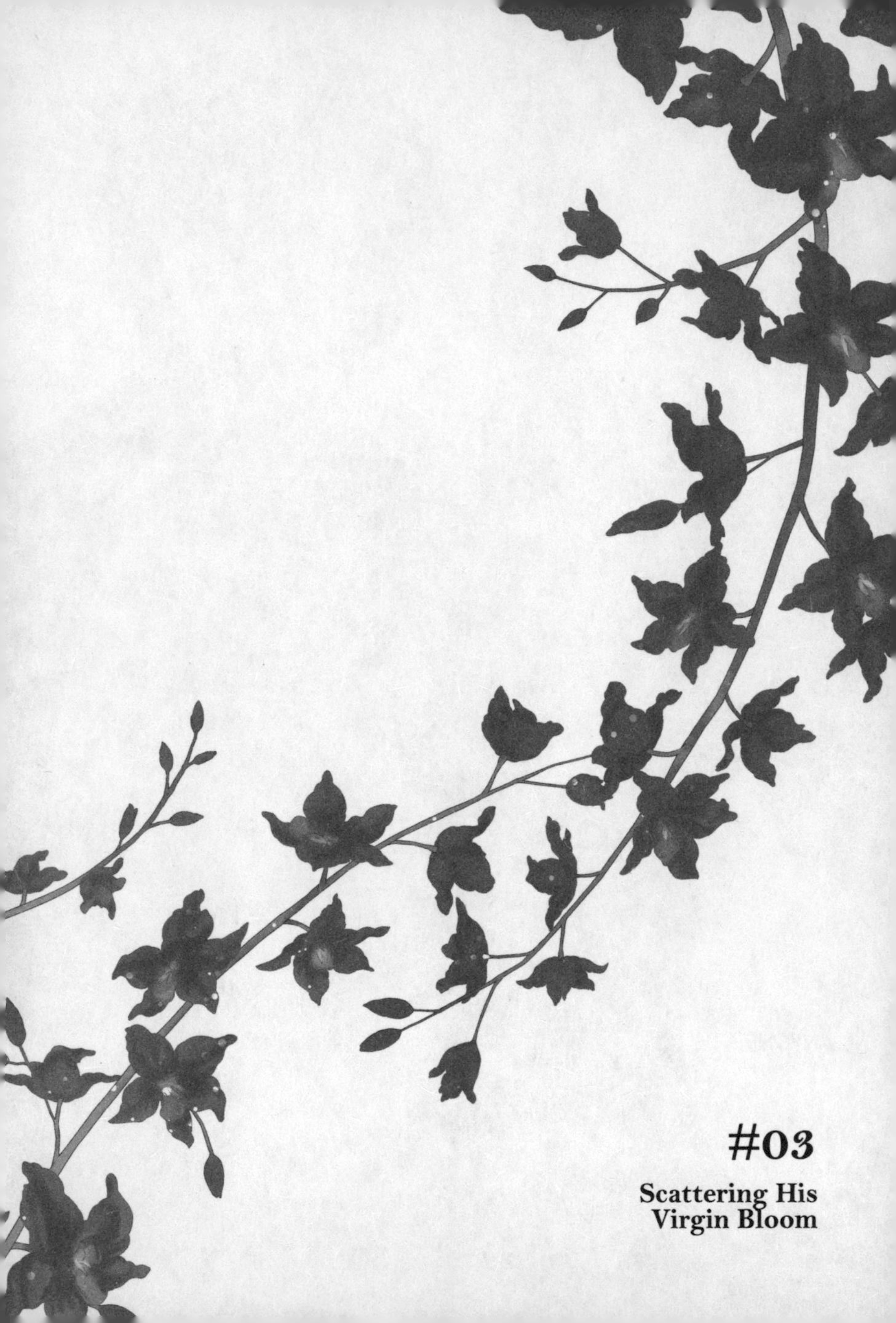

#03

Scattering His Virgin Bloom

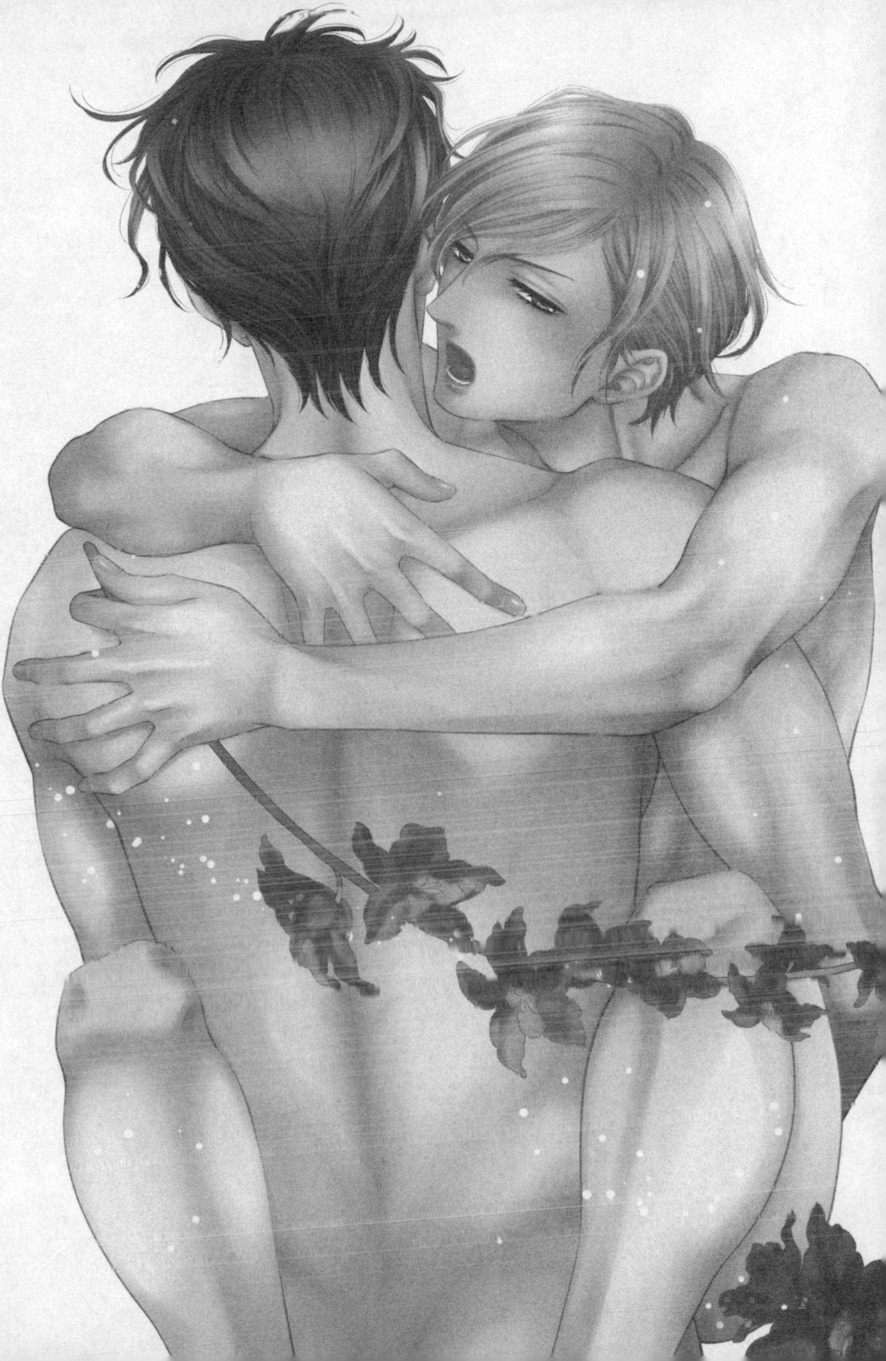

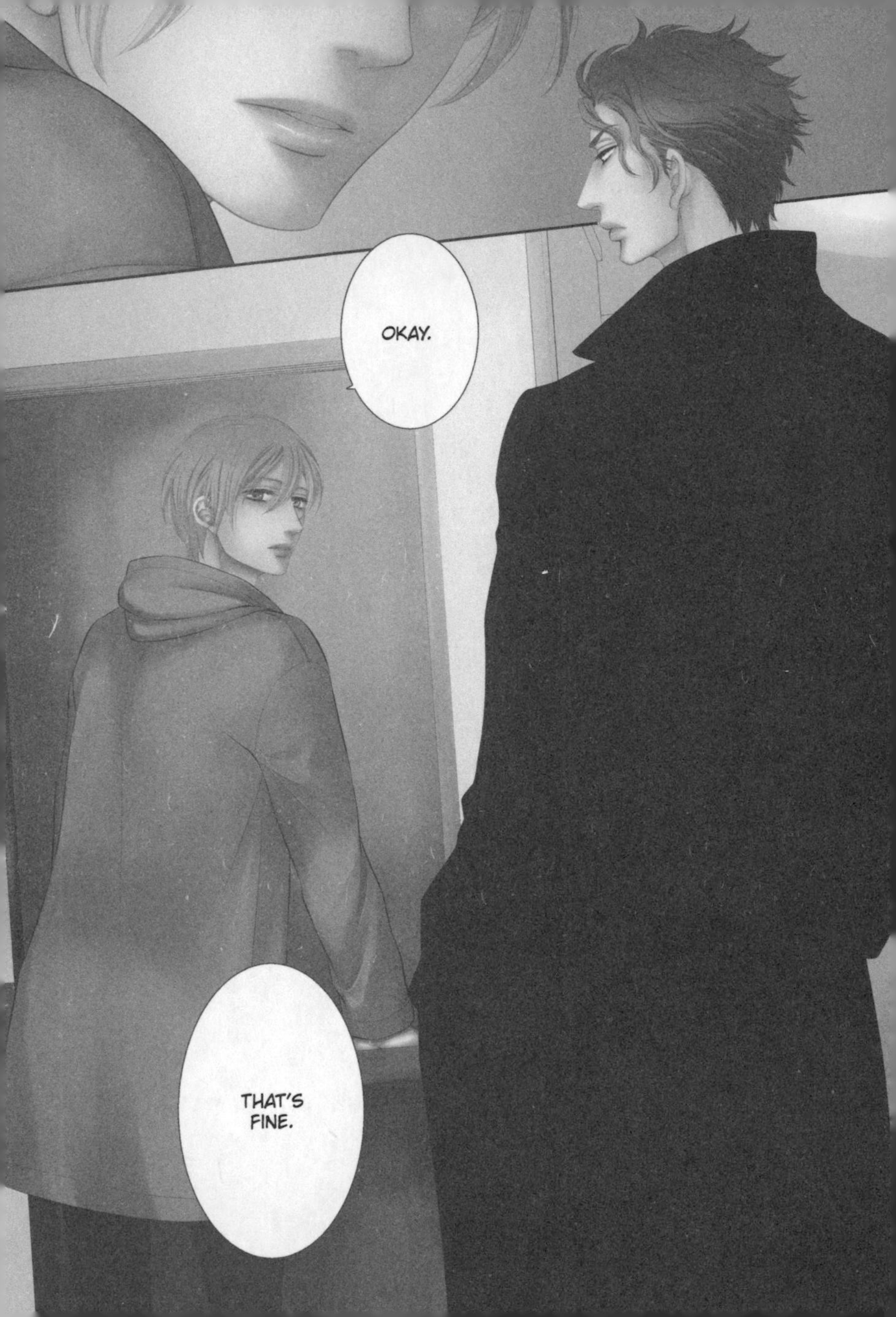
OKAY.
THAT'S FINE.

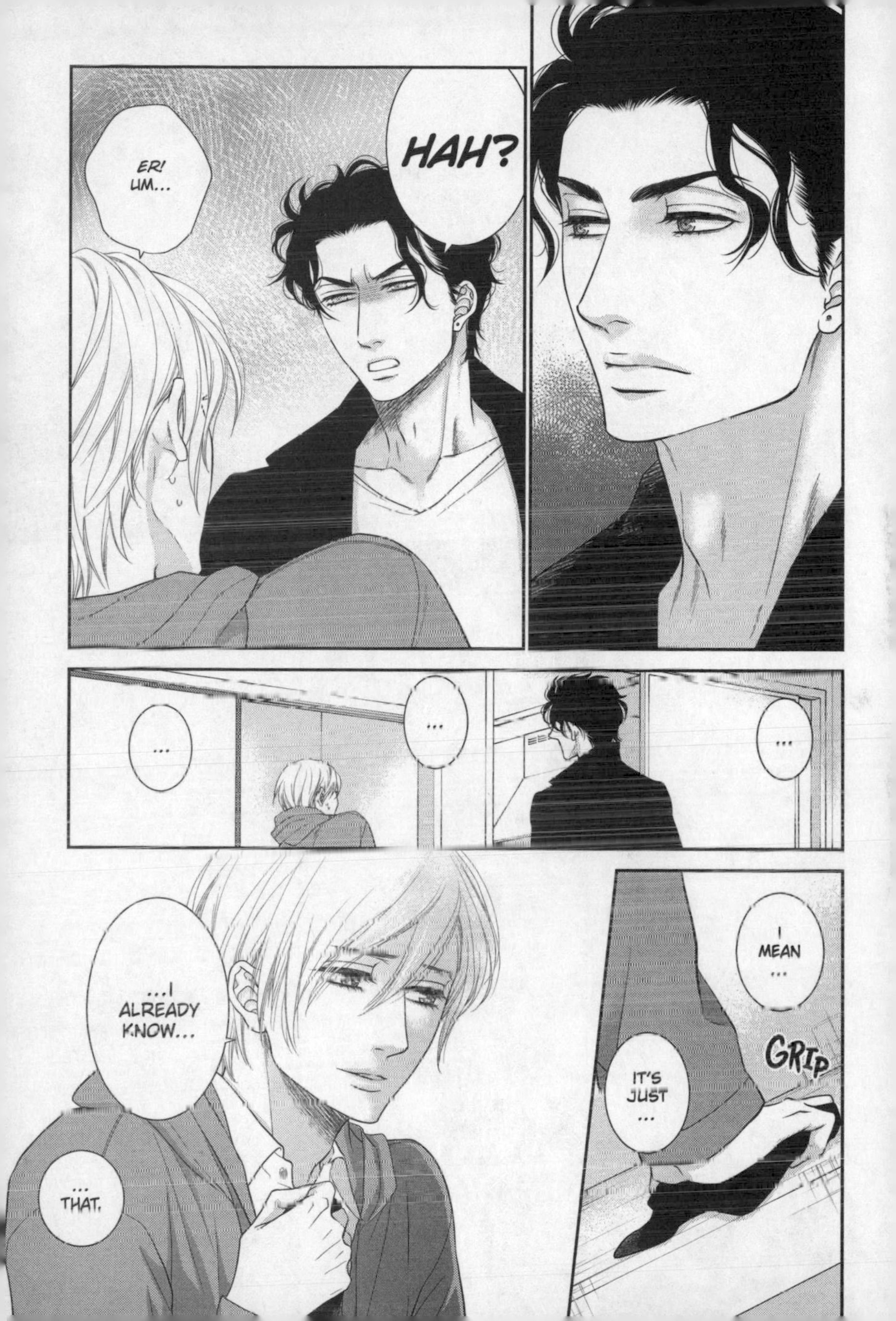
HAH?
ER! UM...
...
...
...
I MEAN...
IT'S JUST...
GRIP
...I ALREADY KNOW...
...THAT.

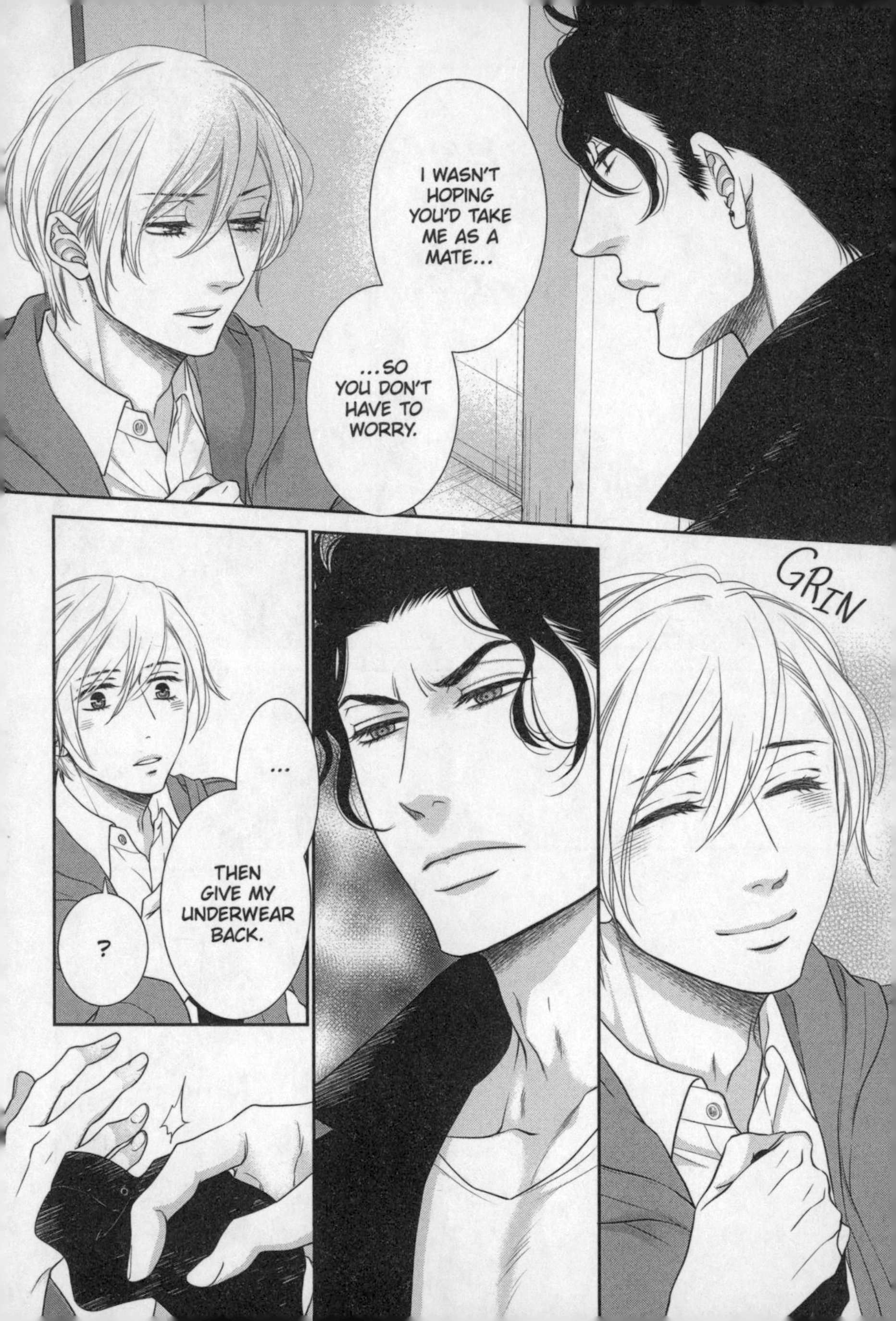
I WASN'T HOPING YOU'D TAKE ME AS A MATE...
...SO YOU DON'T HAVE TO WORRY.
GRIN
...
THEN GIVE MY UNDERWEAR BACK.
?

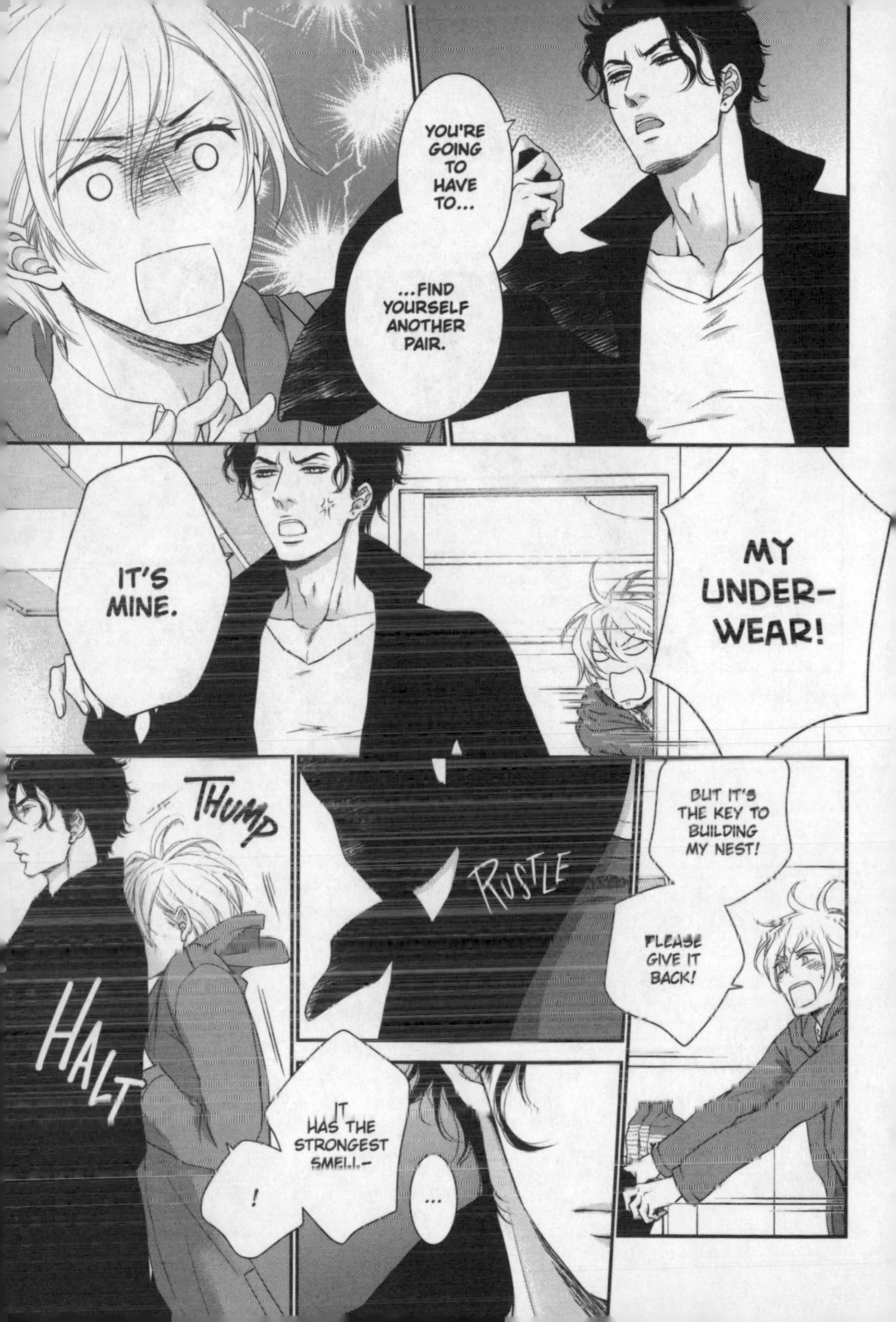
YOU'RE GOING TO HAVE TO...
...FIND YOURSELF ANOTHER PAIR.
MY UNDER-WEAR!
IT'S MINE.
BUT IT'S THE KEY TO BUILDING MY NEST!
PLEASE GIVE IT BACK!
RUSTLE
IT HAS THE STRONGEST SMELL-
!
...
THUMP
HALT

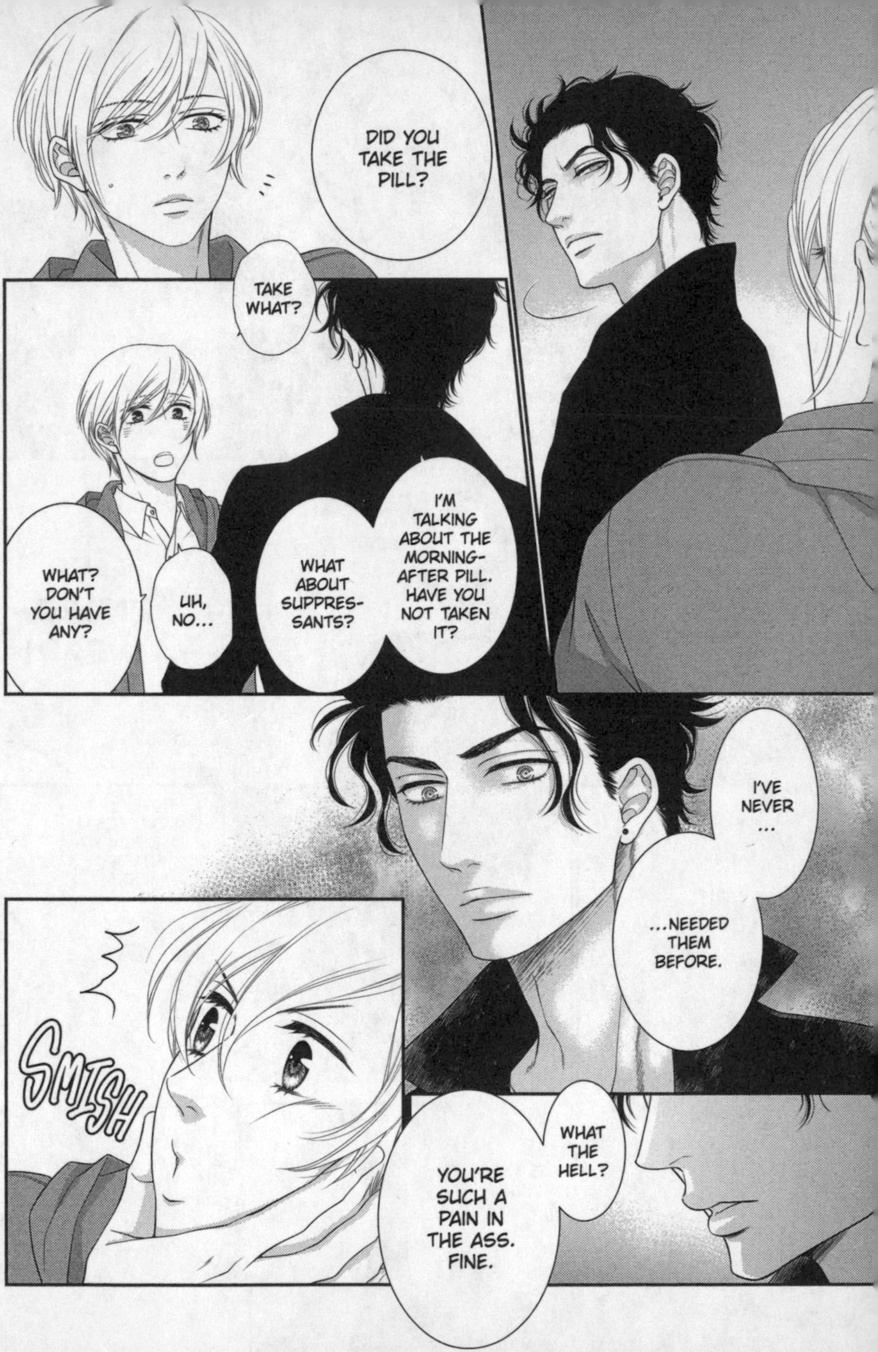
DID YOU TAKE THE PILL?
TAKE WHAT?
I'M TALKING ABOUT THE MORNING-AFTER PILL. HAVE YOU NOT TAKEN IT?
WHAT ABOUT SUPPRES-SANTS?
UH, NO...
WHAT? DON'T YOU HAVE ANY?
I'VE NEVER ...
...NEEDED THEM BEFORE.
WHAT THE HELL?
YOU'RE SUCH A PAIN IN THE ASS. FINE.
SMISH

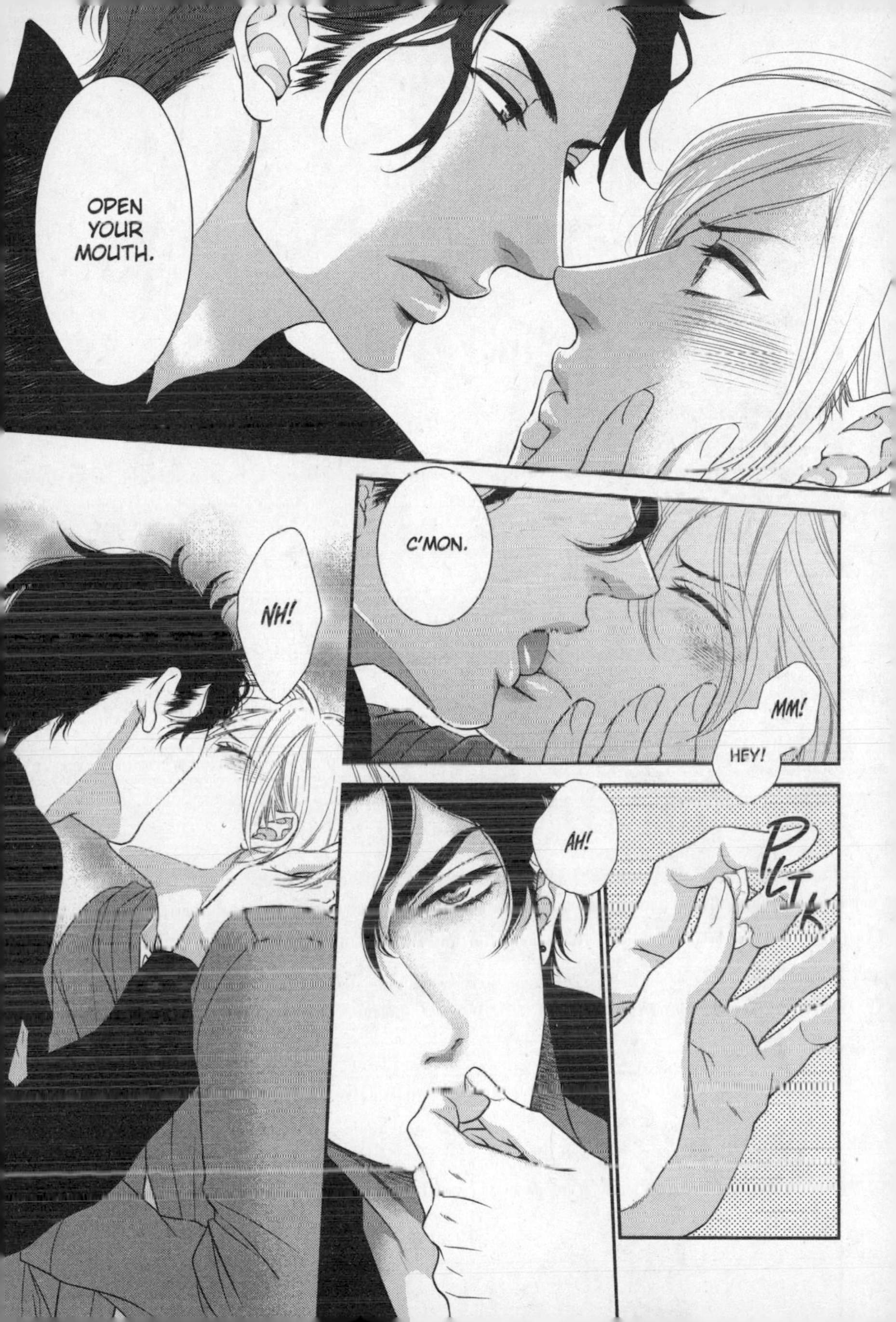
OPEN YOUR MOUTH.
C'MON.
MM!
HEY!
PLTK
AH!
NH!

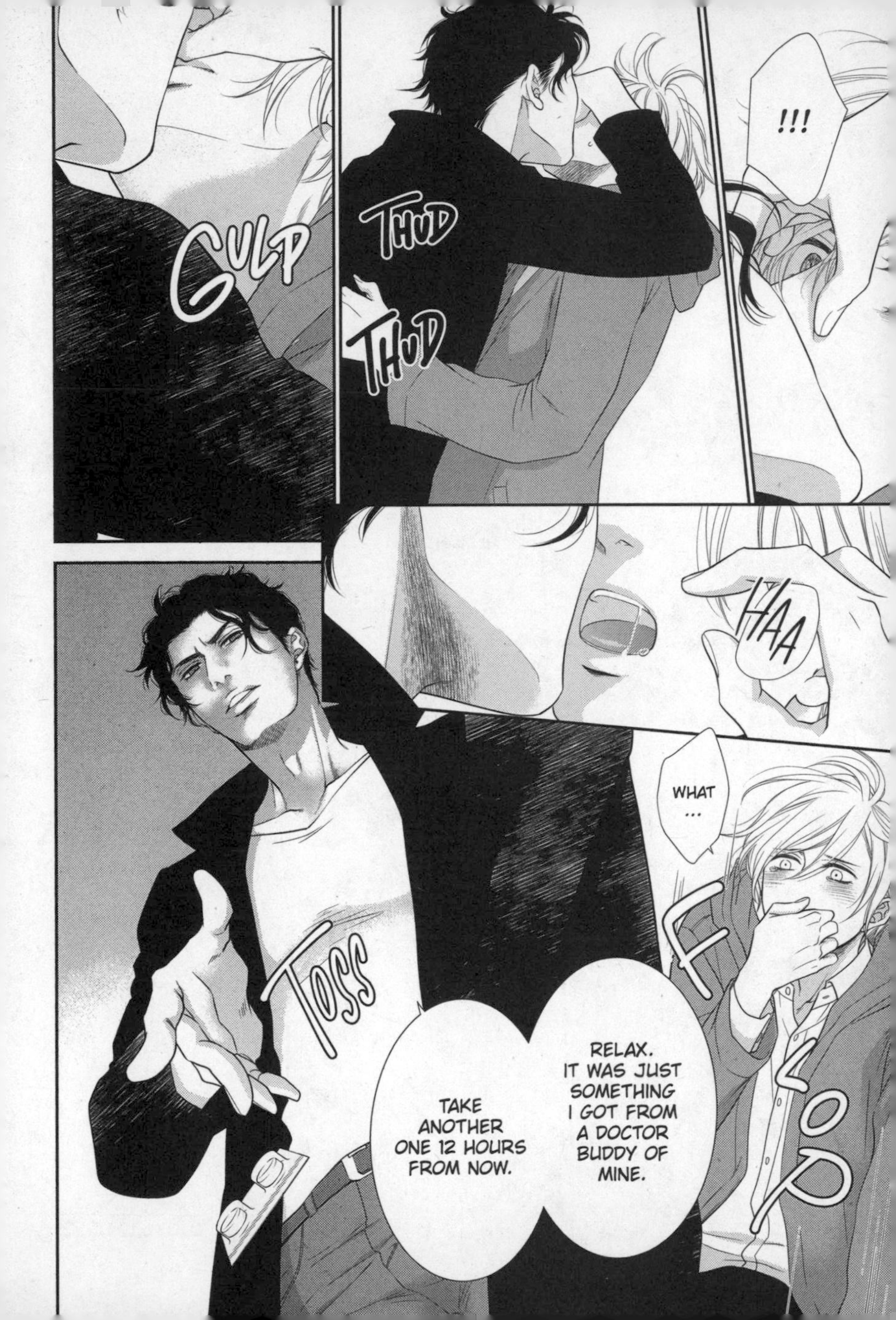
!!!
THUD
THUD
GULP
HAA
WHAT ...
FLOP
TOSS
RELAX. IT WAS JUST SOMETHING I GOT FROM A DOCTOR BUDDY OF MINE.
TAKE ANOTHER ONE 12 HOURS FROM NOW.

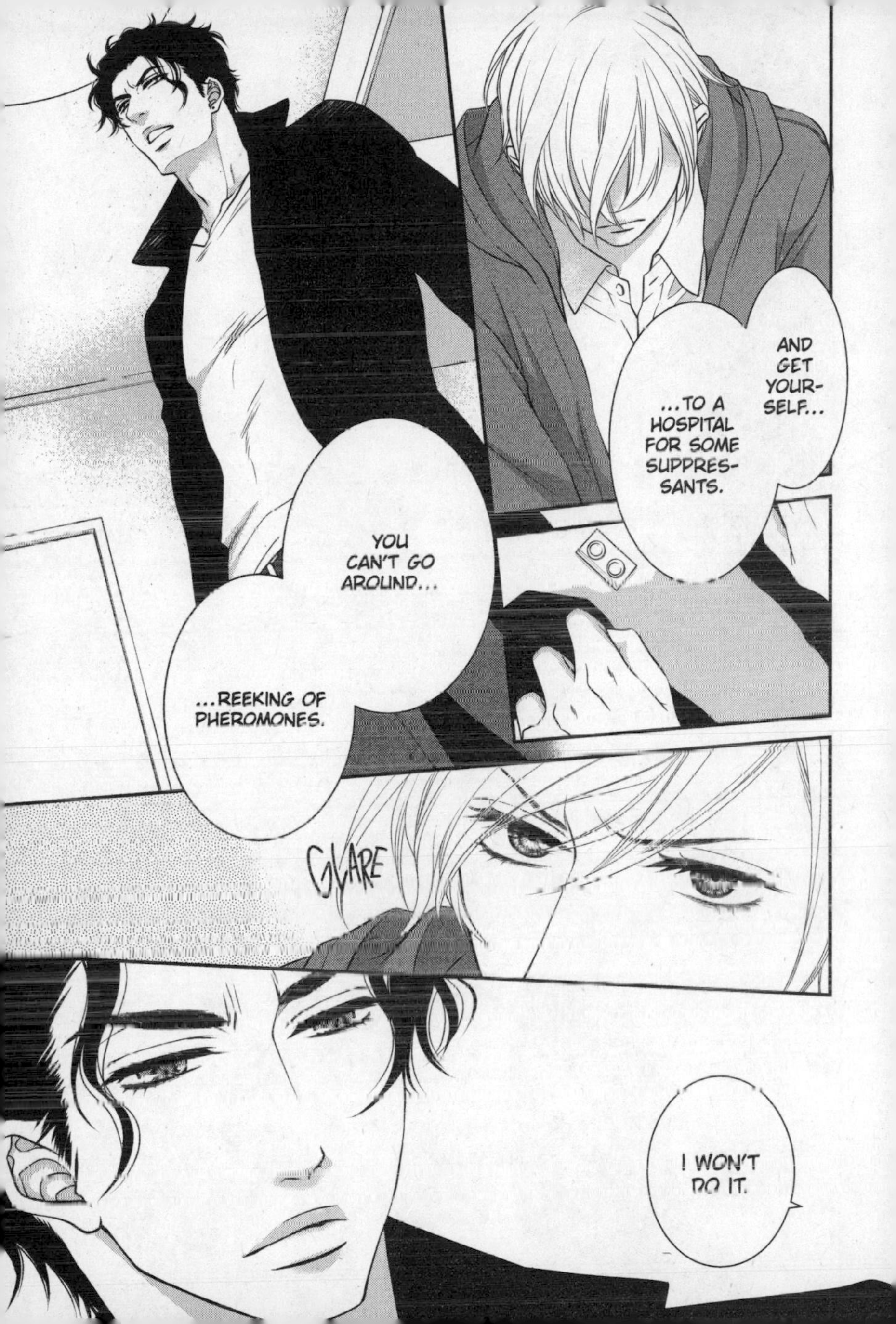
AND GET YOUR-SELF...
...TO A HOSPITAL FOR SOME SUPPRES-SANTS.
YOU CAN'T GO AROUND...
...REEKING OF PHEROMONES.
GLARE
I WON'T DO IT.

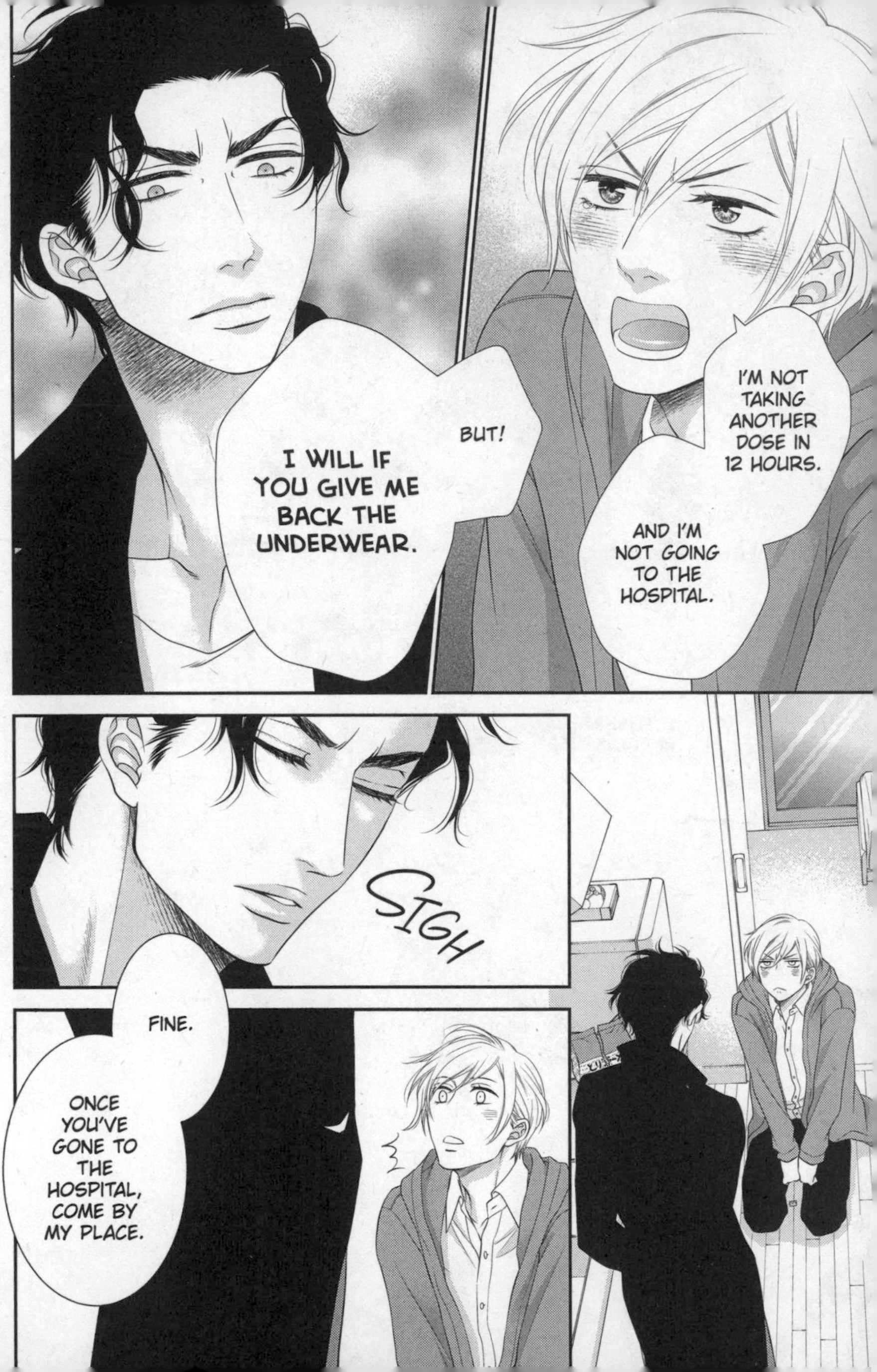
I'M NOT TAKING ANOTHER DOSE IN 12 HOURS.
AND I'M NOT GOING TO THE HOSPITAL.
BUT!
I WILL IF YOU GIVE ME BACK THE UNDERWEAR.
SIGH
FINE.
ONCE YOU'VE GONE TO THE HOSPITAL, COME BY MY PLACE.

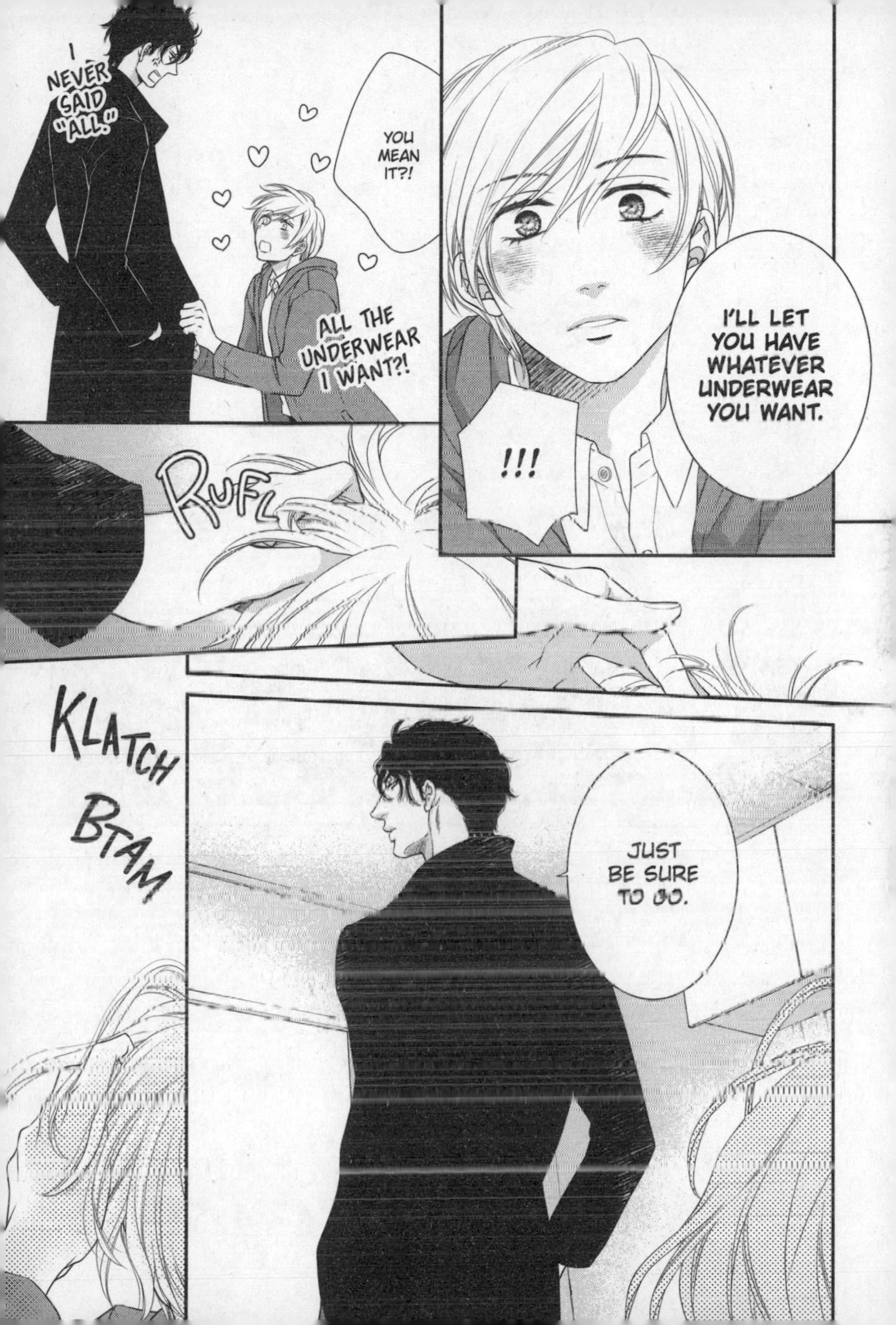
I'LL LET YOU HAVE WHATEVER UNDERWEAR YOU WANT.
!!!
YOU MEAN IT?!
ALL THE UNDERWEAR I WANT?!
I NEVER SAID "ALL."
RUFL
JUST BE SURE TO GO.
KLATCH
BTAM

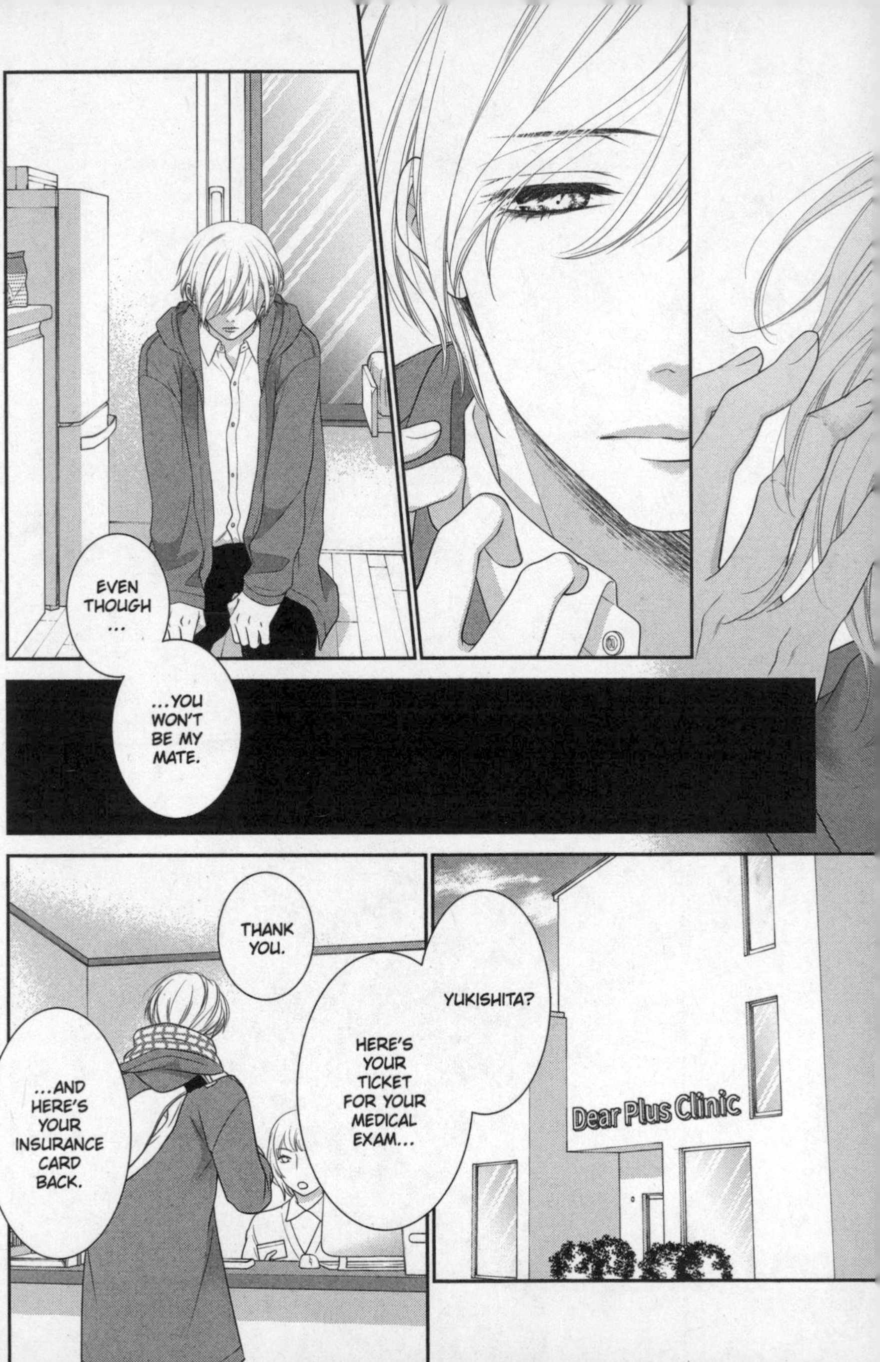
EVEN THOUGH ...
...YOU WON'T BE MY MATE.
Dear Plus Clinic
YUKISHITA?
HERE'S YOUR TICKET FOR YOUR MEDICAL EXAM...
...AND HERE'S YOUR INSURANCE CARD BACK.
THANK YOU.

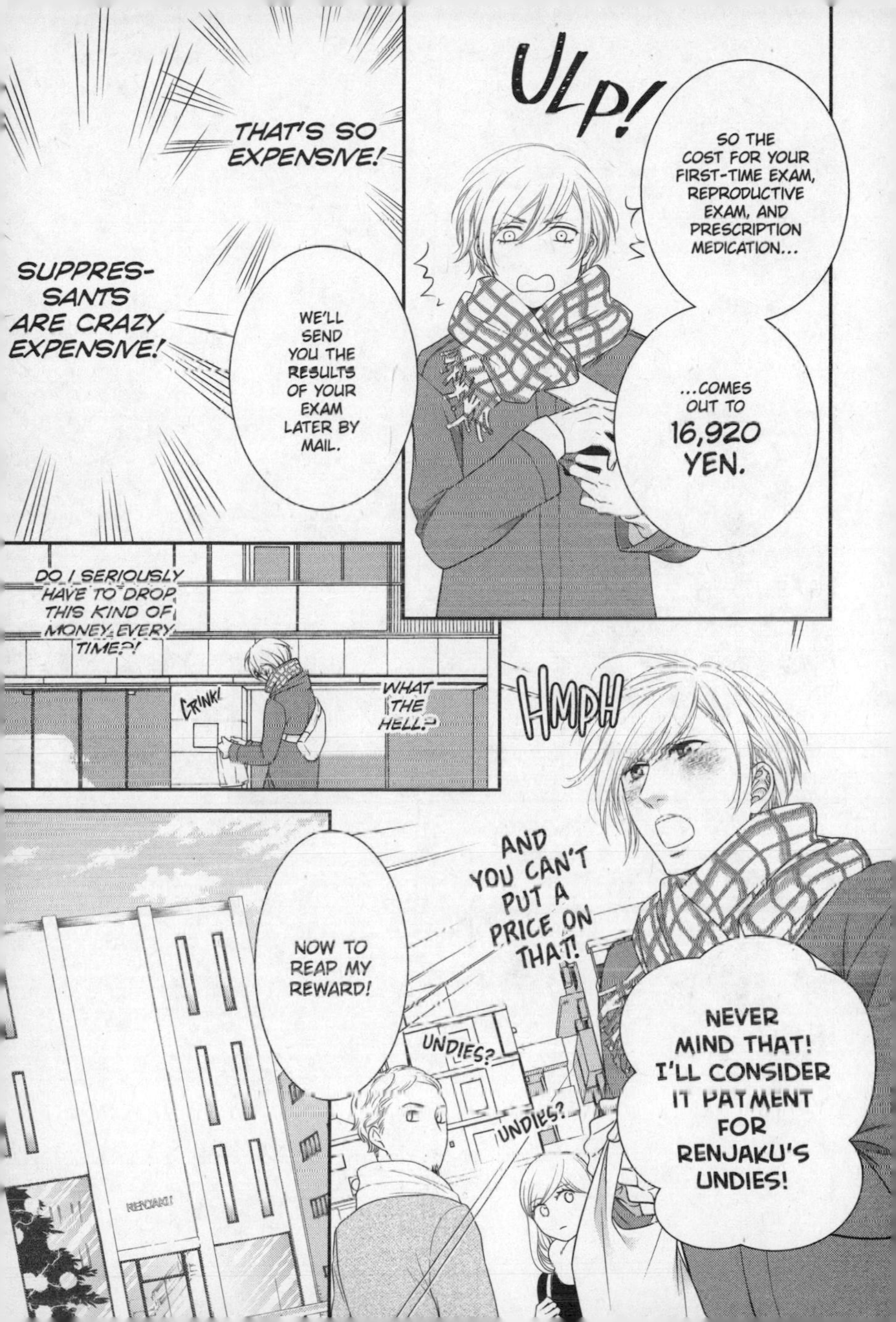
ULP!
SO THE COST FOR YOUR FIRST-TIME EXAM, REPRODUCTIVE EXAM, AND PRESCRIPTION MEDICATION...
...COMES OUT TO 16,920 YEN.
THAT'S SO EXPENSIVE!
WE'LL SEND YOU THE RESULTS OF YOUR EXAM LATER BY MAIL.
SUPPRES-SANTS ARE CRAZY EXPENSIVE!
DO I SERIOUSLY HAVE TO DROP THIS KIND OF MONEY EVERY TIME?!
WHAT THE HELL?
CRINK
NOW TO REAP MY REWARD!
HMPH
NEVER MIND THAT! I'LL CONSIDER IT PATMENT FOR RENJAKU'S UNDIES!
AND YOU CAN'T PUT A PRICE ON THAT!
UNDIES?
UNDIES?
RENJAKU

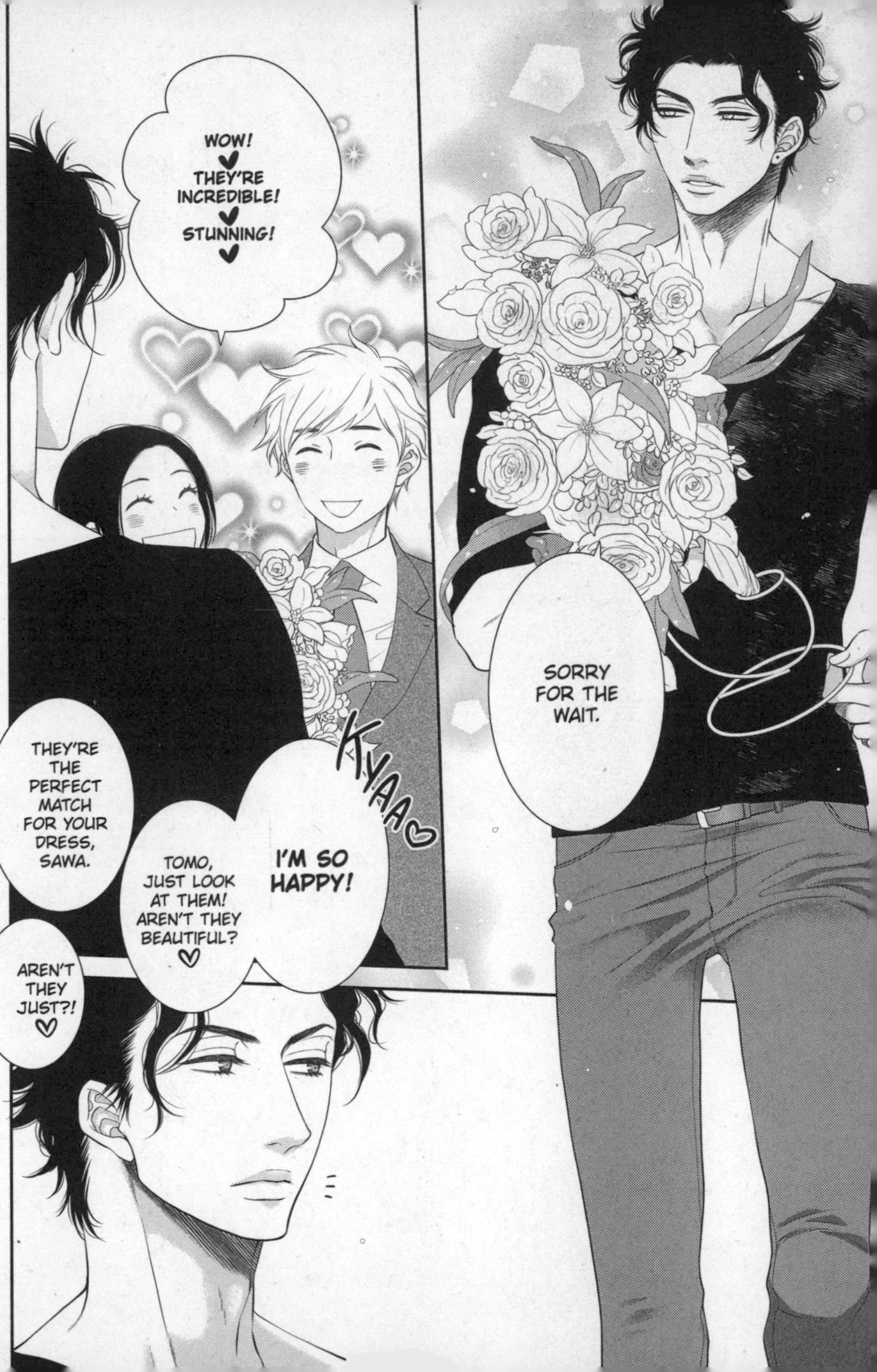
SORRY FOR THE WAIT.
WOW! ♥ THEY'RE INCREDIBLE! ♥ STUNNING! ♥
KYAAA ♥
I'M SO HAPPY!
TOMO, JUST LOOK AT THEM! AREN'T THEY BEAUTIFUL? ♥
THEY'RE THE PERFECT MATCH FOR YOUR DRESS, SAWA.
AREN'T THEY JUST?! ♥

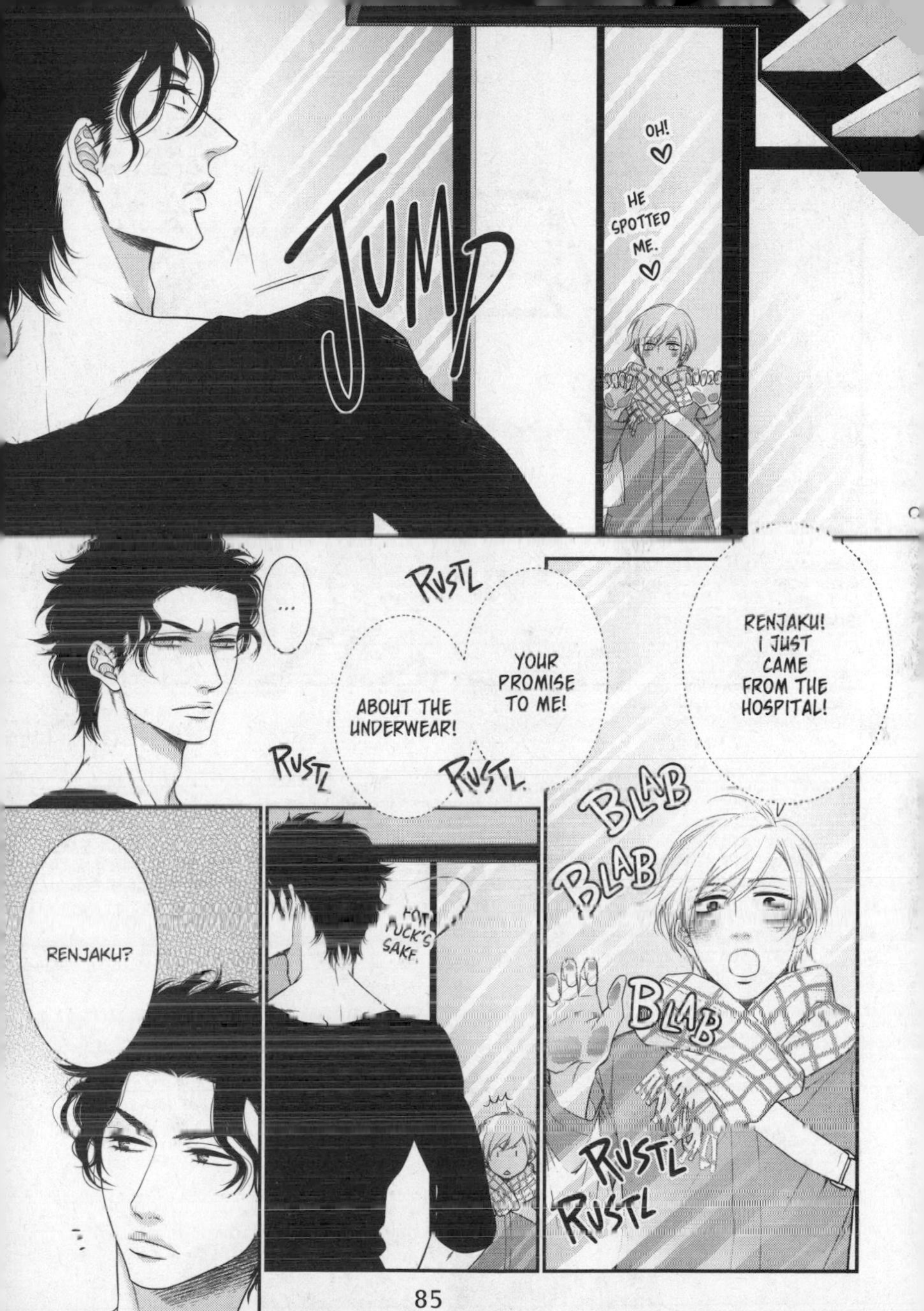

OH! ♥
HE SPOTTED ME. ♥
JUMP
RENJAKU! I JUST CAME FROM THE HOSPITAL!
YOUR PROMISE TO ME!
ABOUT THE UNDERWEAR!
BLAB
BLAB
BLAB
RUSTL
RUSTL
RUSTL
...
RUSTL
RUSTL
FOR FUCK'S SAKE.
RENJAKU?

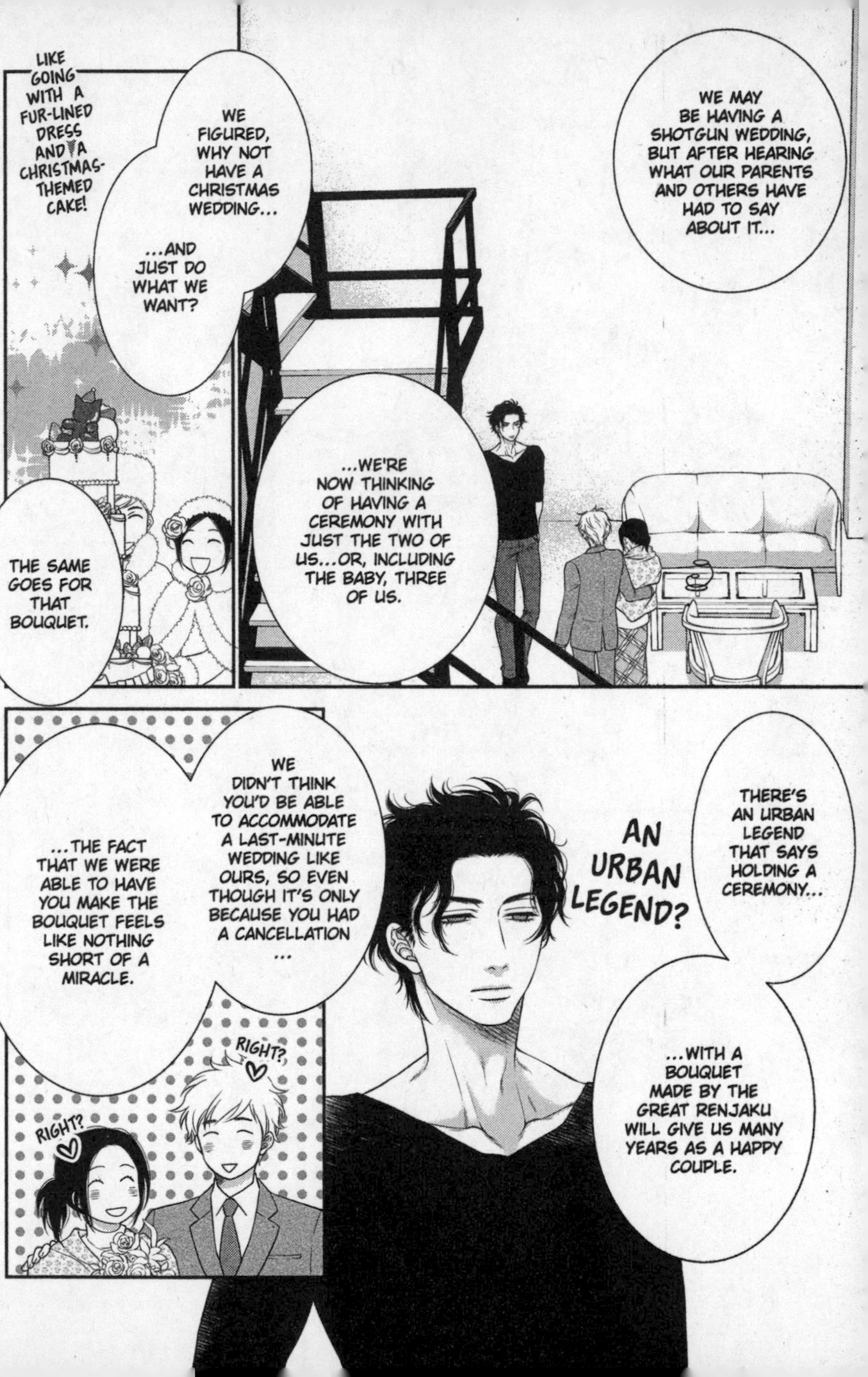
WE MAY BE HAVING A SHOTGUN WEDDING, BUT AFTER HEARING WHAT OUR PARENTS AND OTHERS HAVE HAD TO SAY ABOUT IT...
...WE'RE NOW THINKING OF HAVING A CEREMONY WITH JUST THE TWO OF US...OR, INCLUDING THE BABY, THREE OF US.
WE FIGURED, WHY NOT HAVE A CHRISTMAS WEDDING...
...AND JUST DO WHAT WE WANT?
LIKE GOING WITH A FUR-LINED DRESS AND A CHRISTMAS-THEMED CAKE!
THE SAME GOES FOR THAT BOUQUET.
THERE'S AN URBAN LEGEND THAT SAYS HOLDING A CEREMONY...
...WITH A BOUQUET MADE BY THE GREAT RENJAKU WILL GIVE US MANY YEARS AS A HAPPY COUPLE.
AN URBAN LEGEND?
WE DIDN'T THINK YOU'D BE ABLE TO ACCOMMODATE A LAST-MINUTE WEDDING LIKE OURS, SO EVEN THOUGH IT'S ONLY BECAUSE YOU HAD A CANCELLATION ...
...THE FACT THAT WE WERE ABLE TO HAVE YOU MAKE THE BOUQUET FEELS LIKE NOTHING SHORT OF A MIRACLE.
RIGHT?
RIGHT?

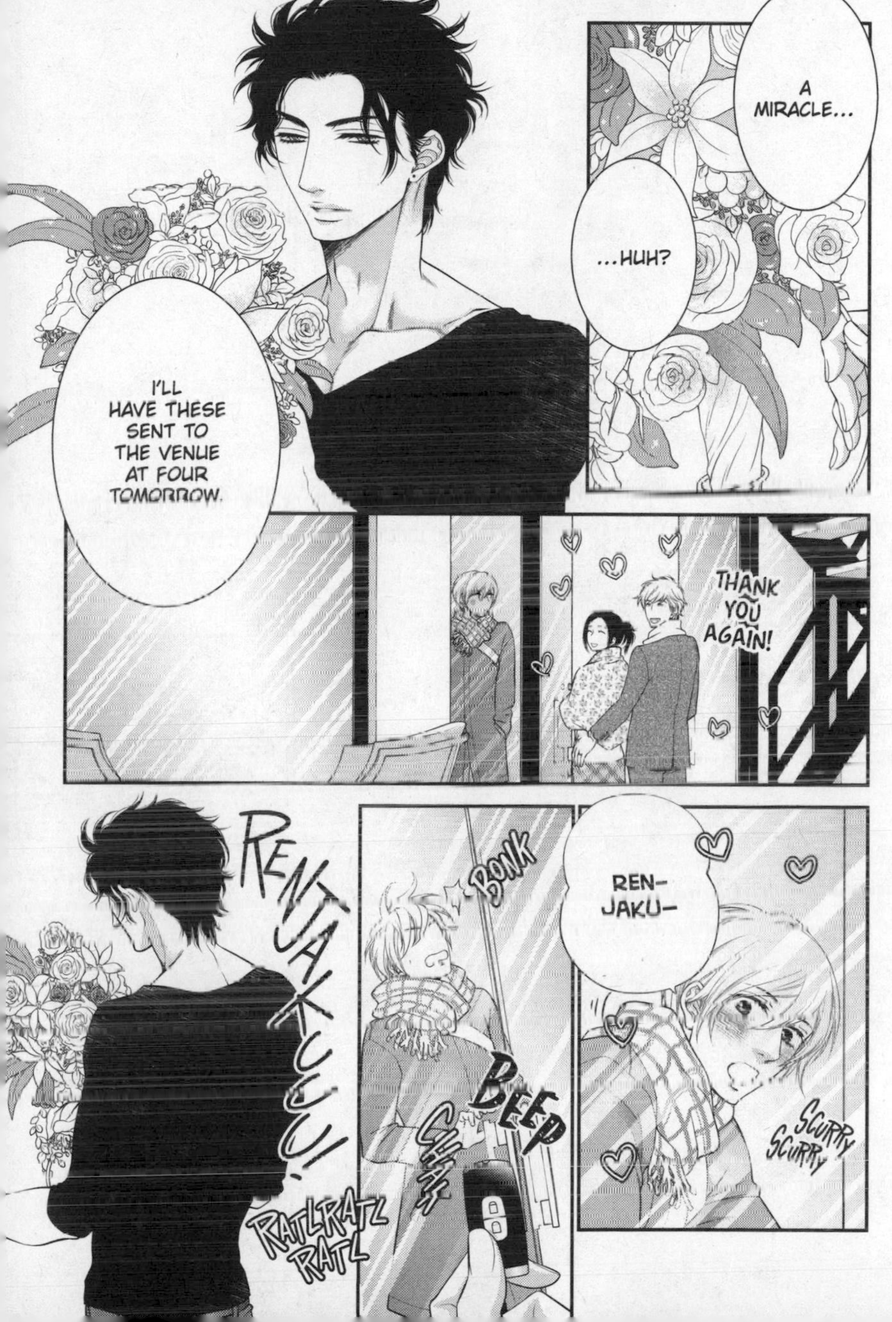
A MIRACLE...
...HUH?
I'LL HAVE THESE SENT TO THE VENUE AT FOUR TOMORROW.
THANK YOU AGAIN!
REN-JAKU-
SCURRY SCURRY
BONK
BEEP
CHAK
RENJAKUUU!
RATLRATL RATL

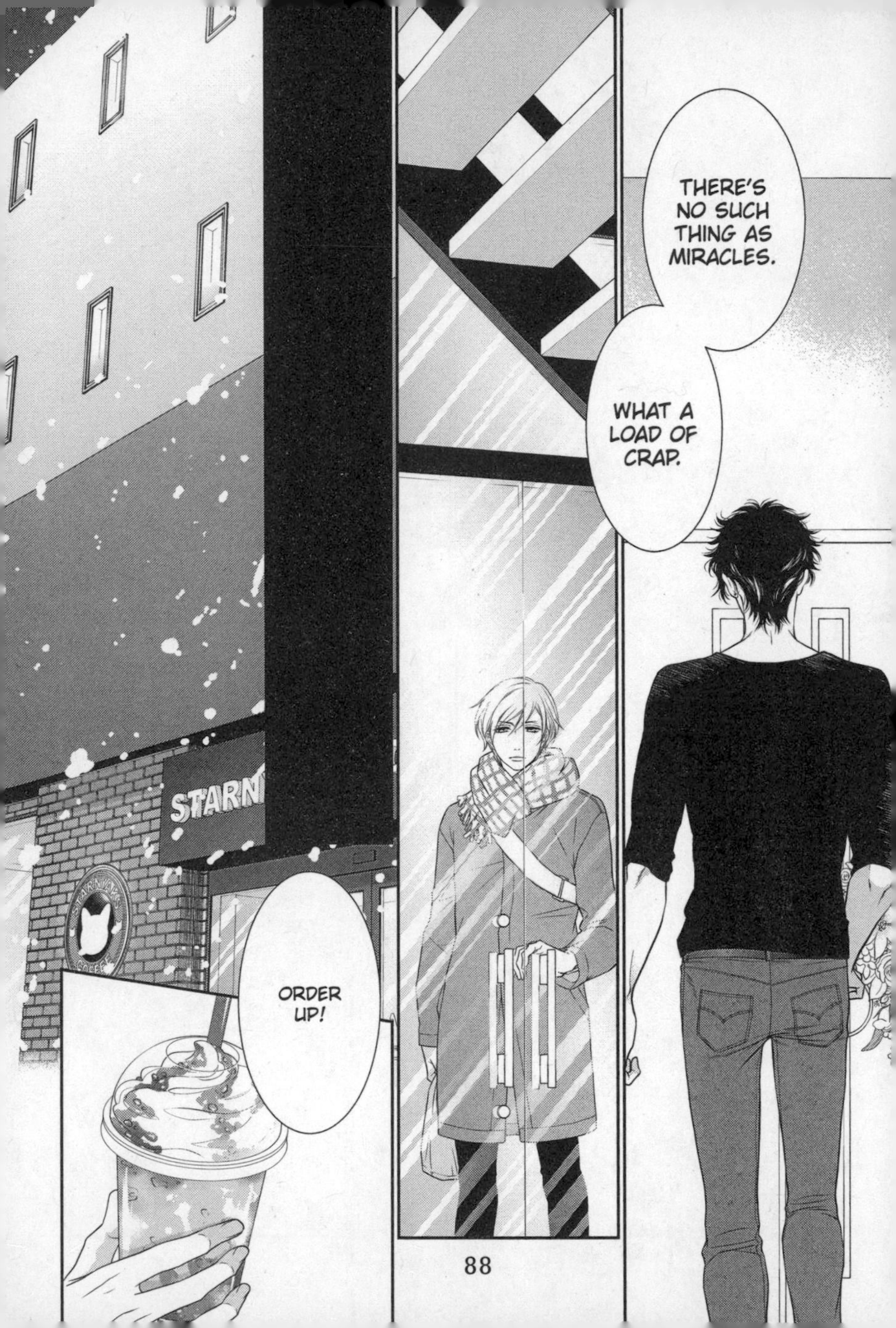
THERE'S NO SUCH THING AS MIRACLES.
WHAT A LOAD OF CRAP.
STARN
ORDER UP!

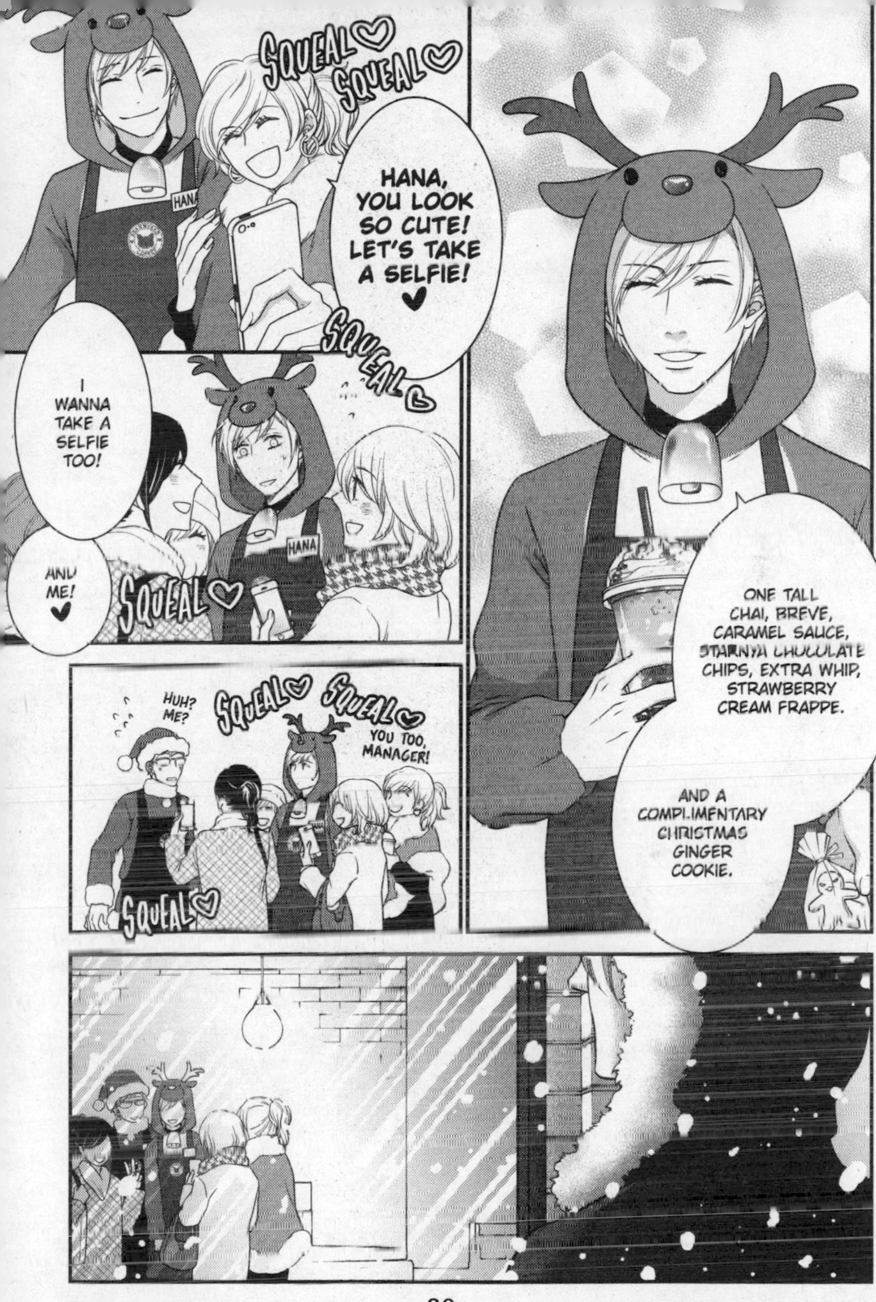

ONE TALL CHAI, BREVE, CARAMEL SAUCE, STARNYA CHOCOLATE CHIPS, EXTRA WHIP, STRAWBERRY CREAM FRAPPE.
AND A COMPLIMENTARY CHRISTMAS GINGER COOKIE.
SQUEAL♡ SQUEAL♡
HANA, YOU LOOK SO CUTE! LET'S TAKE A SELFIE! ♥
HANA
SQUEAL SQUEAL♡
I WANNA TAKE A SELFIE TOO!
AND ME! ♥
HANA
SQUEAL♡
SQUEAL♡ SQUEAL♡
HUH? ME?
YOU TOO, MANAGER!
SQUEAL♡

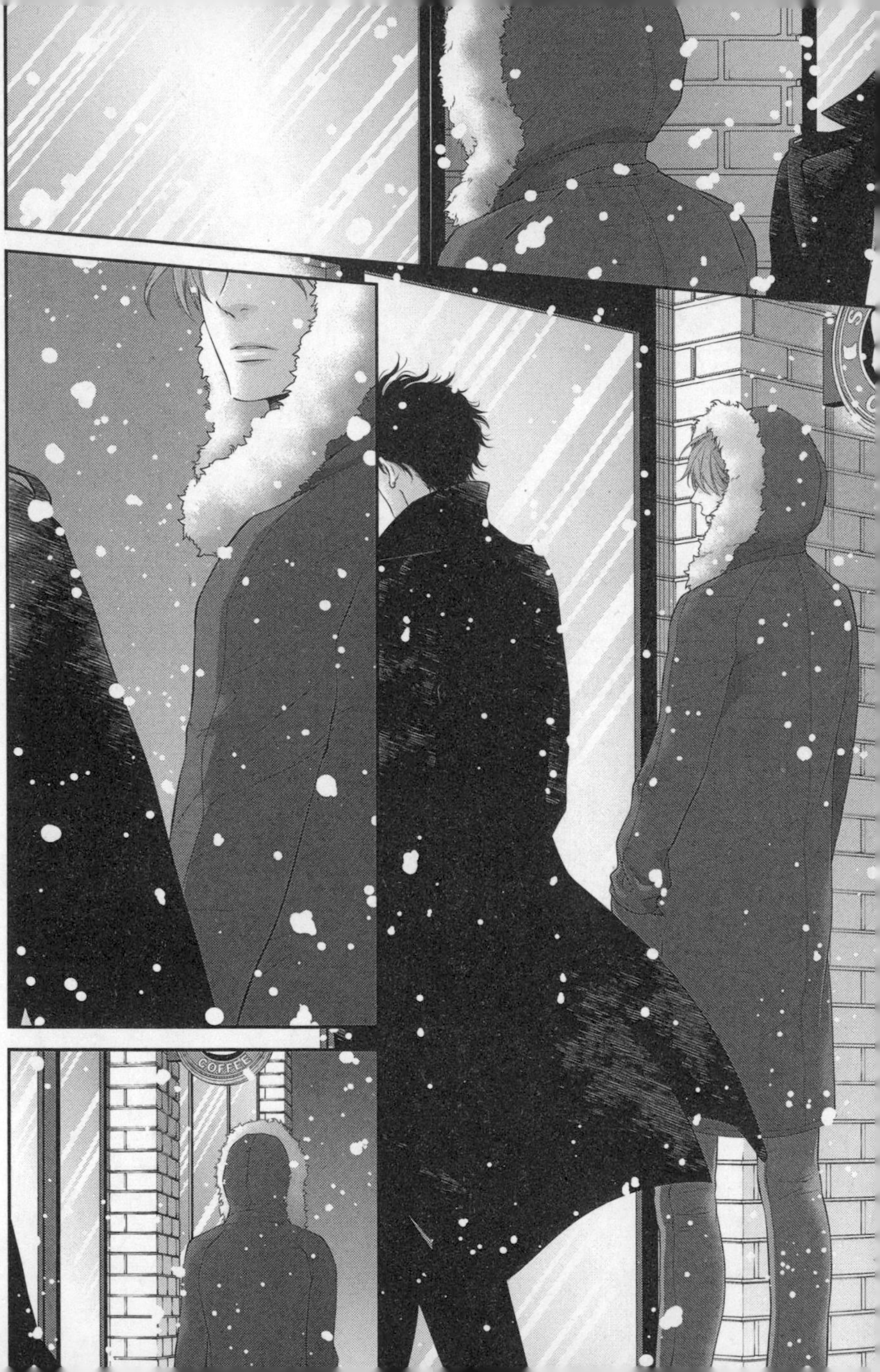
COFFEE

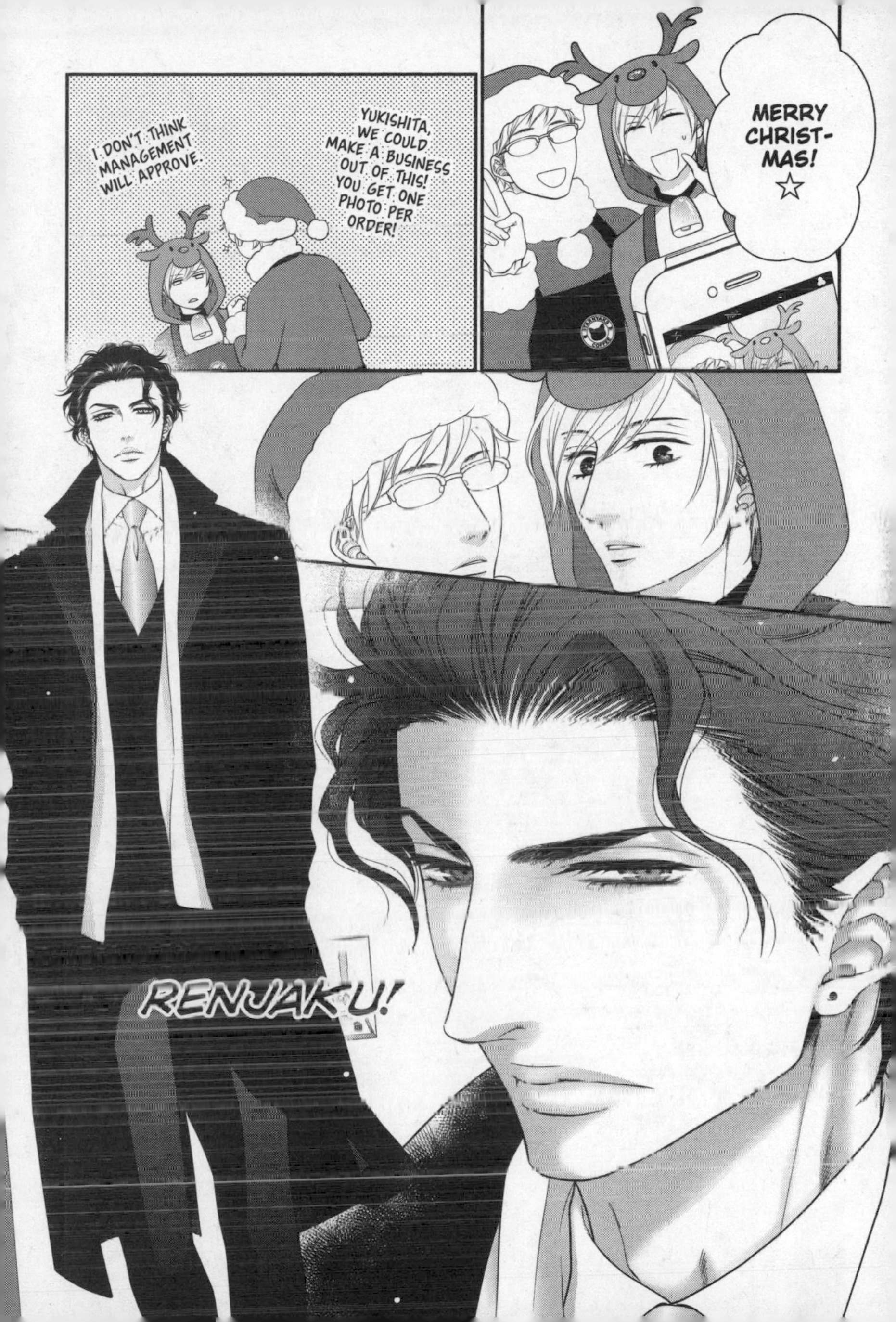
MERRY CHRIST-MAS! ☆
YUKISHITA, WE COULD MAKE A BUSINESS OUT OF THIS! YOU GET ONE PHOTO PER ORDER!
I DON'T THINK MANAGEMENT WILL APPROVE.
RENJAKU!

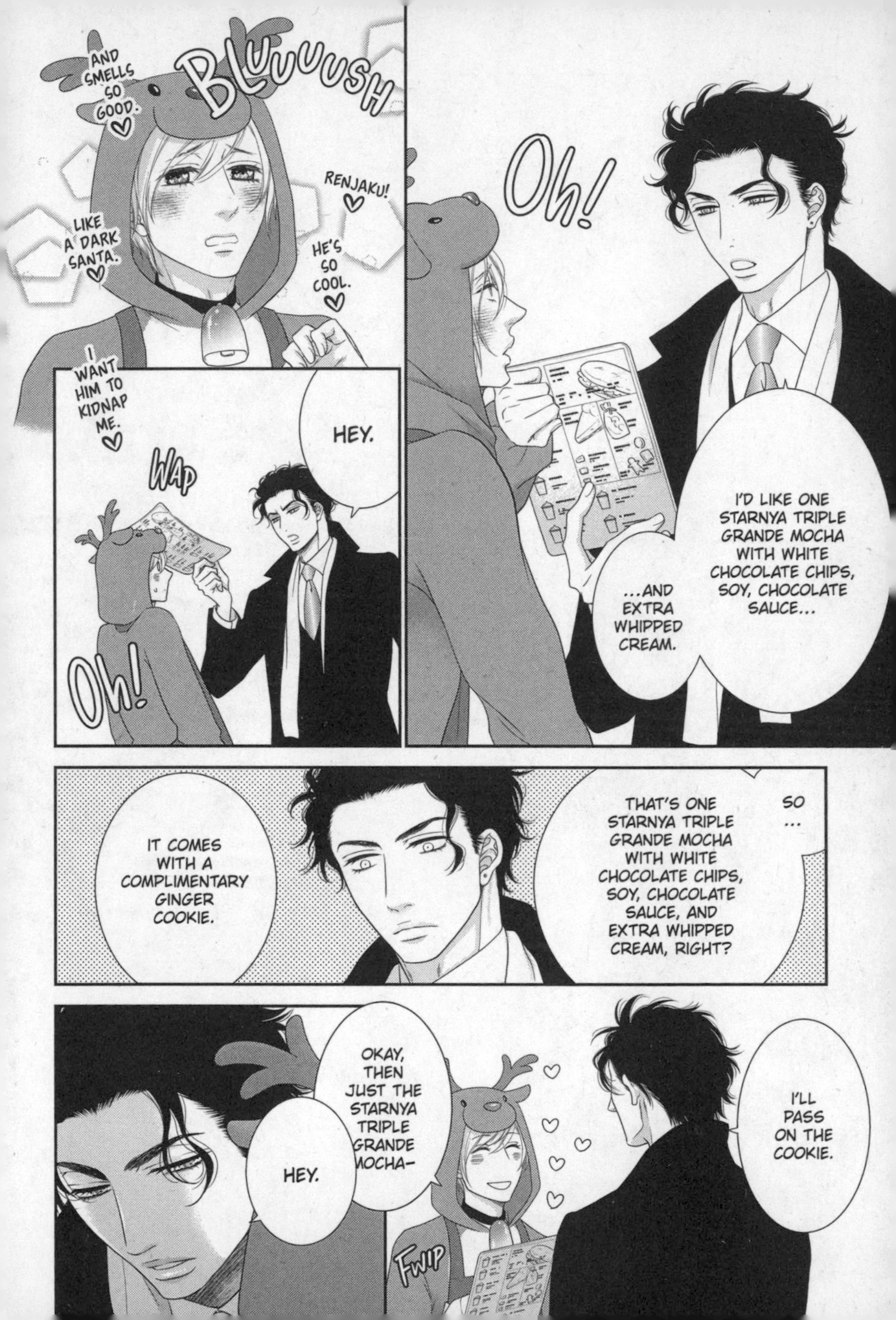
Oh!
I'D LIKE ONE STARNYA TRIPLE GRANDE MOCHA WITH WHITE CHOCOLATE CHIPS, SOY, CHOCOLATE SAUCE...
...AND EXTRA WHIPPED CREAM.
BLUUUUSH
AND SMELLS SO GOOD. ♡
RENJAKU! ♡
LIKE A DARK SANTA. ♡
HE'S SO COOL. ♡
I WANT HIM TO KIDNAP ME. ♡
HEY.
WAP
Oh!
SO...
THAT'S ONE STARNYA TRIPLE GRANDE MOCHA WITH WHITE CHOCOLATE CHIPS, SOY, CHOCOLATE SAUCE, AND EXTRA WHIPPED CREAM, RIGHT?
IT COMES WITH A COMPLIMENTARY GINGER COOKIE.
I'LL PASS ON THE COOKIE.
OKAY, THEN JUST THE STARNYA TRIPLE GRANDE MOCHA—
HEY.
FWIP

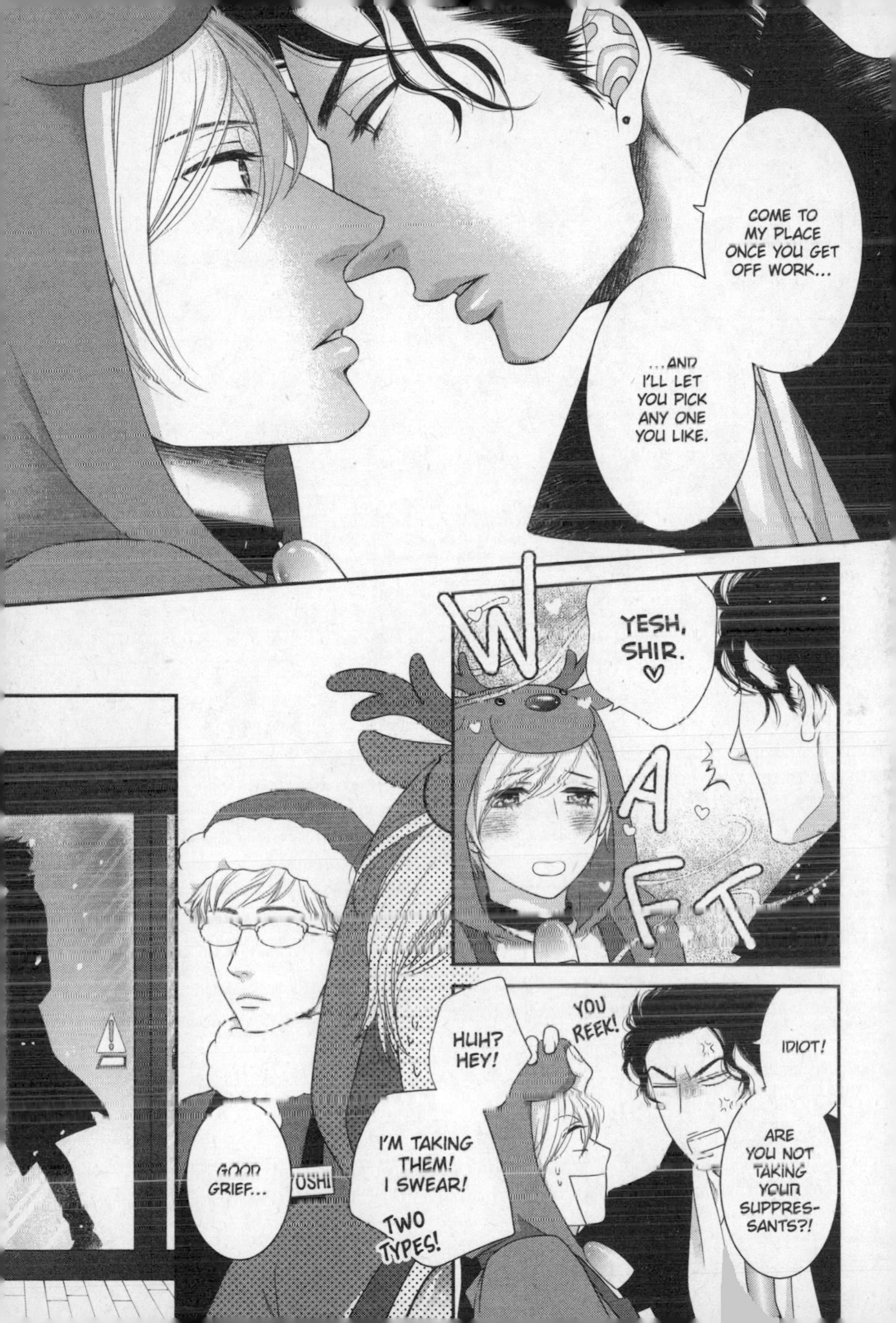
COME TO MY PLACE ONCE YOU GET OFF WORK...
...AND I'LL LET YOU PICK ANY ONE YOU LIKE.
YESH, SHIR. ♥
WAFT
IDIOT!
ARE YOU NOT TAKING YOUR SUPPRES-SANTS?!
YOU REEK!
HUH? HEY!
I'M TAKING THEM! I SWEAR!
TWO TYPES!
GOOD GRIEF...
YOSHI

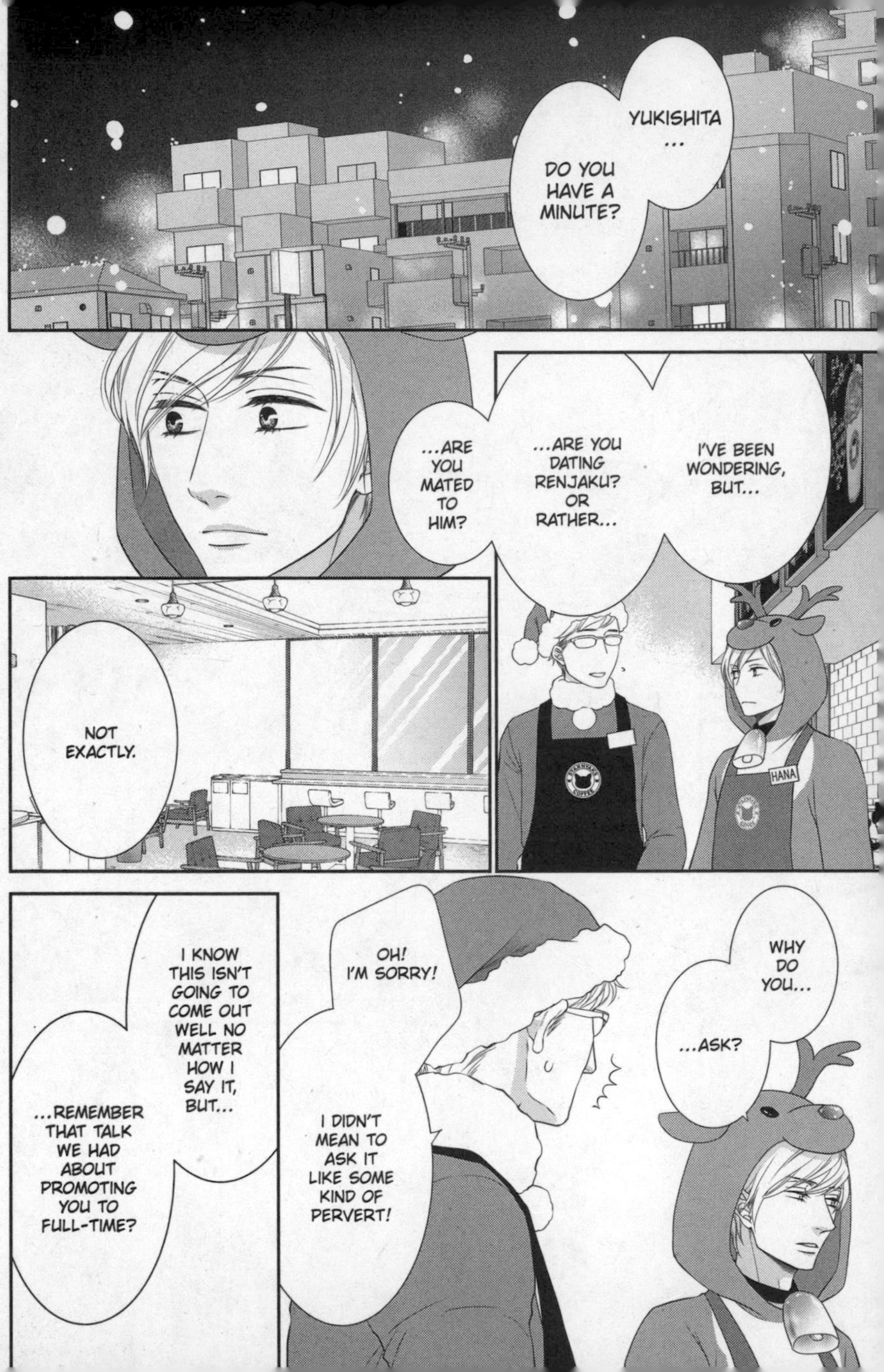
YUKISHITA ... DO YOU HAVE A MINUTE?
I'VE BEEN WONDERING, BUT...
...ARE YOU DATING RENJAKU? OR RATHER...
...ARE YOU MATED TO HIM?
HANA
NOT EXACTLY.
WHY DO YOU...
...ASK?
OH! I'M SORRY!
I DIDN'T MEAN TO ASK IT LIKE SOME KIND OF PERVERT!
I KNOW THIS ISN'T GOING TO COME OUT WELL NO MATTER HOW I SAY IT, BUT...
...REMEMBER THAT TALK WE HAD ABOUT PROMOTING YOU TO FULL-TIME?

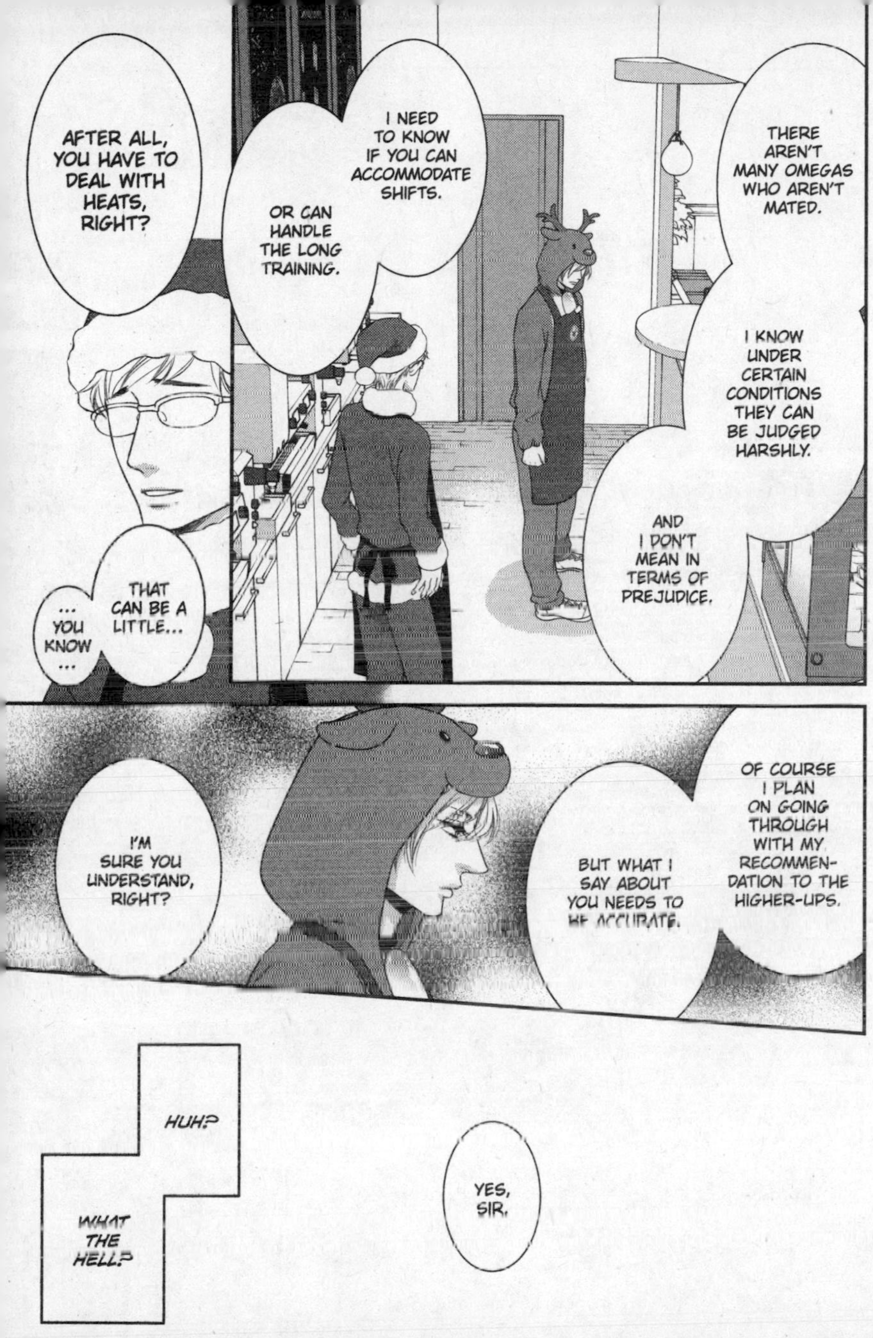
THERE AREN'T MANY OMEGAS WHO AREN'T MATED.
I KNOW UNDER CERTAIN CONDITIONS THEY CAN BE JUDGED HARSHLY.
AND I DON'T MEAN IN TERMS OF PREJUDICE.
I NEED TO KNOW IF YOU CAN ACCOMMODATE SHIFTS.
OR CAN HANDLE THE LONG TRAINING.
AFTER ALL, YOU HAVE TO DEAL WITH HEATS, RIGHT?
THAT CAN BE A LITTLE...
...YOU KNOW...
OF COURSE I PLAN ON GOING THROUGH WITH MY RECOMMEN-DATION TO THE HIGHER-UPS.
BUT WHAT I SAY ABOUT YOU NEEDS TO BE ACCURATE.
I'M SURE YOU UNDERSTAND, RIGHT?
YES, SIR.
HUH?
WHAT THE HELL?

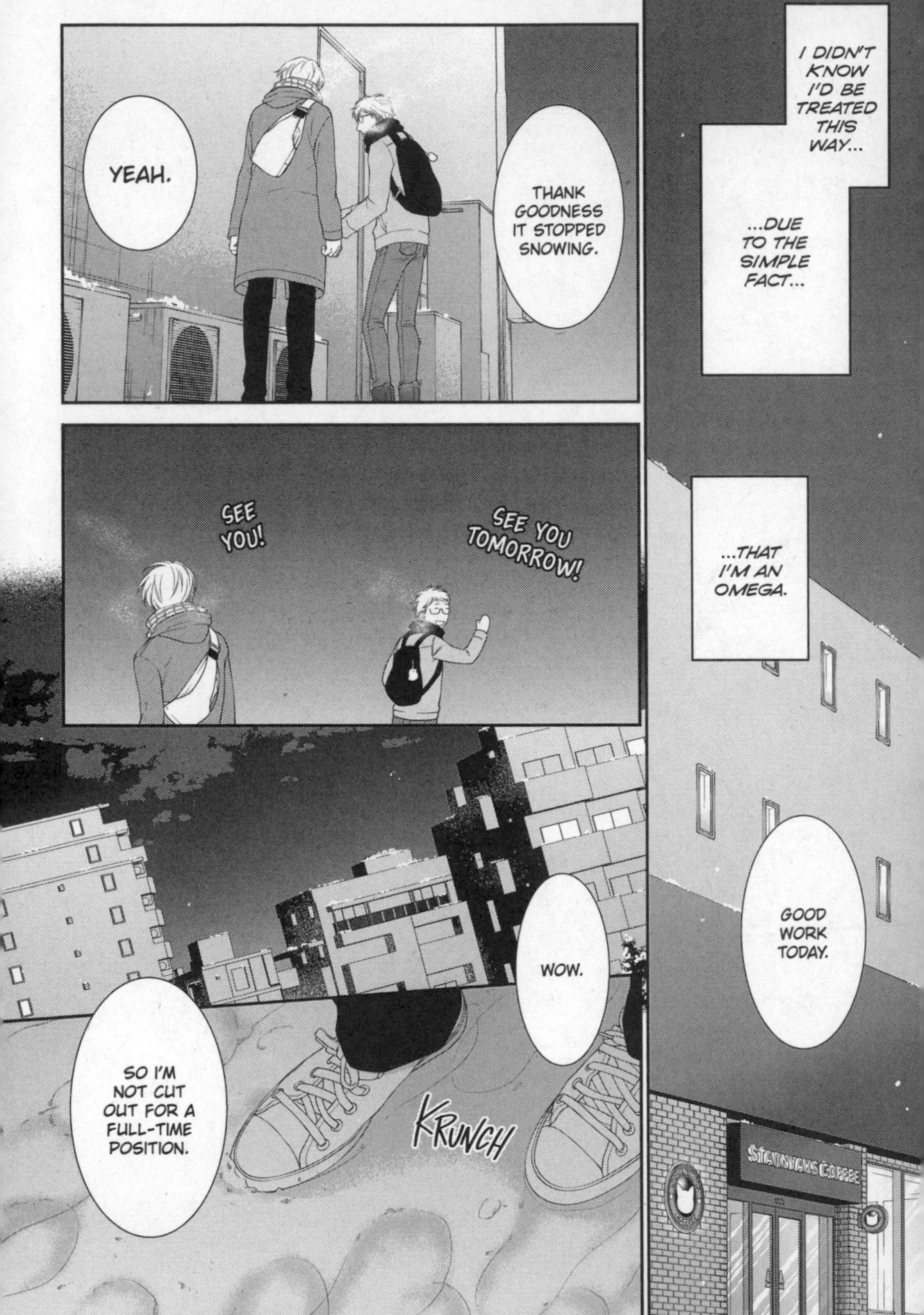
I DIDN'T KNOW I'D BE TREATED THIS WAY...
...DUE TO THE SIMPLE FACT...
...THAT I'M AN OMEGA.
GOOD WORK TODAY.
STARNYAKS COFFEE
THANK GOODNESS IT STOPPED SNOWING.
YEAH.
SEE YOU TOMORROW!
SEE YOU!
WOW.
KRUNCH
SO I'M NOT CUT OUT FOR A FULL-TIME POSITION.

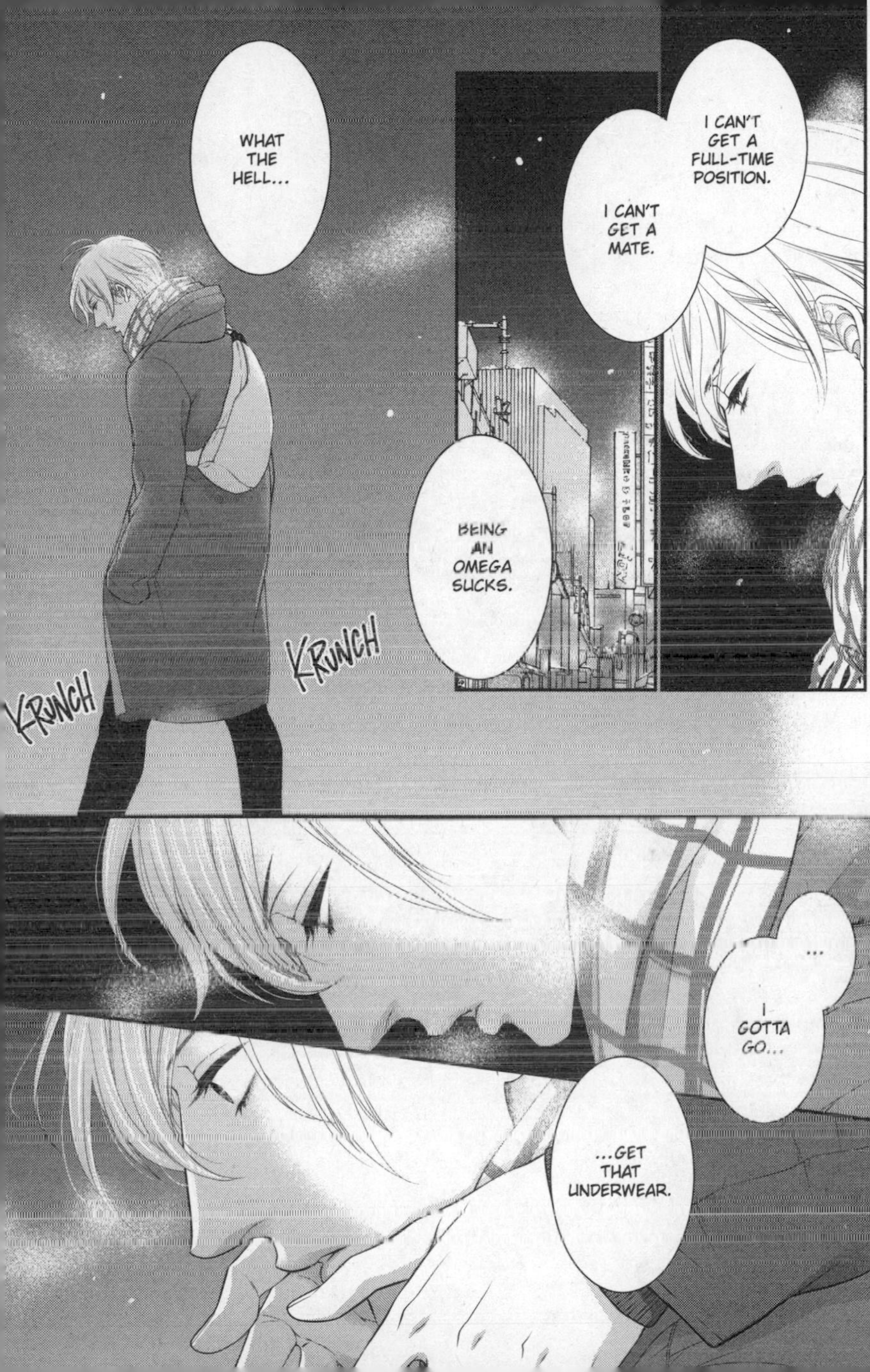
I CAN'T GET A FULL-TIME POSITION.
I CAN'T GET A MATE.
BEING AN OMEGA SUCKS.
WHAT THE HELL...
KRUNCH
KRUNCH
...
I GOTTA GO...
...GET THAT UNDERWEAR.

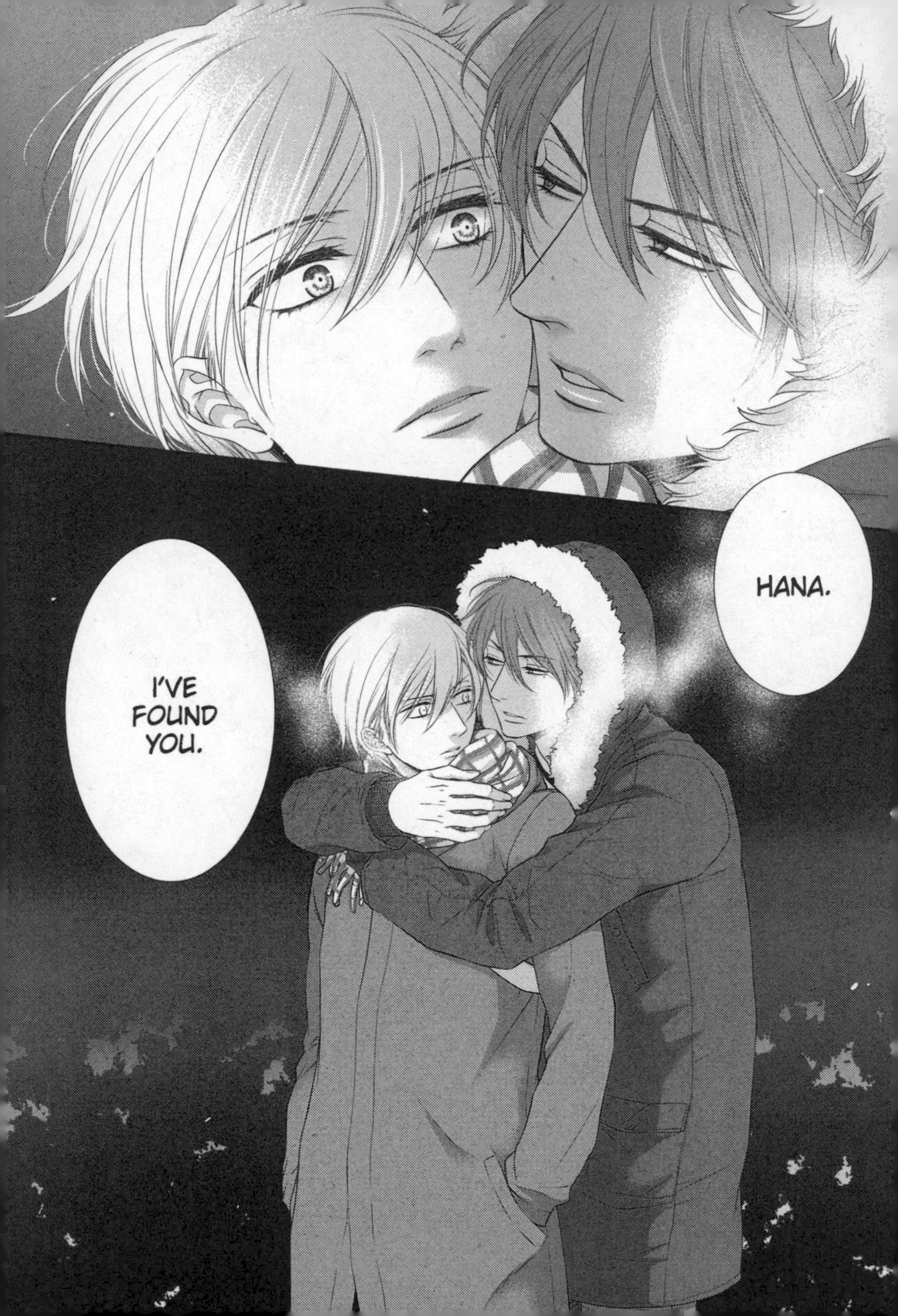
HANA.
I'VE FOUND YOU.

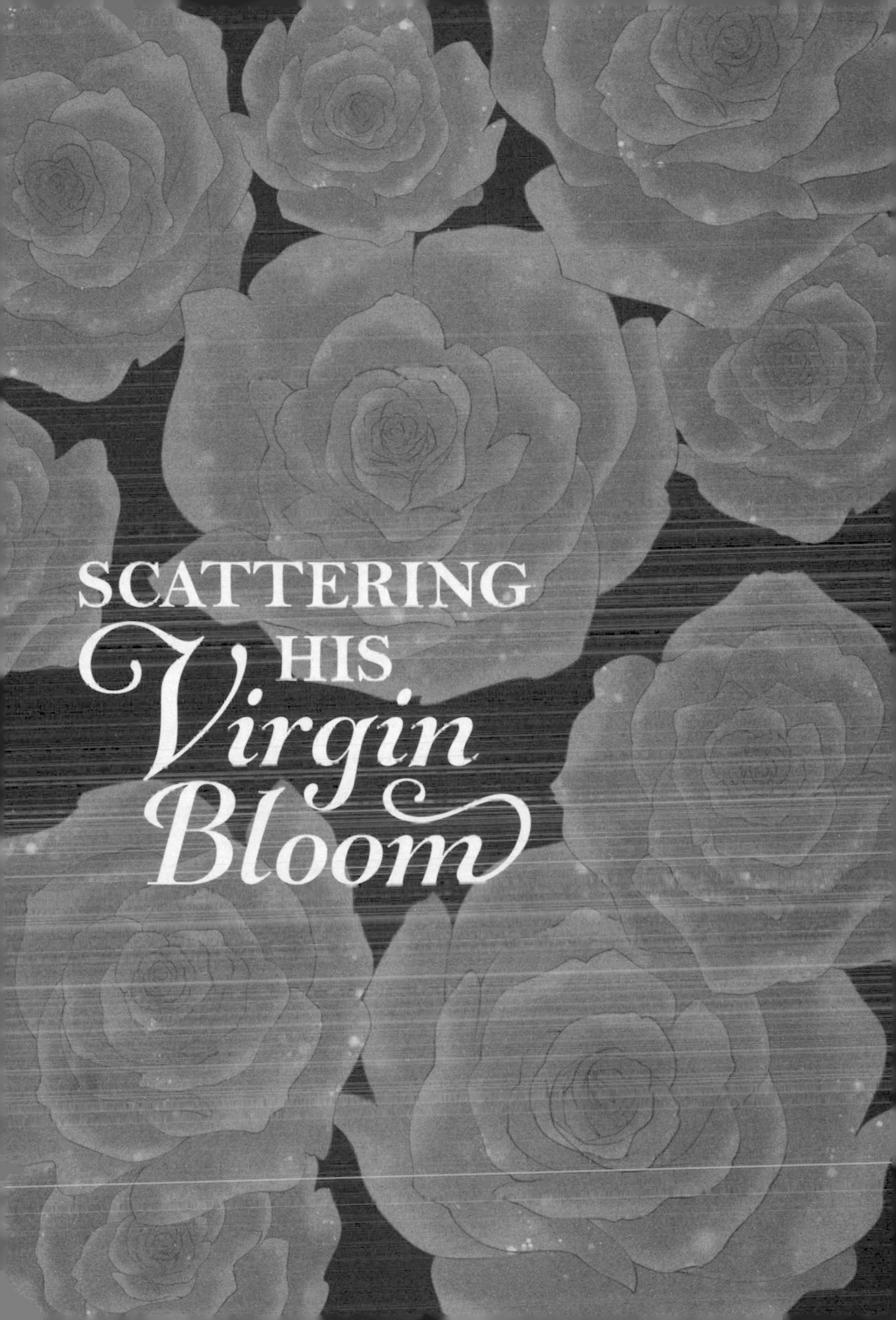
SCATTERING
HIS
Virgin
Bloom

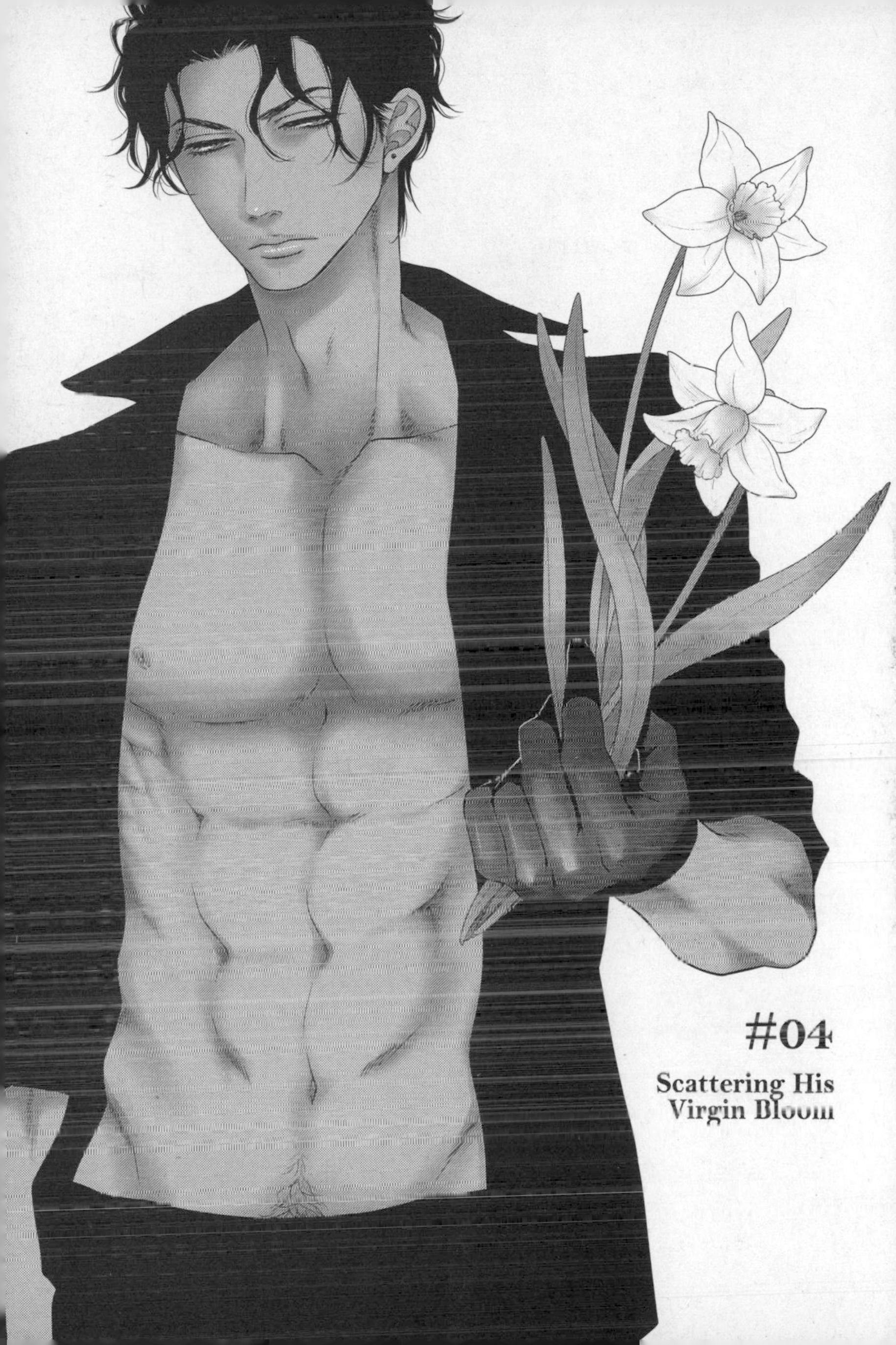

#04

Scattering His Virgin Bloom

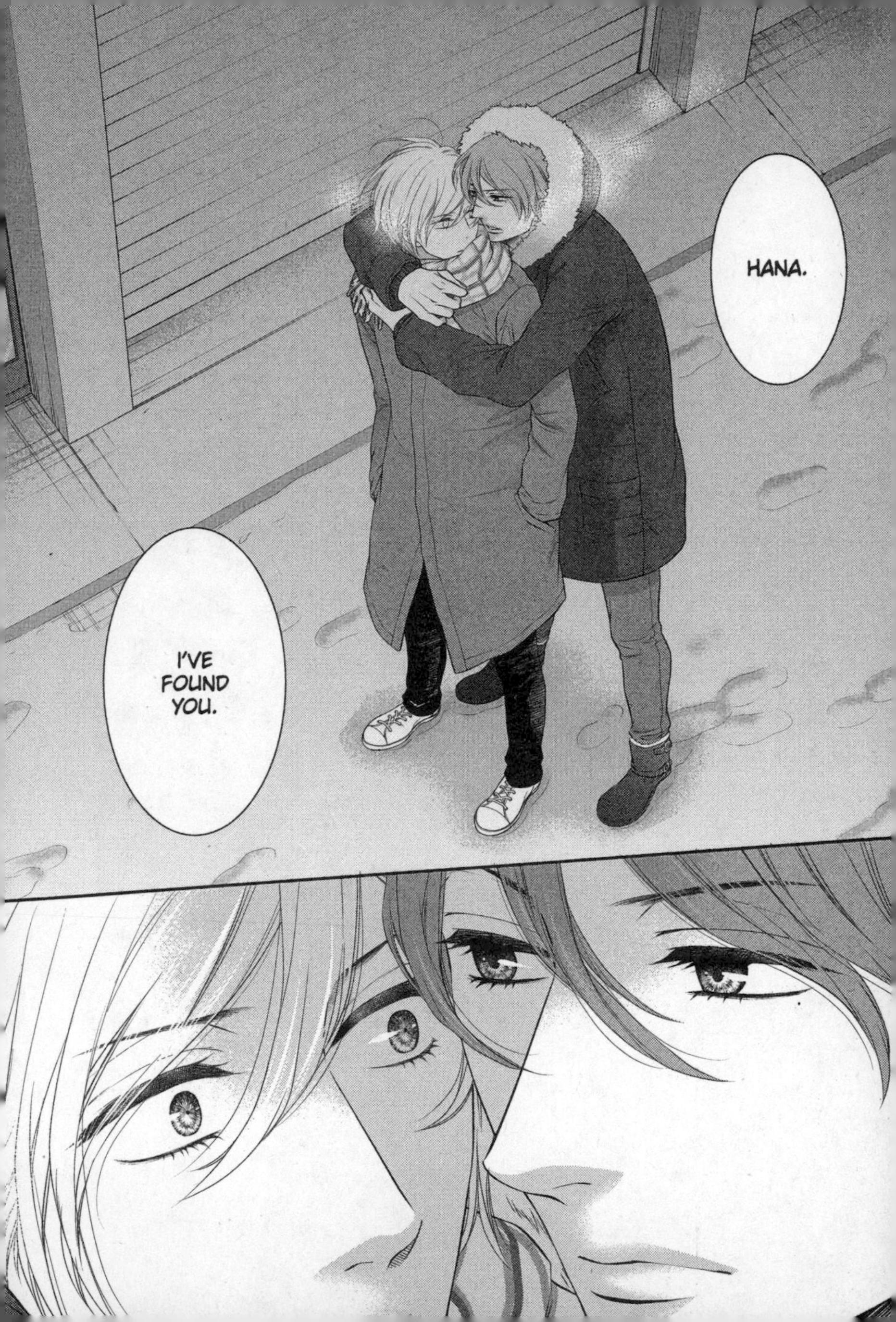
HANA.
I'VE FOUND YOU.

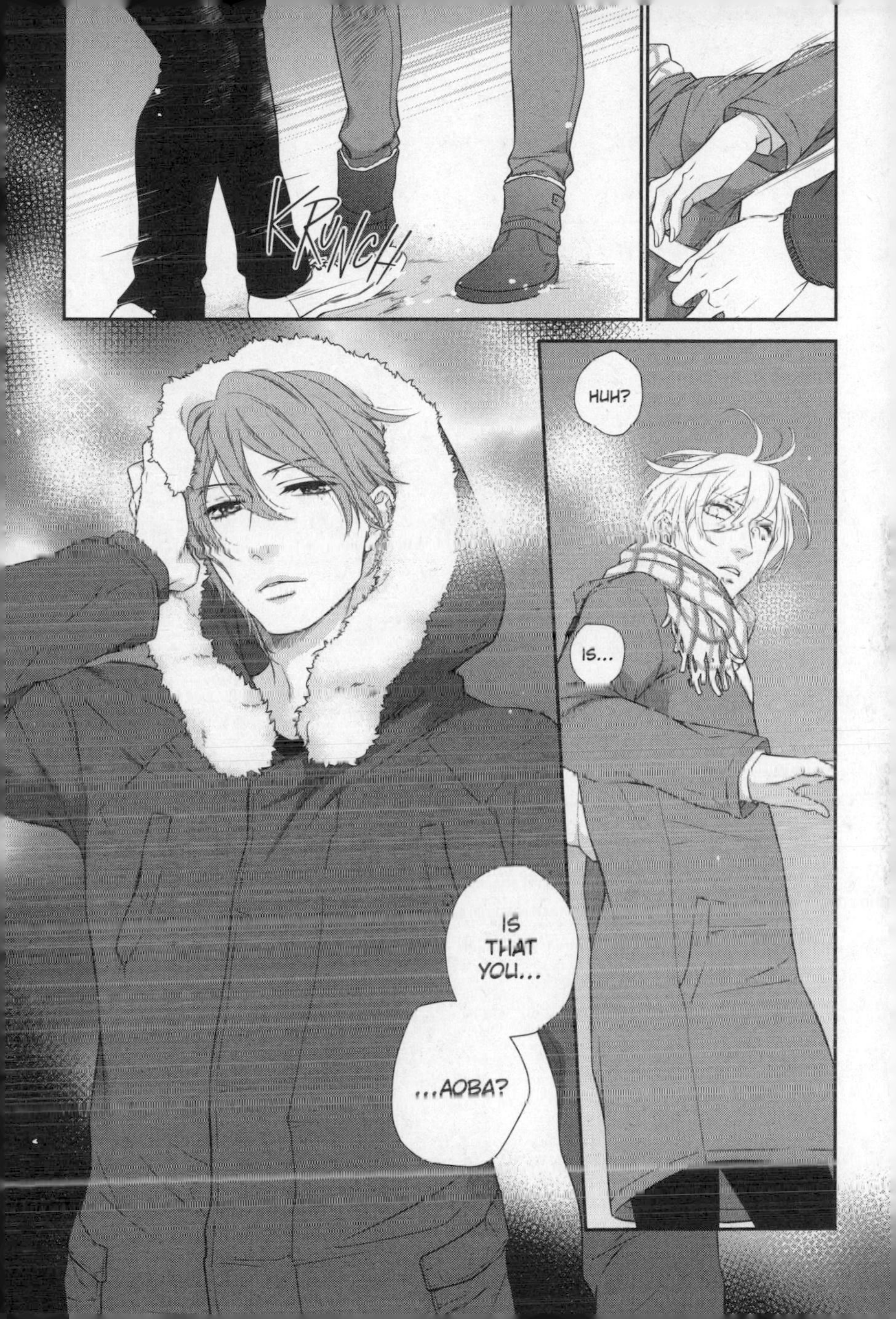
KRUNCH
HUH?
IS...
IS THAT YOU...
...AOBA?

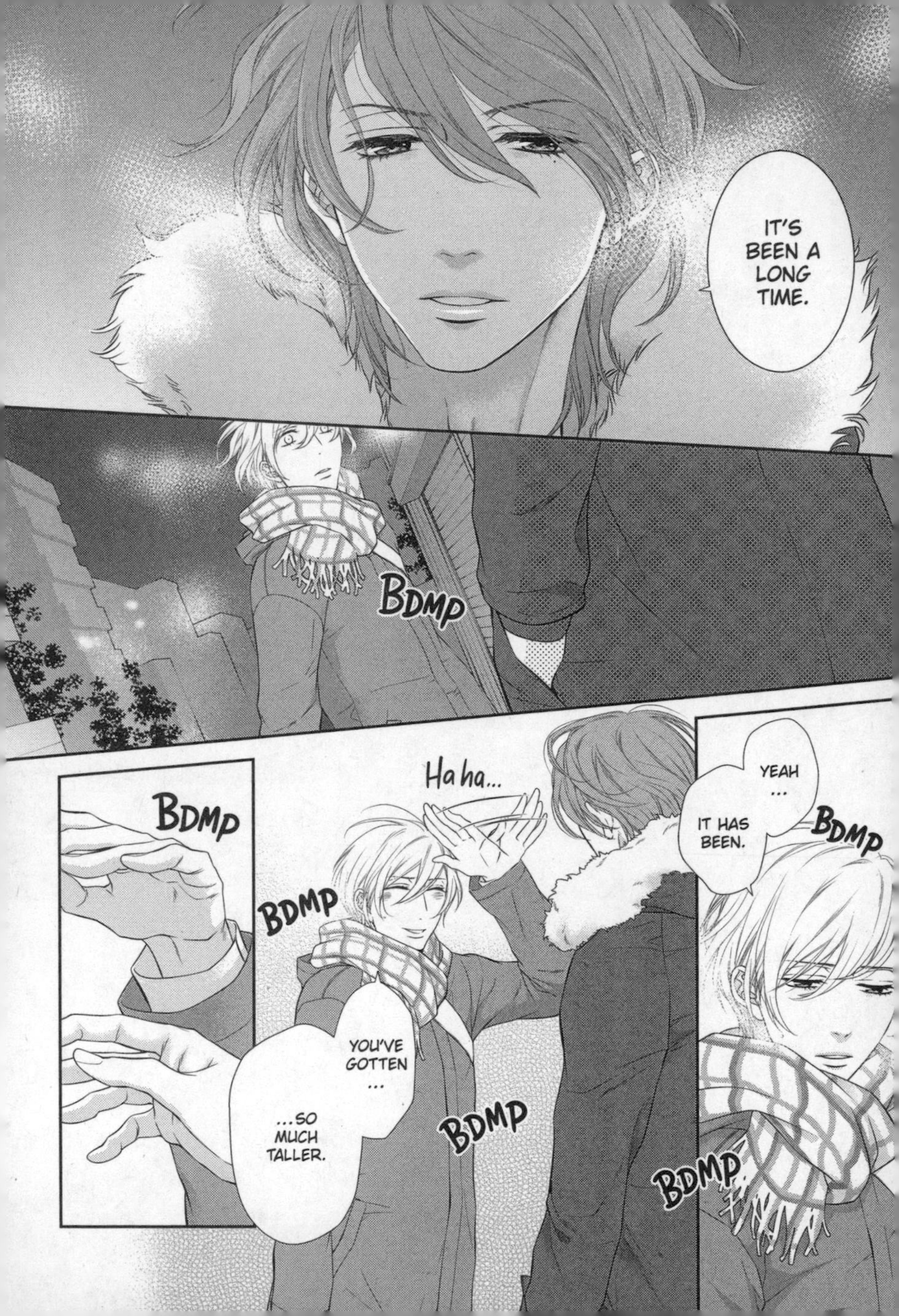
IT'S BEEN A LONG TIME.
BDMP
YEAH ... IT HAS BEEN.
BDMP
BDMP
Ha ha...
BDMP
YOU'VE GOTTEN ...
...SO MUCH TALLER.
BDMP
BDMP

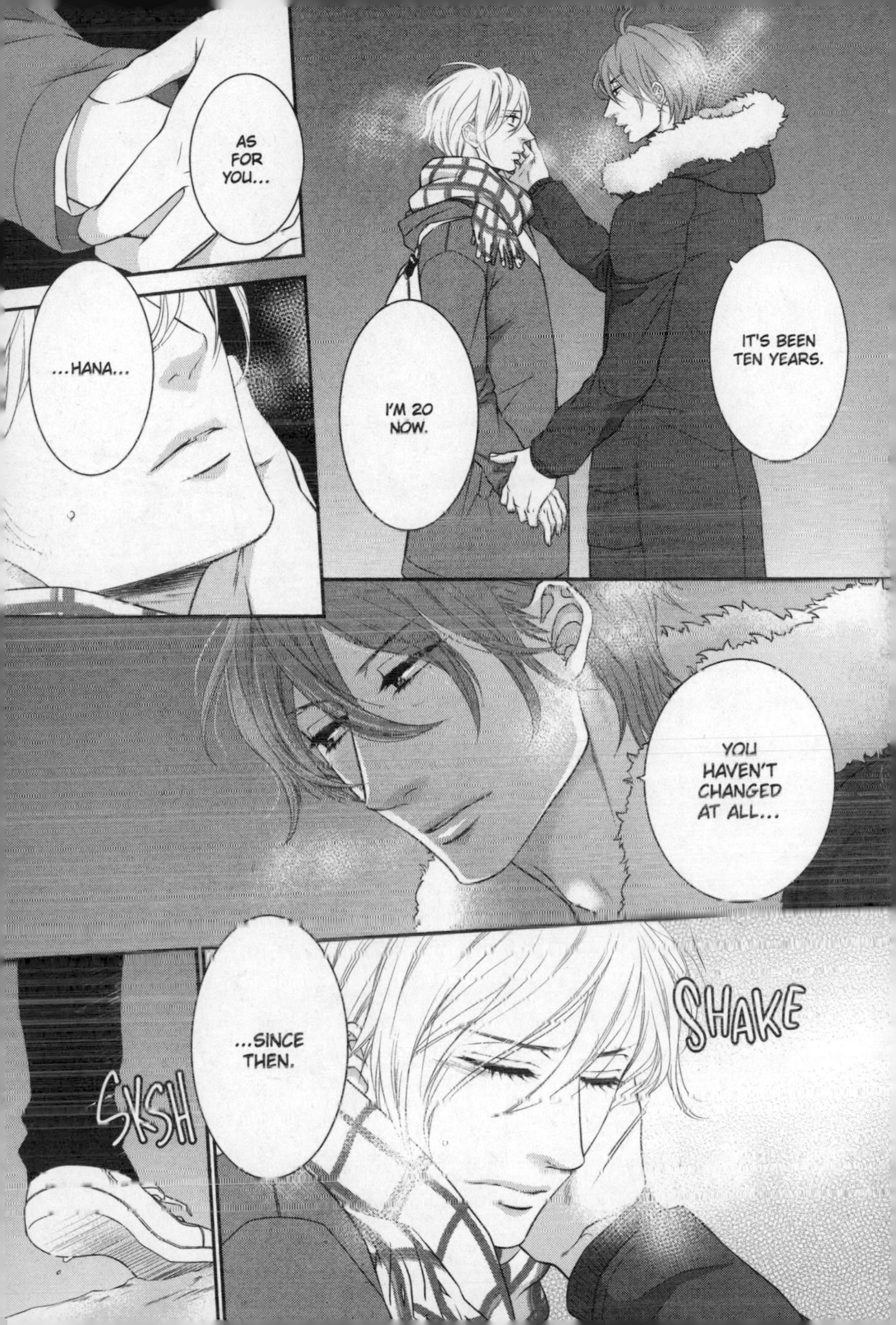
IT'S BEEN TEN YEARS.
I'M 20 NOW.
AS FOR YOU...
...HANA...
YOU HAVEN'T CHANGED AT ALL...
SHAKE
...SINCE THEN.
SXSH

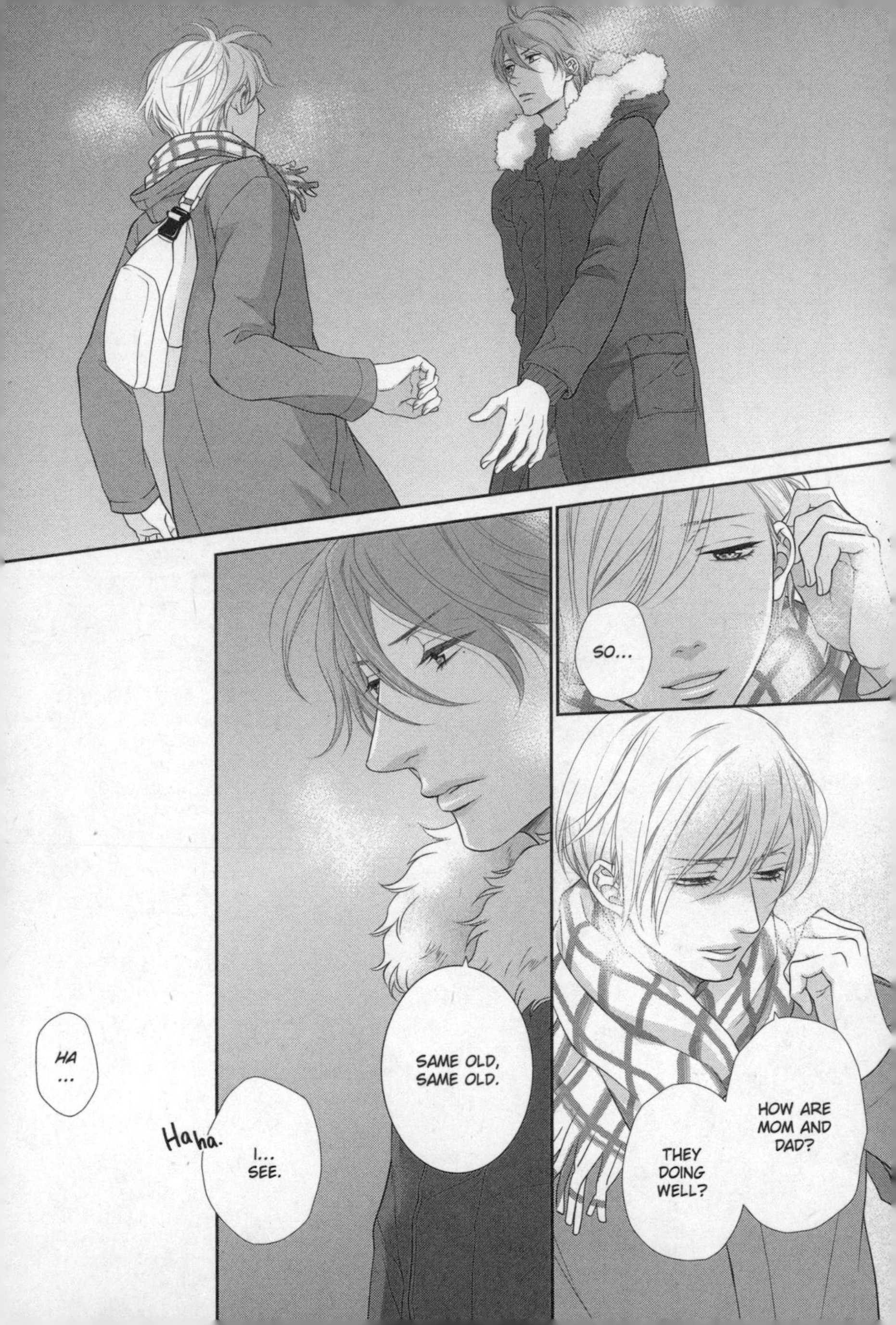
SO...
HOW ARE MOM AND DAD?
THEY DOING WELL?
SAME OLD, SAME OLD.
I... SEE.
Haha.
HA ...

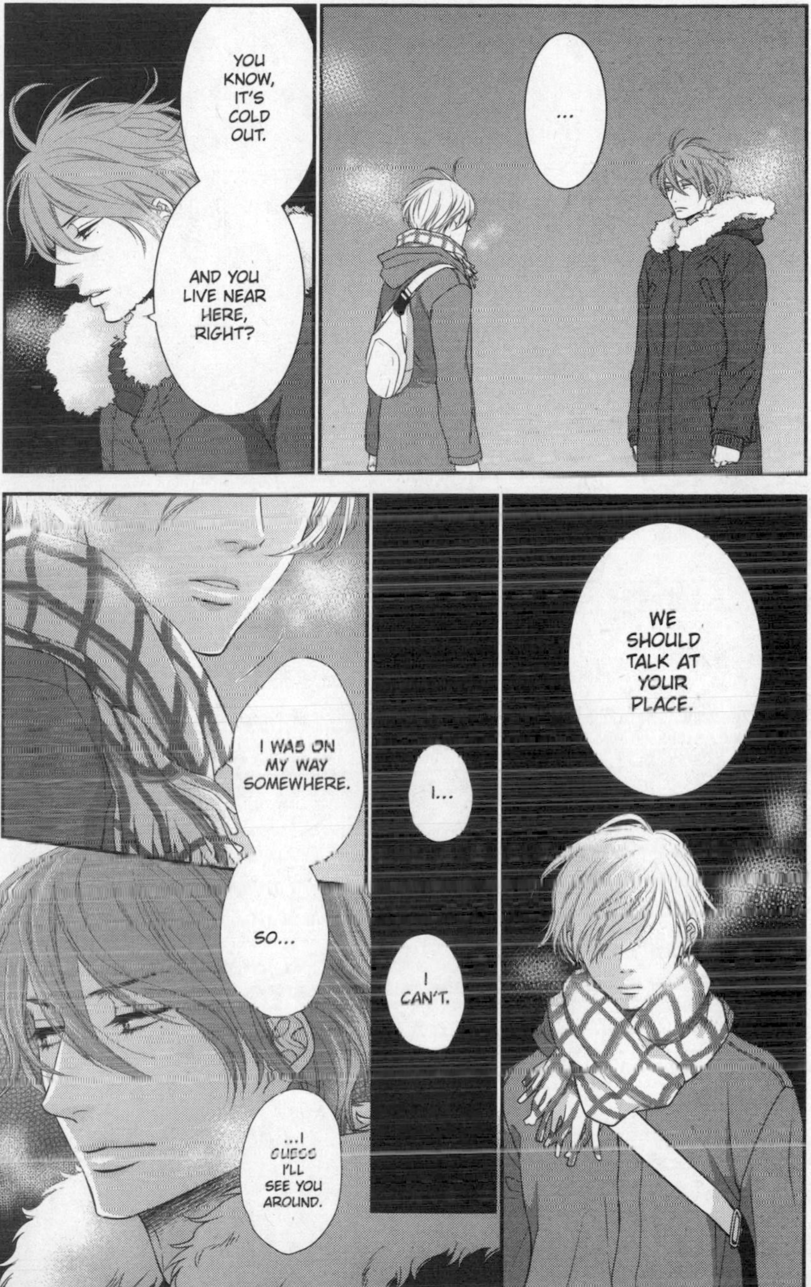
...
YOU KNOW, IT'S COLD OUT.
AND YOU LIVE NEAR HERE, RIGHT?
WE SHOULD TALK AT YOUR PLACE.
I...
I CAN'T.
I WAS ON MY WAY SOMEWHERE.
SO...
...I GUESS I'LL SEE YOU AROUND.

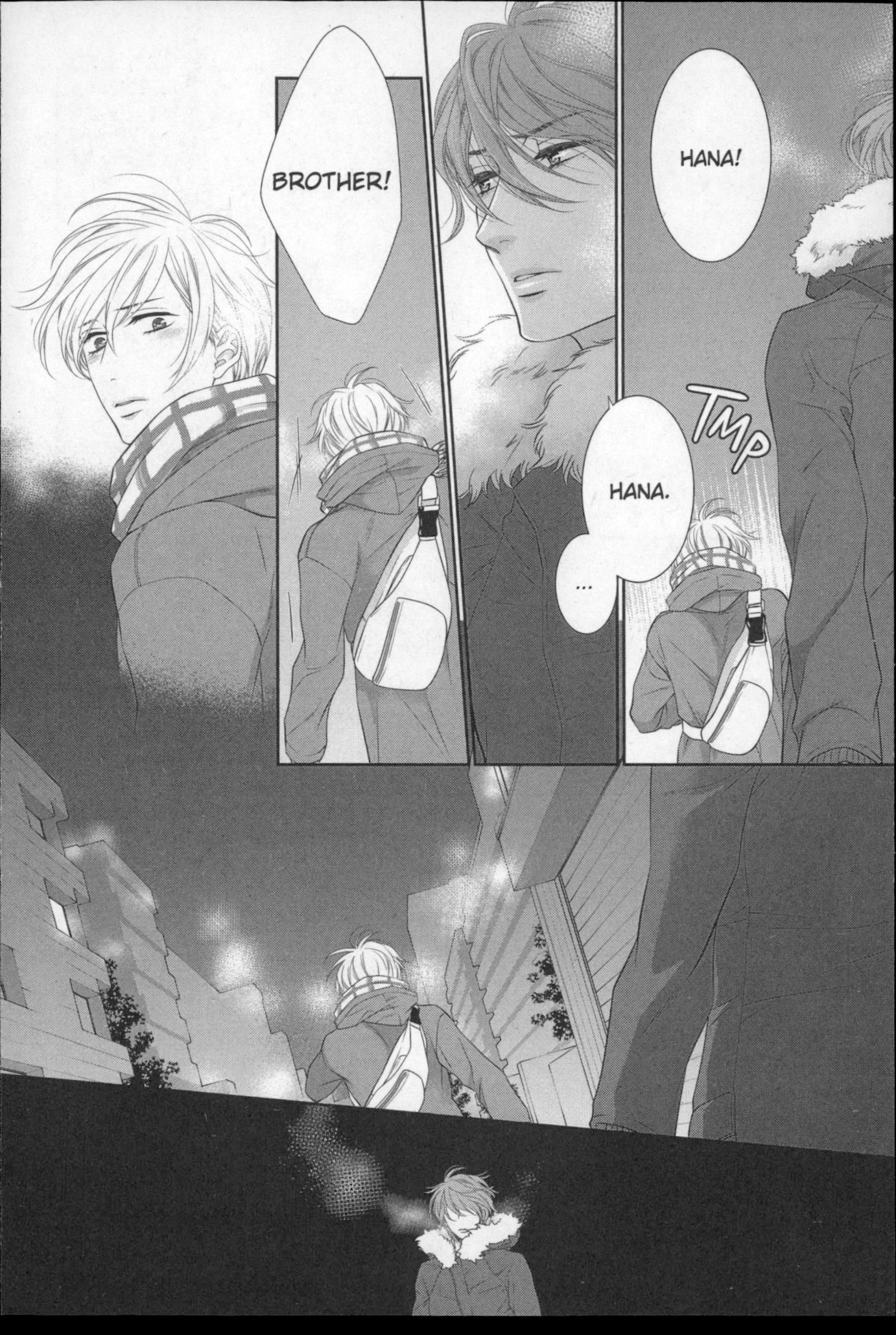
HANA!
TMP
HANA.
...
BROTHER!

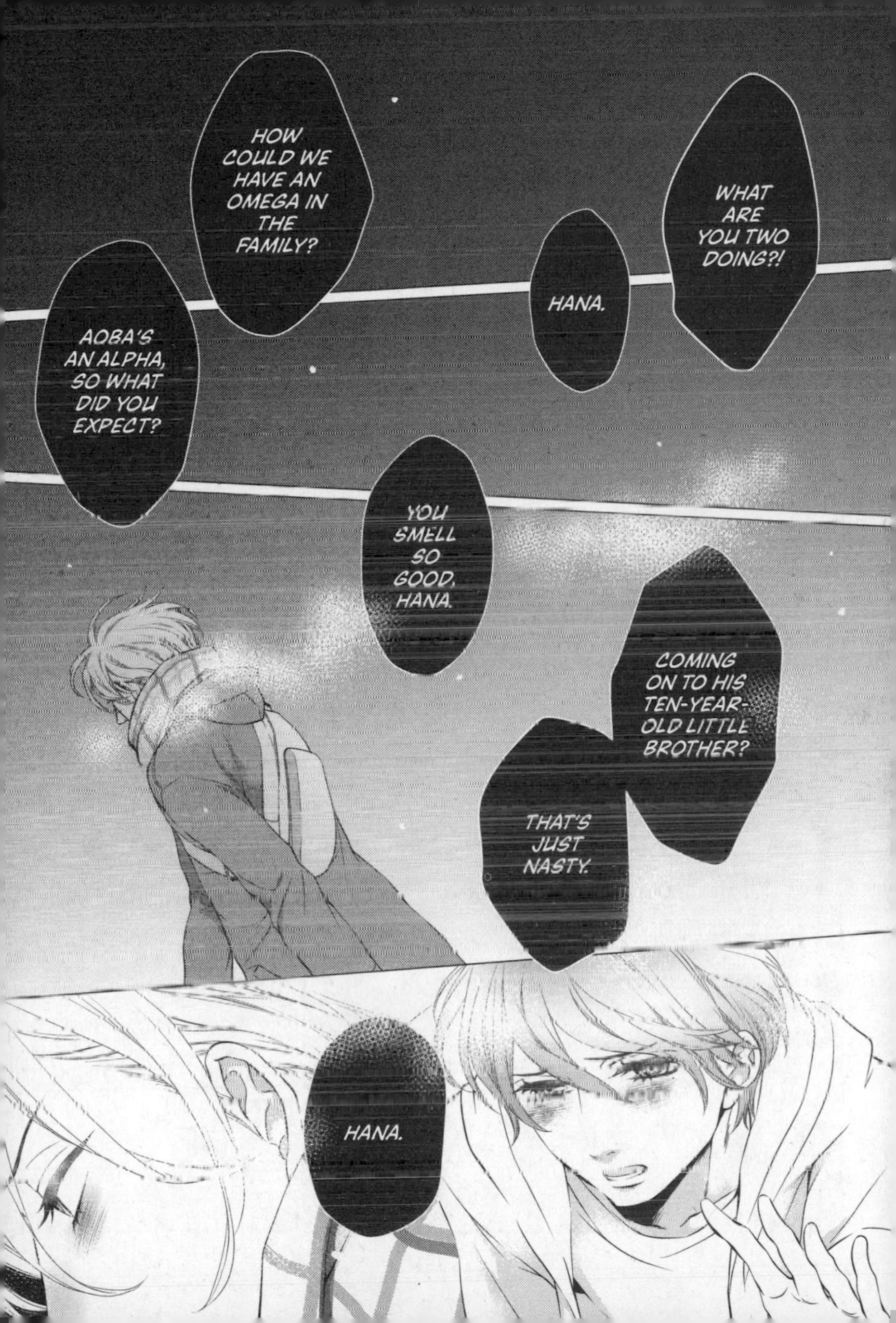
WHAT ARE YOU TWO DOING?!
HANA.
HOW COULD WE HAVE AN OMEGA IN THE FAMILY?
AOBA'S AN ALPHA, SO WHAT DID YOU EXPECT?
COMING ON TO HIS TEN-YEAR-OLD LITTLE BROTHER?
THAT'S JUST NASTY.
YOU SMELL SO GOOD, HANA.
HANA.

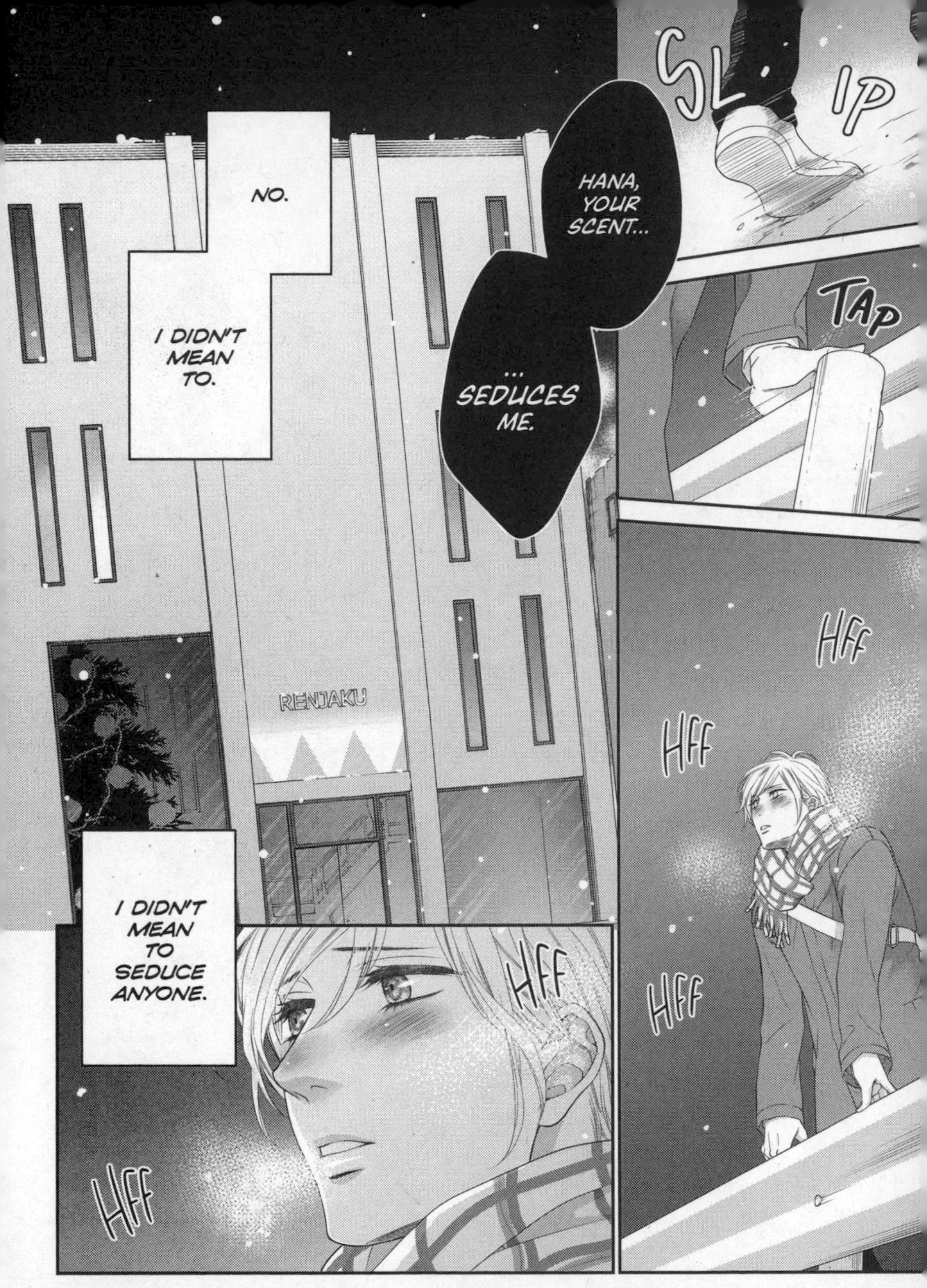
SLIP
HANA, YOUR SCENT...
...SEDUCES ME.
NO.
I DIDN'T MEAN TO.
TAP
HFF
HFF
HFF
I DIDN'T MEAN TO SEDUCE ANYONE.
HFF
HFF

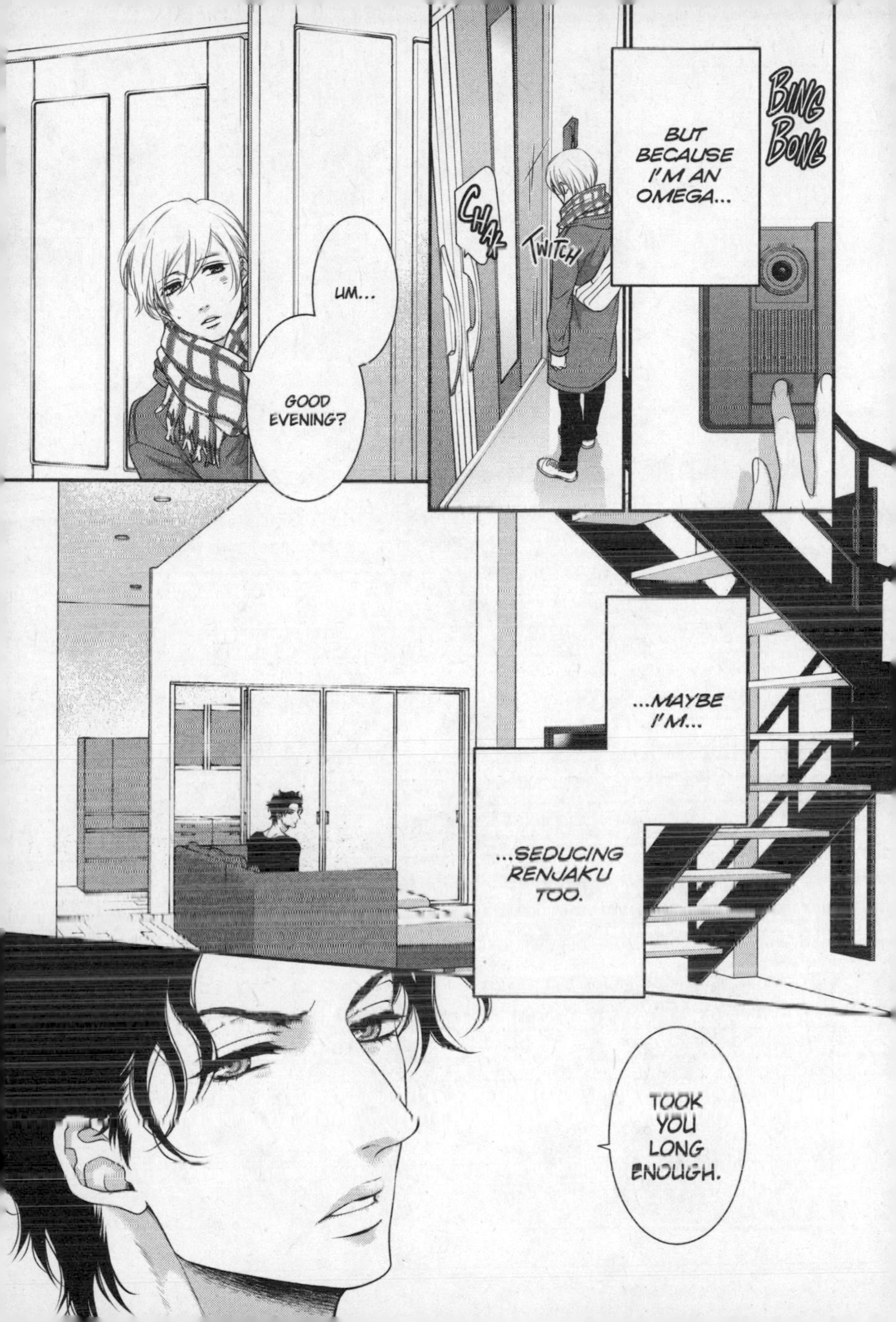
BING BONG
BUT BECAUSE I'M AN OMEGA...
CHAK
TWITCH
UM...
GOOD EVENING?
...MAYBE I'M...
...SEDUCING RENJAKU TOO.
TOOK YOU LONG ENOUGH.

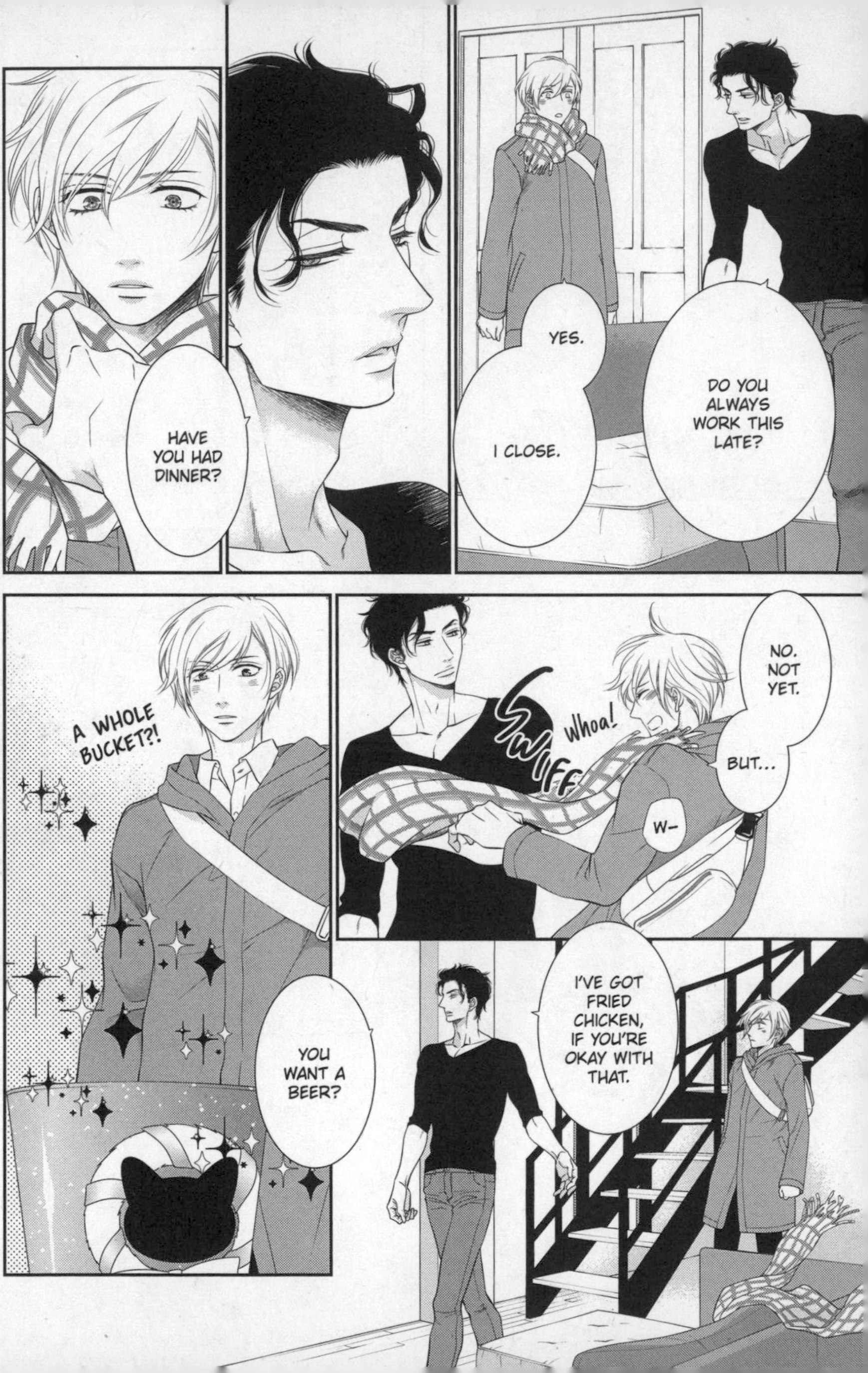
DO YOU ALWAYS WORK THIS LATE?
YES.
I CLOSE.
HAVE YOU HAD DINNER?
NO. NOT YET.
BUT...
W-
SWIFF
Whoa!
I'VE GOT FRIED CHICKEN, IF YOU'RE OKAY WITH THAT.
YOU WANT A BEER?
A WHOLE BUCKET?!

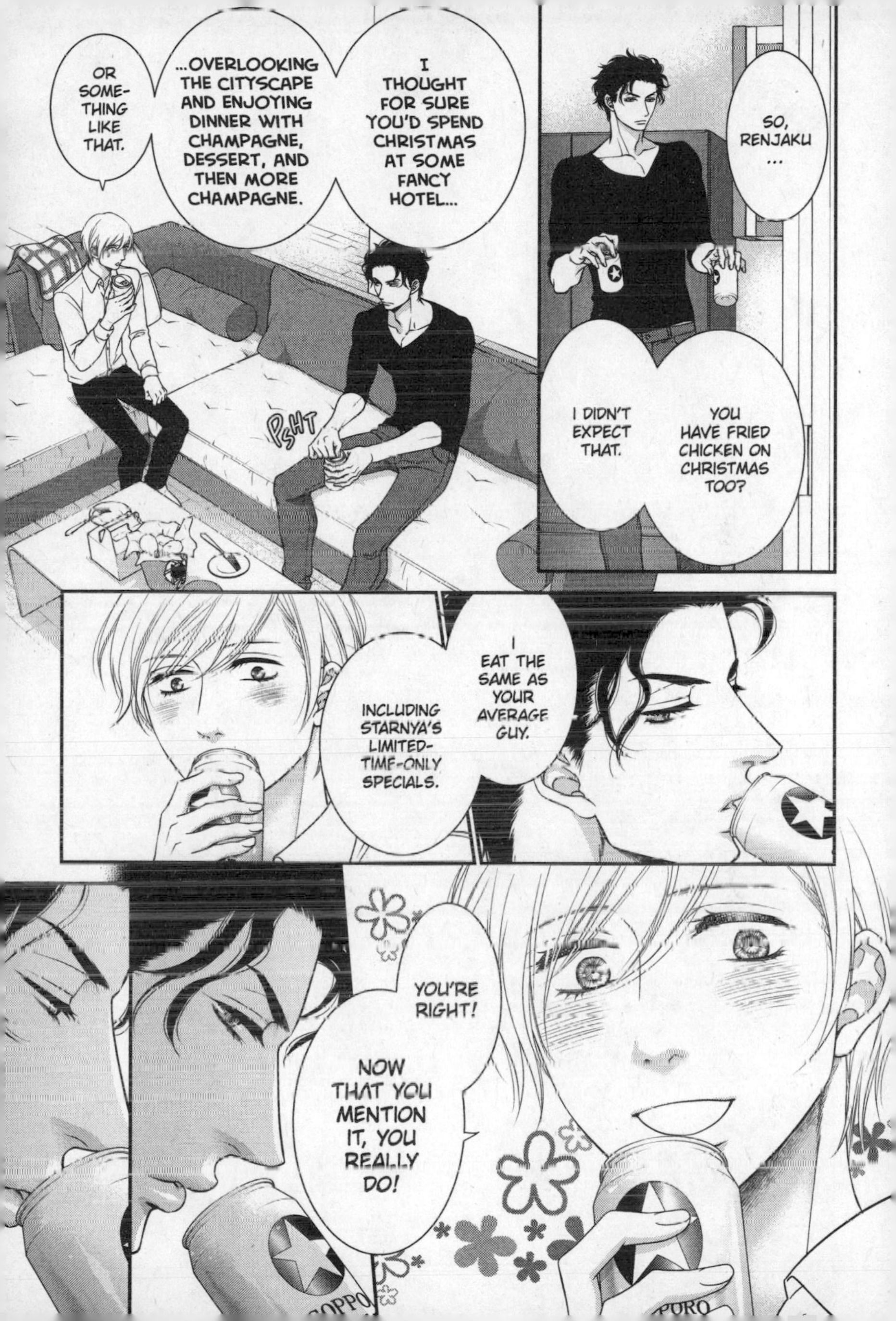

SO, RENJAKU ...
YOU HAVE FRIED CHICKEN ON CHRISTMAS TOO?
I DIDN'T EXPECT THAT.
I THOUGHT FOR SURE YOU'D SPEND CHRISTMAS AT SOME FANCY HOTEL...
...OVERLOOKING THE CITYSCAPE AND ENJOYING DINNER WITH CHAMPAGNE, DESSERT, AND THEN MORE CHAMPAGNE.
OR SOME-THING LIKE THAT.
PSHT
I EAT THE SAME AS YOUR AVERAGE GUY.
INCLUDING STARNYA'S LIMITED-TIME-ONLY SPECIALS.
YOU'RE RIGHT!
NOW THAT YOU MENTION IT, YOU REALLY DO!

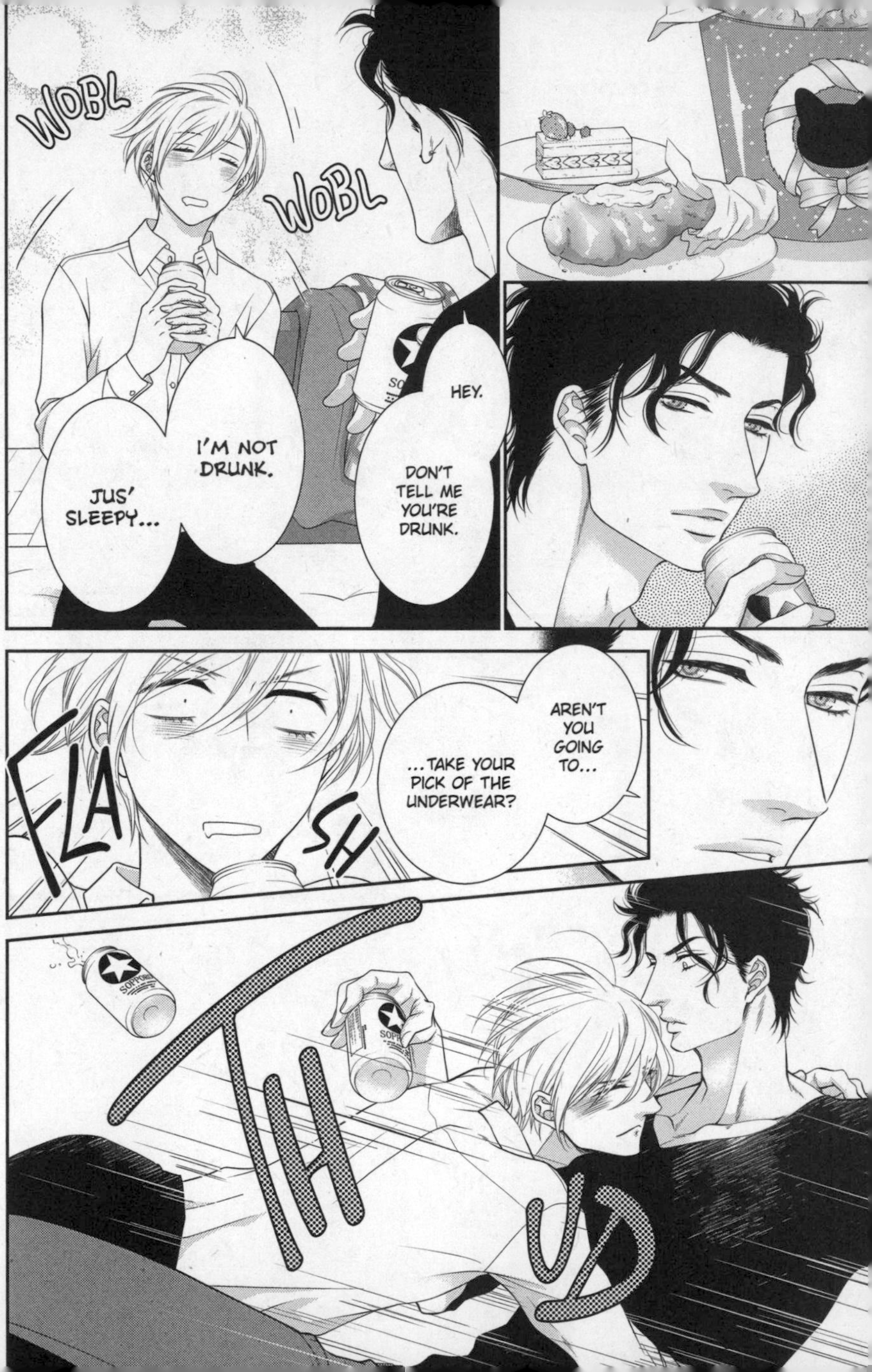
WOBL
WOBL
HEY.
DON'T TELL ME YOU'RE DRUNK.
I'M NOT DRUNK.
JUS' SLEEPY...
AREN'T YOU GOING TO...
...TAKE YOUR PICK OF THE UNDERWEAR?
FLASH
THUD
SOPPORO

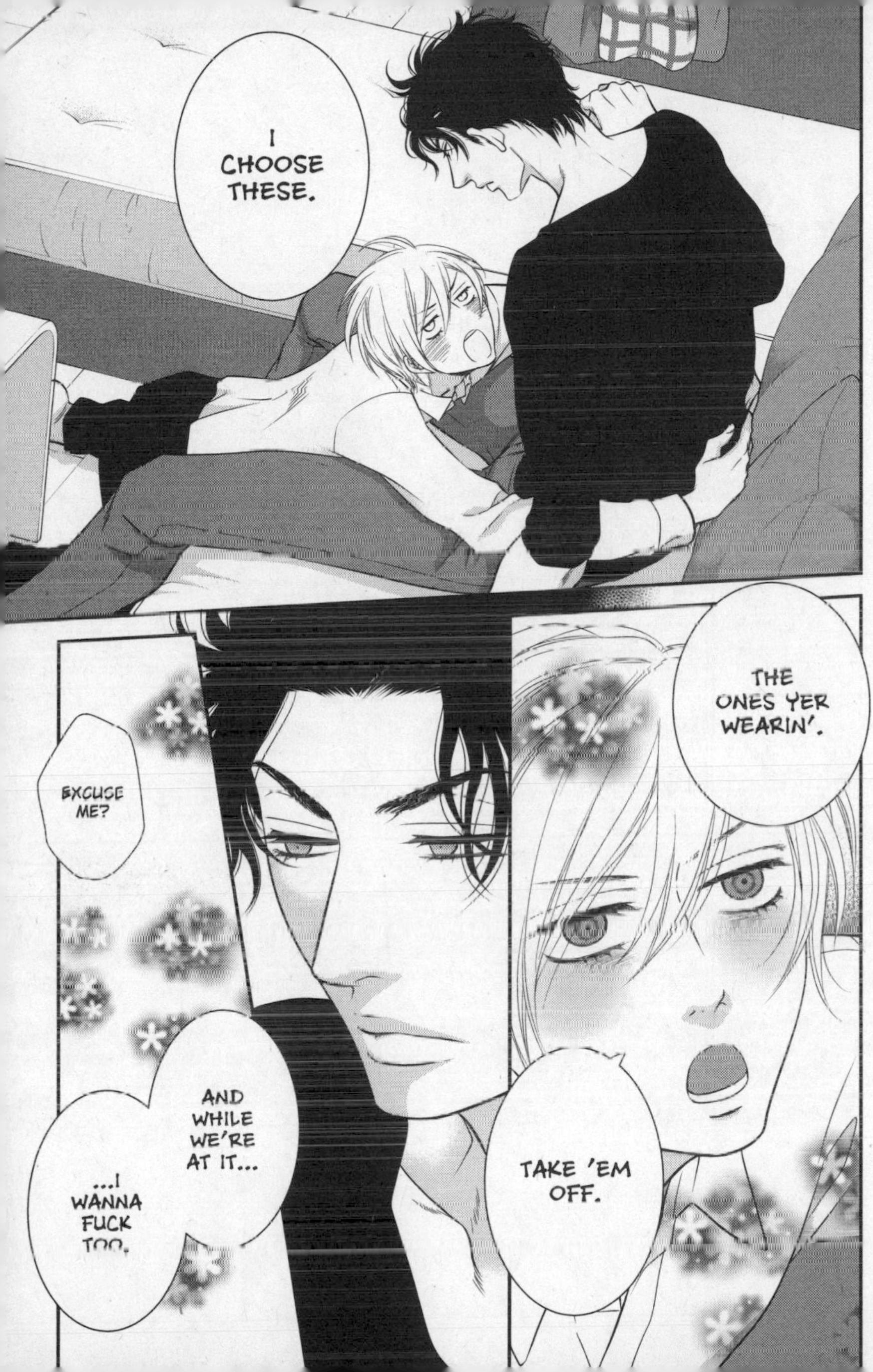
I CHOOSE THESE.
THE ONES YER WEARIN'.
EXCUSE ME?
TAKE 'EM OFF.
AND WHILE WE'RE AT IT...
...I WANNA FUCK TOO.

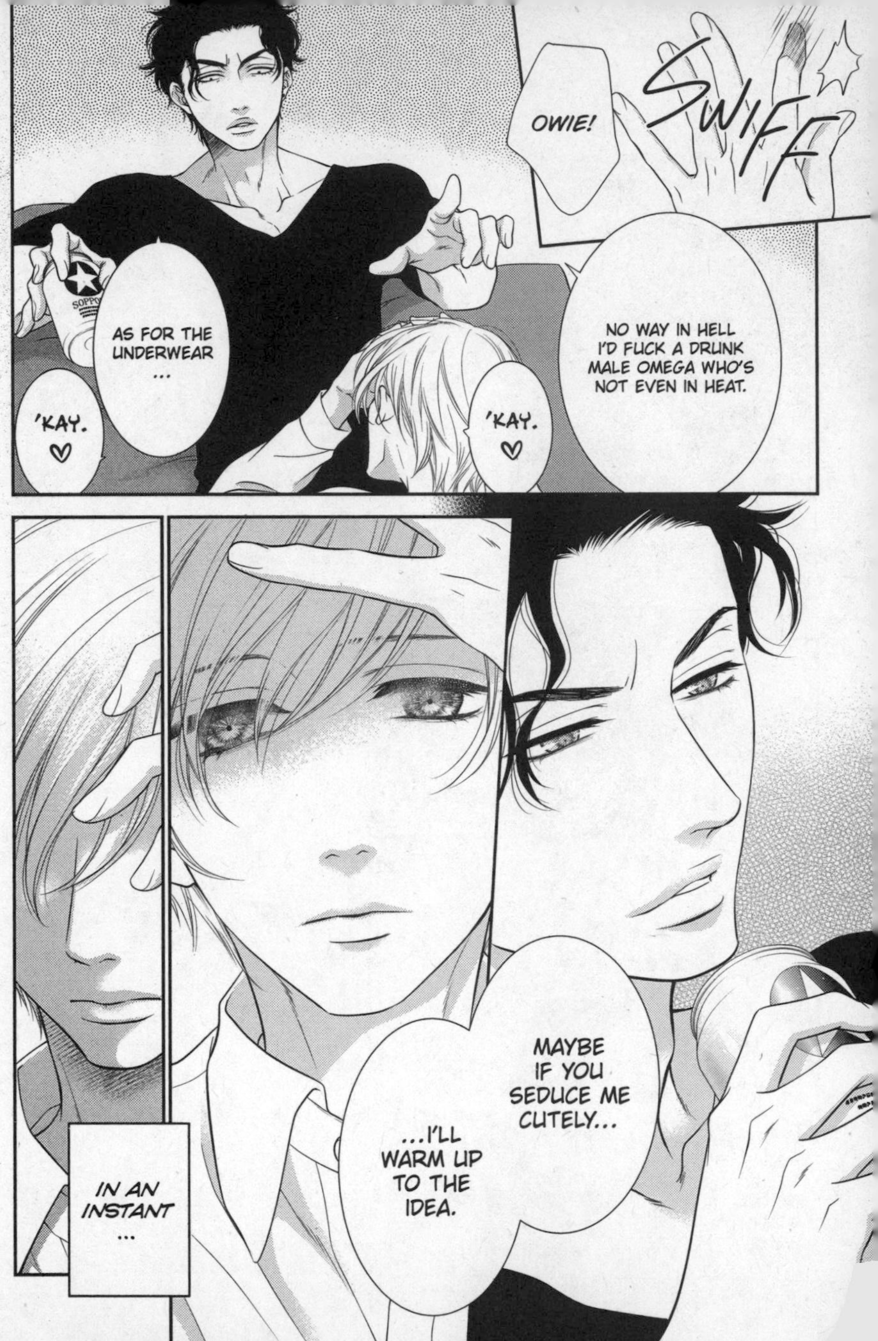
OWIE!
SWIFF
NO WAY IN HELL I'D FUCK A DRUNK MALE OMEGA WHO'S NOT EVEN IN HEAT.
'KAY. ♡
AS FOR THE UNDERWEAR ...
'KAY. ♡
MAYBE IF YOU SEDUCE ME CUTELY...
...I'LL WARM UP TO THE IDEA.
IN AN INSTANT ...

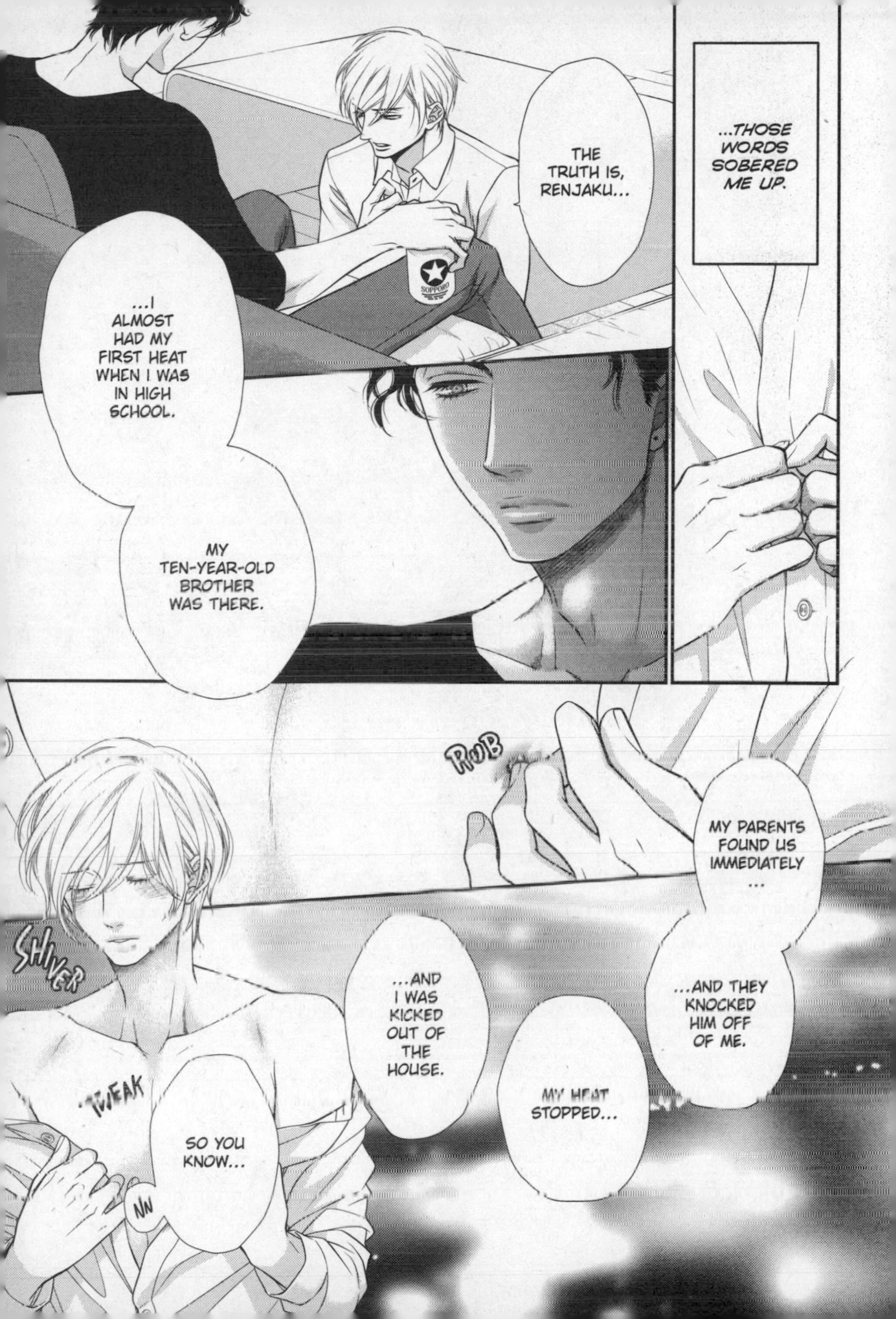
...THOSE WORDS SOBERED ME UP.
THE TRUTH IS, RENJAKU...
...I ALMOST HAD MY FIRST HEAT WHEN I WAS IN HIGH SCHOOL.
MY TEN-YEAR-OLD BROTHER WAS THERE.
RUB
MY PARENTS FOUND US IMMEDIATELY...
...AND THEY KNOCKED HIM OFF OF ME.
MY HEAT STOPPED...
...AND I WAS KICKED OUT OF THE HOUSE.
SHIVER
TWEAK
SO YOU KNOW...
NN

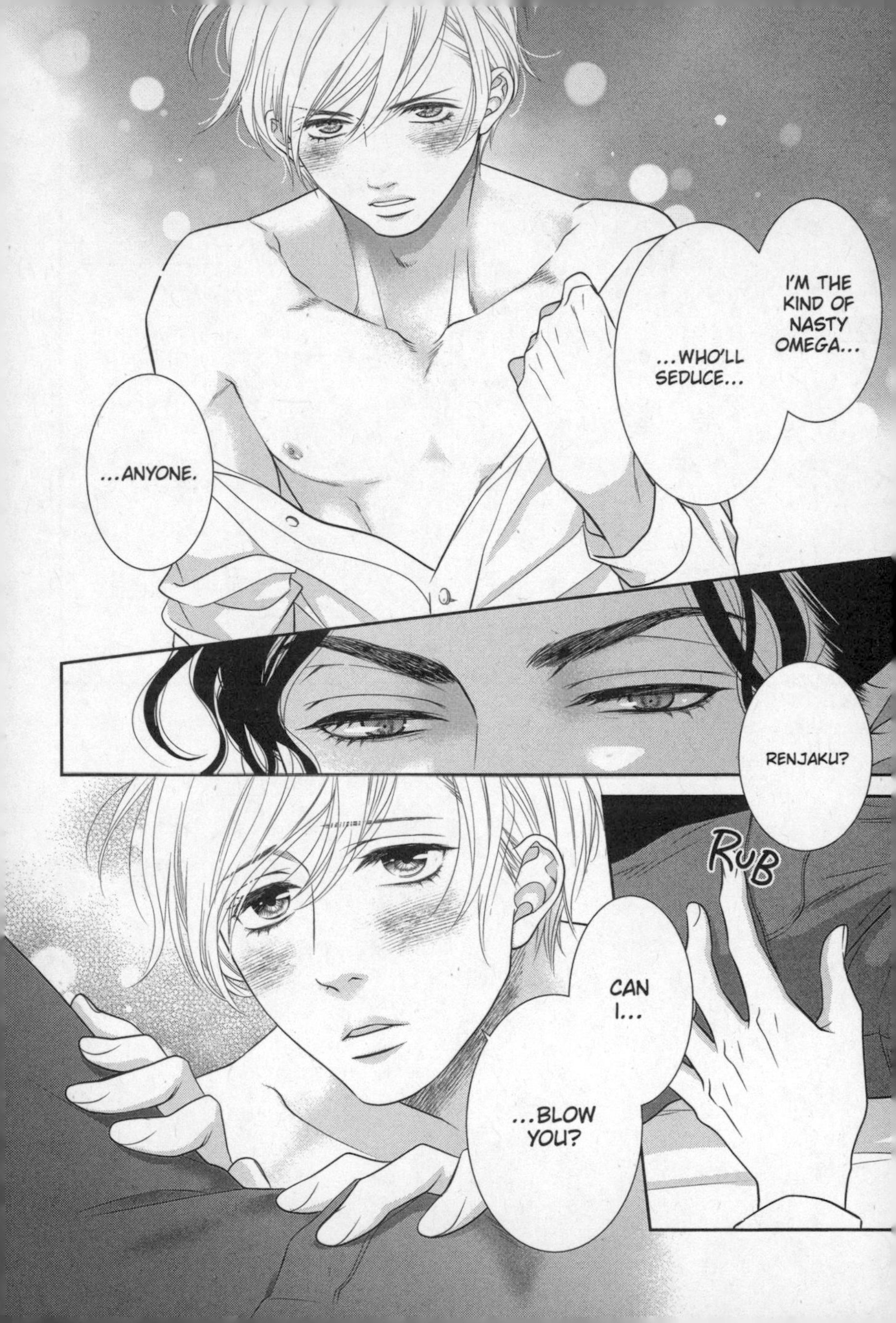
I'M THE KIND OF NASTY OMEGA...
...WHO'LL SEDUCE...
...ANYONE.
RENJAKU?
RUB
CAN I...
...BLOW YOU?

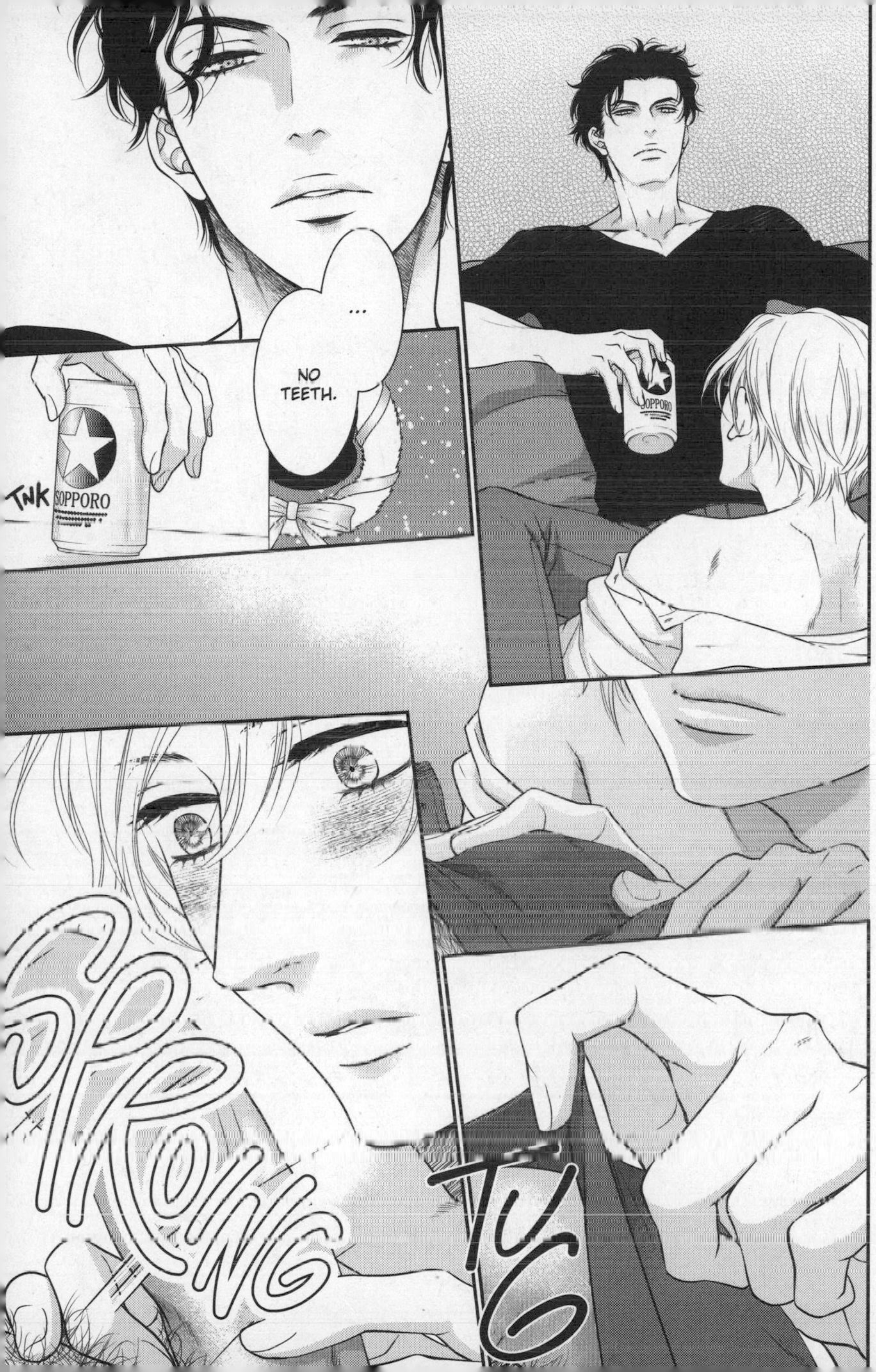
...
NO TEETH.
TNK
TUG
PRONG

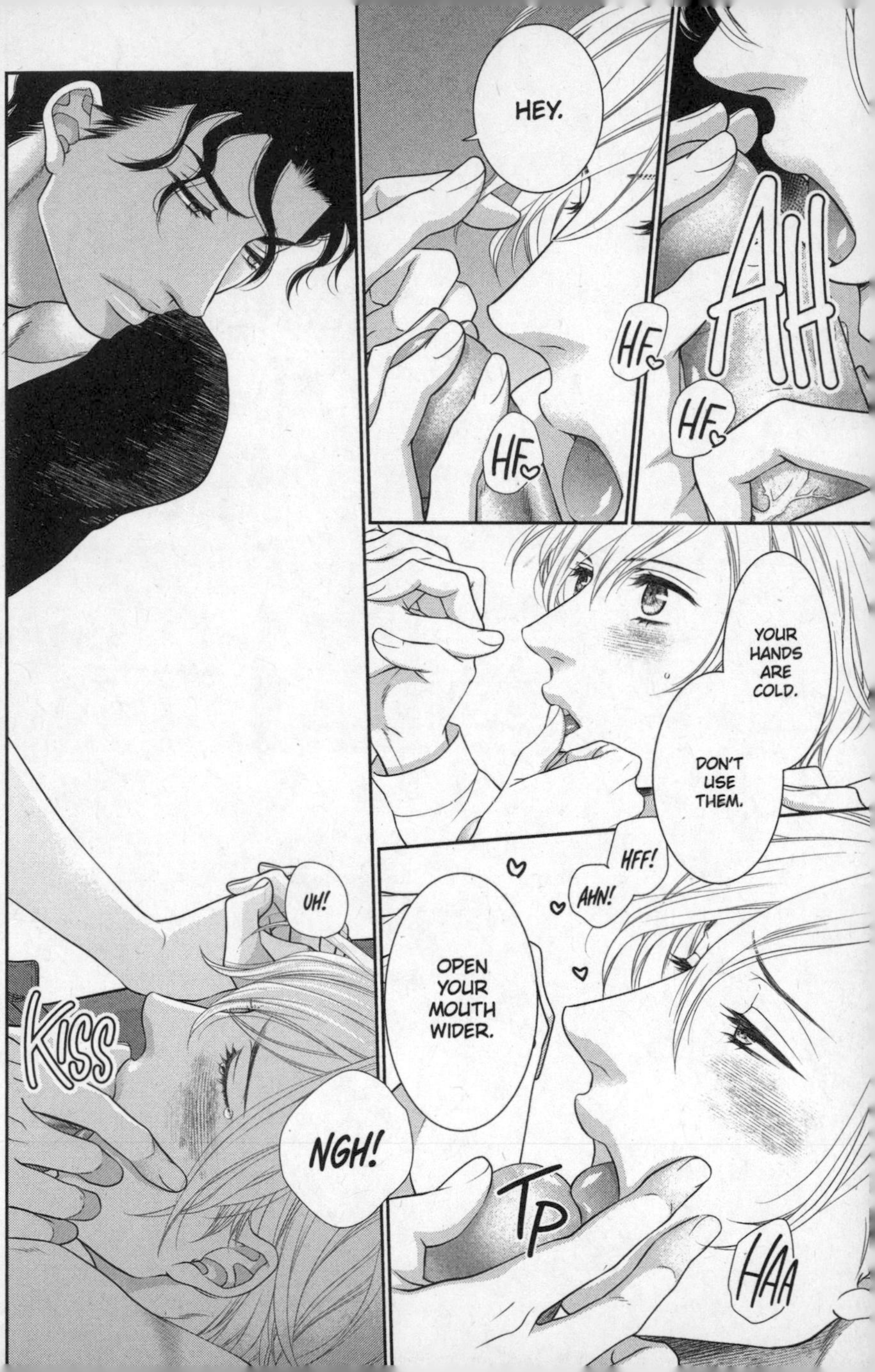
AH
HF
HEY.
HF
HF
YOUR HANDS ARE COLD.
DON'T USE THEM.
HFF!
AHN!
OPEN YOUR MOUTH WIDER.
TP
HAA
UH!
KISS
NGH!

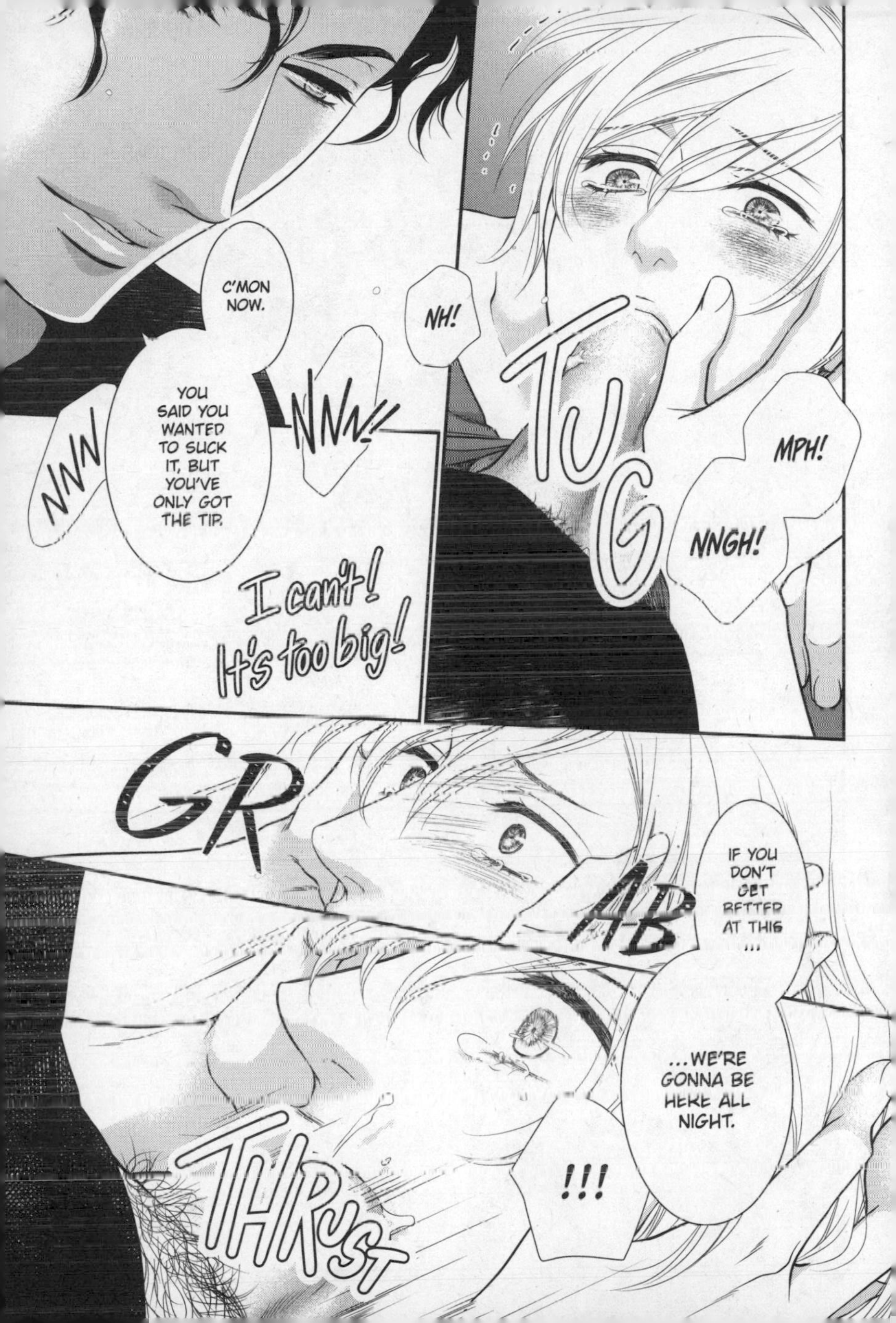
NH!
TUG
MPH!
NNGH!
C'MON NOW.
YOU SAID YOU WANTED TO SUCK IT, BUT YOU'VE ONLY GOT THE TIP.
NNN
NNN!!
I can't! It's too big!
GR
AB
IF YOU DON'T GET BETTER AT THIS...
...WE'RE GONNA BE HERE ALL NIGHT.
!!!
THRUST

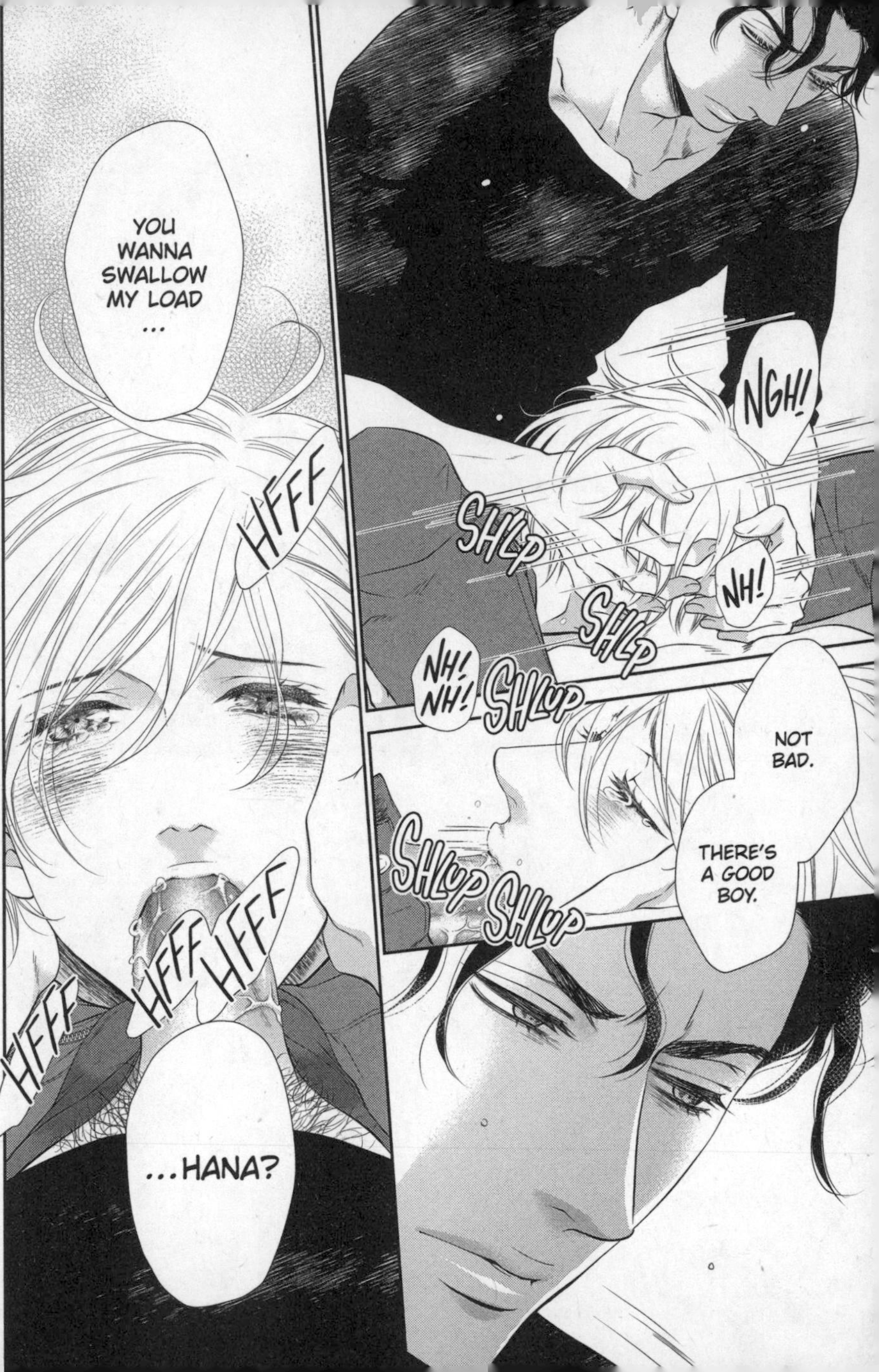
NGH!
SHLP
NH!
SHLP
NH! NH!
SHLUP
NOT BAD.
THERE'S A GOOD BOY.
SHLUP SHLUP
YOU WANNA SWALLOW MY LOAD ...
HFFF
HFFF
HFFF
HFFF
...HANA?

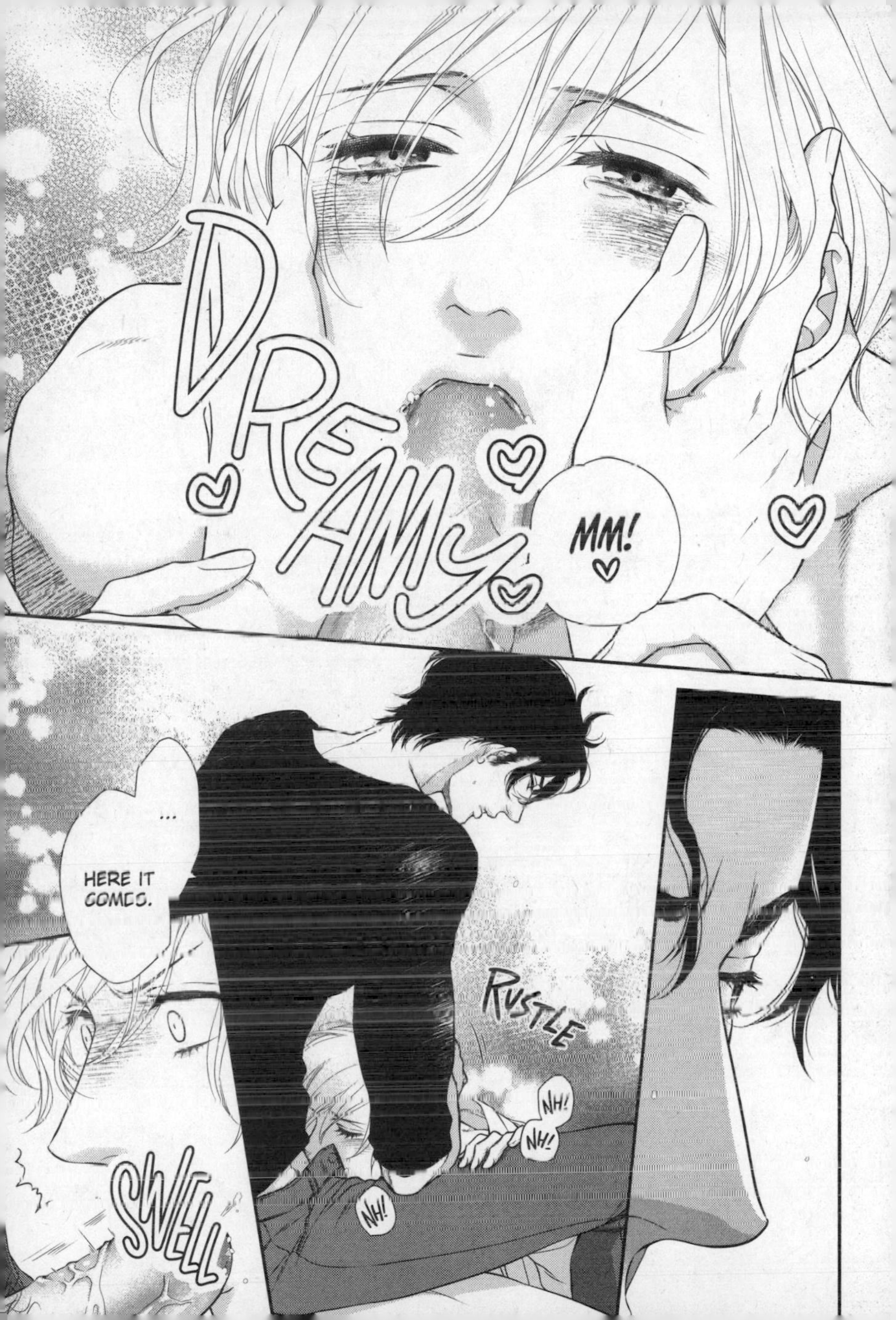
DREAMY
MM!
...
HERE IT COMES.
RUSTLE
NH!
NH!
NH!
SWELL

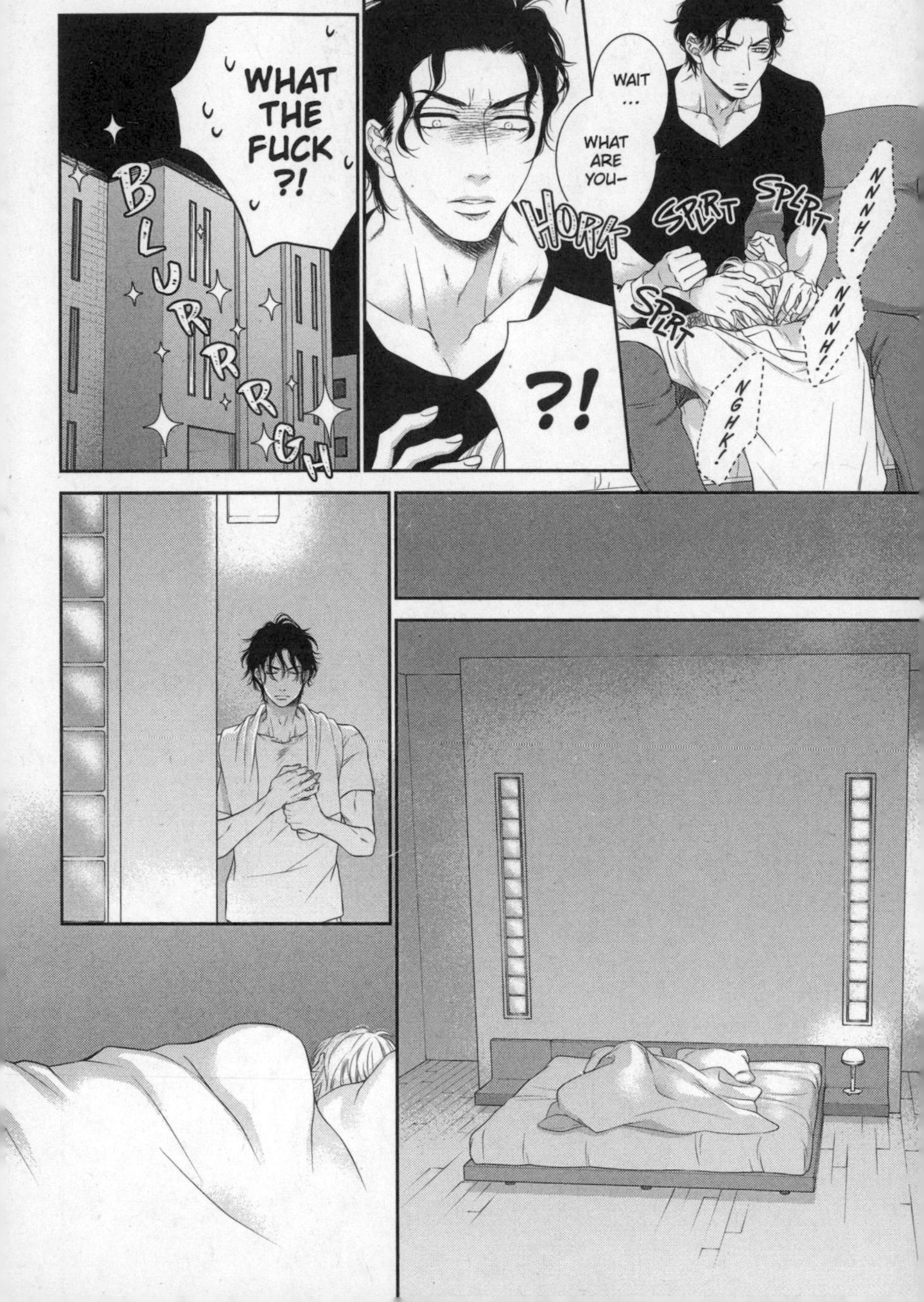
WAIT...
WHAT ARE YOU–
HORK
SPLRT
SPLRT
SPLRT
NNNH!
NNNH!
NGHK!
?!
WHAT THE FUCK?!
BLURRRRGH

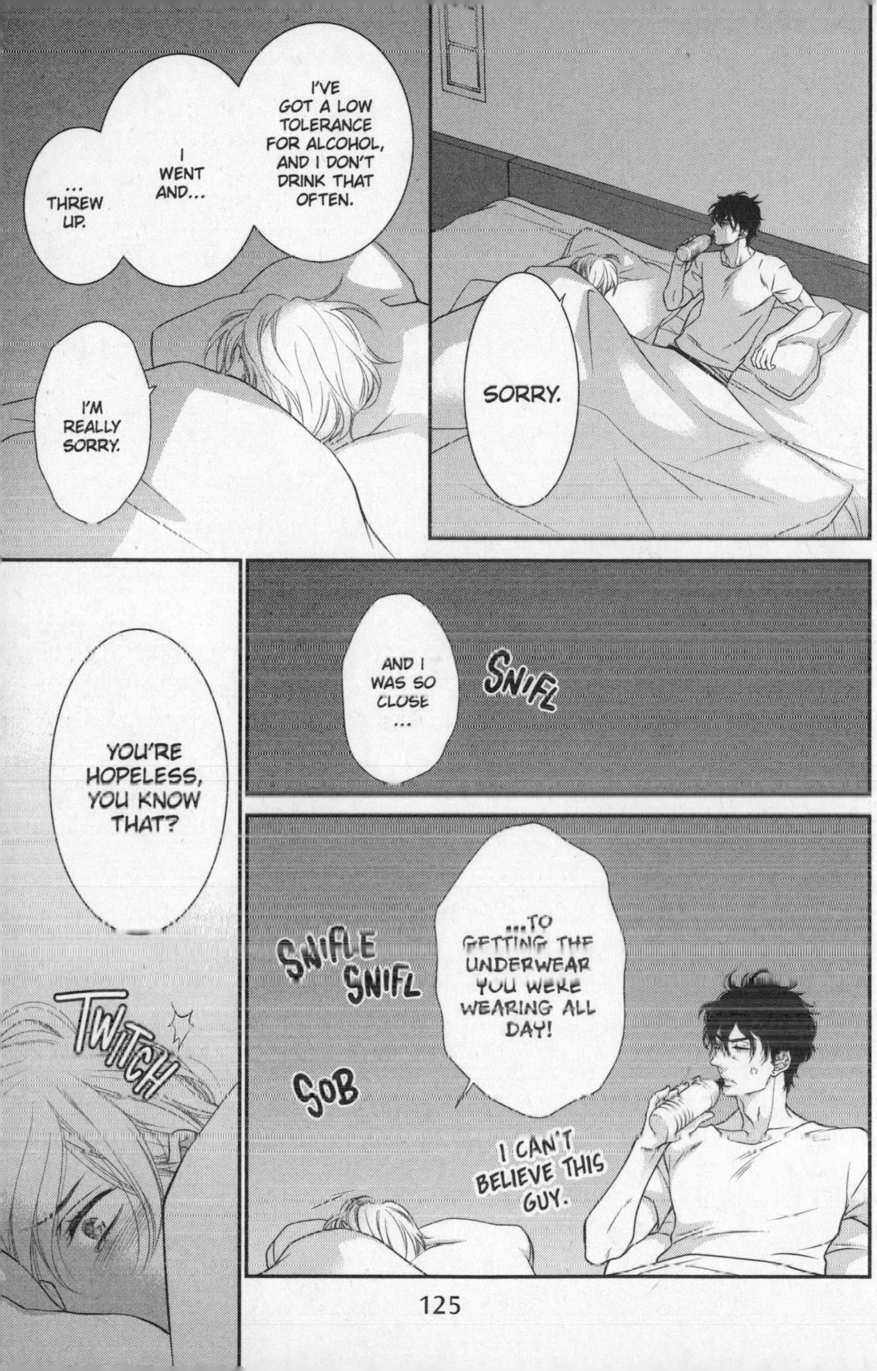
SORRY.
I'VE GOT A LOW TOLERANCE FOR ALCOHOL, AND I DON'T DRINK THAT OFTEN.
I WENT AND...
...THREW UP.
I'M REALLY SORRY.
AND I WAS SO CLOSE...
SNIFL
...TO GETTING THE UNDERWEAR YOU WERE WEARING ALL DAY!
SNIFLE SNIFL
SOB
I CAN'T BELIEVE THIS GUY.
YOU'RE HOPELESS, YOU KNOW THAT?
TWITCH

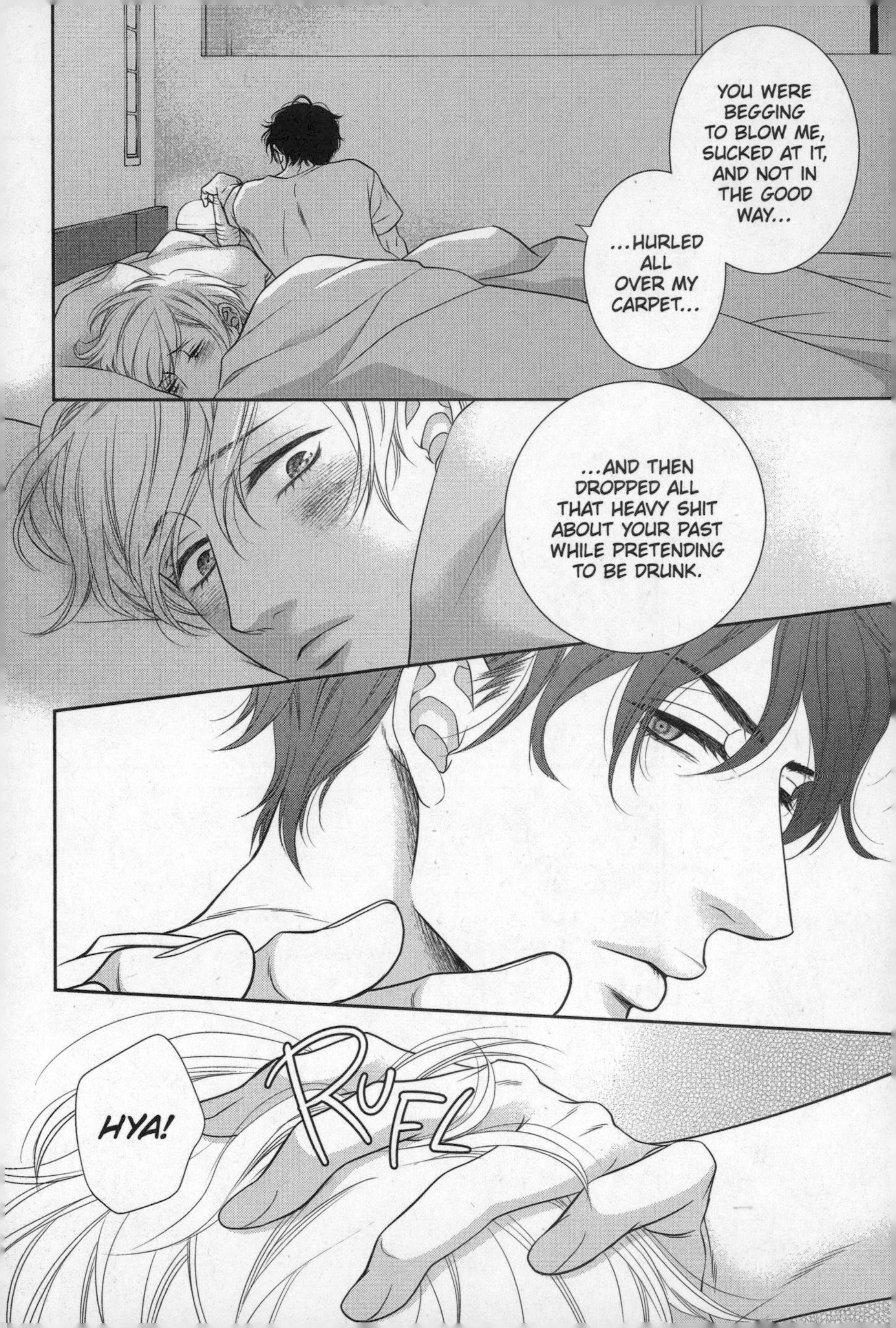
YOU WERE BEGGING TO BLOW ME, SUCKED AT IT, AND NOT IN THE GOOD WAY...
...HURLED ALL OVER MY CARPET...
...AND THEN DROPPED ALL THAT HEAVY SHIT ABOUT YOUR PAST WHILE PRETENDING TO BE DRUNK.
RUFL
HYA!

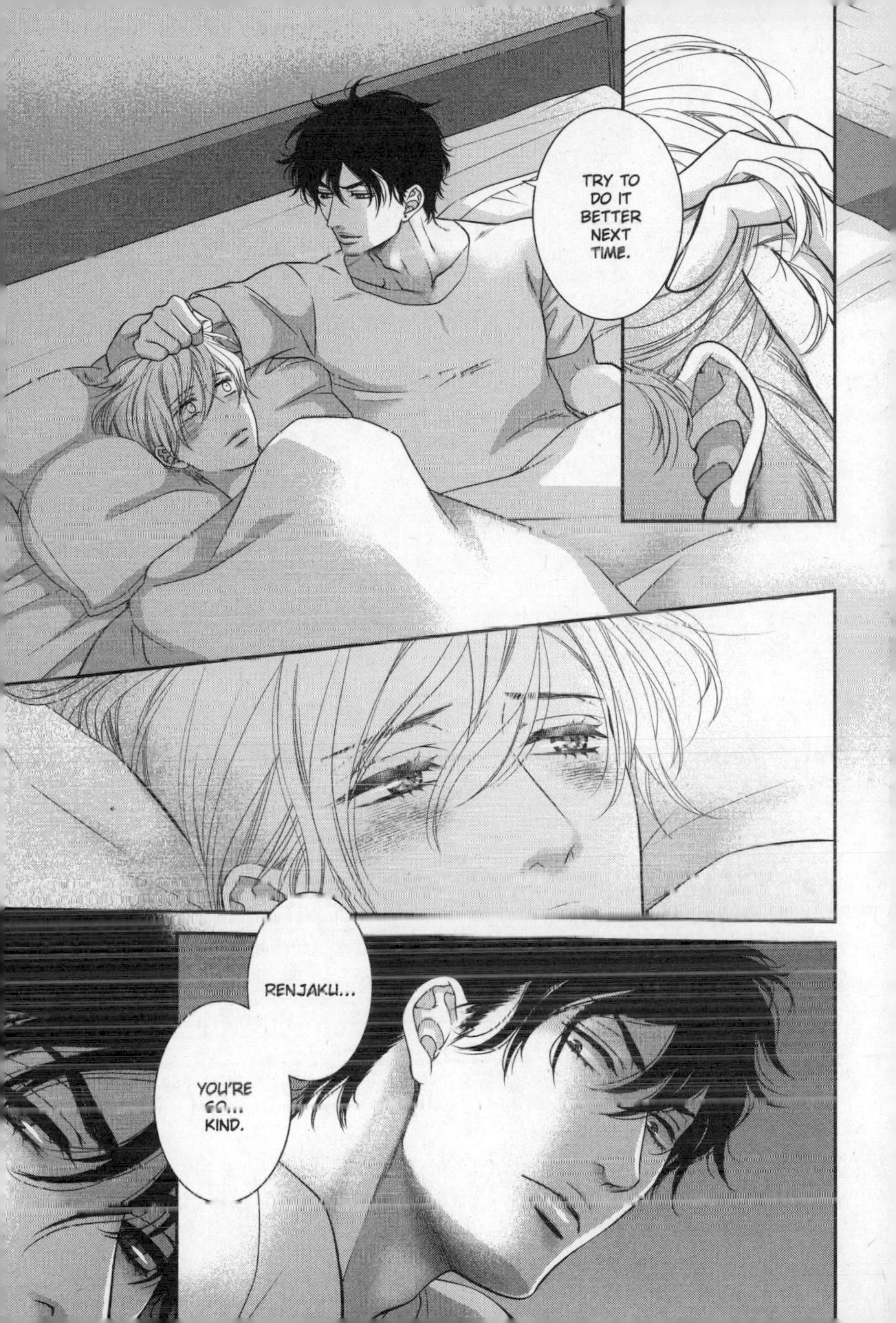
TRY TO DO IT BETTER NEXT TIME.
RENJAKU...
YOU'RE SO... KIND.

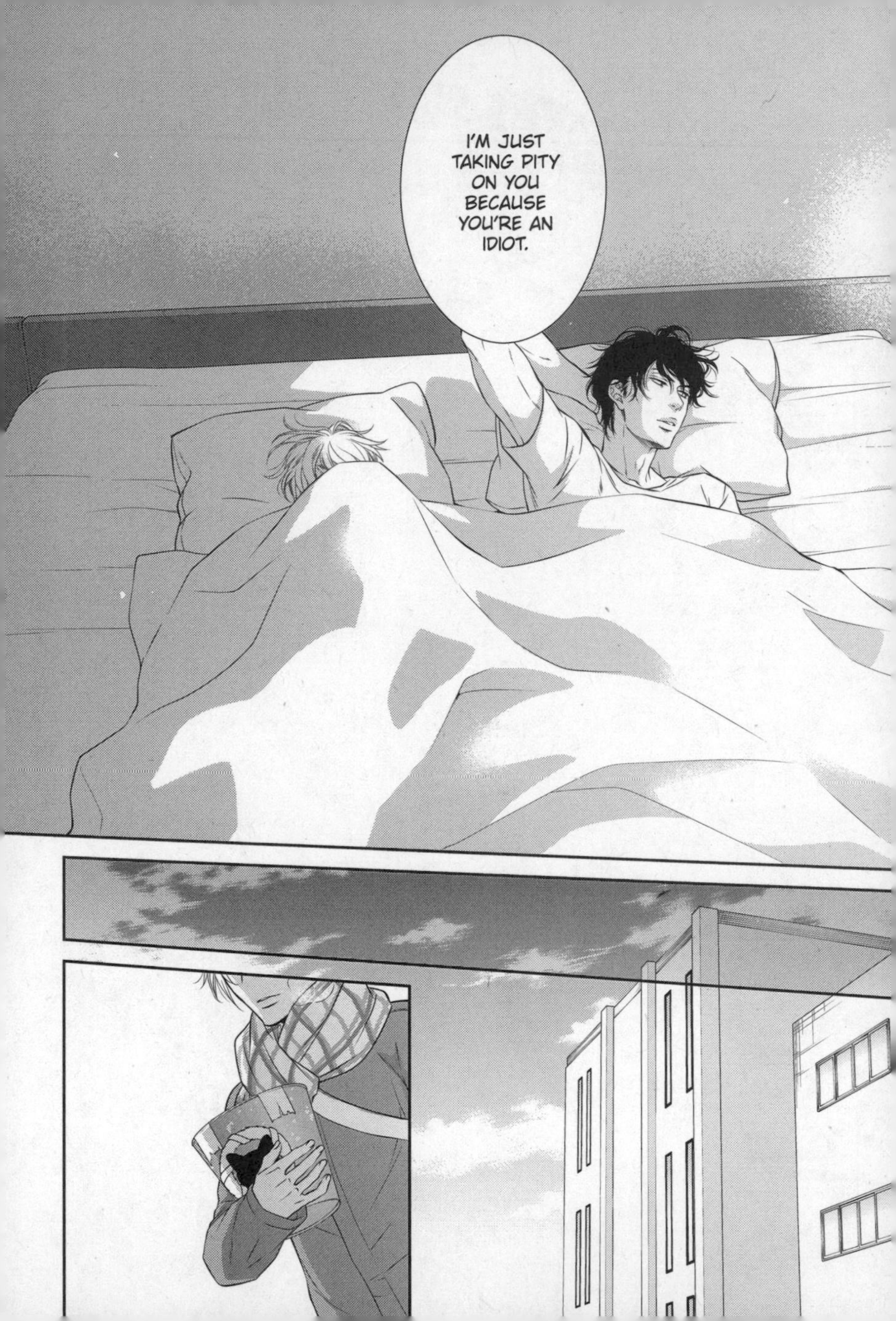
I'M JUST TAKING PITY ON YOU BECAUSE YOU'RE AN IDIOT.

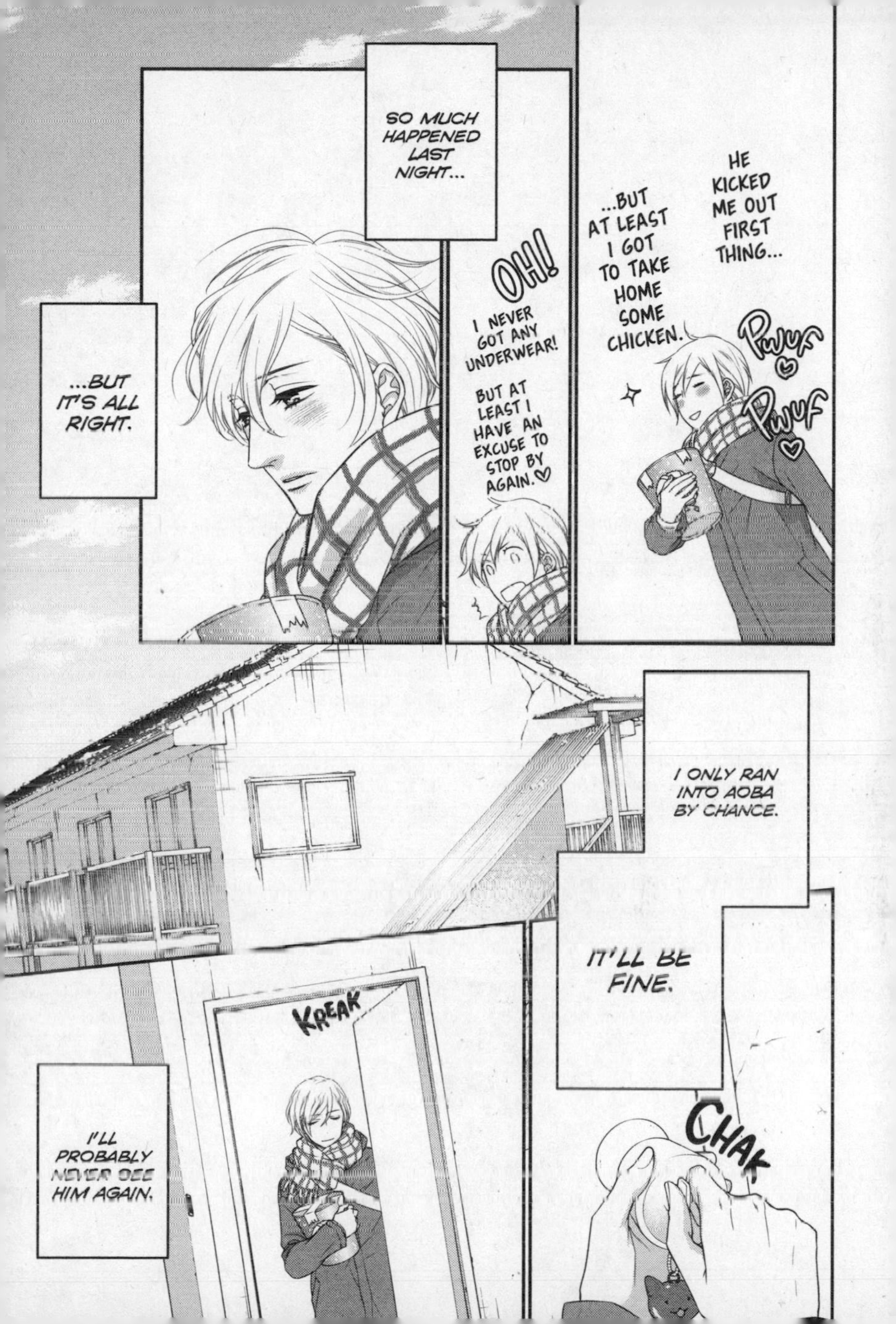
HE KICKED ME OUT FIRST THING...
...BUT AT LEAST I GOT TO TAKE HOME SOME CHICKEN.
PWUF ♡
PWUF ♡
OH!
I NEVER GOT ANY UNDERWEAR!
BUT AT LEAST I HAVE AN EXCUSE TO STOP BY AGAIN. ♡
SO MUCH HAPPENED LAST NIGHT...
...BUT IT'S ALL RIGHT.
I ONLY RAN INTO AOBA BY CHANCE.
IT'LL BE FINE.
CHAK
KREAK
I'LL PROBABLY NEVER SEE HIM AGAIN.

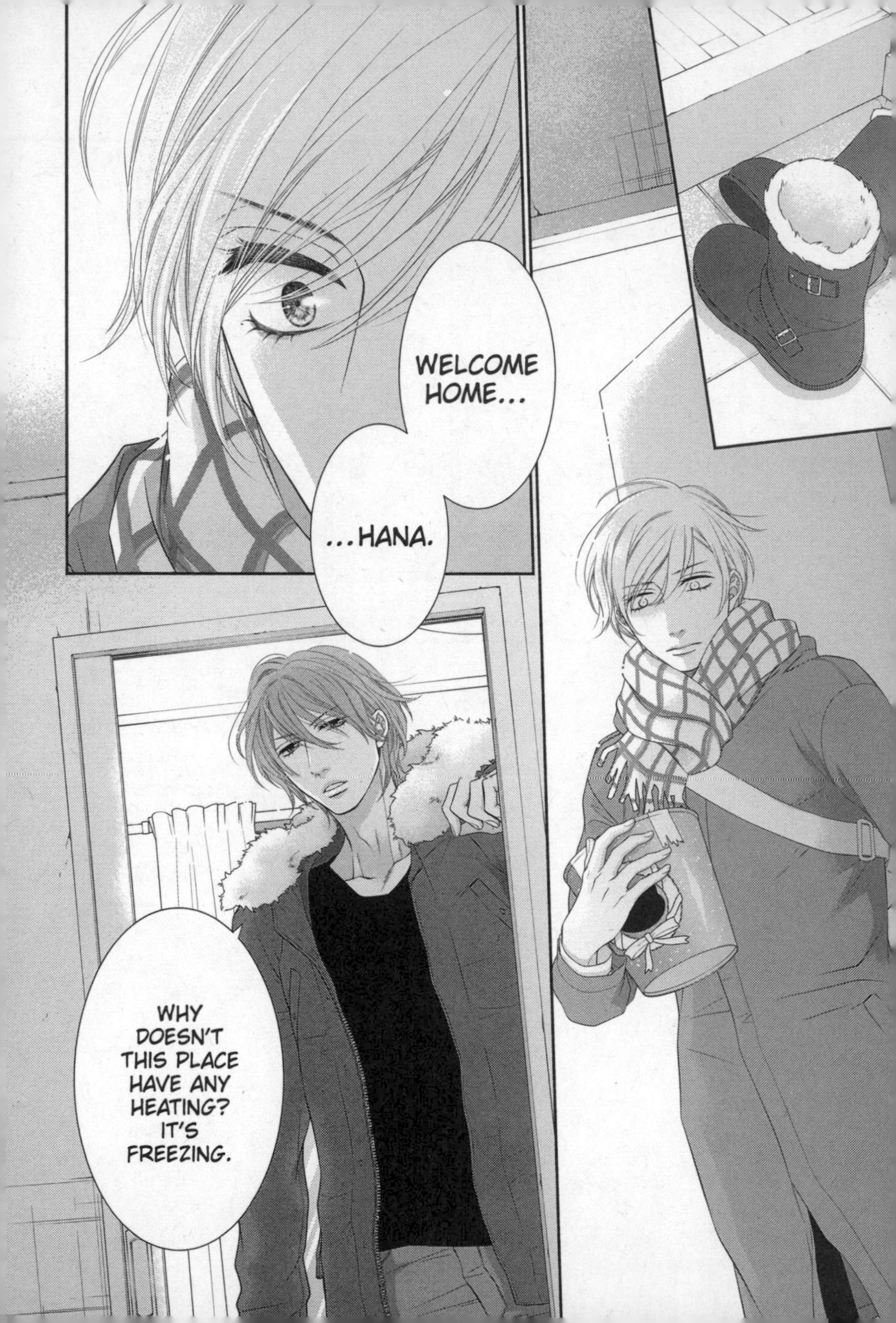
WELCOME HOME...
...HANA.
WHY DOESN'T THIS PLACE HAVE ANY HEATING? IT'S FREEZING.

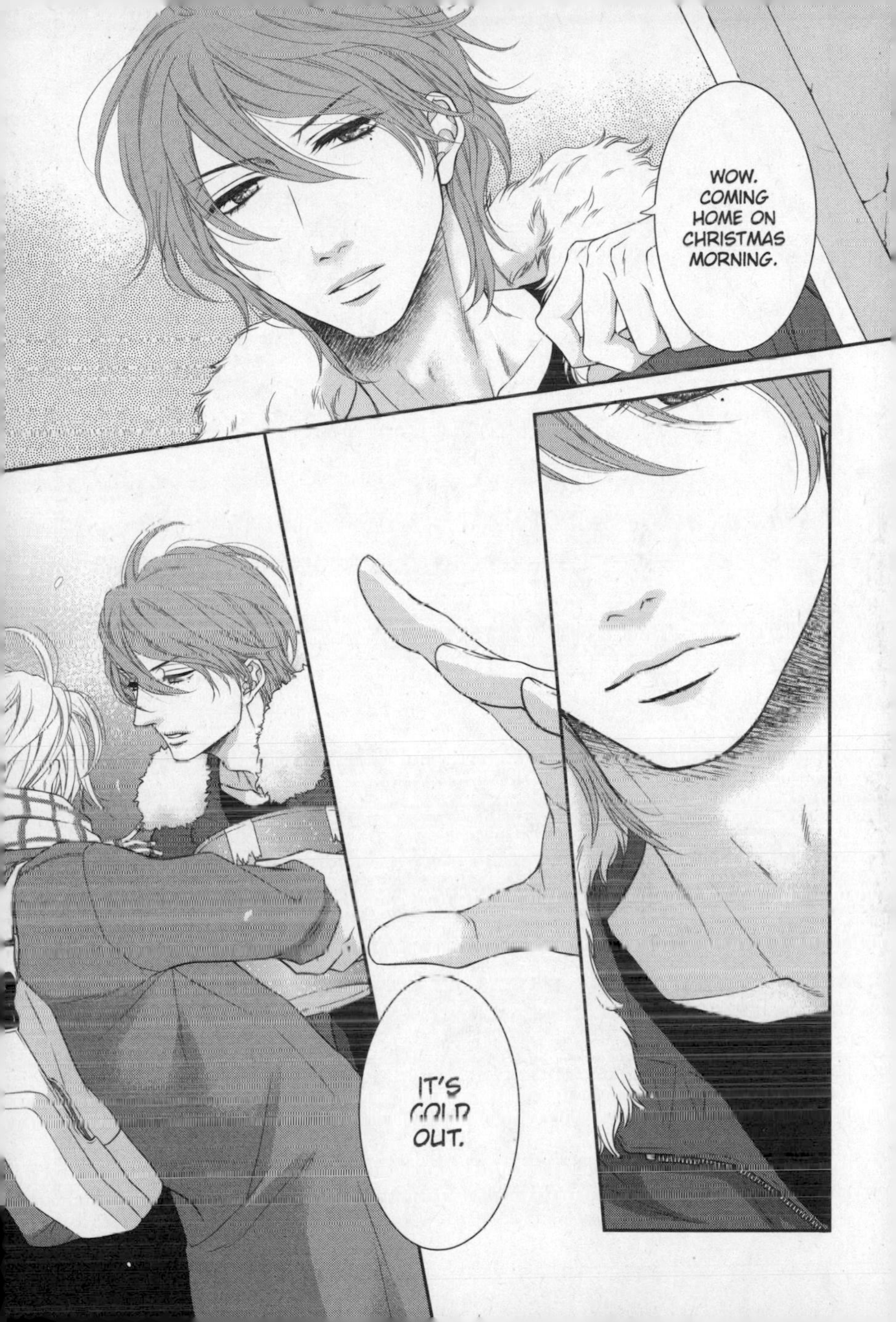
WOW. COMING HOME ON CHRISTMAS MORNING.
IT'S COLD OUT.

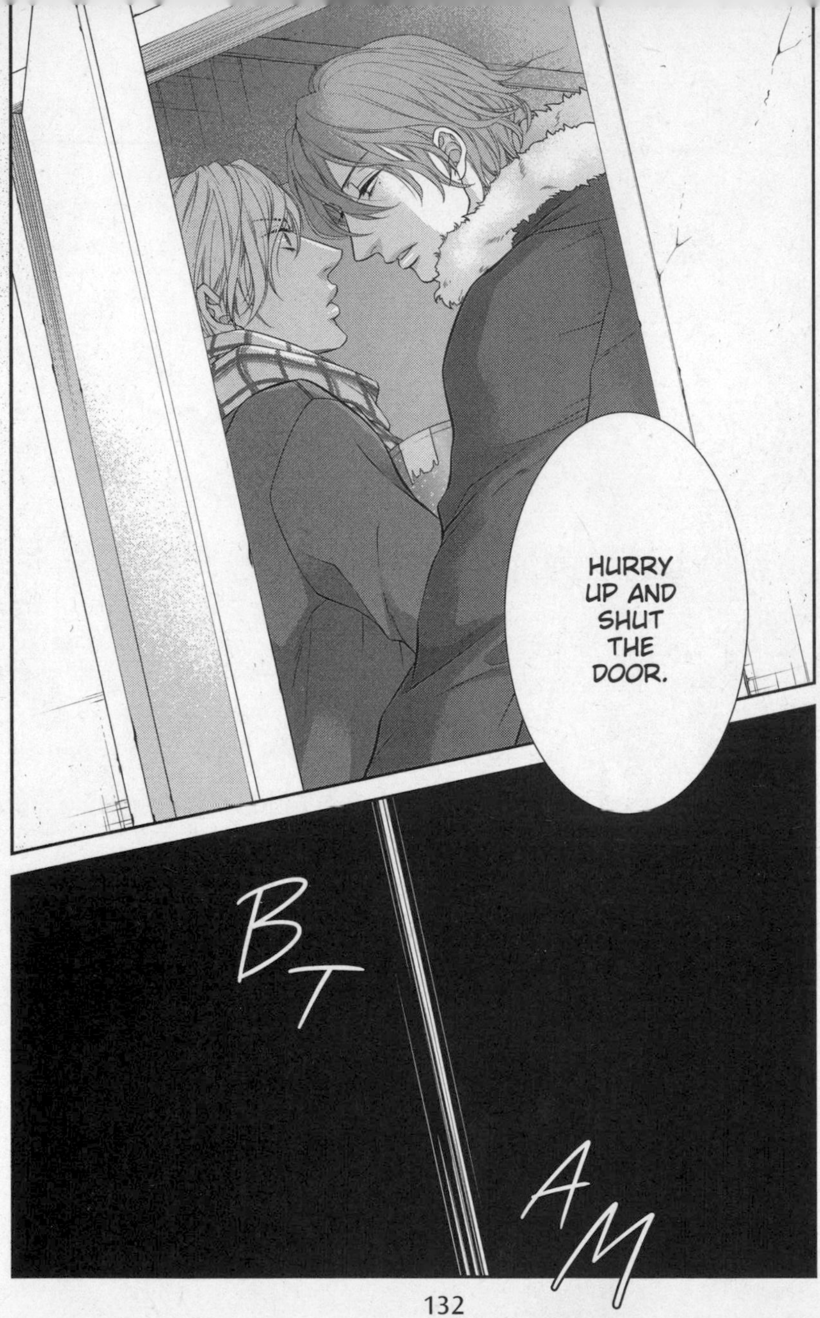
HURRY UP AND SHUT THE DOOR.
BTAM

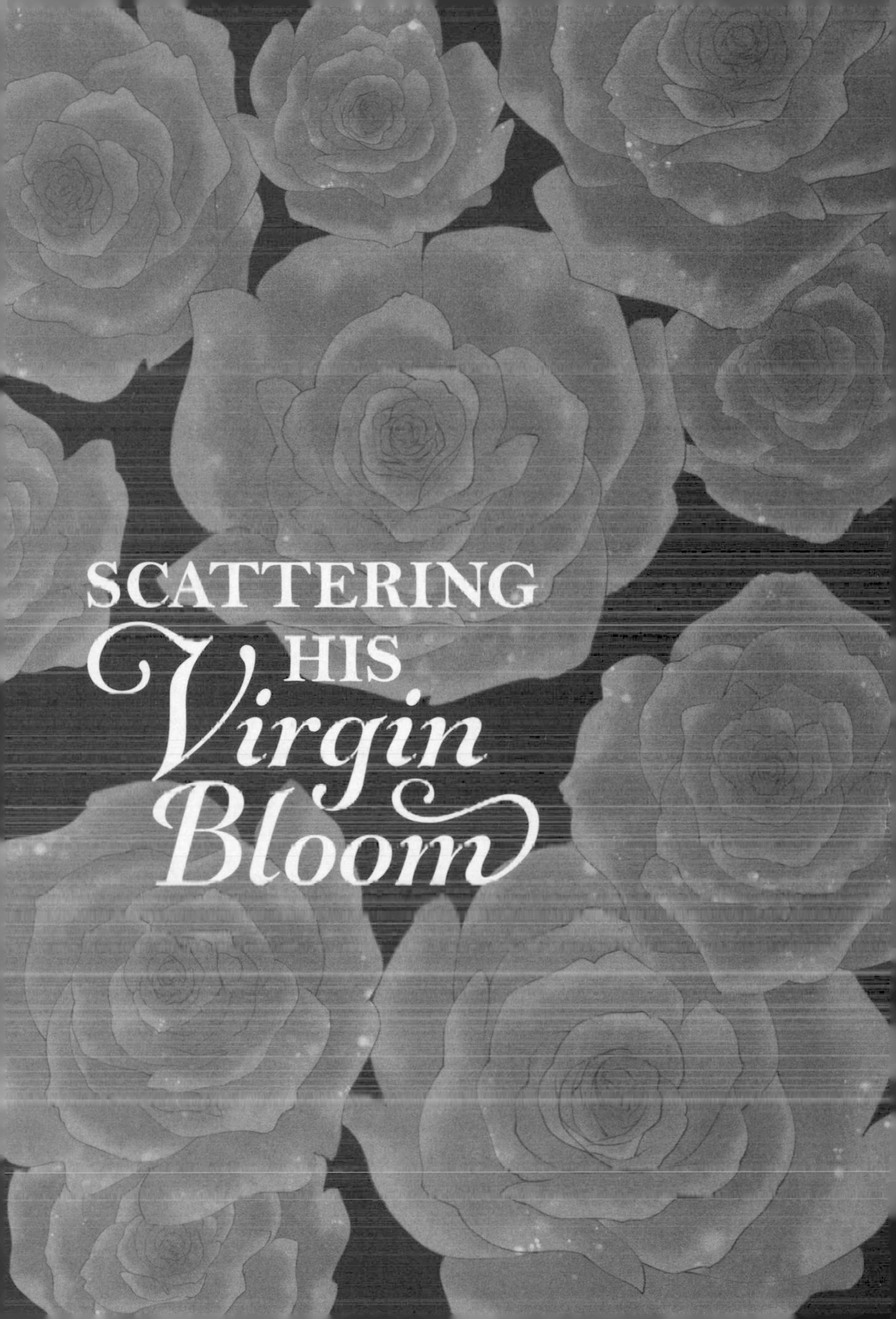
SCATTERING HIS
Virgin Bloom

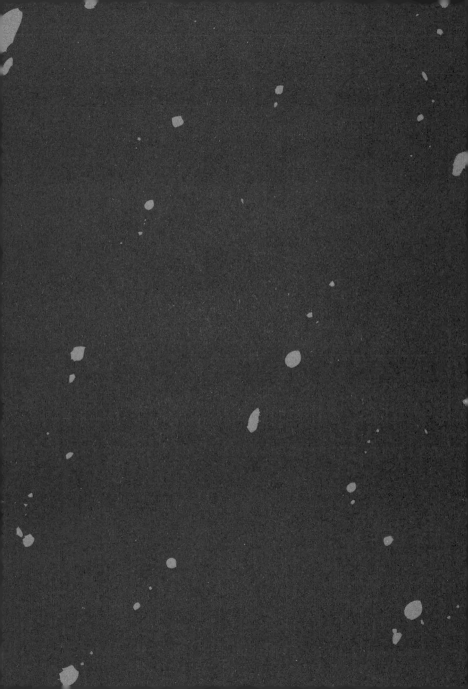

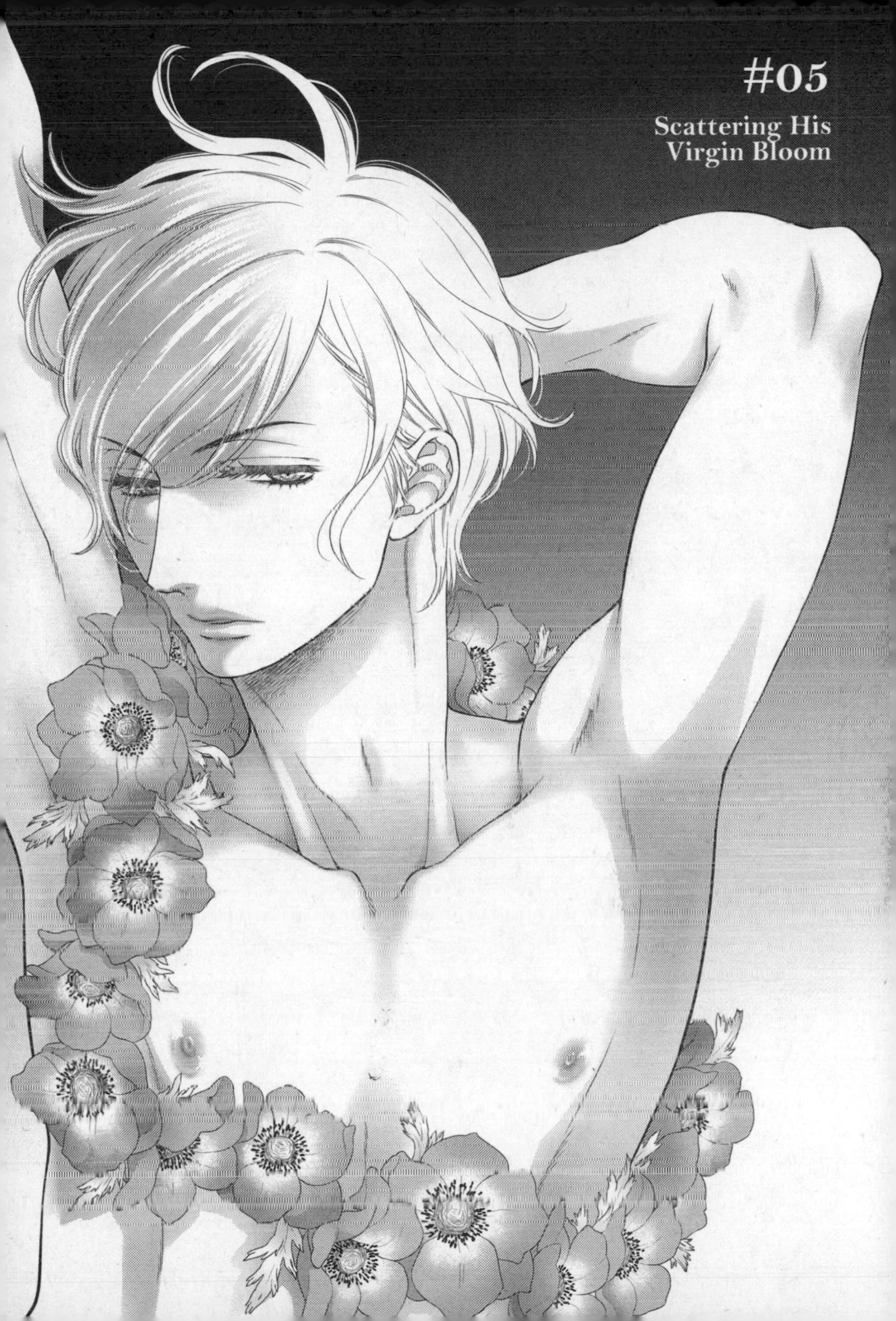
#05
Scattering His
Virgin Bloom

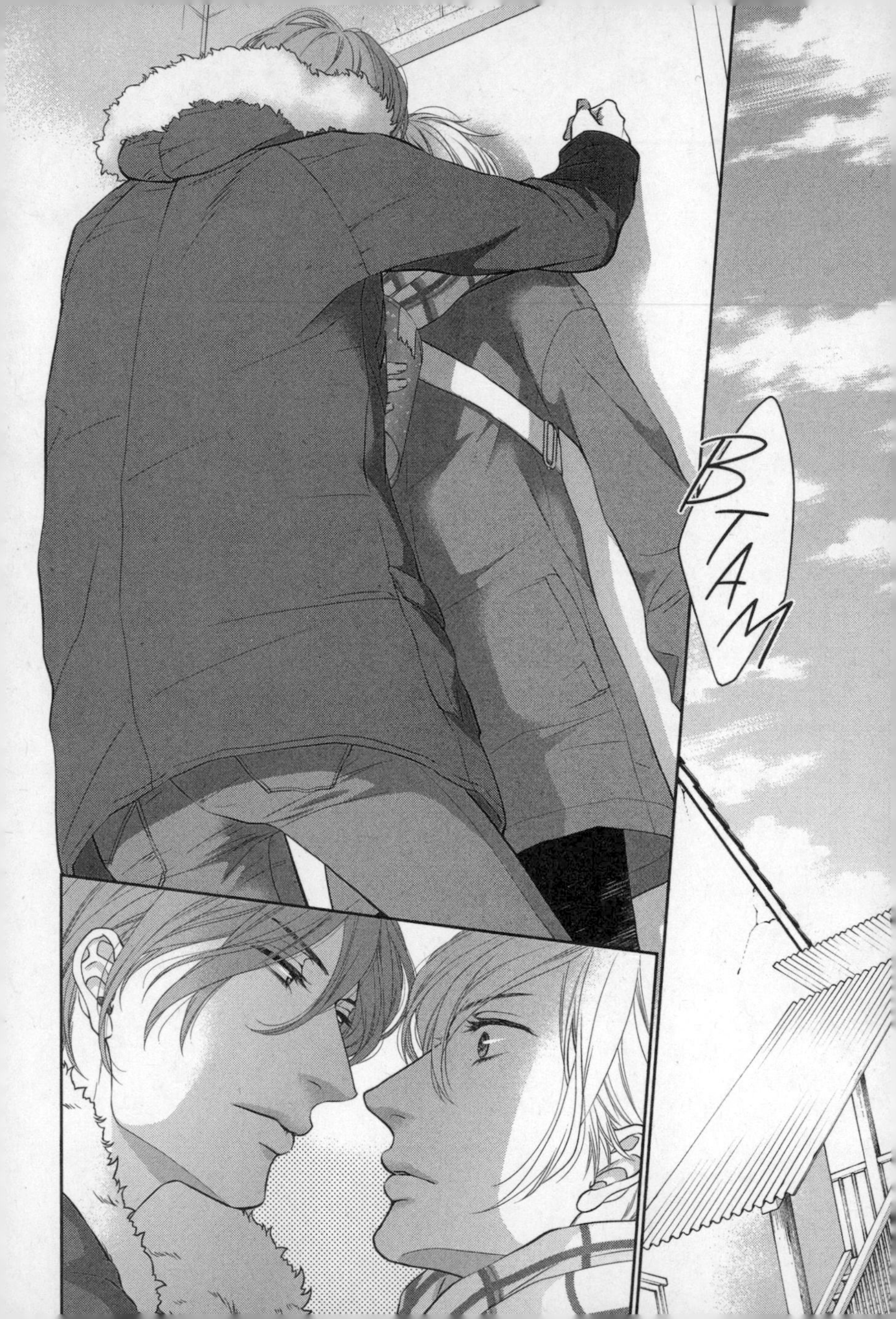
BTAM

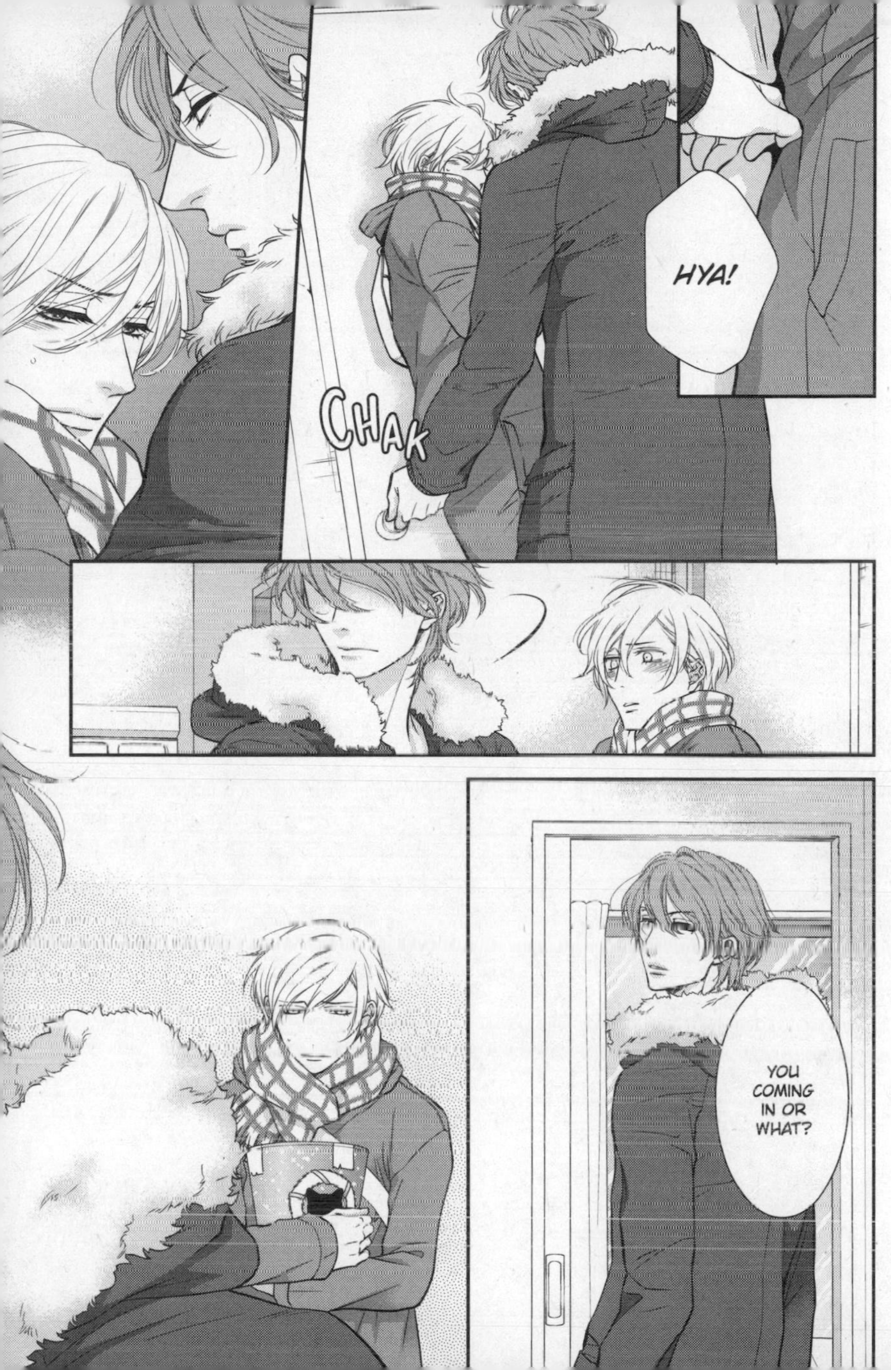
HYA!
CHAK
YOU COMING IN OR WHAT?

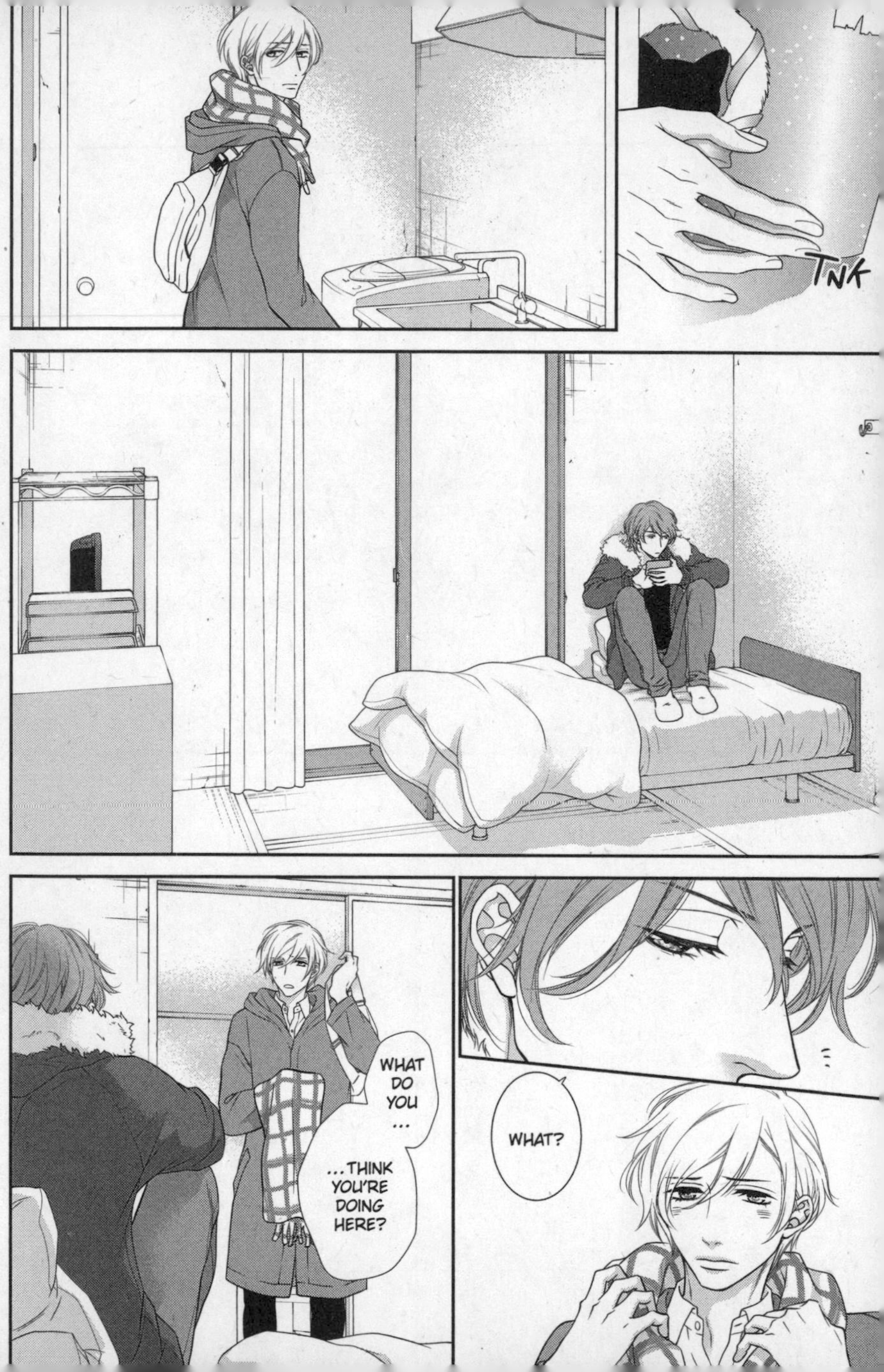
TNK
WHAT?
WHAT DO YOU ...
...THINK YOU'RE DOING HERE?

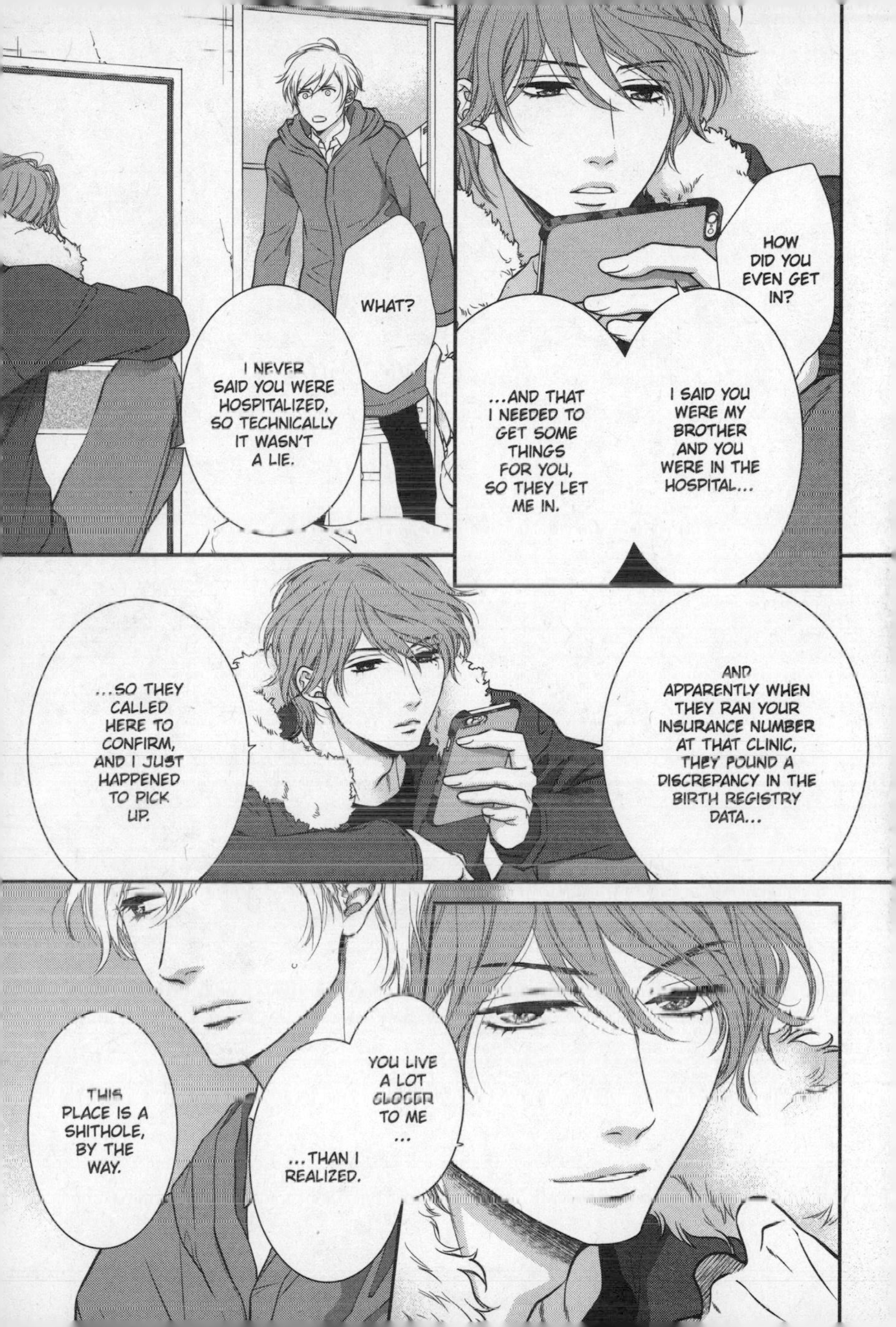
HOW DID YOU EVEN GET IN?
I SAID YOU WERE MY BROTHER AND YOU WERE IN THE HOSPITAL...
...AND THAT I NEEDED TO GET SOME THINGS FOR YOU, SO THEY LET ME IN.
WHAT?
I NEVER SAID YOU WERE HOSPITALIZED, SO TECHNICALLY IT WASN'T A LIE.
AND APPARENTLY WHEN THEY RAN YOUR INSURANCE NUMBER AT THAT CLINIC, THEY FOUND A DISCREPANCY IN THE BIRTH REGISTRY DATA...
...SO THEY CALLED HERE TO CONFIRM, AND I JUST HAPPENED TO PICK UP.
YOU LIVE A LOT CLOSER TO ME ...
...THAN I REALIZED.
THIS PLACE IS A SHITHOLE, BY THE WAY.

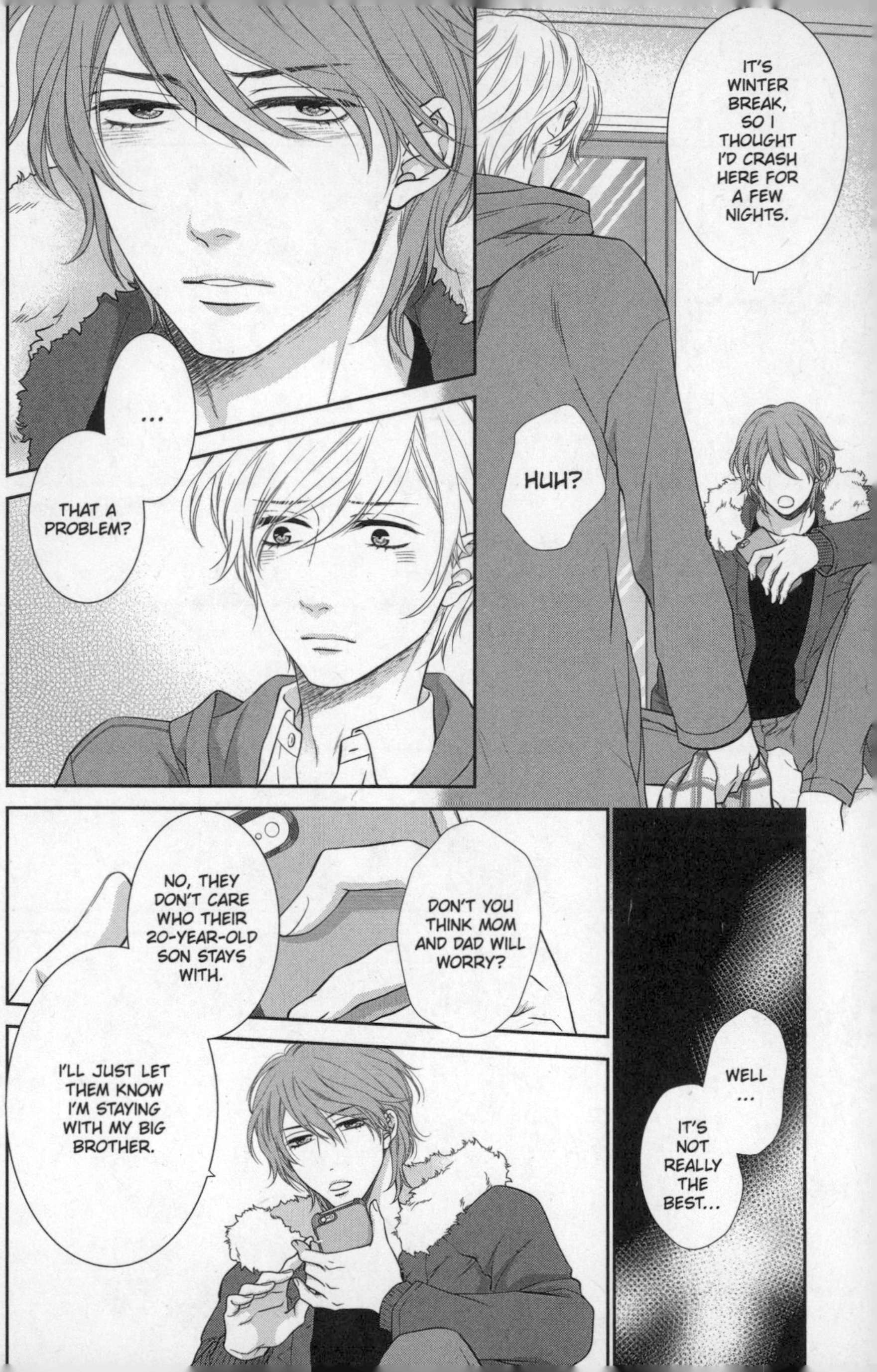
IT'S WINTER BREAK, SO I THOUGHT I'D CRASH HERE FOR A FEW NIGHTS.
HUH?
...
THAT A PROBLEM?
WELL ... IT'S NOT REALLY THE BEST...
DON'T YOU THINK MOM AND DAD WILL WORRY?
NO, THEY DON'T CARE WHO THEIR 20-YEAR-OLD SON STAYS WITH.
I'LL JUST LET THEM KNOW I'M STAYING WITH MY BIG BROTHER.

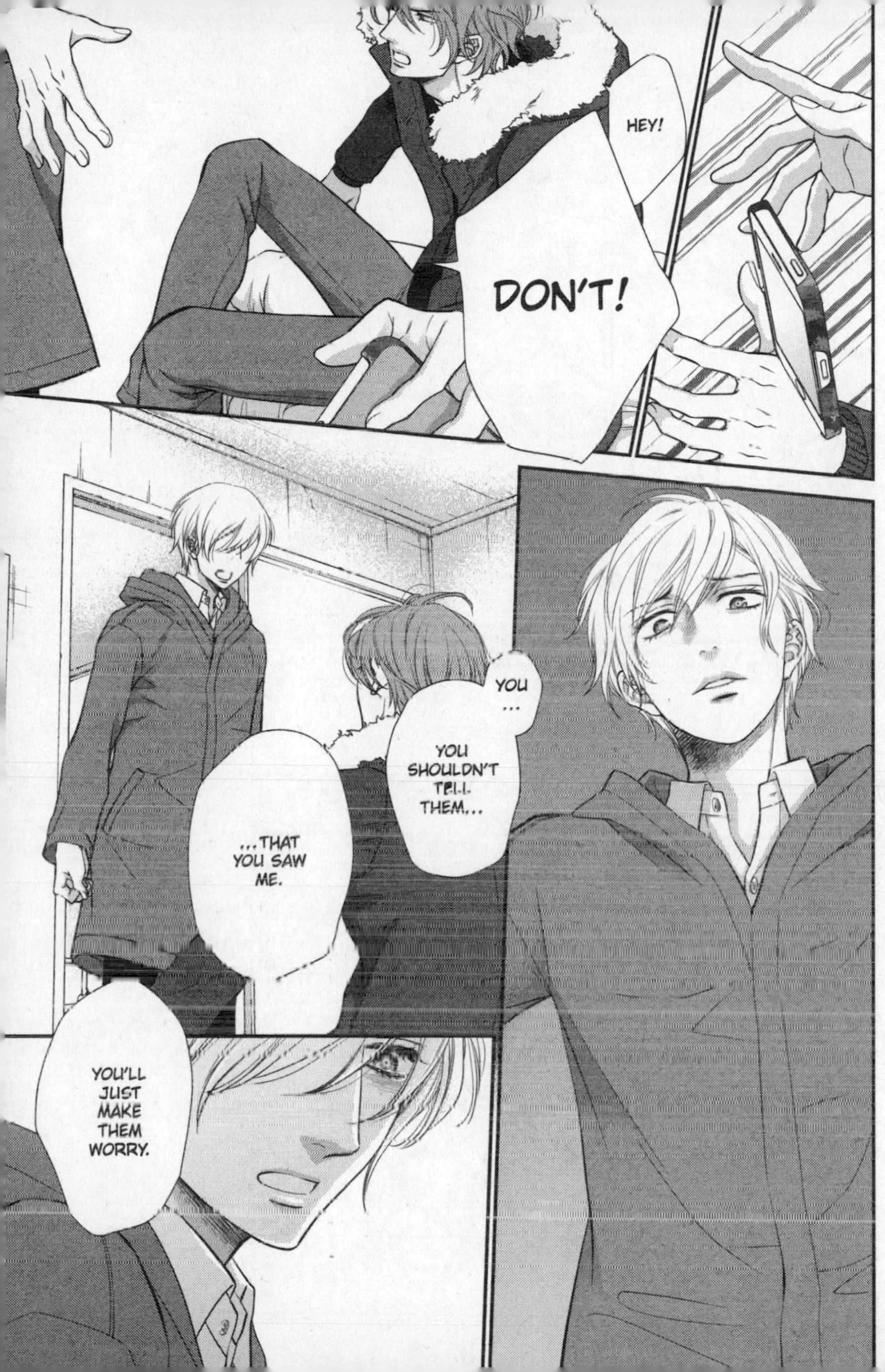
HEY!
DON'T!
YOU ...
YOU SHOULDN'T TELL THEM...
...THAT YOU SAW ME.
YOU'LL JUST MAKE THEM WORRY.

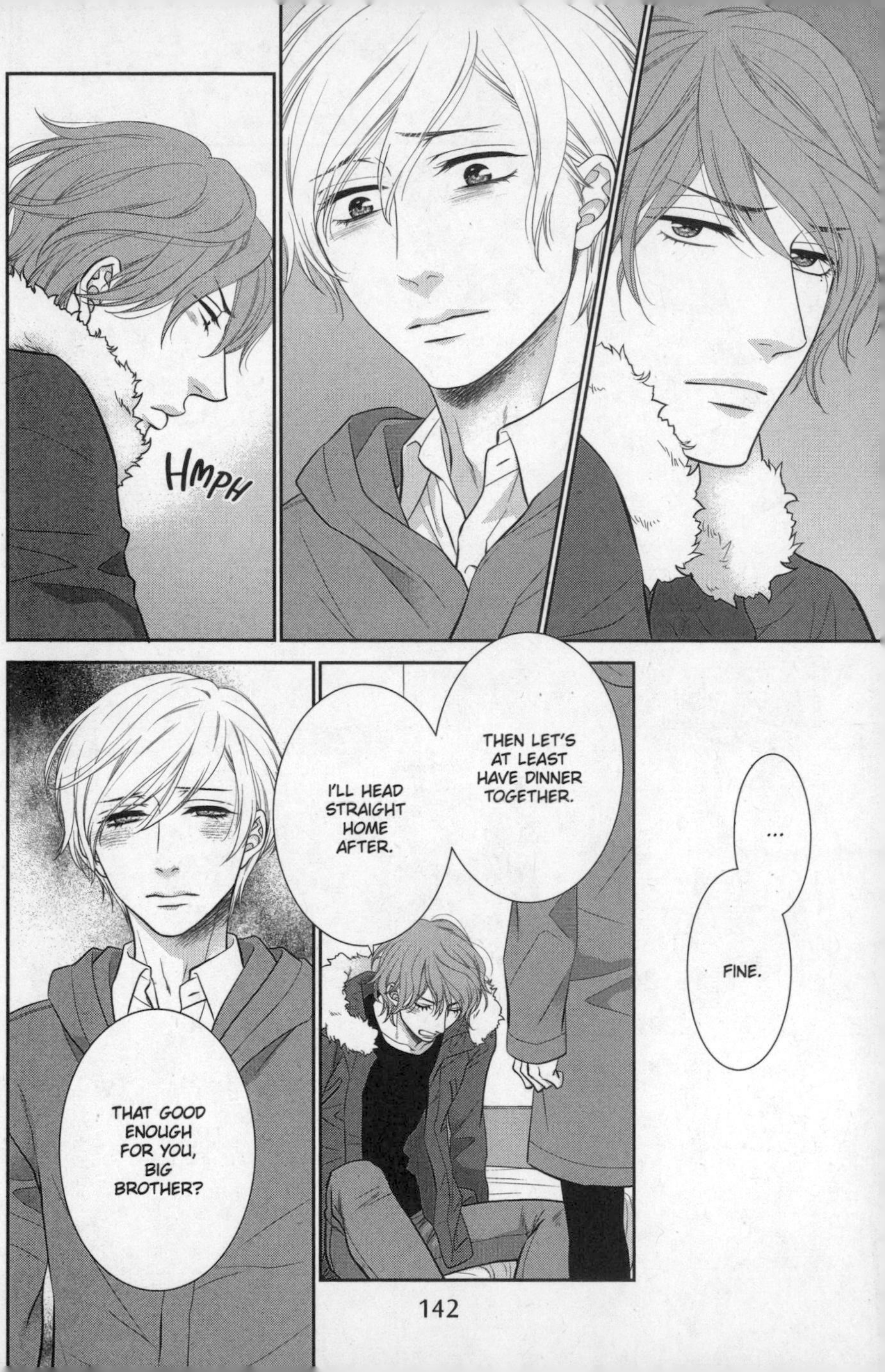
HMPH
...
FINE.
THEN LET'S AT LEAST HAVE DINNER TOGETHER.
I'LL HEAD STRAIGHT HOME AFTER.
THAT GOOD ENOUGH FOR YOU, BIG BROTHER?

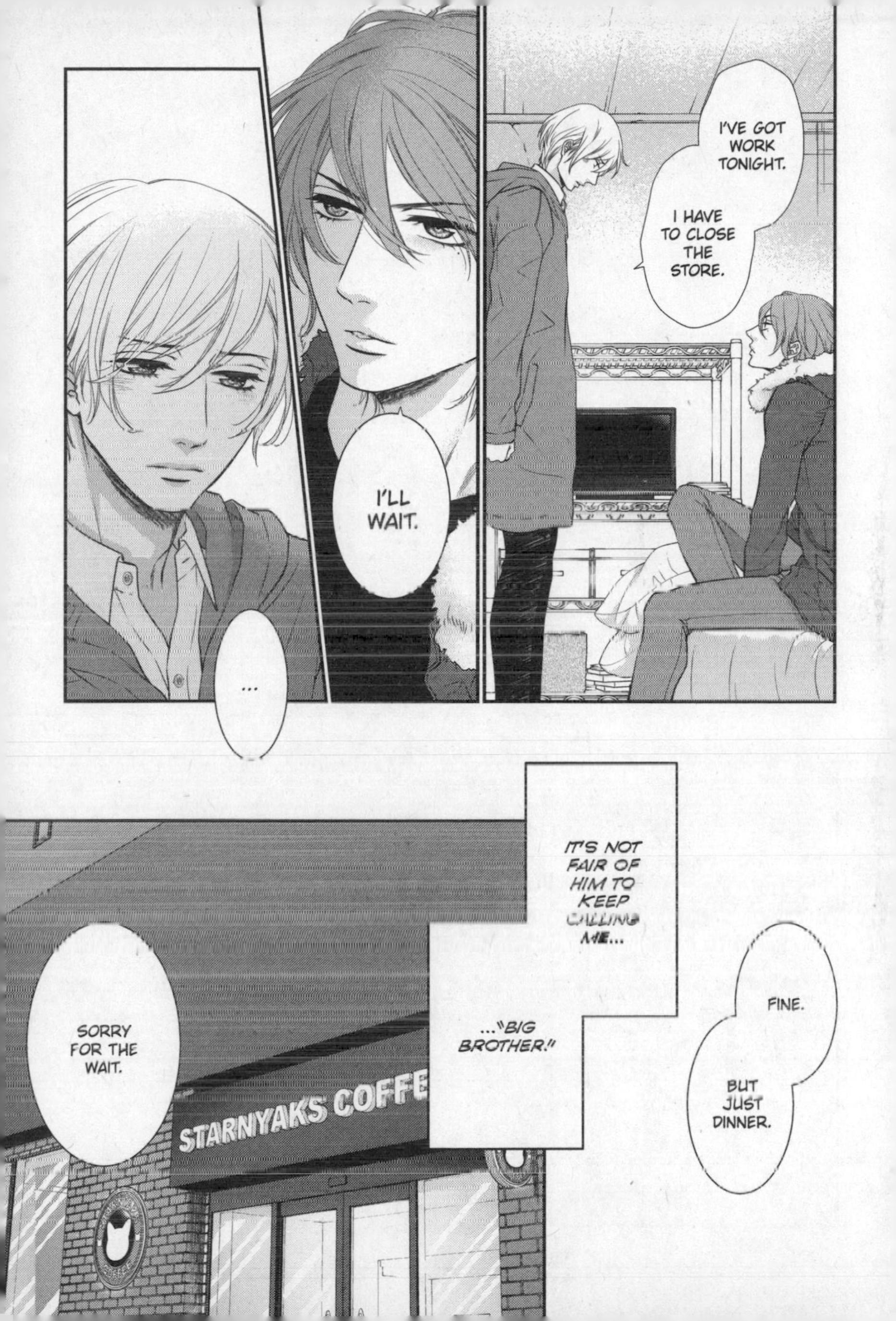
I'VE GOT WORK TONIGHT.
I HAVE TO CLOSE THE STORE.
I'LL WAIT.
...
FINE.
BUT JUST DINNER.
IT'S NOT FAIR OF HIM TO KEEP CALLING ME...
..."BIG BROTHER."
SORRY FOR THE WAIT.
STARNYAKS COFFE

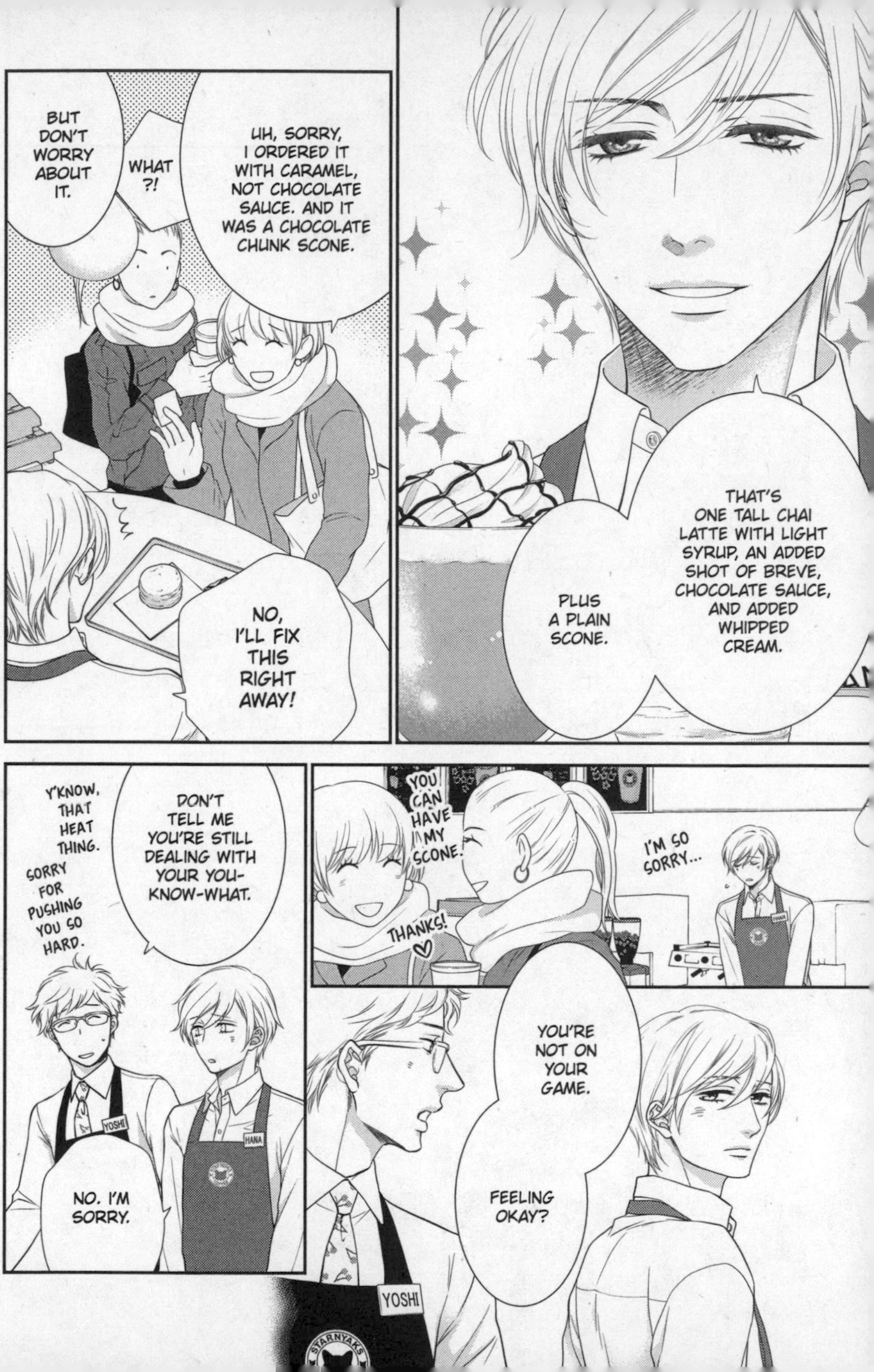
THAT'S ONE TALL CHAI LATTE WITH LIGHT SYRUP, AN ADDED SHOT OF BREVE, CHOCOLATE SAUCE, AND ADDED WHIPPED CREAM.
PLUS A PLAIN SCONE.
UH, SORRY, I ORDERED IT WITH CARAMEL, NOT CHOCOLATE SAUCE. AND IT WAS A CHOCOLATE CHUNK SCONE.
WHAT ?!
BUT DON'T WORRY ABOUT IT.
NO, I'LL FIX THIS RIGHT AWAY!
I'M SO SORRY...
YOU CAN HAVE MY SCONE.
THANKS!
YOU'RE NOT ON YOUR GAME.
FEELING OKAY?
DON'T TELL ME YOU'RE STILL DEALING WITH YOUR YOU-KNOW-WHAT.
Y'KNOW, THAT HEAT THING.
SORRY FOR PUSHING YOU SO HARD.
NO. I'M SORRY.

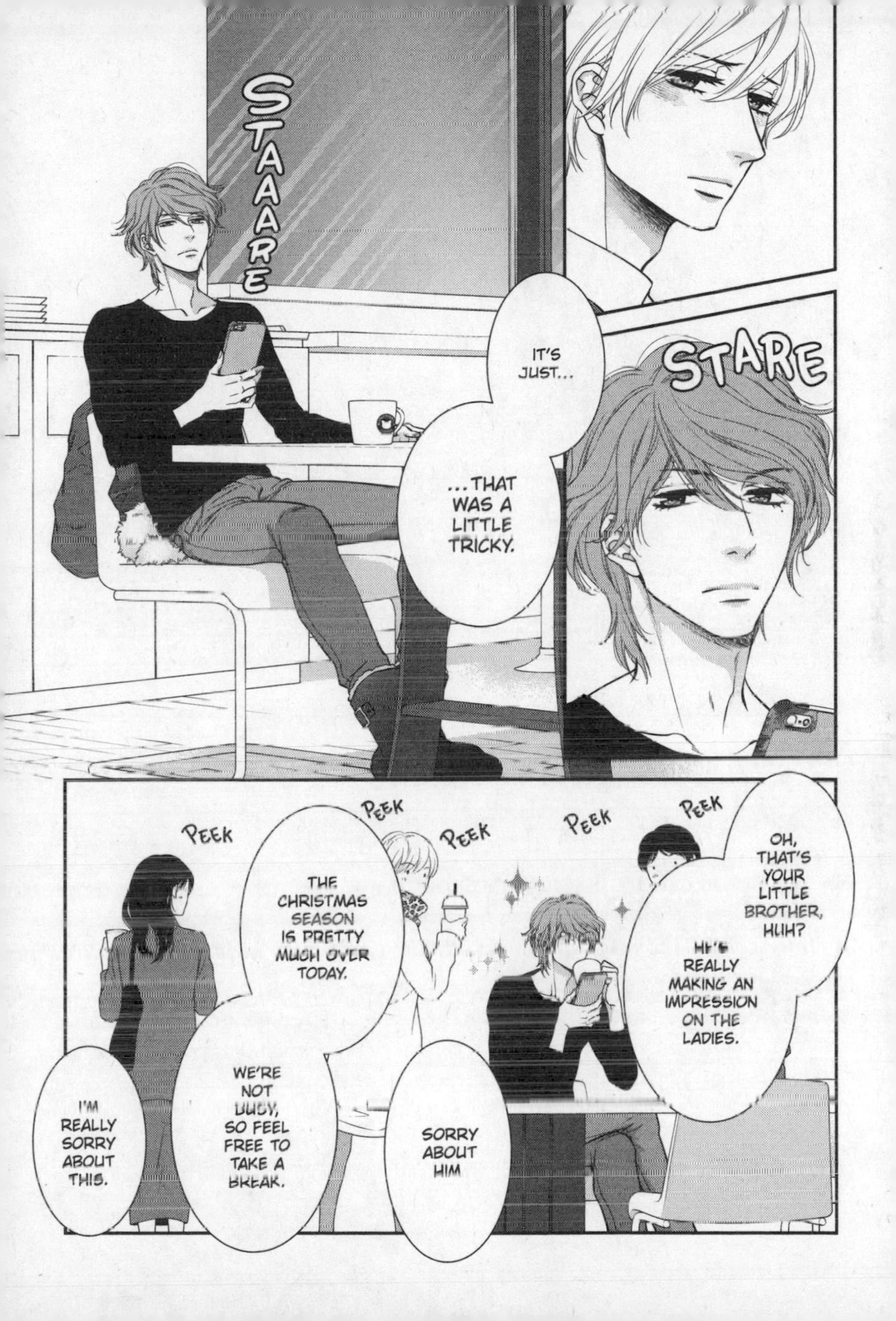
IT'S JUST...
...THAT WAS A LITTLE TRICKY.
STARE
STAAARE
PEEK
OH, THAT'S YOUR LITTLE BROTHER, HUH?
HE'S REALLY MAKING AN IMPRESSION ON THE LADIES.
PEEK
PEEK
PEEK
THE CHRISTMAS SEASON IS PRETTY MUCH OVER TODAY.
PEEK
SORRY ABOUT HIM
WE'RE NOT BUSY, SO FEEL FREE TO TAKE A BREAK.
I'M REALLY SORRY ABOUT THIS.

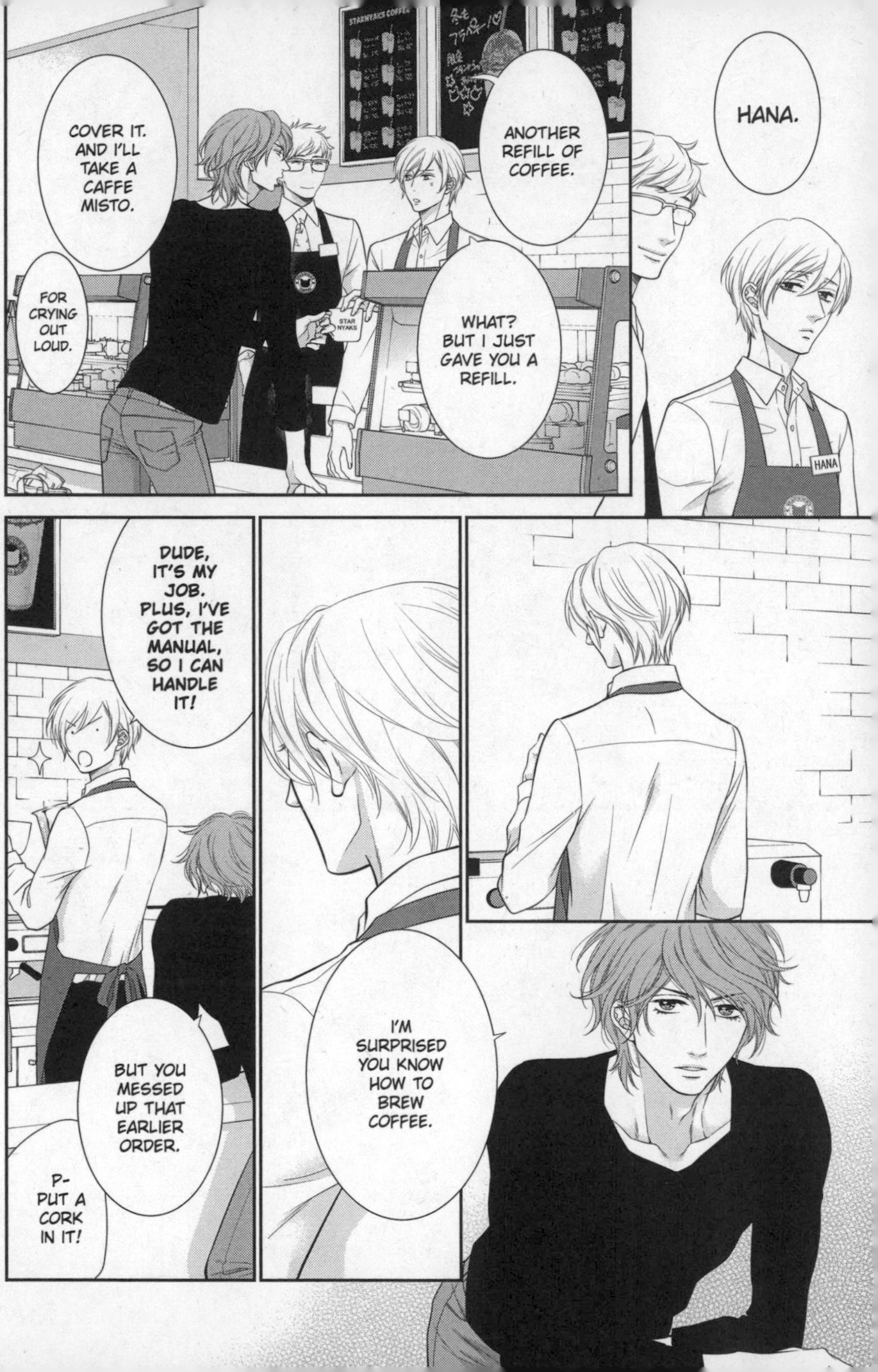
HANA.
ANOTHER REFILL OF COFFEE.
WHAT? BUT I JUST GAVE YOU A REFILL.
COVER IT. AND I'LL TAKE A CAFFE MISTO.
FOR CRYING OUT LOUD.
STAR NYAKS
HANA
I'M SURPRISED YOU KNOW HOW TO BREW COFFEE.
DUDE, IT'S MY JOB. PLUS, I'VE GOT THE MANUAL, SO I CAN HANDLE IT!
BUT YOU MESSED UP THAT EARLIER ORDER.
P- PUT A CORK IN IT!

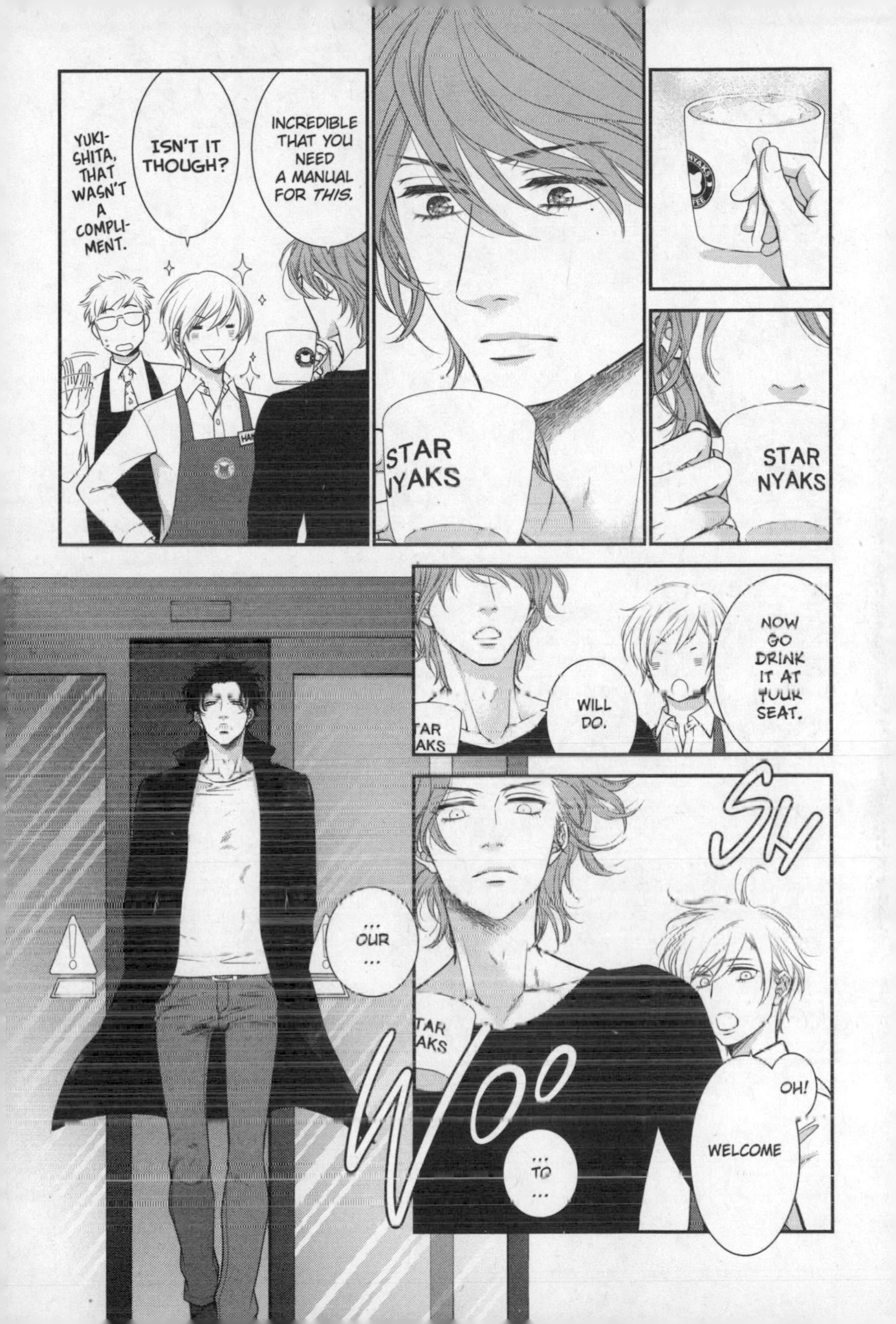
STAR NYAKS
STAR NYAKS
INCREDIBLE THAT YOU NEED A MANUAL FOR *THIS.*
ISN'T IT THOUGH?
YUKI-SHITA, THAT WASN'T A COMPLI-MENT.
NOW GO DRINK IT AT YOUR SEAT.
WILL DO.
SH
OH!
WELCOME
... TO ...
WOO
... OUR ...

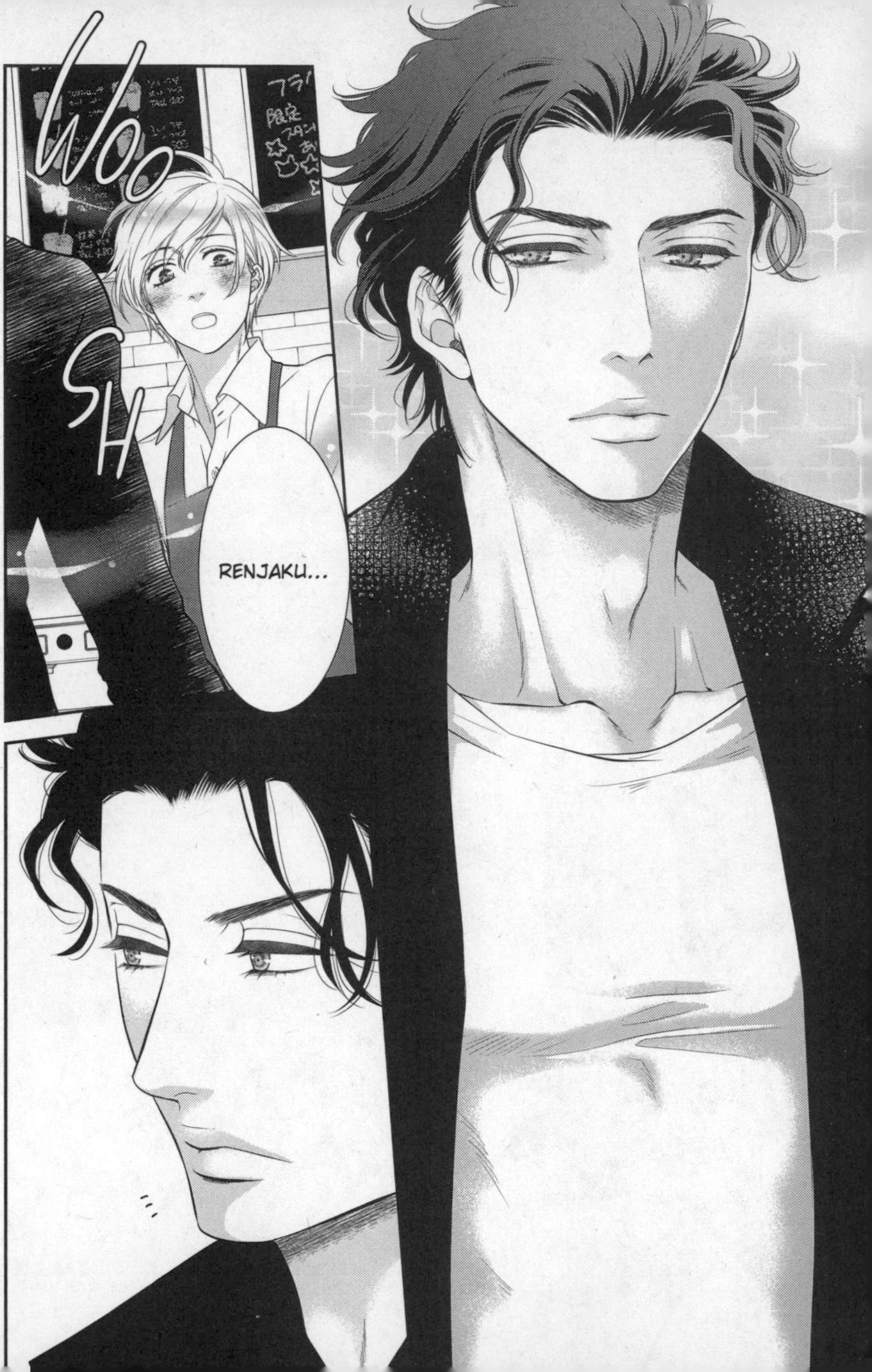
WOOSH
RENJAKU...

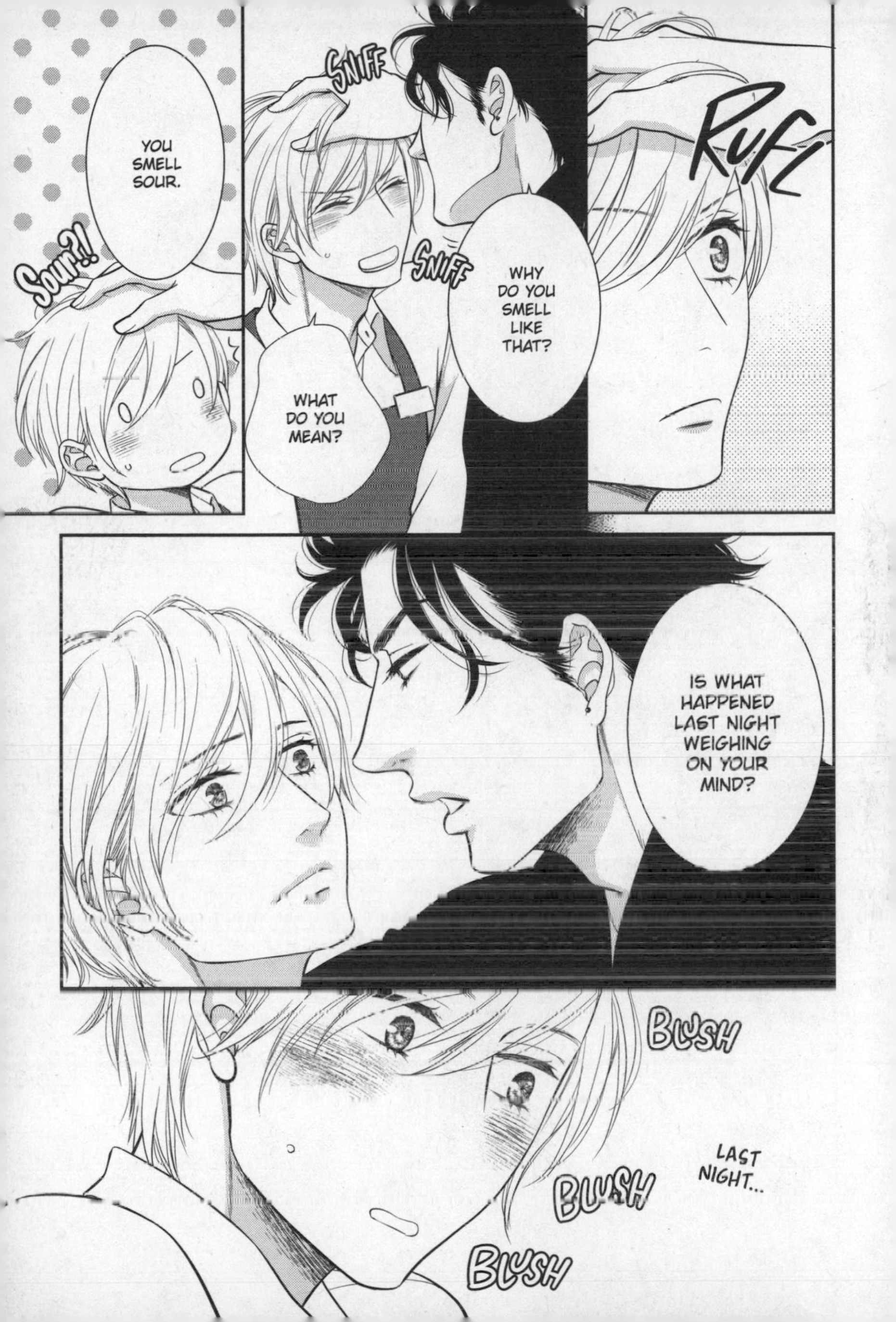
RUFF
SNIFF
WHY DO YOU SMELL LIKE THAT?
SNIFF
WHAT DO YOU MEAN?
YOU SMELL SOUR.
Sour?!
IS WHAT HAPPENED LAST NIGHT WEIGHING ON YOUR MIND?
BLUSH
LAST NIGHT...
BLUSH
BLUSH

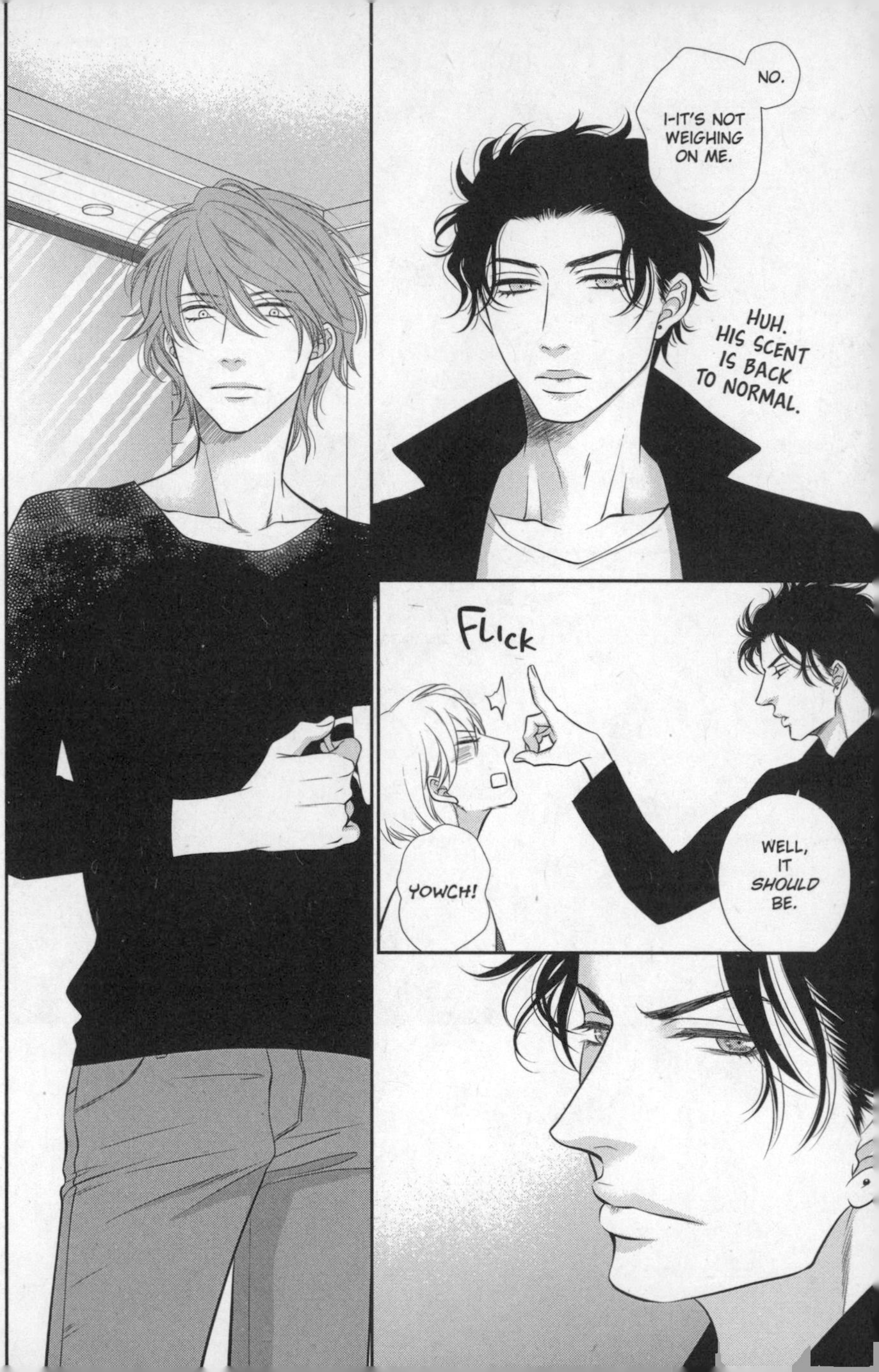
NO.
I-IT'S NOT WEIGHING ON ME.
HUH. HIS SCENT IS BACK TO NORMAL.
FLICK
WELL, IT SHOULD BE.
YOWCH!

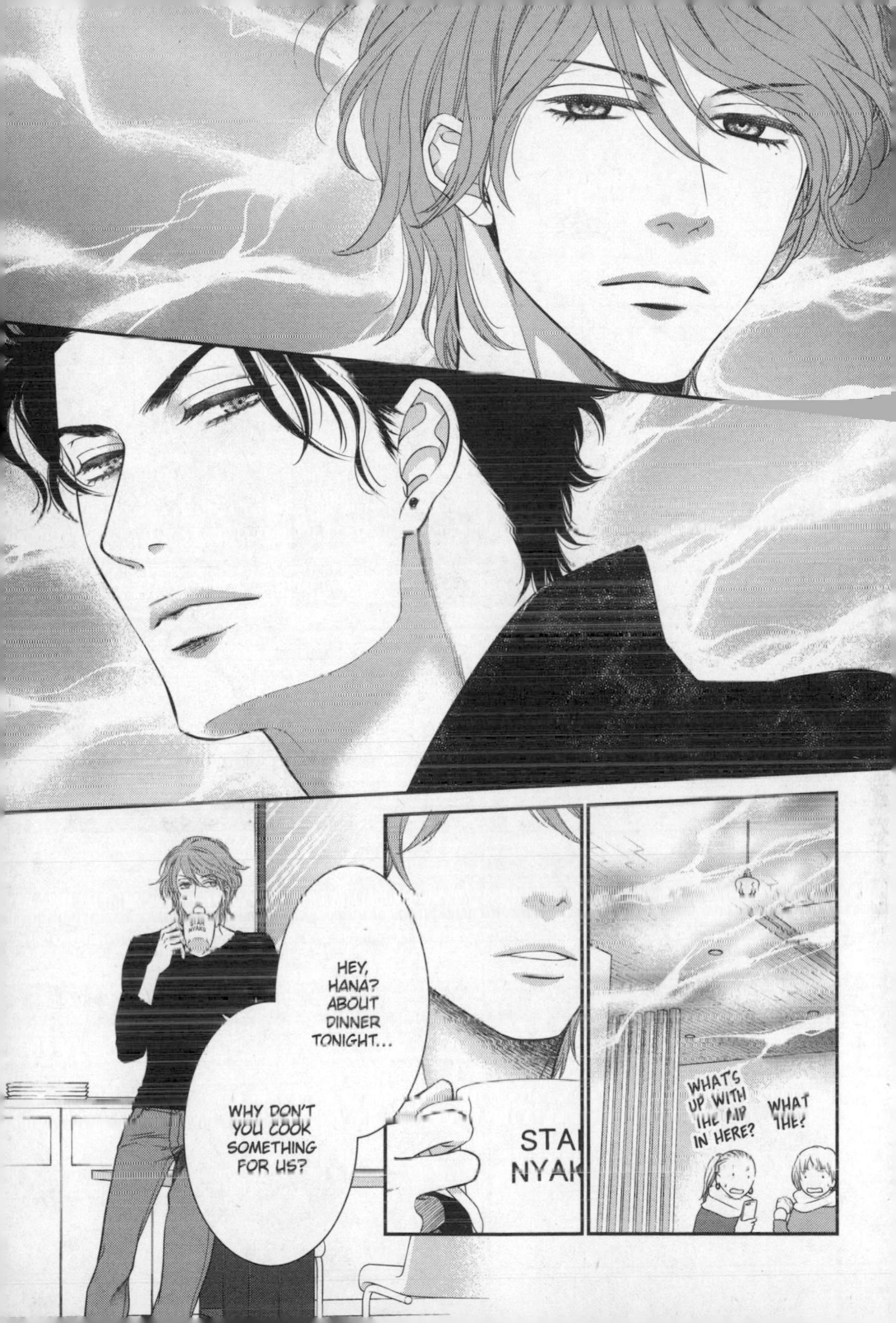
WHAT THE?
WHAT'S UP WITH THE AIR IN HERE?
HEY, HANA? ABOUT DINNER TONIGHT...
WHY DON'T YOU COOK SOMETHING FOR US?

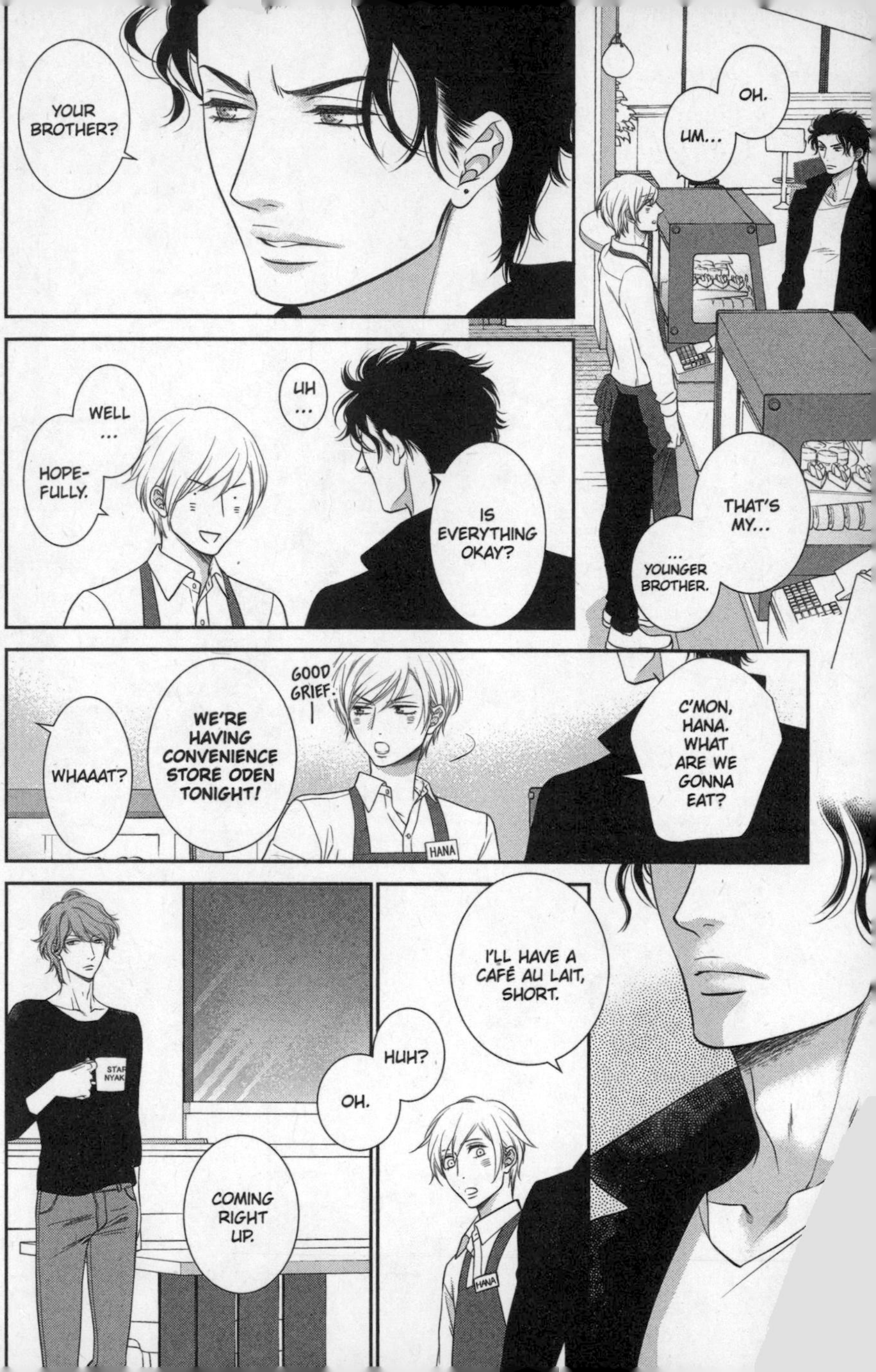
OH.
UM...
THAT'S MY...
...YOUNGER BROTHER.
YOUR BROTHER?
UH ...
IS EVERYTHING OKAY?
WELL ...
HOPE-FULLY.
C'MON, HANA. WHAT ARE WE GONNA EAT?
GOOD GRIEF.
WE'RE HAVING CONVENIENCE STORE ODEN TONIGHT!
WHAAAT?
I'LL HAVE A CAFÉ AU LAIT, SHORT.
HUH?
OH.
COMING RIGHT UP.

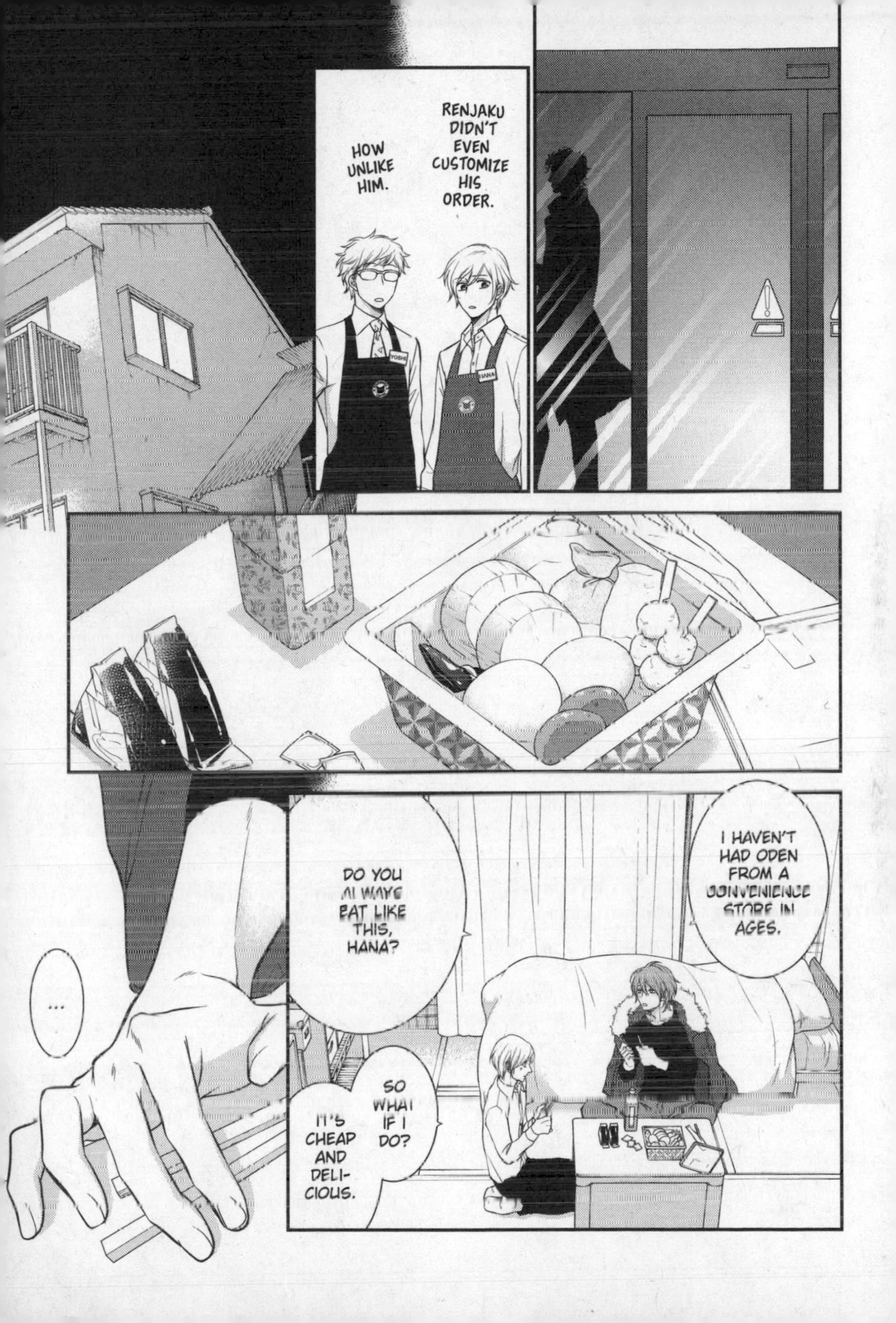
RENJAKU DIDN'T EVEN CUSTOMIZE HIS ORDER.
HOW UNLIKE HIM.
I HAVEN'T HAD ODEN FROM A CONVENIENCE STORE IN AGES.
DO YOU ALWAYS EAT LIKE THIS, HANA?
SO WHAT IF I DO?
IT'S CHEAP AND DELI-CIOUS.
...

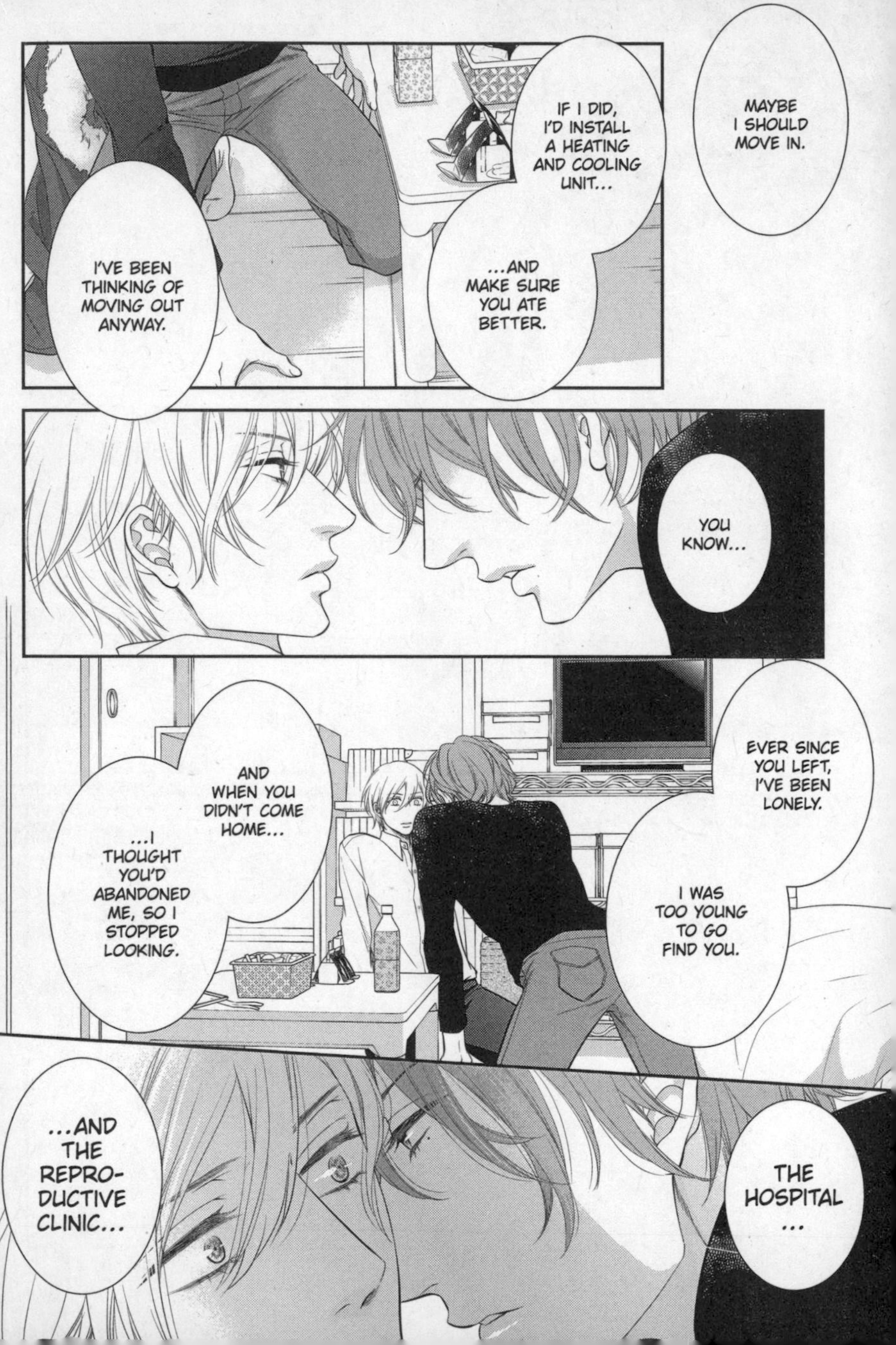
MAYBE I SHOULD MOVE IN.
IF I DID, I'D INSTALL A HEATING AND COOLING UNIT...
...AND MAKE SURE YOU ATE BETTER.
I'VE BEEN THINKING OF MOVING OUT ANYWAY.
YOU KNOW...
EVER SINCE YOU LEFT, I'VE BEEN LONELY.
I WAS TOO YOUNG TO GO FIND YOU.
AND WHEN YOU DIDN'T COME HOME...
...I THOUGHT YOU'D ABANDONED ME, SO I STOPPED LOOKING.
THE HOSPITAL...
...AND THE REPRO-DUCTIVE CLINIC...

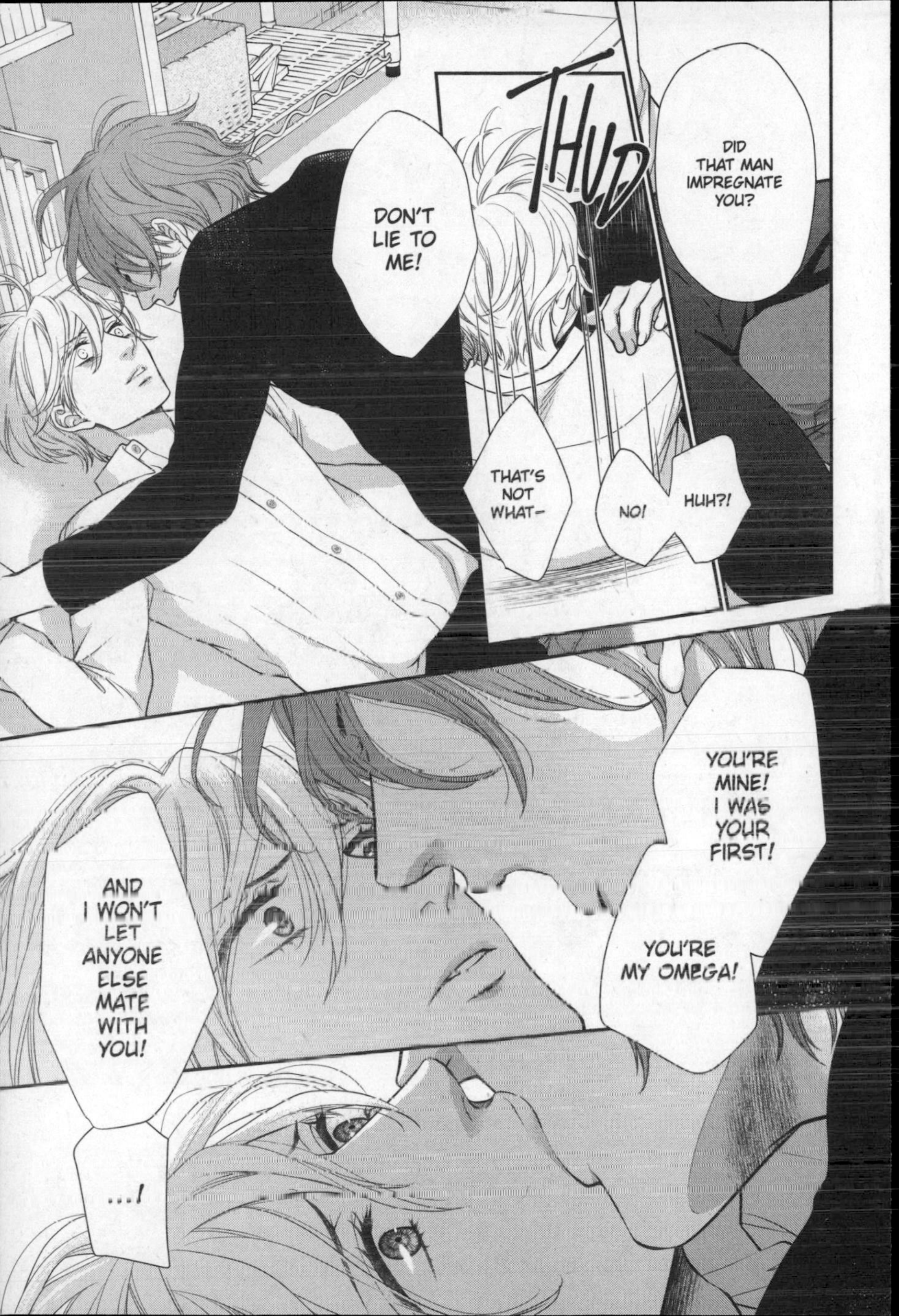
DID THAT MAN IMPREGNATE YOU?
THUD
HUH?!
NO!
THAT'S NOT WHAT-
DON'T LIE TO ME!
YOU'RE MINE! I WAS YOUR FIRST!
YOU'RE MY OMEGA!
AND I WON'T LET ANYONE ELSE MATE WITH YOU!
...!

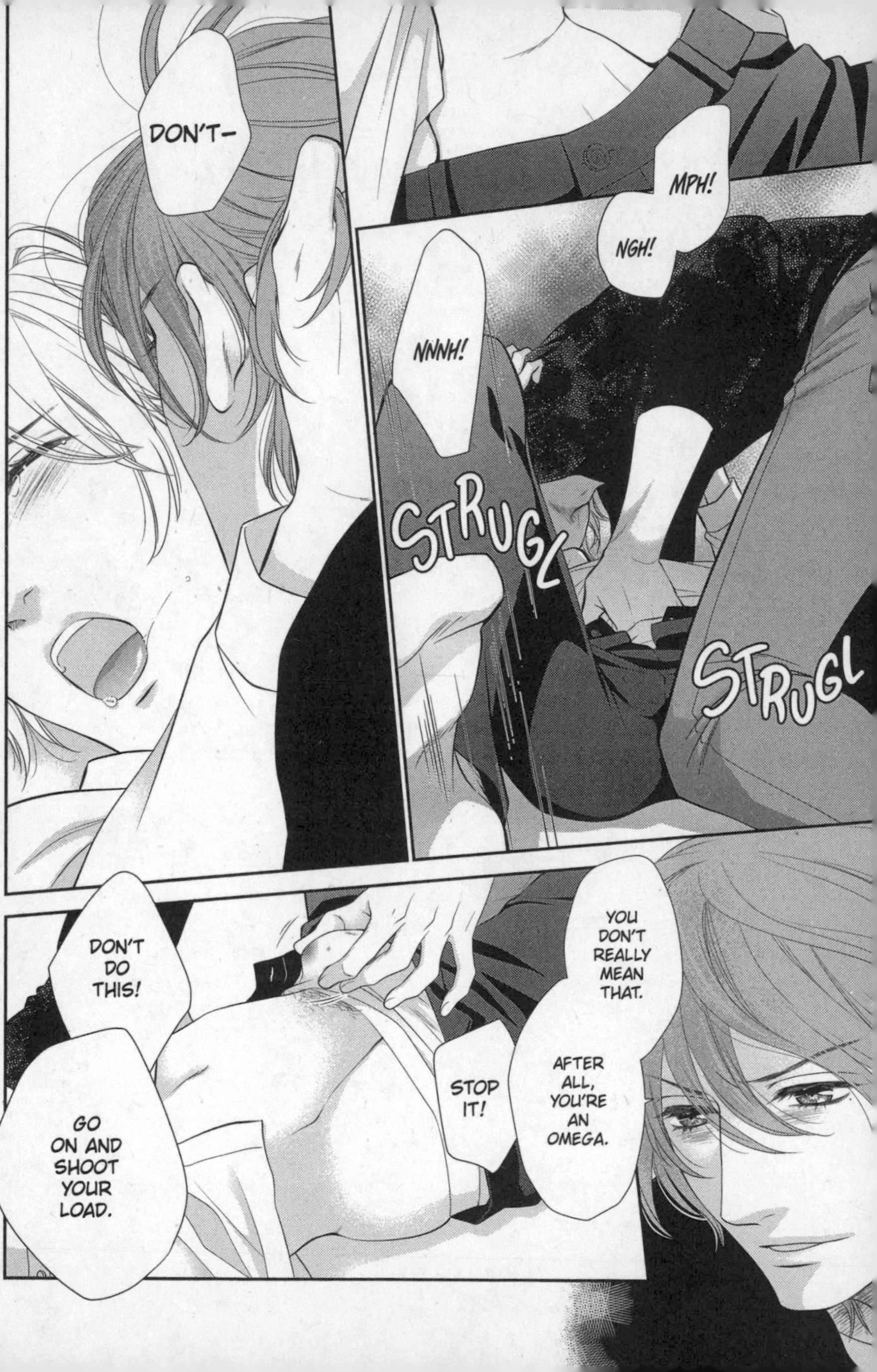
MPH!
NGH!
NNNH!
STRUGL
STRUGL
DON'T-
YOU DON'T REALLY MEAN THAT.
DON'T DO THIS!
AFTER ALL, YOU'RE AN OMEGA.
STOP IT!
GO ON AND SHOOT YOUR LOAD.

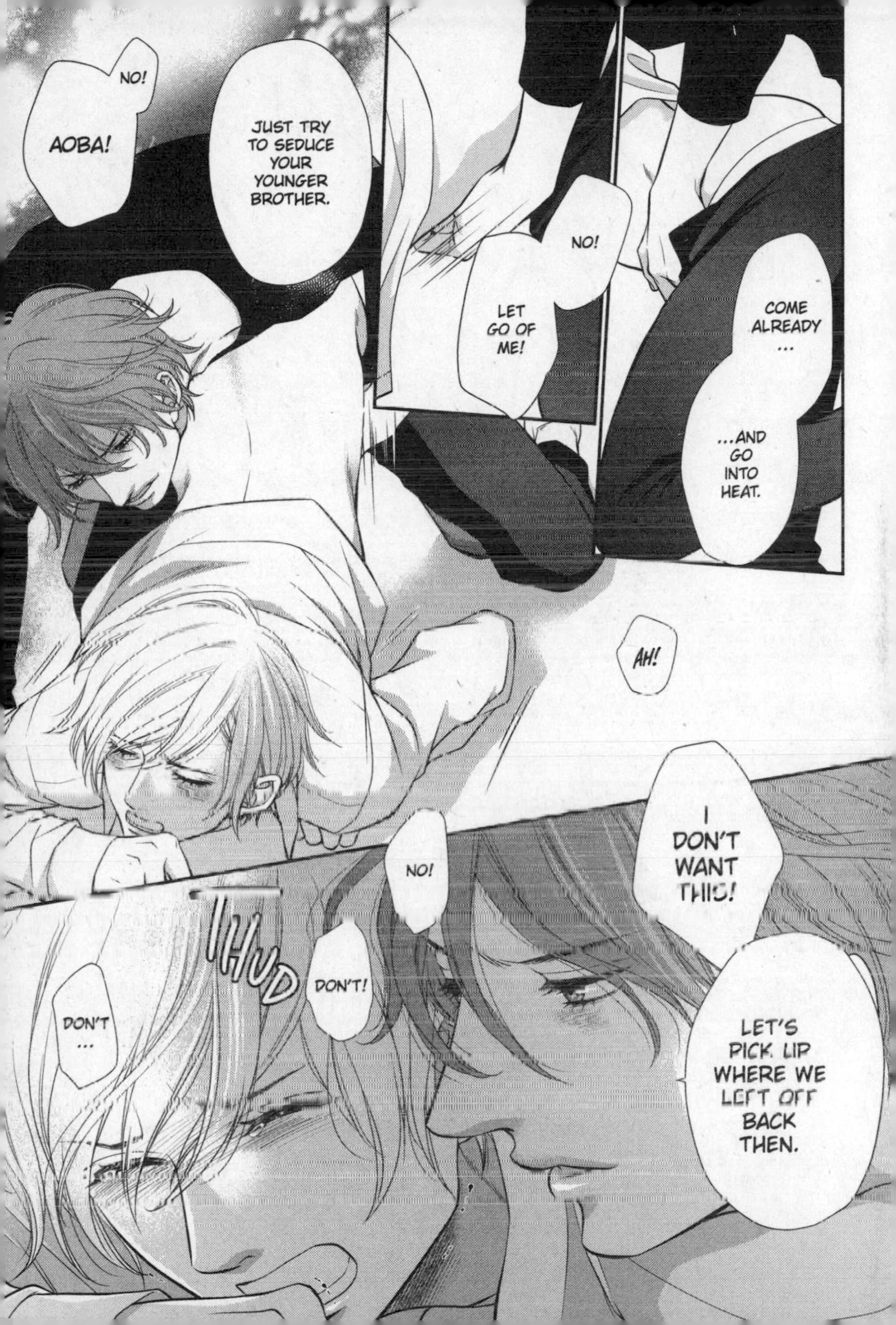
COME ALREADY ...
...AND GO INTO HEAT.
NO! LET GO OF ME!
JUST TRY TO SEDUCE YOUR YOUNGER BROTHER.
NO! AOBA!
AH!
I DON'T WANT THIS!
NO!
LET'S PICK UP WHERE WE LEFT OFF BACK THEN.
DON'T!
THUD
DON'T ...

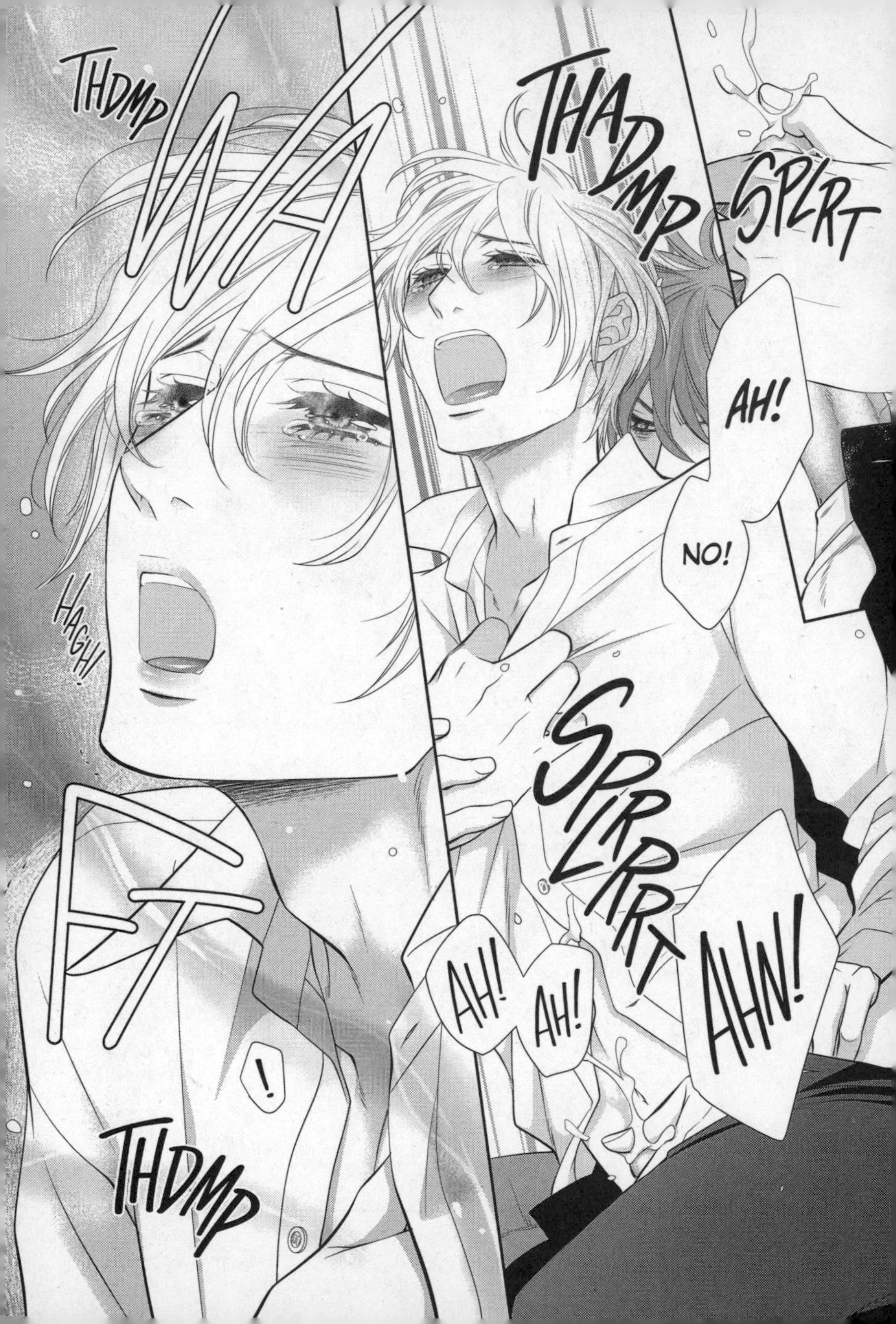
SPLRT
AH!
NO!
THADMP
SPRLRRT
AHN!
AH!
AH!
THDMP
WAFT
HAGH!
!
THDMP

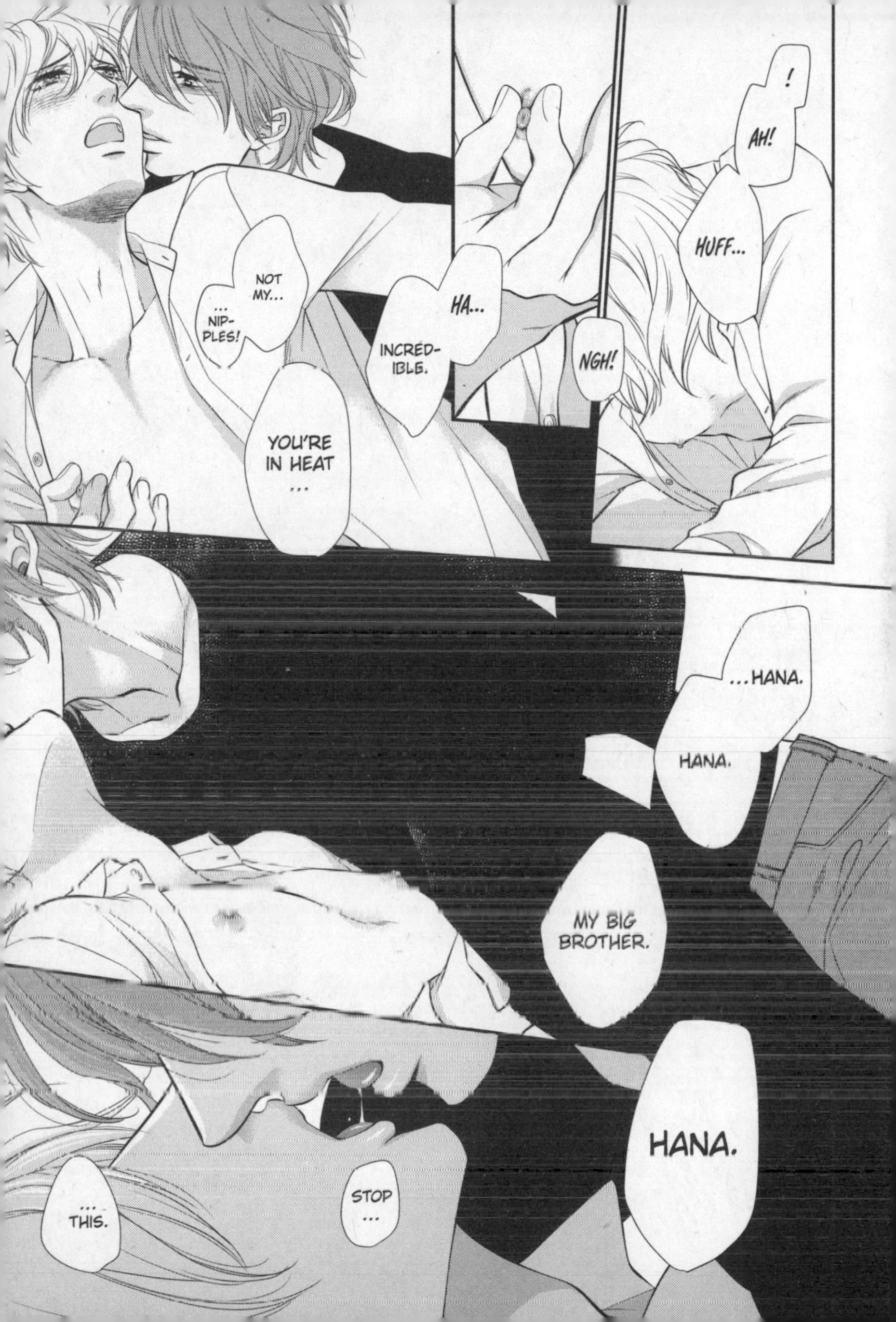
!
AH!
HUFF...
NGH!
HA...
INCRED-IBLE.
NOT MY...
... NIP-PLES!
YOU'RE IN HEAT ...
...HANA.
HANA.
MY BIG BROTHER.
HANA.
STOP ...
... THIS.

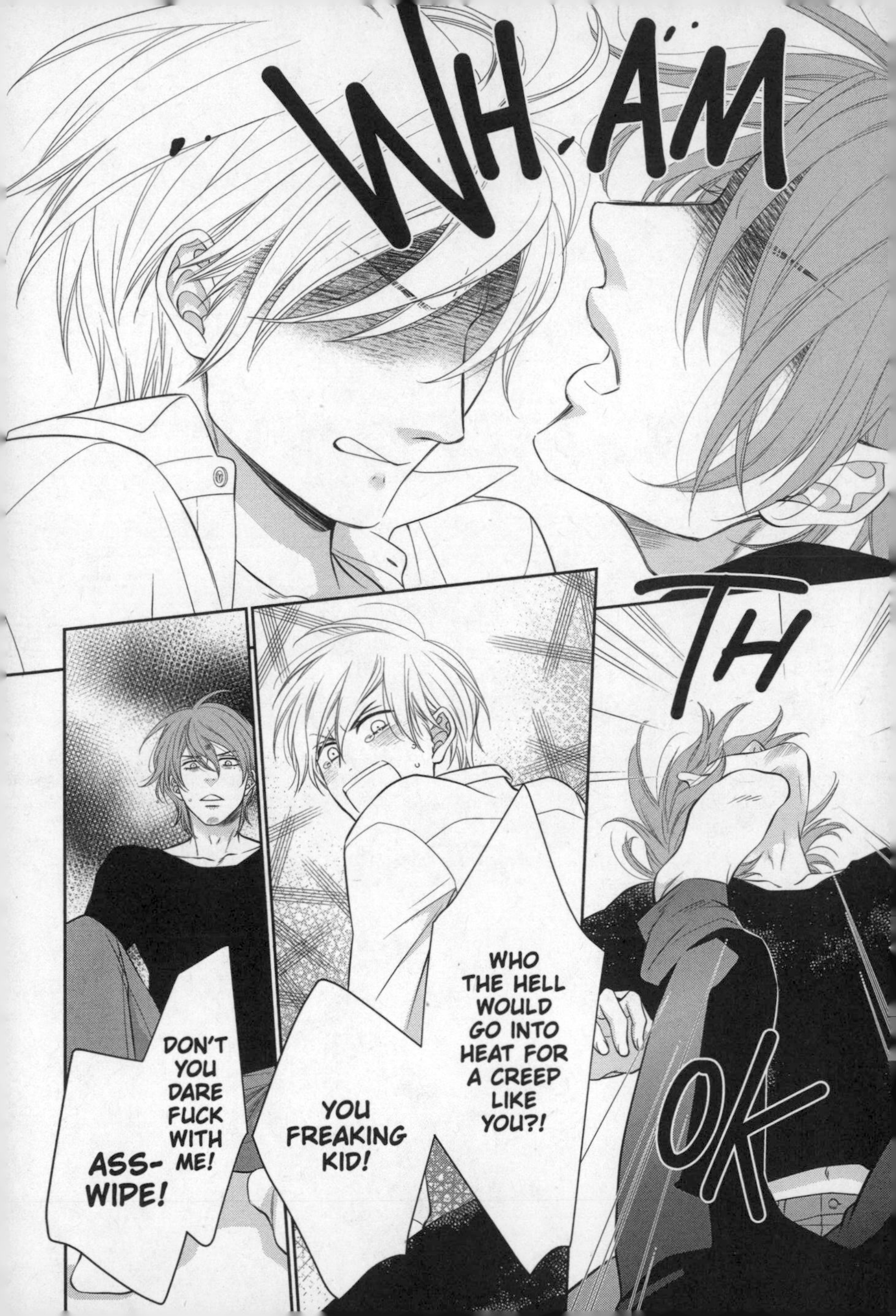
WHAM
THOK
WHO THE HELL WOULD GO INTO HEAT FOR A CREEP LIKE YOU?!
YOU FREAKING KID!
DON'T YOU DARE FUCK WITH ME!
ASS-WIPE!

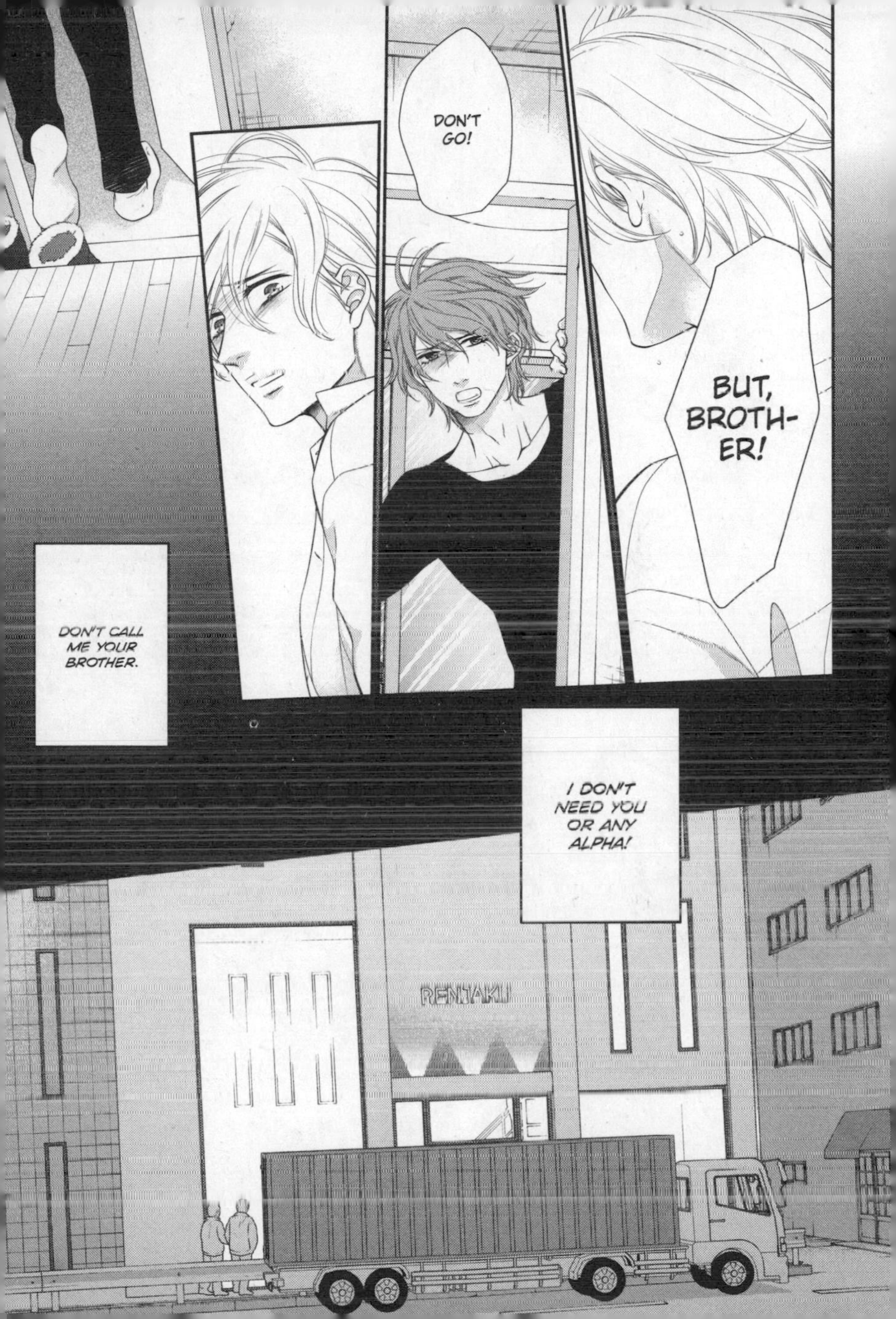
BUT, BROTHER!
DON'T GO!
DON'T CALL ME YOUR BROTHER.
I DON'T NEED YOU OR ANY ALPHA!
RENJAKU

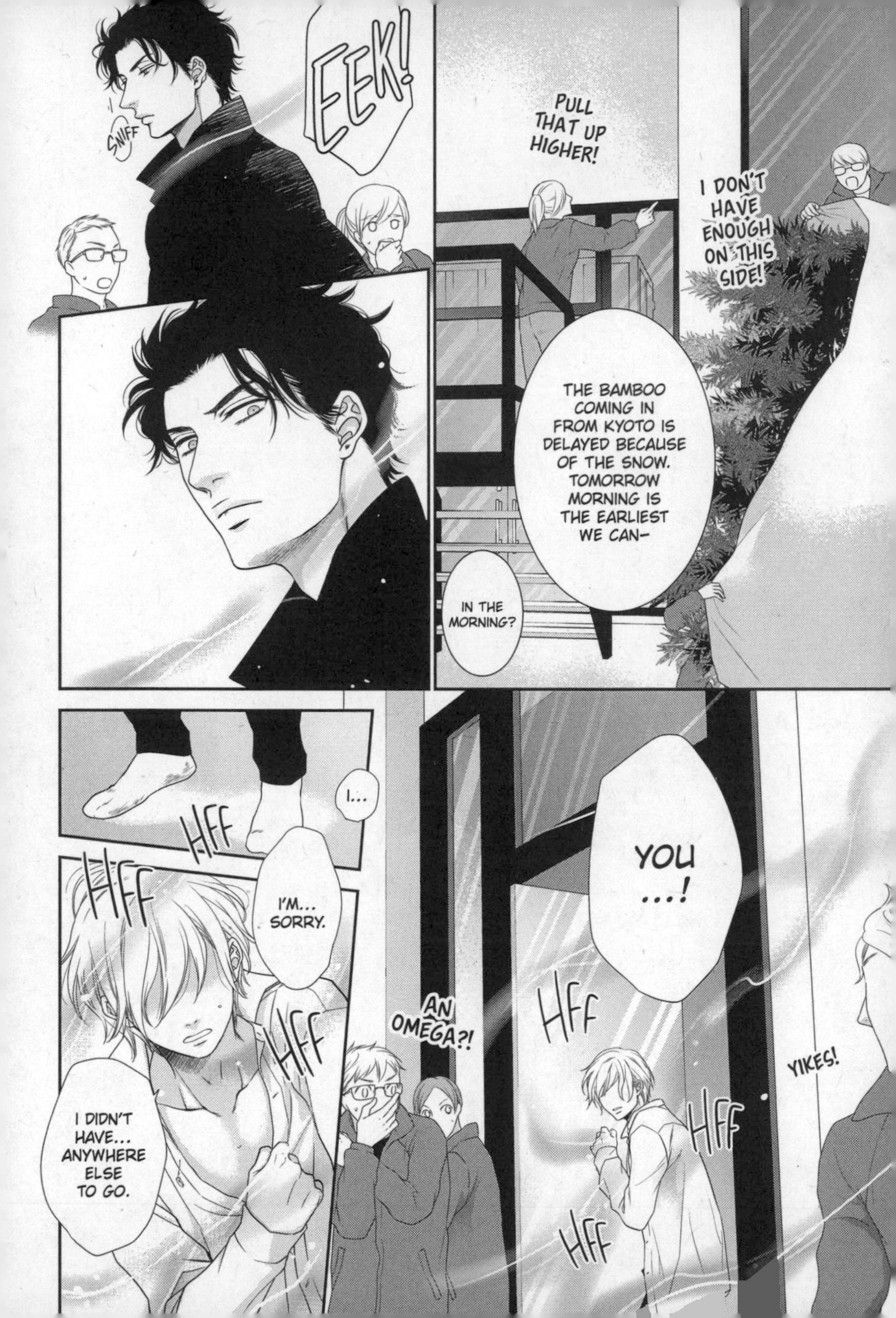
PULL THAT UP HIGHER!
I DON'T HAVE ENOUGH ON THIS SIDE!
THE BAMBOO COMING IN FROM KYOTO IS DELAYED BECAUSE OF THE SNOW. TOMORROW MORNING IS THE EARLIEST WE CAN-
IN THE MORNING?
EEK!
SNIFF
YOU ...!
YIKES!
HFF
HFF
AN OMEGA?!
HFF
I...
HFF
HFF
I'M... SORRY.
HFF
I DIDN'T HAVE... ANYWHERE ELSE TO GO.

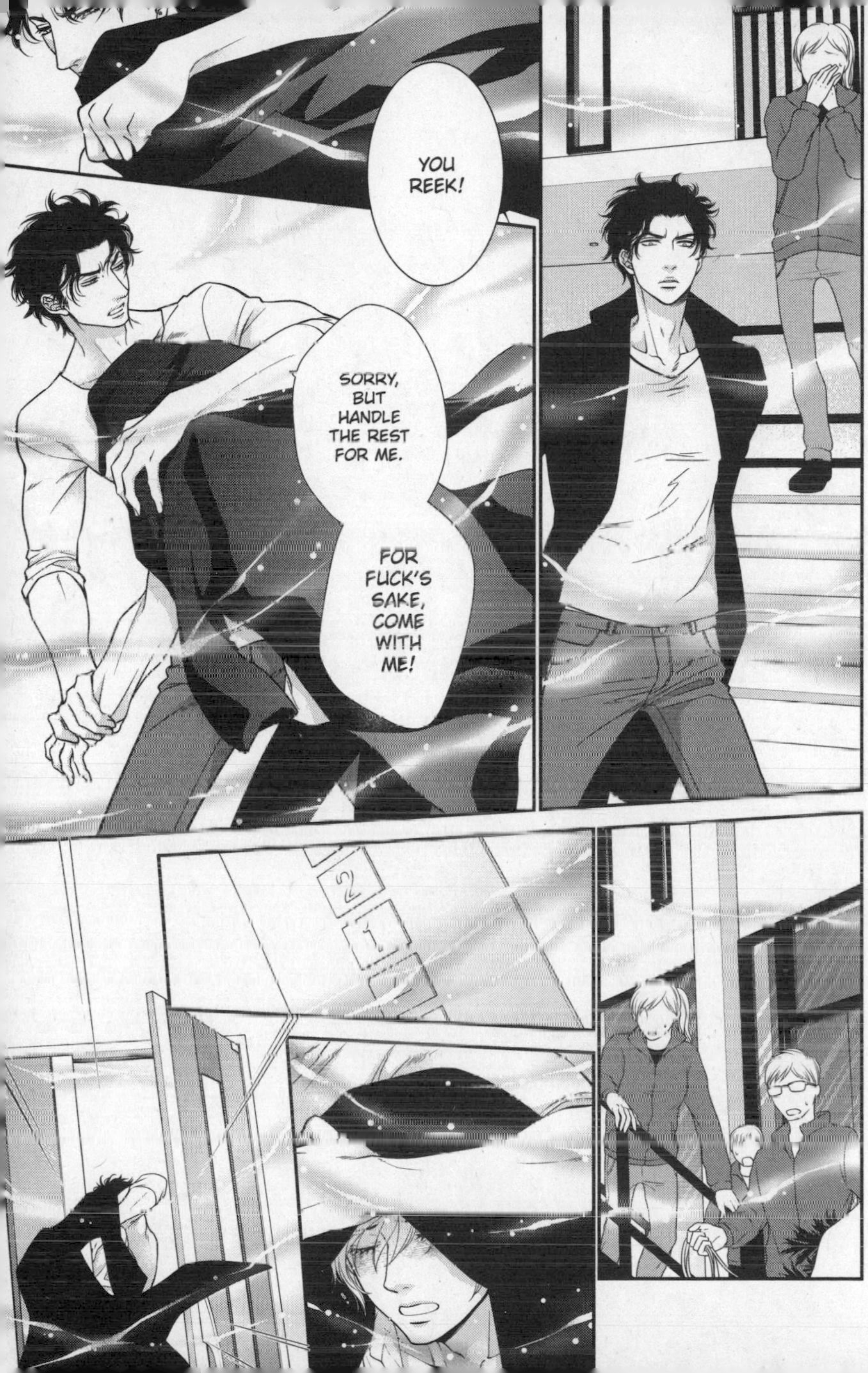
YOU REEK!
SORRY, BUT HANDLE THE REST FOR ME.
FOR FUCK'S SAKE, COME WITH ME!

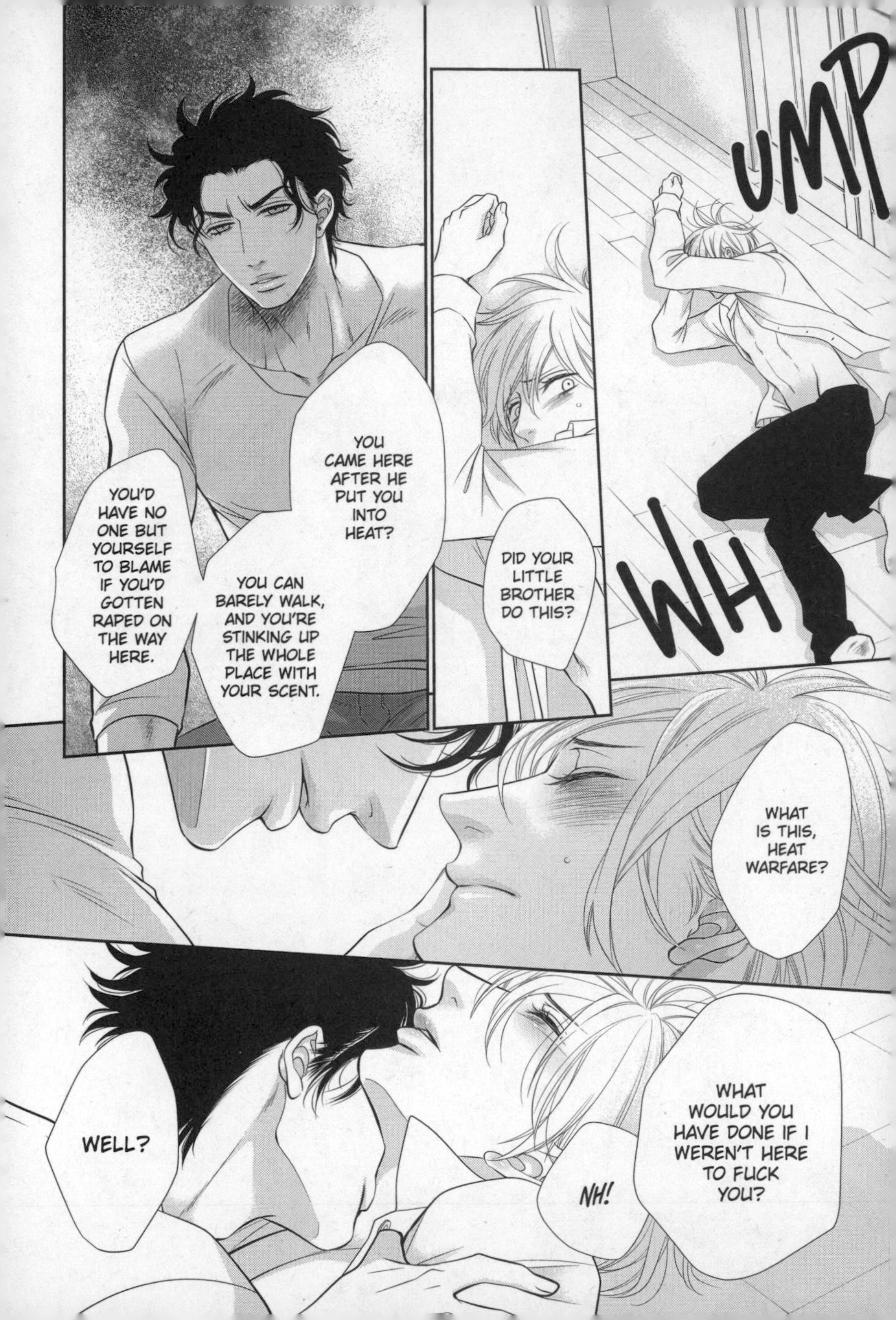
WHUMP
DID YOUR LITTLE BROTHER DO THIS?
YOU CAME HERE AFTER HE PUT YOU INTO HEAT?
YOU CAN BARELY WALK, AND YOU'RE STINKING UP THE WHOLE PLACE WITH YOUR SCENT.
YOU'D HAVE NO ONE BUT YOURSELF TO BLAME IF YOU'D GOTTEN RAPED ON THE WAY HERE.
WHAT IS THIS, HEAT WARFARE?
WHAT WOULD YOU HAVE DONE IF I WEREN'T HERE TO FUCK YOU?
NH!
WELL?

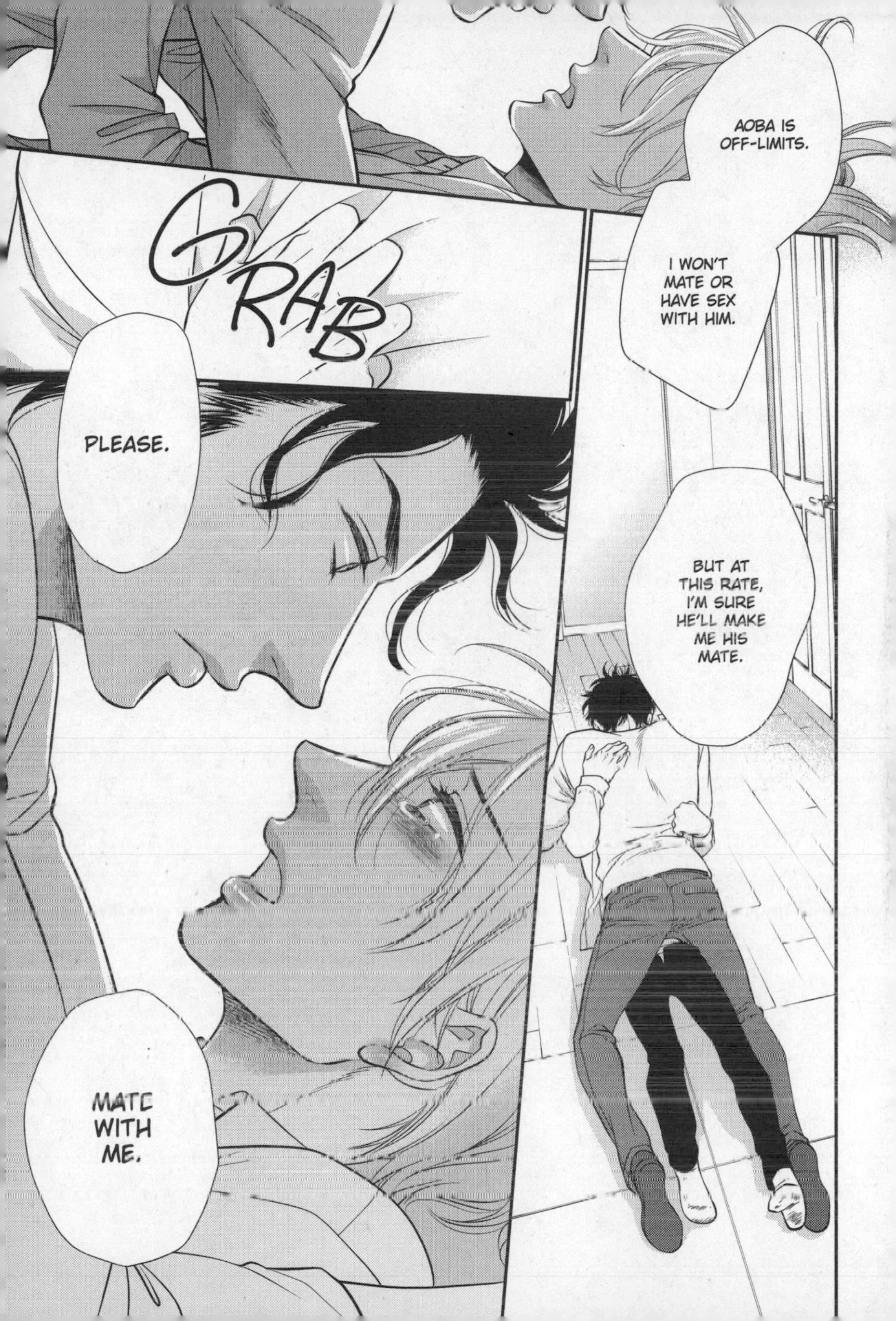
AOBA IS OFF-LIMITS.
I WON'T MATE OR HAVE SEX WITH HIM.
BUT AT THIS RATE, I'M SURE HE'LL MAKE ME HIS MATE.
GRAB
PLEASE.
MATE WITH ME.

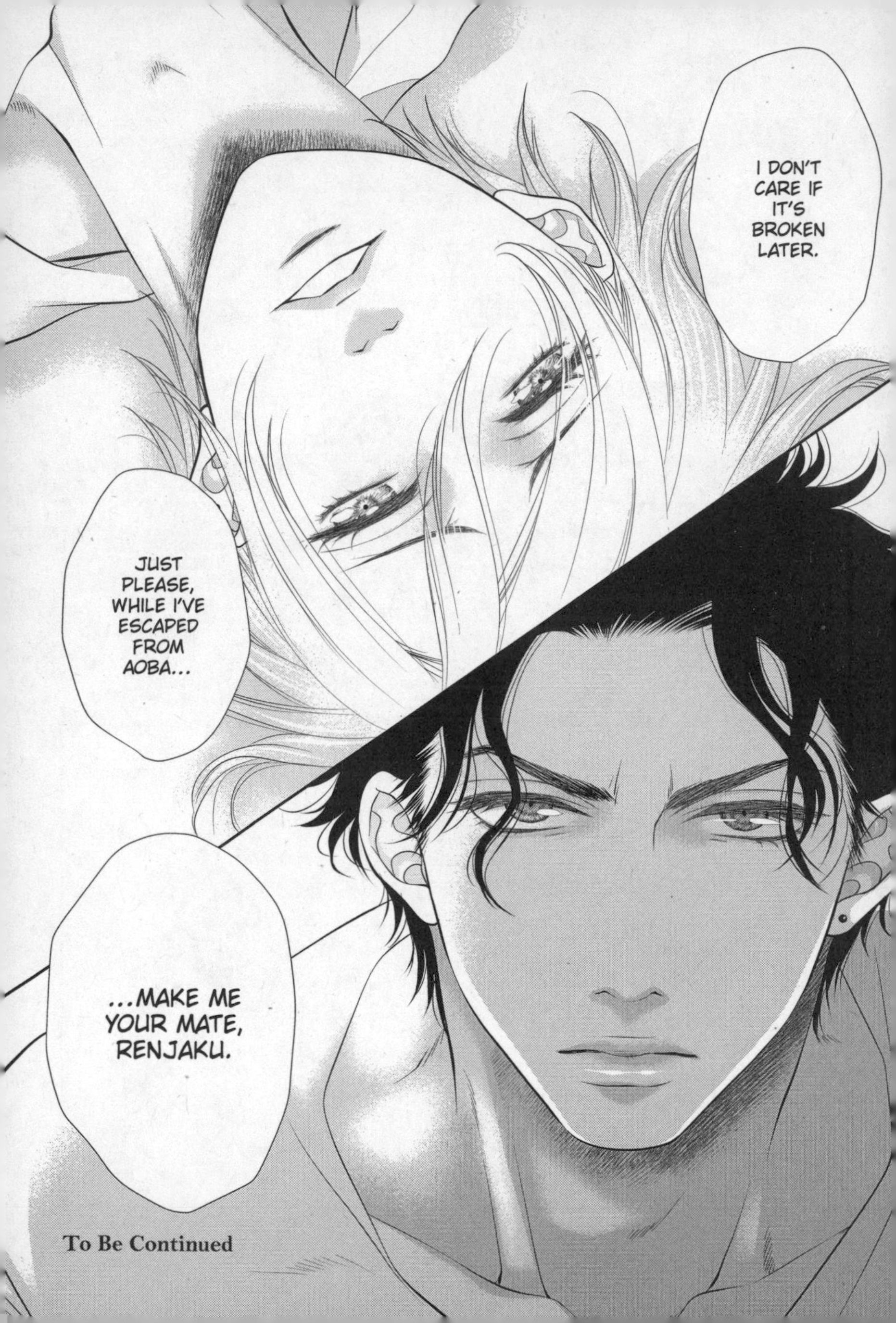
I DON'T CARE IF IT'S BROKEN LATER.
JUST PLEASE, WHILE I'VE ESCAPED FROM AOBA...
...MAKE ME YOUR MATE, RENJAKU.

To Be Continued

What Is Omegaverse?

Omegaverse is a hybrid concept, combining wolf pack hierarchies, m-preg, and other unique elements that were made popular on Western fan fiction sites. Because there are no official standards, different creators have different interpretations and systems.

Three Keywords to Understanding Omegaverse

(This is a general explanation. Please note that some works may not utilize these standards.)

1 There are six sexes in this universe—
male/female alphas, male/female betas, and male/female omegas

 Alpha

 Beta

 Omega

Superior in physique, ability, and pedigree, they're the high-spec type. Elite with natural-born charisma and leadership skills, they are sometimes written as occupying the highest echelons of society. There are relatively few in the general population.

The general population, they lack the heightened abilities of alphas or the special physiological attributes of omegas.

Both males and females are capable of becoming pregnant and giving birth. They experience periodic heats that can interfere with their daily living, limiting their options for livelihoods. They are even rarer than alphas.

2 Heats
Omegas go through periodic heats during which they release powerful pheromones designed to attract alphas (and sometimes betas). In the world of omegaverse, medicines like suppressants and contraceptives have been invented to help control their heats.

3 Mated relationships
Once bonded in a mated relationship—one that can only be forged between an alpha and an omega—the makeup of the omega's pheromones change to attract only their mated partner and no longer arouse others indiscriminately. Further, although an alpha can mate with other omegas even after bonding, it is said an omega can form only one bond in their lifetime.

Soul Mates A one-of-a-kind relationship where an alpha and omega are said to be attracted to each other on a soul level. Legend has it that they are able to recognize each other instantly at the slightest touch.

TRIVIA

Secondary Sex Examination
An examination intended to ascertain whether someone is an alpha, beta, or omega. Typically carried out at school or in a medical institution.

Omega Nest
A unique behavior of omegas is that they will subconsciously collect the scented clothing and belongings of their mate during a heat.

Heat Suppressants
A medicine for suppressing the symptoms of a heat. Intended for dealing with periodic heats, they can be taken in pill form, and many omegas walk around with them on hand to suppress unexpected heats.

Rut
An alpha's heat triggered by an omega's pheromones. They will be overcome by violent sexual urges and seek out an omega.

About the Author

Aya Sakyo is a prolific boys' love and shojo mangaka who also writes under the pen name Ukyou Ayane. Her likes include the color orange, sour foods, and pachinko. Born August 25 in Aichi Prefecture, she's a Virgo with an AB blood type. You can find out more about Aya Sakyo on her Twitter page, **@ukyoayane**.

Scattering His Virgin Bloom
Volume 1
SuBLime Manga Edition

Story and Art by **Aya Sakyo**

Translation—**Christine Dashiell**
Touch-Up Art and Lettering—**Mary Pass**
Cover and Graphic Design—**Joy Zhang**
Editor—**Jennifer LeBlanc**

新書館
SHINSHOKAN

Printed in the U.S.A.

Published by SuBLime Manga
P.O. Box 77010
San Francisco, CA 94107

10 9 8 7 6 5 4 3 2 1
First printing, April 2022

PARENTAL ADVISORY
SCATTERING HIS VIRGIN BLOOM is rated M for Mature and is recommended for mature readers. This volume contains graphic imagery and mature themes.

M
MATURE

SUBLIME
SuBLimeManga.com

For more information

on all our products, along with the most up-to-date news on releases, series announcements, and contests, please visit us at:

SuBLimeManga.com

twitter.com/**SuBLimeManga**

facebook.com/**SuBLimeManga**

instagram.com/**SuBLimeManga**

SuBLimeManga.tumblr.com

SUBLIME
MANGA

YARICHIN BITCH CLUB

OGERETSU TANAKA

At an all-boys' boarding school deep in the mountains, hapless transfer student Takashi Tono joins the Photography Club, only to learn too late that the club's main extracurricular activity is offering its sexual services to the student body! Now that Takashi's surrounded by bedroom aces, can this virgin survive a day, much less the whole school year, as part of the school's most lascivious club?

Today's top could be tomorrow's bottom when playing the caste game!

Caste Heaven

STORY AND ART BY **Chise Ogawa**

School is hard enough as it is, but when students are forced to play a cutthroat game to determine their social ranks—and subsequent treatment—all bets are off.